# FOR THE
# GOOD
## OF THE
# GAME

THE OFFICIAL HISTORY OF

PROFESSIONAL FOOTBALLERS ASSOCIATION

**THE PROFESSIONAL
FOOTBALLERS' ASSOCIATION**

# FOR THE
# GOOD
## OF THE
# GAME

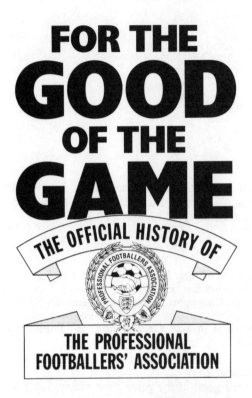

THE OFFICIAL HISTORY OF

PROFESSIONAL FOOTBALLERS ASSOCIATION

### THE PROFESSIONAL
### FOOTBALLERS' ASSOCIATION

## JOHN HARDING

Robson Books

First published in Great Britain in 1991 by
Robson Books Ltd, Bolsover House, 5-6
Clipstone Street, London W1P 7EB

**British Library Cataloguing in Publication
Data**

Harding, John
For the good of the game : the official history
of the Professional Footballers' Association.
  I. Title
  796.3340941

ISBN 0 86051 770 5

Photoset in North Wales by
Derek Doyle & Associates, Mold, Clwyd.
Printed and bound in Great Britain by
St Edmundsbury Press, Bury St Edmunds,
Suffolk.

# Contents

Acknowledgements      vii
Foreword by Bobby Charlton      ix
Introduction by Gordon Taylor      xi

1   *A Profession in Chains* 1888–1900      1
2   *'An Ambitious Scheme'* 1897      6
3   *Charlie Saer's Transfer Scheme* 1898      15
4   *'A Practical Failure'* 1901      25
5   *Revival – Meredith and Manchester* 1901–7      34
6   *The New Union* 1907–8      40
7   *Confrontation* 1909      51
8   *Summer of the Outcasts* 1909      65
9   *Settlement and Survival* 1909      75
10   *Masters and Servants* 1910–11      84
11   *Kingaby* 1912      95
12   *Edwardian High Summer* 1912–14      105
13   *Roberts Revives the Union* 1918–19      116
14   *Good Times* 1920–22      127
15   *The Leddy Case* 1923      142
16   *Hard Times* 1923–28      157
17   *Jimmy Fay Takes Over* 1929–34      170
18   *Lost Opportunities* 1934–36      186
19   *Approaching Storm* 1936–39      196

| 20 | *Post-war Militancy* 1946–47 | 207 |
| 21 | *Chairman Guthrie* 1947–51 | 220 |
| 22 | *Troubled Times* 1951–57 | 237 |
| 23 | *The Fall of Guthrie* 1957 | 252 |
| 24 | *Enter Jimmy Hill* 1957–61 | 266 |
| 25 | *New Deal – and Eastham* 1961–63 | 276 |
| 26 | *A Sort of Freedom* 1963–67 | 289 |
| 27 | *Chester and Dougan* 1968–71 | 299 |
| 28 | *CIR – and Hard Bargaining* 1971–73 | 309 |
| 29 | *Freedom at Last?* 1974-81 | 319 |
| 30 | *Gordon Taylor's Baptism of Fire* 1982–84 | 329 |
| 31 | *Building for the Future* 1985–88 | 342 |
| 32 | *Taylor of the League?* 1989–90 | 354 |

| Epilogue | 367 |
| Appendix One:   PFA Chairmen | 375 |
| Appendix Two:   PFA Secretaries | 385 |
| Appendix Three: Team Line-ups for the Three Scottish Union vs. English Union Fundraising Matches | 389 |
| Bibliography | 391 |
| Index | 393 |

# Acknowledgements

There are many people I have to thank for helping me with gathering information for this book. John Litster, Pat Woods and Bob Crampsey provided Scottish facts and figures; Harry Glasper, Sam Rendell, Stewart Beckett, Mr E Griffiths, Ian Rigby, William Powell, Denis Turner, David Smith, Harry Berry, Mark Skoal, Ron Gould, M J Spinks, Phil Tooley, Keith Warsop, Mrs K Ashcroft, J McCormick, Miss K Holdsworth, Duncan Carmichael, T Waite, R Shepherd, John Relish, Derek Higton, F G Jeavans, Phil Soar, Brian Truscott, Brian Horsnell, Peter Cullen, Andy Ward, Alan Futter all provided valuable photographs, statistics and information, while Denis Clarebrough's inexhaustible supply of cigarette cards has proved invaluable.

Braham Dabscheck's excellent papers on the PFA and Simon Inglis's Official League history have been invaluable and essential guides across the terrain, while I am especially indebted to Dr Tony Mason for reading through the manuscript and offering pertinent and constructive advice.

Ex-Management Committee members have been very helpful; in particular I would like to thank Tony Ingham, Frank and Elsa Broome, Danny Winter, Harry Hough, Jack Campbell, Ian Dargie, Tommy Cummings, Keith Peacock, Maurice Setters, A Robertson, Jimmy Hill, Terry Neill, Alan Gowling, Steve Coppell, Brian Talbot, Garth Crooks and the late Joe Mercer OBE.

Relatives of ex-Management Committee men have also kindly contributed photos and memories: in particular, Mrs Hinchcliffe, F Robbie, Mrs Crooks, Stuart Crooks, Will and Chris Roberts, and Christine Kerry, while journalist Dave Caldwell and ex-players Tom Finney OBE and Jack Crayston also contributed fascinated anecdotes.

The late George Davies, PFA solicitor for many years, was both kind and encouraging – his death is a great loss to the PFA and to football in general. David Green, once of the Davies law firm, was extremely helpful in explaining the intricacies of the Eastham Case.

At the PFA offices, I would like to thank Brendon Batson, Micky Burns and Mick McGuire for all their time, patience and friendly assistance. Likewise, a special thank you must also go to Karen Evans, Carol Brown, Anne Stephenson and Zöe Holmes.

One man in particular deserves special mention – Cliff Lloyd. I know Cliff has been keen to have a history of the PFA produced for many years. He has been most helpful and generous to me with his time and knowledge and I only hope this book will serve in some way as a tribute to the many years he devoted to the Association as Secretary.

I must also pay tribute to the PFA Chief Executive, Gordon Taylor, for his enthusiasm for and commitment to the book. Gordon is a keen student of the game's history and without his considerable help the book most certainly could not have been written.

Lastly, I would like to thank Louise Dixon, Editor at Robson Books, for her patience and good humour.

# Foreword

## by Bobby Charlton

I joined the Player's Union back in 1956 when I signed on as a professional for Manchester United. As I recall, the great Roger Byrne was Union representative at the club, although in truth I felt at the time that the Union was more for lower-division players, those who didn't receive the 'perks' and better conditions that went with Division One.

My opinion changed on that in 1961 with the campaign led by Jimmy Hill for the removal of the maximum wage. I can still recall the meetings we held – even Stan Matthews came to one! It was an exciting time and I saw then how important the Union was to all players.

Later on Cliff Lloyd – who in many ways *was* the Union in those days – invited me to serve on the Management Committee along with good friends like Terry Venables, Nobby Lawton, Tony Leighton and Terry Neill. We realized then how crucial education was for professional players – in fact, I went on one of the first Management courses set up by the FA at Lilleshall.

Today the Association is recognized as being a key player in football politics. Superbly led by Gordon Taylor, it holds the balance between League and FA and its views can no longer be ignored.

So I wish both the PFA and its official history all the very best of luck!

Bobby Charlton OBE

# Introduction

# by Gordon Taylor

When I became secretary of the Association in 1981 we were situated across the city of Manchester in offices in the old Corn Exchange – a lovely old building but a little bit antiquated. Indeed, I remember one day coming across a camera crew in the corridor filming an episode of *Sherlock Holmes*! I knew then that it was time for a move to somewhere that reflected a more modern image of professional football and yet, ironically, by transferring to our new home – a spacious and purpose-built Georgian-style office block off Lower Mosley Street – we were moving back next to the site of the PFA (then the Players' Union) office in 1907, in St Peter's Square. Thus whilst moving forward, we were retaining our links with the past.

The Union has always had strong links with Manchester. My predecessor, Cliff Lloyd, told me of his visit to Welsh wizard Billy Meredith – one of the Union's founders – a Manchester City and United player and a true servant of the Union right up until his death in 1958. Billy was ill and destitute yet beneath his bed he kept a battered old suitcase filled with caps and medals, his only reward after an incredible career that spanned thirty years. 'Always remind your members that those caps and medals didn't look after me in my old age', he said. The difference between what Billy was left with at the end of his career and what the vast majority of today's players at all levels can look forward to when they retire is a measure of the great strides the Association and the profession have made.

Looking through the papers that came to light during the move, I was struck by the way the battles of long ago so closely mirrored those of recent years. Back in the early 1900s the Union that was so dear to Billy Meredith's heart was trying to prove itself as an organization with credibility and respectability that looked to advance not just the status of players but also the overall interests and health of the game as well. Today, the PFA has a high media profile, expects to be involved in all matters concerning players, is consulted by Government Departments and Parliamentary Committees, by clubs, by chairmen, and by managers and has a liaison with or seat on all major football bodies including the Football Trust, a body now empowered with implementing the Taylor Report and dispensing some £30m per year in Government and Pools money. In fact, the PFA can no longer be ignored in any matter affecting professional players – and while there may still be some critics who choose to cling to a caricature image of professional footballers – low on IQ, high on misbehaviour – reality usually paints a different picture perhaps best illustrated by the performance of Gary Lineker at the Oxford Union.

It was to document as fully as possible the way in which the PFA has achieved such radical alterations in both the public's perception and the status of the professional footballer, that we have collaborated with John Harding, biographer of Billy Meredith, to produce this extensive history. John has worked closely not only with myself, but also with Cliff Lloyd, like Meredith, a great servant of the Union – and we hope the results will not only inform and educate but also – in the best traditions of professional football – entertain.

Gordon Taylor

# 1

# *A Profession in Chains* 1888–1900

In 1885 professionalism in football was reluctantly 'legalized' by the game's ruling body, the Football Association, a group of men drawn from the upper echelons of British society – honourable men but, as Percy Young has written: 'Men of prejudice, seeing themselves as patricians, heirs to the doctrine of "leadership" and so law-givers by at least semi-divine right.'

Three years later, the Football League was founded by a group of very different men – shopkeepers, minor government officials, small businessmen – not for the purpose of encouraging football but, as a journalist of the period put it, 'so that allied clubs may make more money than they already do …'

William McGregor, the architect of the League, had seen that professional football as a commercial venture was in danger of destroying itself. Clubs were too concerned to compete on individual terms – to lure the best players, to attract the best crowds – with no concern as to the economic fate of opponents.

Fixtures were haphazard, smaller clubs often finding games cancelled at the last moment because a larger club had arranged what was likely to be a more profitable match. With the FA Cup – the only national, prestigious competition – being organized on a knock-out basis, eliminated clubs often had nothing exciting other than, perhaps, County Cups to offer their patrons. In short, there was no pattern and, increasingly, no credibility to competition.

The League simply repackaged in a clever and novel way a potentially lucrative product and it was immediately successful, growing rapidly from twelve teams in 1888 to thirty-six in 1900. From being a predominantly North/Midlands organization, it soon embraced all areas of the country until no football club of substance or ambition could afford to remain outside it.

Membership brought with it so many benefits: a regular flow of income derived from a guaranteed number of fixtures; sustained competition that kept interest high throughout the season, thus attracting large crowds; plus rules and regulations designed to bind members together for their own protection. It was a cartel, which rapidly assumed monopoly powers; only the Southern League offered any sort of competition over the years but even it was eventually absorbed.

For the newly recognized professional player the rise of the League proved to be both a blessing and a curse. Not that players were against the establishment of the League system: far from it – the League was seen at the outset as being of great benefit. Pro-players increasingly desired security of employment, regular pay and a good working environment. The League appeared to produce all these. Indeed, without it, professional football might not have survived into the twentieth century.

In 1885, however, the player had been as free as the next man to sell his labour to the highest bidder; yet by 1900 he was being described as a bonded slave, a chattel, no better than a piece of merchandise. For in rescuing the professional game from financial ruin, the founders of the Football League had created a category of workman like no other before or since.

League administrators would argue down the years that the success of the League depended on balance – teams of near-equal ability in competition, the outcome of games uncertain, the entertainment factor consequently high, resulting in large, enthusiastic crowds. But with the rapid growth of the League in centres of large population, imbalances appeared. Small town clubs, no matter how successful on the pitch, could never earn as much as big town clubs at the turnstile. Unable to pay sufficiently high wages to attract the best players, they seemed doomed to struggle, facing dwindling crowds and eventually the spectre of bankruptcy.

'Survival of the fittest', although the law of the business world, was nevertheless anathema to League philosophy because the folding of smaller clubs, it was contended, would destroy the essential balance. It might even lead to a Super League which, in turn would mean less variety and, once again, smaller and smaller attendances.

Therefore, almost from the start of their phenomenally successful competition, the founders and administrators of the League saw the maintenance of the shape and size of the League as one of the principal tasks.

The obvious method of achieving this was the sharing of gate-money. A club situated in a centre of a large population was merely fortunate; playing no better football than a team from a smaller town, it could earn three, four times as much – yet it depended on the small town team for competition. Both, it was argued, should share in the financial results.

Yet from the outset this idea (favoured by William McGregor) was resisted by a majority of clubs, for the adventure of earning massive amounts of money and building an edifice to one's own memory was more appealing to directors and owners than the less tangible concept of brotherly love. The only realistic alternative to pooling, therefore, was to control (and share) the raw material of the game – the players.

If clubs – especially smaller clubs – could be certain of keeping their players from season to season instead of having them snatched by bigger, wealthier clubs, then talent would remain equally spread and thus no team could dominate the competition. But how to secure such control? Fortunately for the League, the FA had, unwittingly, created a perfect mechanism.

The amateur – professional split was a profound one, reflecting deeply held class prejudices. Certain key members of the FA were extremely disturbed by professionalism in sport and had only accepted it if they could somehow 'control' it and, in their view, safeguard the principles essential to 'true' sport.

In the eyes of the FA, football would always be a sport, never a business, while those who played it would always be 'sportsmen', never workmen. That the pro-player *was* a workman with a legal contract and recognized as such (after a struggle) by the law of the land, would make no practical difference. For the FA, football was a world within a world, and they were its rulers.

To ensure that pro-players remained under the FA's control, a regulation was passed that compelled all pro-players to register annually. No player was allowed to play until he was registered, nor was he free to change clubs during the same season without the FA's permission.

Clearly the FA intended that once the season was over, players could move on if they wished; the League, however, quickly realized that to achieve the necessary control, it had to go one step further. Thus it insisted that any pro-player who had signed for a particular club and wished to move on to another club had to obtain the permission of his present club.

More controversial still, however, was the League rule that, once signed, a player was tied to his club for as long as the club wanted him (and even beyond that point). Thus, the season would end, the player might refuse to sign a new contract, but he could sign for no one else unless the club gave permission.

The smaller clubs, it was argued, could thus be sure of keeping their 'assets'; if a larger club wanted a particular player, then it would have to compensate the smaller club by offering money with which the latter might buy a replacement or service its debt. Although, admittedly, it was not the *man* who was being bought, merely his registration, the point was a technical one. Within a year or two of the League's formation, men were being bought and sold. The retain and transfer system had been created.

In years to come this uncomfortable truth would be justified on many grounds, not least the insistence that the chaos of pre-League days had been caused by the players and their excessive financial demands; that clubs, fearful of losing 'star' players, had been blackmailed into paying whatever had been demanded; that many clubs had bankrupted themselves in the process while the players had moved on to pastures new.

This was, of course, a convenient fiction. Some men certainly had behaved unscrupulously, treating contracts like so much confetti. But it had been club managements that had created the atmosphere in which such 'mercenaries' had been able to flourish. Clubs – or their directorates – in their anxiety to fill grounds and make money, had broken whatever rules had then existed and in the process had reduced the game to a shambles. Nevertheless, the myth of the greedy, grasping player would prove a powerful and convenient one.

From 1893, therefore, players in the Football League were not free to negotiate a new contract on anything like equal terms with their employers. In fact, if a player wanted to leave a League club, perhaps to earn a better wage, he could be prevented from doing so; to continue playing in League football, he would have to sign a new contract with his original club – hardly a situation in which a player could make demands for better conditions.

In effect, the Football League abolished the free market where players' wages and conditions were concerned; indeed, once the question of retention had been settled, it was not long before clubs began clamouring for an 'equal' wage – a maximum that a player, any player, might be able to earn.

At first the situation did not look too grim for players. During the early 1890s the Football League, though growing fast, was also racked by controversy and dissent which appeared to herald its demise. Furthermore, imitation leagues sprang up all over the country (and in Scotland and Ireland).

Thus, there were 'escape routes' to clubs and countries where a player could ply his trade freely and earn a reasonable (indeed, where some Southern League clubs were concerned, highly lucrative) wage. But as the League expanded, or struck up deals with rival Leagues, that freedom began to disappear.

It was then that professional players began to think of protecting themselves, of speaking out to suggest alternative methods of running League football. During the late 1890s, there was lively debate as to the future of professional League football in England. It was in order that players could participate effectively in such discussions and to clarify their position in a rapidly changing 'industry', that the first players' organizations were formed.

# 2
# 'An Ambitious Scheme' 1897

The earliest mention of a possible Players' Union came in the columns of the *Athletic News* in late 1893. 'Old Fogey', who penned the paper's Midland column, reported that 'Billy' Rose, the Wolves goalkeeper, was finding it harder than he had anticipated eliciting a response from his fellow professionals.

Rose had sent a circular to every League club suggesting a conference of leading players to discuss 'a possible cutting down of wages'. The players, he felt, 'must have a voice in these matters'.

But in November 'Old Fogey' reported that only a few clubs had replied to the circular and that Rose had given up the idea. The reason for the poor response was because the question of wages – the threat of a maximum wage plus cuts in summer pay – had been swiftly dispensed with.

Derby County had put forward the idea of a £140 a year maximum in September 1893, but few clubs were then in favour and the proposal had been thrown out at the League AGM. League minutes suggest that the president, J J Bentley, did discuss the idea with certain players, though whether Rose was among them is not known.

Yet although the maximum wage issue appeared to have been settled, it would not go away. The fact that clubs were anxiously discussing such cost-cutting ideas just eight years after the official acceptance of professionalism suggested that all was not well where football finances were concerned.

Attendances were rising – the 1890s saw a veritable boom in gates – yet the problems posed by such a rapid rise in popularity were becoming apparent. Individual League clubs' grounds were too small and inadequate, and during the 1890s a great deal of football finance would be ploughed into improving them – enclosures, grandstands, terracing etc. In fact, the whole business climate of professional football changed during these years. In 1893 only seven clubs were limited companies – that number would rapidly rise.

Thus it was inevitable that League clubs, especially the smaller ones, were being forced to consider running costs and, as the League was ostensibly a collective enterprise, its members bound together for mutual benefit, proposals to regulate wages (in the absence of agreement on pooling gate money) would affect all clubs, no matter what their size and profitability.

For the majority of players, however, a maximum wage of £4 a week (the Derby proposal) would have made little difference to their lives. Many players then still had trades and jobs; few actually

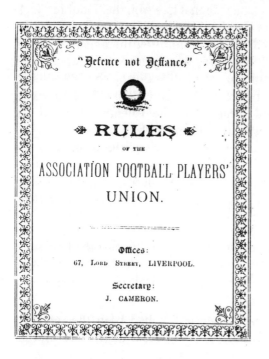

*Rule book of the old Union, circa 1898*

earned more than £4 a week anyway – while the concept of football as a 'profession' was still a weak one.

Yet within a few years conditions would have changed so rapidly in the football industry that the question of organization would be raised again, this time more urgently, and with dramatic results.

In the *Lancashire Daily Post* of 22 December 1897 there appeared a headline: Football Professionals Form a Union. An Ambitious Scheme Floated. The sudden appearance of the Union came as a surprise to many observers. There had been little advance publicity, no circulars to leading players. Yet the men involved were all 'stars' and the authoritative *Cricket and Football Field* was certainly impressed, commenting in the same month, 'They are representative in every way and men who would do credit to any organization as its champions.'

Champions they undoubtedly were. They included Bob Holmes and Jimmy Ross of Preston; John Devey of Aston Villa; John Somerville of Bolton Wanderers; Jack Bell of Everton; Hugh McNeill of Sunderland and Harry Wood of Wolves.

Holmes was almost ever-present in the England team during the early 1890s while both he and Ross had been members of the 'Invincibles', that classic Preston side that had won the 'Double'. Jack Bell would win ten caps for Scotland between 1890 and 1900, while Wood and Dave Calderhead (another committee member) were both respected internationals. John Devey was Aston Villa's captain and there was no more powerful team than Villa during the 1890s – five times League champions between 1894 and 1900. McNeill was a member of the Sunderland 'Team of all the Talents' – three times champions in four years between 1892 and 1895.

Here were men who had been at the top of the profession for almost as long as the League had been in existence. Thus they were well aware of the disturbing changes taking place and in the opening lines of the first report on a Players' Union meeting, the *raison d'être* of the Union was clearly stated:

> The recent international agreement arrived at between the English and Scottish League has had the effect of stimulating the professional players in England to take action whereby to safeguard their own interests.

The international agreement referred to had been the result of moves by the Football League to 'co-ordinate matters of mutual interest' (as the League historian put it). The two Leagues had agreed to make the retain and transfer system binding on both sides of the border. Thus players were no longer free to cross the border and sign a contract on their own behalf.

The League had thus closed a significant loophole in its defences; what was more, it was reportedly talking to representatives of the Southern League to see if a similar agreement could be arranged with them. Therefore, although the aims of the new Union included the establishment of a widows' and orphans' fund, and a permanent disablement fund, it was the transfer system ('that horrid business', as a contemporary journalist described it) that was the Union's primary target.

At this early stage it could count on a number of influential FA figures to support its stance. The FA was equally disgusted by the way the League had developed the transfer system – indeed, there was a real question mark over its legality.

The Union thus began life with a fund of moral indignation to fuel its progress – particularly as it took a deliberately non-controversial (non-political) stance, John Devey declaring, 'We're not taking up the question of wages and we are not taking any strike business.'

It had also secured a useful means of communicating its aims and activities to the wider world. The *Lancashire Daily Post* correspondent 'Abaris' was a friend of both Devey and Holmes. The Union therefore granted his paper exclusive rights to report on its affairs. Within weeks of that first meeting, Abaris was able to reveal that meetings had taken place between English and Scottish players with a view to establishing a Scottish branch.

Bearing in mind that it had been the establishment of an International Board by the English and Scottish Leagues that had led to the creation of the Union, such a move was inevitable. It was not, however, universally welcomed and it sounded the first controversial note in the proceedings. As the *Cricket and Football Field* reported in early 1898: 'The desires of some of those consulted [in Scotland] are scarcely met by the moderate and pacific programme adopted in England.'

The Scottish branch had been mooted during a trip to Glasgow by Everton to play Ranger in a friendly match. Old friendships appear to have been re-established, in particular with Dan Doyle, ex-Evertonian, and now with Celtic.

Doyle, said to be one of the Scottish committee members, had been at the centre of many a controversy in the late 1880s and early 1890s. In fact, he virtually represented all that had once been wrong with the professional football system.

A genuine 'rolling stone', he had signed for many English clubs, sometimes for more than one at a time. Leaving Hibernian in the late 1880s, he had played for, among others, Sunderland Albion, Grimsby Town and Bolton Wanderers (for just a few months) before finally moving to Everton.

The last move had angered J J Bentley, League president and Bolton committee member, because Doyle had concealed his intention to move to Everton and had broken a contract.

After a successful period with the Liverpool club, where he teamed up at fullback with George Hannah, he had suddenly decamped to Scotland, breaking his contract once again. Celtic had lured him with the promise of a public house; subsequent legal action by Everton failed to bring him back.

Thus the appearance of Doyle as a Union executive must have given many a League official pause for thought. Exactly what the 'desires' of the Scots members were that had caused the *Cricket and Football Field* correspondent such disquiet were never revealed. Nevertheless, it did not go unremarked that Doyle's arrival at Celtic had sparked off a strike for higher wages (this when officially no Scottish club actually paid wages!).

The Scottish link was important for the new Union, however, where the question of funds was concerned. For the next three years Scottish Union members would play English Union members in benefit matches to raise cash – with varying degrees of success.

Back in England, the organizational work continued apace. An Emergency Committee consisting of Holmes, Bell, Somerville, Wood and Charlie Saer of Leicester was elected to meet monthly, and the list of clubs claiming members was reported to embrace almost every club in the two divisions. Only Sheffield seemed reluctant. According to Fred Spikesly, England international winger: 'There appears to be a disinclination to let the committee of their clubs know that they are in any way concerned with the movement.'

Such wariness, however, appears to have been rare. Intimidation by management was reported to be non-existent, while 'every member is pledged to a course of missionary work each to prosecute his efforts wherever there is pro football'.

By late February 1898 the Union rules had been drawn up and these were announced at a meeting of the Emergency Committee at the Spread Eagle Hotel, Manchester.

The Union – now known officially as the Association Footballers' Union – had been advised to register under the Trades Union Act rather than the Friendly Society Act, and already the Union was involving itself in the day-to-day administration of the game. A case was cited where a member had come to the Union for advice regarding a dispute between himself and his club concerning his contract, and the matter had been settled after consultation.

Union secretary John Cameron of Everton announced that membership stood at 250 – all members of League clubs, although he insisted that the Union was open to 'all men who played football for a livelihood'.

What is interesting about the Union's tactics at this point is that, even where the vexed question of transfers was concerned, a gradualist, moderate approach was insisted upon. Thus Cameron explained: 'The Union has decided to touch upon what appears to be only the fringe of the question.' In other words, they wanted any negotiations regarding transfers to be between the interested club and the player concerned – not between club and club with the player excluded. Abolition of the system was not at that point on the agenda.

The suggestion was going to be put to the Football League at the latter's AGM in May 1898. As Abaris commented: 'Evidently it is the intention of the Union not to permit time to elapse before they commence a programme of active work. They are opening by tackling one of the knottiest points that could engage their attention. And the League club managers will not receive the news with complete composure.'

League club managers – or more accurately for this period, directors and shareholders – might well have felt apprehension at the prospect of having to deal with a strong, well-organized and determined body of players. However, even at this early, relatively optimistic stage, it was evident that the AFU was beginning to show signs of internal discontent.

The fact that so many Union activists were members of either Liverpool or Everton caused a certain amount of resentment among other members at what appeared to be an exclusive 'clique' of players – and when many of them later in the season moved on to the Southern League at apparently fabulous salaries, the disillusion would be almost complete.

As April approached, however, the AFU confidently put forward its rules and constitution for ratification by the Football Association at the latter's traditional eve-of-Cup Final meeting. This was a necessary step given that the FA was the supreme governing body in the game; if the AFU wanted to thrive and be allowed to hold fund-raising matches, then FA blessing was crucial. Given the FA's opposition to the transfer system and its apparent espousal of players' rights, few problems were anticipated.

The Union was in for a rude shock.

The announcement that the FA had refused to sanction the rules of the AFU – in fact, had refused to recognize the Union until it changed its rules – made no headlines in the sporting press. The news gradually filtered into various columns of sporting chatter just at the point in the year when cricket was taking over, when the majority of players were heading off on holiday or back to full-time work. There were no interviews with Union officials; instead, 'Gossip' in the *Cricket and Football Field* of June 1898 speculated:

> Considerable astonishment must have been caused by the reception accorded by the Council of the FA to the rules of the Players' Union. I know that the bulk of the Union members feared some difficulty so far as the League is concerned but they thought the Association would be strongly in their favour.

The Union had made the mistake of thinking that FA support for its case regarding the reform of the transfer system meant support for the idea of the Union itself; whereas, unionism in football (in the FA's eyes) only threatened yet more financial wrangling, possibly even in court. As the *Cricket and Football Field* editors accurately put it:

> They [the Union] must now recognize that the FA does not intend to abrogate its authority or to lightly permit anything which might easily make certain phases of professionalism very squalid indeed.

The FA spelled out its objections a week or so later. According to their interpretation, Union Rule 2c ('To protect the interests of members against undue or arbitrary measures adopted or to be adopted by the FA, the Football League or any other recognized football authority') assumed a position antagonistic to the FA's jurisdiction. Moreover, the FA felt that the rules relating to the provision of legal assistance 'may be detrimental to the interests of true sport'. Legal proceedings, the FA declared, would be a last resort and then only if the FA gave its permission.

Alteration or deletion of the objectionable rules would enable the FA to recognize the Union and, more important, to sanction the benefit match for which arrangements had already been made. There was little the Union could do at that point to accept the FA's decision and water down its rules accordingly.

It reasoned that to attract members, particularly the rank and file, an accident or insurance scheme of some sort was essential. To help finance this, funds were needed, and the only method – Union subscriptions being negligible at that point – was a prestigious match. It was, after all, through the receipts from international matches or inter-League games that the League and the FA financed themselves.

Unfortunately, the benefit match played at Ibrox Park on 28 April was a flop. Poor weather and weak teams (for England, no Steve Bloomer, Fred Spikesly or Earnest Needham, for they were not, apparently, Union members) led to an indifferent match watched by a poor crowd.

To make matters worse, it was at about this point that the first rumblings of discontent from certain players were heard concerning the way the Union was being run. 'Olympic' in *Athletic News* reported that several members had not yet received copies of the Union rules and that money spent on committee meetings was excessive.

John Cameron replied via an open letter in the press in which he rebutted such 'uncalled for comments'. The rule-books had been sent out some months ago and the expenses had been no more than might have been expected during a period of formation. The Union books, he declared, were open for anyone to inspect:

> The Union has quite sufficient difficulties to contend with without the addition of unfair criticisms and insinuations by the press. In fact, the Union rather looks to the press for assistance in its efforts to protect the interests of its members.

Nothing seemed to be going right for the Union and the summer of 1898, instead of proving to be a breathing space in which to regroup and consolidate, would only bring further body-blows to what appeared to be an ailing organization.

# 3

# *Charlie Saer's Transfer Scheme* 1898

The Southern League, having failed to reach an agreement with the Football League regarding amalgamation, now posed itself as a rival.

At a time when League club finances were stretched, with accompanying complaints about existing wage levels, Southern League clubs began enticing Football League stars to defect with promises of up to £100 signing-on fees plus £4–£5 a week all the year round.

Tottenham Hotspur, in particular, were searching for talented men and offering the likes of Billy Meredith, the new star of Wales and Manchester City, unheard-of sums to break their contracts.

Unfortunately for the AFU's image, some of the most notable Southern League captures turned out to be its own Management Committee men.

First to go was Harry Wood of Wolves, whom Southampton signed in May for a reputed £100 a year increase in wages. Next to depart were McNaught of Newton Heath and Bradshaw of Liverpool – both of them Management Committee men, both signing with Tottenham Hotspur for substantial sums.

In July John Bell left Everton for London to see what Spurs might offer, but eventually signed with Celtic for £300, a move that brought predictable press criticism. How, it was asked, could Bell, the Union chairman, complain about the morality of the system when he appeared willing to be sold 'like a chattel' provided he received a substantial lump sum himself?

A more serious blow was struck that same month when John Cameron, the Union secretary, moved from Everton to Tottenham Hotspur. An amateur player who had represented Scotland in 1896 while playing for Queen's Park, he had spent no more than two seasons with Everton, much of the time in the reserves. He had worked as a clerk for the shipping line Cunard; however, towards the end of the 1897-8 season he had established himself in the Everton side and appeared on the point of signing professional forms. He was still only 26, an astute ball-playing inside forward – but Everton suddenly swung against 'the Scottish element'. It was a time of great change at the club, with great players retiring and moving on. Cameron found himself on the transfer list.

Not being a star player, his move to Tottenham was scarcely remarked upon. But for the Union it meant yet further dislocation and confusion. Membership – now pitifully low – was practically nil in the South, and with its secretary 'stranded' in London, things were beginning to look bleak.

In mid-July, Bob Holmes, interviewed in the *Lancashire Daily Post*, gave the impression that the Union, barely a year old, was on the point of collapse, saying, 'I am not quite sure that we shall succeed in attaining all the objects with which we set out; it is not a certainty that we shall carry any .... The break-up of the Everton team as we knew it last season may have a good deal in influencing the future of the Union. With Cameron, Jack Bell, Robertson, Holt, Stewart, Storrier, Meecham of Everton as well as Hartley and Bradshaw of Liverpool gone, our centre has lost strength. Liverpool was our headquarters, you know, and our registered offices were there. But the secretary, John Cameron, has gone to London and Bell the chairman will not, so far as we know, play for anybody. Cameron says the office will be transferred to London but that cannot be done until next December and I don't fancy that even after that it will come off.'

Could not a successor to Cameron be appointed? he was asked. 'Yes, but that's not the whole of it,' he replied. 'Our position as to members is not what it ought to be. At first the players all over the country seized on the idea with the eagerness of a child for a new toy.

*'My boy,' said the lady, 'I don't like to see that kind of bird being sold. You'll let them go, to please me, won't you?'*

*'Yes, Lady,' said the boy, 'course I will.' (M'yes! Lots of it!)*

But now there no longer comes any addition to our membership and those who do remain members seem to have entirely to have lost interest in the concern. We shall know at the end of this year whether the thing is to live or not, because if the players do not continue their membership – and it is not certain that they will – well, then, there remains nothing but the name of the National Association Football Players' Union.'

A week later, in the same paper, Jimmy Ross was asked for his opinion of the Union. Yes, he agreed, it was a doomed body: 'We never hear anything of it and don't want to. We are so well protected by the rules of the Football Association as to need no Union. I am the delegate for North East Lancashire but since the second meeting of the Union I have heard nothing from it.'

Thus the Management Committee meeting at the Maypole, Nottingham, in August 1898 should have been little more than a wake. In fact, it proved to be something of a resurrection.

Those present, principally Charlie Saer, Bob Holmes and Harold Munroe of Gainsborough Trinity were clear as to what had gone wrong: 'Too much had been expected and too little sweeping changes effected'. However, there was still a little money left and it was decided that fresh efforts should be made to keep the Union alive: 'Some fresh paths must be trodden.'

Holmes was once again elected to the chair, and announced that the transfer system 'is a grave and many-sided problem – and one that must not be hastily disturbed'. Saer, appointed secretary to replace John Cameron, appeared to disagree with Holmes on this point and wasted no time in reopening the debate on the subject. Indeed, in a letter to the *Lancashire Daily Post* some two weeks after the Maypole meeting, Saer launched into a full-scale assault on the transfer system, calling the League regulations 'a mass of inconsistency and injustice' and asserting that 'the object of the transfer system is to prevent competition and to give each club the power to monopolize the services of its players as long as it chooses. I claim this monopoly is in direct contravention to the rules of the FA.'

The system, he continued, caused players to 'appear as prospectuses, as more or less valued assets of a limited liability company'. It had 'destroyed the old personal bond of friendly feeling between us and club managers ... and brought the latter to regard us as chattels to be bought and sold. What wonder that the loyalty of players to their clubs is a diminishing quantity year by year? We have to thank the transfer system for bringing us down to the level of beasts in the market place. The commodity – the player – has no locus standing. The part that the League has played in settling the transfers question may be compared with that of an arbitrator in a difference between the purchaser and the seller of a horse. The horse is not allowed a say as to the price to be paid for him. Neither is the player. But in one respect the horse is better off than the player, for until he is sold his owner is bound to keep him in food and shelter. But the club can hold the player for sale for an indefinite period without doing anything to maintain him ...' The League system, he concluded, 'in its present form, must go!'

With a nice touch of unconscious irony the *Lancashire Daily Post* sports editor placed Saer's column alongside the first in a series of profiles of Famous Men In Football, the inaugural subject being C.E. Sutcliffe. A line drawing of Sutcliffe accompanying the text had this formidable League official and administrator almost turning his back in disdain on Saer's impassioned argument. It could not have summed up the forthcoming tussle between the two men more succinctly.

Not surprisingly, Saer's emergence as secretary and thus chief spokesman of the AFU galvanized the near moribund organization to such an extent that, for a few brief months, the Union was to play

FAMOUS MEN IN FOOTBALL.

NO. VIII.—MR. CHARLES SAER,
SECRETARY OF THE PLAYERS' UNION.

Lancashire Daily Post, *September 1898.*

a central role in football politics, standing between the League and the FA, if not as mediator then certainly as a repository of common sense.

In many respects, Saer was ideally suited to the post. His playing career had been moderate but respectable. Trained initially as a teacher, he played for three years as an amateur for Fleetwood Rangers, a non-League side. A fine goalkeeper, he had once had ambitions to represent Wales (having been born in a small village in West Camarthenshire) but had been unfortunate to be playing during the reign of James Trainer, 'Prince of Deepdalia' in the Welsh goal. Towards the end of 1897-8 he went to First Division Blackburn Rovers and from there to Second Division Leicester City. The following season saw him injured and in dispute with Leicester regarding back-pay. In fact, he would never play League football again, ultimately preferring to take up a position under the Fleetwood School Board.

Saer was thus freer than most of his more illustrious colleagues to devote his time and energy to the job and the fact that he had been trained and educated beyond board school level was essential; he saw a strategy where most of his colleagues simply saw red.

In early October at a Management Committee meeting in Preston, Saer's importance was emphatically underlined. Present at the meeting were some familiar faces: John Bell, now with Celtic; Hugh McNeill, Sunderland captain; John Devey, Aston Villa; Bob Holmes of Preston and Harold Munroe of Gainsborough. Holmes was voted into the chair and immediately invited an accountant named Rushton to submit the Provident and Accident scheme suggested at the last meeting.

Having listened patiently to the scheme, John Devey, declared, 'that unfortunately it was a direction in which they would move in the not very distant future, but at present it could scarcely be considered ripe for the acceptance of so considerable a responsibility'. Instead, 'they must do something to prove to existing and possible members that the Union exists for some real object.... Let them show the general body of players that there was a Union capacity for effecting reforms and an earnest desire to bring about such improvements in their lot as all desired to see.'

That led, inexorably, to the transfer system – its reform, if not its abolition. 'That is all we joined for', declared McNeill, confirming Devey's estimation of the general mood. As Mr Rushton rolled up his plans and left the room, Charlie Saer took centre stage.

Saer outlined an alternative transfer system, based on the logical notion of tying a man's fee to what his club considered he was worth in terms of wages offered. He then went on to the practical politics, referring critically to a plan C E Sutcliffe had outlined a week or so earlier concerning the extension of the League to take in the Southern League. This, Saer declared, 'meant the complete hemming-in of the players.... The men would be absolutely tied and their liberty worse restricted than was the case now.' They must, he continued, not calmly submit to such a thing and he proposed that the Union approach the League with his new scheme *before* the Southern League amalgamation was completed. If the League turned down the Union idea, 'the Union has a powerful weapon to wield'.

The FA had to give its sanction to any extension of the League; if the League refused to reform the transfer system, the Union would apply to the Association to refuse the League permission to extend its borders.

The delegates were enthusiastic; they now had something to work with – a scheme and a strategy. Saer then put before the committee a letter he had drafted to the *Lancashire Daily Post* outlining the scheme. It was approved. Something was happening!

Charlie Saer's transfer system:

I If a club offers a player no terms for the ensuing season, no fee shall be charged for his transfer. An offer of less than £1 a week – £52 a year – shall not be considered a bona-fide one.

2 If a club offers a player a sum exceeding £52 a year then should he refuse, half the difference between £52 and the sum offered shall be the maximum fee chargeable for his transfer.

The following table shows at a glance how the maximum transfer fee is arrived at in the cases of players offered various weekly wages:

| Player | Weekly salary offered Winter 35 weeks £ | Summer 17 weeks £ | Total annual salary £ | Less £52 £ | Half the difference or max. transfer fee £ |
|---|---|---|---|---|---|
| A | – | – | – | S | – |
| B | 1 | 1 | 52 | – | |
| C | 2 | – | 70 | 18 | 9 |
| D | 2 | 2 | 104 | 52 | 26.10 |
| E | 3 | 2 | 139 | 87 | 43.10 |
| F | 3 | 3 | 155 | 104 | 52 |
| G | 4 | 4 | 208 | 156 | 78 |
| H | 5 | 5 | 260 | 208 | 104 |

Lancashire Daily Post, *October 1898.*

Saer certainly managed to capture the high-ground; his ideas were soon being discussed and mulled over in editorial offices up and down the country. The *Lancashire Daily Post* ran an editorial on the day of the unveiling of the scheme beneath a headline, 'The Impending Crisis', and for a while it looked as though the League's bluff might be called. The editor wrote:

The fact that so many players change their situation between one season and another and that one hears no protests from them as to transfer matters induces the impression that existing conditions are agreeable to the general body of players. But when men like John

Devey, Hugh McNeill, John Bell, Charles Saer and others, each speaking for a wider constituency, utterly condemn the systems it becomes apparent that though on the surface there may seem contentment and satisfaction there is, beneath the veneer of indifference, a deep-seated dissatisfaction.

Saer, in his letter, played on this apparent tendency of the League to stifle debate, to pretend that all was well within their domain, and proceeded to involve the FA:

> One of the rules of the Association is that after 30 April of each year a player is free to sign for any club he pleases. By the operation of the League laws, however, the above rule is already partially a dead letter and the proposed amalgamation would make it completely useless. For a League player is NOT free to sign for any club after 30 April ...

The approaching monopoly of the League, its apparent refusal to revise transfer prices on the appeal of players – all this, Saer claimed, made the players apprehensive. The FA, he was sure, 'would undoubtedly refuse to allow its own rules to be over-ridden by a syndicate of Leaguers'.

In that, he would be sadly mistaken.

However, his broadside (during which he likened League clubs holding players to ransom in the manner of Italian banditti) had one immediate consequence. It forced C E Sutcliffe himself to put pen to paper.

The short, carefully worded article was the first of many that Sutcliffe would pen over the next forty years or more, and already the characteristic tone was present – seemingly down to earth, rational and calm, yet tinged with a sarcasm that the powerful occasionally enjoy using on lesser mortals. And Sutcliffe was, even by November 1898, probably the most powerful man in League football.

He had been involved in League administration for only five years, but since 1893 his progress, according to Abaris, had been phenomenal:

> Look at his record. Five years ago he was unknown or forgotten in football circles; today he is chairman of the Burnley club, League representative of that club; a member of the League management committee; a committee-man of the Lancashire Association;

ex-secretary and present committee-man of the Lancashire Combination; member of the executive of the Lancashire Referees Association; and last and perhaps most important of all, one of the four delegates from the English League to the International League Board.

Sutcliffe's *Lancashire Daily Post* article, though apparently all sweet reasonableness, was in fact a warning. Declaring his willingness to meet and talk to Mr Saer, he continued: 'May I point out, however, there is no need for either threats or fears.' He did not desire the end of freedom of movement for players. Rather, he wanted a system in which clubs should have a 'maximum of interest at a minimum of cost so that clubs can pay their way and all players receive a generous remuneration for their services'.

Furthermore, he had no desire to see the Players' Union die. 'It has only been my desire that the Union do good work on the right lines for the benefit of the club and the player alike. There is plenty of room for the players union but to set up in antagonism to the League and the Association is to court death and certain failure ...'

He was certain, however, that it was the will of the 'new' union to keep peace with the League, 'notwithstanding Mr Saer's war-like attitude'. And he concluded by asserting once again that he and the League would listen carefully to what Mr Saer had to say and would not prejudge the issues. But, 'afterwards I may have something to say on the system Mr Saer so much abominates but which appears to be an integral part of the success of so many clubs.'

The League, in the person of Sutcliffe, was certainly not going to change the transfer system unless it was forced to; and Charlie Saer's alternative system, though a reasonable enough talking point, was never going to prove attractive to League clubs and their directorates. By tying the fee of a player to the wages he might be offered, Saer's scheme drastically reduced the amounts clubs might hope to 'earn' on the sale of a good player.

This, according to an unnamed club manager writing to the *Lancashire Daily Post* a few days later, would stop clubs spending money on discovering and nurturing players. As for Saer's other rule, that if a player was offered no wages, then he should be allowed to leave the club with no fee payable, this, according to 'Club Manager', would simply lead to players 'playing for their papers', i.e. not playing at all, thus forcing the management to get rid of them. There was little to support such accusations, and little chance that they would be put to the test.

The promised meeting between Union officials and the League Management Committee did, in fact, take place but resulted in a meaningless exchange of views – a delaying tactic the League would employ with numbing regularity for the next sixty years or more.

And within a few weeks of the meeting with the League, Charlie Saer tendered his resignation from the Union. Although it was explained at the first Players' Union AGM in December that 'Mr Saer had no alternative but to retire as his scholastic duties precluded the possibility of his devoting the necessary time to the office', it was clear that Saer had rapidly grown tired of football politics.

The *Bolton Cricket and Football Field* pointed to his disputes with Leicester Fosse concerning the wages owed to him. He had, 'now severed his connections with Stockport County under circumstances which may cause Stockport County to appear before the FA'. Saer, the correspondent claimed, 'is said to have sickened of the game'.

The Union Management Committee declared its support for his scheme and hoped he would be able to play a part in subsequent Union affairs – but Charlie Saer had seen enough of football's problems.

# 4

# 'A Practical Failure' 1901

With the departure of Charlie Saer, John Cameron resumed as full-time secretary and presented the financial and political balance sheet at the Union's first AGM held at the Spread Eagle Hotel, Manchester on 12 December 1898.

The Union now claimed to represent a little over 400 players and possessed a cash balance of £132.8.10. Bob Holmes was once again elected chairman. In his address, the day-to-day work of the Union was emphasized: sums of money had been sent to relatives of players who had died; a campaign had been conducted amongst non-League professionals informing them of their rights. Apparently agreements were unheard of outside the League and some players were being induced to play for clubs on the promise of a percentage of the gate money. Of course, many received nothing at all.

Holmes was always particularly keen on such 'missionary' work. Later in the year he was to claim a significant victory in a case brought against Notts County where the club was forced to pay a player wages and expenses after the latter had had to undergo treatment for an injury received while playing. The Players' Union as watchdog, forcing recalcitrant clubs to fulfil their contractual obligations – this, Holmes felt, was the Union's true purpose, not conducting 'political' campaigns against the transfer system.

Holmes thus placed great store by the FA's earnest attempts during 1899 to grapple with the transfer 'problem'. Although the League had poured cold water on the Players' Union scheme, the FA – in the person of J C Clegg – was determined to confront the issue, and so in March 1899 a formal conference was called to which all interested parties were invited: the Football League, the Lancashire League, the Southern League, the United League, etc. – and the Players Union.

A circular containing some of Clegg's conclusions following the conference was produced, and the Players' Union must have been encouraged. Clegg was known for his dislike of the transfer system and was adamant that it was contrary to the laws of the Association. He therefore suggested that transfers be abolished and longer contracts be instituted – of two or three years in length. John Cameron would have been extremely pleased at that – for he had put just such an idea to the Union AGM in December.

It soon became clear, however, that the League was not going to budge. Suggestions by the FA that if the transfer system was to remain in place, players should at least receive a share of the fee, were greeted with incredulity by League officials. Many clubs were already agitating for the abolition of bonuses. A slice of the transfer fee, it was claimed, would result in chaos – the inherent greed of players would lead to their conniving at transfers in order to enrich themselves.

Faced with endless League prevarication, the FA resolved to take action. A special committee was set up to look into the system, and reported: 'The buying and selling of players in the name of sport is both discredited and contrary to the rules of the Association.' It made two recommendations – that the present rules be amended so that players for whom a fee had already been paid could be sold again, but at a fee no higher than the original one; second, that in future, no transfer fees of more than £10 be paid.

In some ways, the FA's attitude was even more radical than that of the Players' Union; and it appeared certain that a grand collision was imminent. As 'Perseus' in the *Lancashire Daily Post* announced: 'Breakers Ahead!' But outright war never occurred. Although there were suggestions that the League might break away from the FA, that its teams should withdraw from the FA Cup, such drastic measures were never seriously contemplated. The League's resolve, however, was not in doubt. J J Bentley declared: 'The serious battle will be fought on what the League considers a principle and that is being allowed to work its own particular competition in its own particular way whilst at the same time observing the rules of the parent body.'

During November and December 1899, League after League voted on the FA's proposals and all rejected the idea of abolishing the transfer system. In February 1900 the Players' Union met in Manchester to consider its response. The statement it finally issued captures the prevailing air of helplessness and futility: 'That whilst recognizing the injustices of the present system the Union could not possibly see how it could be abolished in all fairness to the clubs in one fell swoop. Alterations and improvements could be made to it and the players look to the Association and League to remedy the present defects at least.'

It was now clear that C E Sutcliffe was setting the agenda for the debate – indeed, he went as far as to issue a challenge to those FA legislators 'who have written and said so much about the sale of flesh and blood and slavery of the professional footballer and who are so anxious that the last shred of true sport should not be eliminated from the game might give some thought to the wages question and propound a scheme whereby the paying of a player £10 a week throughout the year would become an impossibility'.

He appeared to be saying that if wages were controlled, then large clubs could not so easily tempt good players from smaller clubs and thus the 'difficulty' of the transfer system would soon diminish. Add to that some scheme whereby League gates might be pooled and 'equality of exchequer be obtained' and the financial fears of smaller clubs would be alleviated: thus the idea that players were simply 'assets' to be sold for hard cash whenever necessary would become irrelevant.

The FA could not, of course, legislate where the pooling of gates was concerned, but it could deal with wages. And whether in response to Sutcliffe's goading or simply – as suggested by the League's own historian – the FA wanted to get back at the League for having refused to take up its transfer system reforms, the FA, urged on by some smaller League clubs, did indeed pass a rule at its May 1900 AGM setting a maximum wage of £4 a week – and abolishing all bonuses at the same time.

The Players' Union could only look on in disbelief. The FA had

Mr. Football Legislator:—"You'll have to come down; this one is quite high enough for you."

Lancashire Daily Post, *circa 1900*.

been its main hope in the battle for freedom. Now it was adding yet more restrictions. Indeed, the FA now had powers to investigate League clubs and their finances, powers that it would use with all the determination and distaste of a body inherently opposed to professionalism.

John Cameron, interviewed by *Football Chat* in London where he had now taken on the job of secretary of Tottenham Hotspur, expressed his surprise and dismay:

> In my opinion, the FA have not acted with their usual discretion over the wages question. Surely the matter of wages is for club legislation alone? Every club knows, or ought to know, what it can afford to pay and if they go above their means I should certainly call it bad management and the club who does that deserves to be stranded. I noticed with a little amusement that it was those clubs that had paid more than they could afford that fought hard to carry the new measures through. Now look here, how would any man in business like to have his wages reduced by 25% if his employers could well afford better terms?

For John Cameron, however, the most pressing problem was no

longer the maximum wage nor the transfer system. As the new century got under way, it was now a matter of the very survival of the Players' Union.

It is ironic that the Players' Union, the weakest of all the football organizations, should have possessed in its secretary, John Cameron, one of the most talented and intelligent of administrators. Fortunately for Cameron, he was able to realize his talents at Tottenham Hotspur where, in an eight-year period initially as player, then as manager, he succeeded in building the first truly great professional side in southern England. Had Tottenham not proved such a triumph, the Players' Union might perhaps have survived – it can be no coincidence that 1901, the year the Union was finally wound up, was also the year that Tottenham won the FA Cup.

The Union's demise, however, was no fault of Cameron's. The year 1900 saw intense activity in football politics, with the FA and the League at loggerheads over the transfer system and with a maximum wage threatened for the following year. But instead of finding himself at the heart of things, Cameron was appealing to football's professionals to support their own organization. An editorial in the *Lancashire Daily Post* commented on Cameron's dilemma:

> It must be a very great disappointment to the officials that the membership is so low. Only some two hundred footballers are on the books of the English branch at the present time – roughly speaking, little more than the number actually playing First Division football each Saturday.

This, the paper pointed out, was half what it had been a year before.

No solid reasons were advanced as to why the Union was floundering. In fact, many editors of sports pages could only see reasons why it ought to have flourished. As Cameron's circular pointed out, there was now a Benevolent Fund in existence that had paid out loans and donations to needy players – more than was being done by the FA's own Benevolent Fund; there had been matches played in aid of families of men who had died leaving no provision; and there had been many cases where advice and legal help had resulted in clubs fulfilling contracts that might otherwise have been torn up.

'ECP' of *Football Chat* in October 1990, ventured to suggest that it was poor communication that was failing to publicize the Union's virtues, even its existence:

> The association has hid its light under a bushel so persistently that to many hundreds of professionals it is quite an unknown body; or if known by name only considered to be an association for the higher grade class of players. Clubs and club managers recognize that football papers are the mediums to make their positions known, but the Players' Union appear never to have recognized this.... Ever since its inception and struggling infancy, never do I recollect receiving a single communication from any officials of the Union.... A season or so back they made my greatly esteemed friend 'Abaris' their press mouthpiece; but at that time he was shut up in proud Preston and quite unable to record the doings of the Union throughout the length and breadth of the United Kingdom and consequently much of his excellent work for the pros was never seen outside a small radius round Preston.

The *Lancashire Daily Post* column had, in fact, ended a year previously with the removal of Abaris to the *Morning Herald*. However, although, when secretary, Charlie Saer had complained of being muzzled by the *Athletic News*, the League mouthpiece and most influential sporting paper, information concerning the Union had regularly appeared in the columns of that and other sports papers, notably the *Bolton Cricket and Football Field* whose editor – not necessarily unsympathetic – was also nonplussed by the poor state of the Union:

> For myself, I cannot understand men failing to join now that they are assured of the permanence of the organization and the soundness of the basis on which it rests. It has proved itself able to achieve sound work in the interests of the men. It has brought cases before the authorities which could otherwise have scarcely reached their ears; and if it hasn't been as aggressive as some of its more pugnacious ones desire it has gained rather than lost as a result of the wise discretion which has marked its doings.... The Union would doubtless have made more noise by a policy of truculence but it would have irreparably damaged its own interests.

All of which sounds logical but perhaps suggests a reason why the Union, despite its apparent achievements, was dying. 'Wise discretion' causes no ripples; 'quiet diplomacy' can also appear as inactivity.

There can be no doubt that the existence of the Union had altered the chemistry of events. Yet whatever it achieved by the diplomatic method had been claimed by others. 'The 'amendments' to the working of the transfer system, for instance, trumpeted by Sutcliffe and the League Management Committee as a generous response to calls for reform, had in truth been the result of Players' Union pressure and lobbying.

As John Cameron admitted to *Football Chat* in November 1900, 'It is nigh three years since we took the matter before the powers that be and until last Friday night when the FA Council met nothing material had been done. Can you wonder therefore that the players grow sceptical?'

By now, Cameron was a manager himself, with a foot in both camps. He could sympathize with League clubs where the transfer system was concerned but he also knew that alternatives were possible:

> Time has made the system almost indispensable to the League clubs. Their finances are wrapped around it for their players are looked upon practically as assets; and when a club is paid a large sum of money for a player you cannot blame them for so doing. They say the system working from the club point of view is a good one, for it gives the clubs a great hold upon the players and perhaps saves a wholesale shifting of players every year which would not be good for the game.... I admit there is some truth in that, but the price is much too heavy on the players. In the Southern League there is no transfer system and yet Southampton, Portsmouth and my own club Tottenham Hotspur and others retain their players year after year; so why not the League?

Ultimately, the answer was that no one seemed able to force the League to change or even to think seriously of a better system. The FA was proving unequal to the task of enforcing its own rules and the League, growing in strength from year to year, was arrogant enough to feel it knew all the answers. As an unnamed club manager put it in October 1898:

> It seems to me the Players' Union wants to govern football and have the League clubs under its finger and thumb. I admire its honesty but the League clubs are in the hands of the men who have made football. The League is governed by men who know something of

club management ... and who can conduct their business without the unsolicited intervention of the Players' Union.

By late 1900, however, the Players' Union was proving unable even to organize its own meetings, let alone intervene in League affairs. And the man who might just have managed to hold things together was increasingly caught up in Tottenham's bid to win the FA Cup. As player-manager, Cameron was taking more and more responsibility for the club's affairs – the Union inevitably suffered. No one else, it seemed, was able to step into Cameron's shoes.

By April 1901, however, preparations for a fourth fund-raising 'international' to be held at Middlesborough on 23 April were said to be well under way. A big conference was scheduled to follow when 'the very existence of the Union would be considered'. At the last moment, however, John Cameron telegraphed to the organizers that, due to the replay of the Cup Final, the whole affair was to be cancelled. At least four members of the Union were taking part in the final who might well have played in the Union match: Kirwan, Priest, Needham and Cameron himself.

In effect, this decision ended the first Players' Union.

The FA Cup won, Cameron was reported in June to be on holiday in Scotland. At its AGM that summer, the FA confirmed the wages 'ceiling' experiment. The Union, it was confidently reported, 'was a practical failure'.

The 'old Union', as it subsequently became known, disappeared so swiftly and completely that it might never have existed. Its achievements were minimal, its membership never more than 50 per cent of League players, its administration rudimentary and generally ineffective. It was a sickly child and was buried in an unmarked pauper's grave.

Nevertheless it cannot be completely dismissed.

The union idea had been given credibility by men of the quality of Cameron, Devey, Holmes and Saer, men who by their intelligence and good sense had demonstrated to the many sceptics that professional footballers were not feckless layabouts nor selfish near-inebriates incapable of concentrating on anything more complicated than kicking a ball. Such attitudes would, of course, persist. They were convenient and served a variety of purposes. The failure of the Union naturally confirmed the sceptical outlook. But a standard had been set; lessons had been learned.

Many of the original Players' Union men went on to greater things. John Cameron proceeded to build a series of superb Tottenham sides following the historic FA Cup win, luring many Football League players away from their clubs in the process, thus causing a great deal of pain and anguish to some of those who had delighted in attacking and belittling the Union when Cameron had been its secretary. Cameron's efforts eventually resulted in Tottenham joining the Football League in 1908; he himself left the club in the previous year to return to Scotland.

Cameron never left football entirely however: he wrote articles and contributed to books (the prestigious *Association Football and the Men Who Made It*, published in 1906, contains an article by him on how to run a football team) as well as writing a small book on tactics and rules. In 1914 he went to Germany to coach the game and was stranded by the outbreak of war. Interned, he continued to organize football teams and even played alongside the famous Steve Bloomer who had also been interned. Following the Armistice, he returned to Scotland to take over Ayr United in 1919 and succeeded in turning the club around within a season before retiring from the game to write a football column.

John Devey was appointed a director of the Aston Villa club once his playing days were over. He also became a successful businessman, joining forces with another famous Villa player, Harry Hampton, to form the Winson Green Picture House Company – opening a 1500-seat cinema in 1915. When he died in 1940 he left an estate worth over £2000.

Jack Bell, after spending a season or so with Celtic, returned to Liverpool where he had a small bicycle business. But he was soon playing again, this time helping to revive the fortunes of fallen giants Preston North End. As captain he helped them back into the First Division and to runners-up position in the First Division in 1906 – it would be another 46 years before Preston would equal that.

Poor Dan Doyle on the other hand, the scourge of many an English League club manager, came to a predictably sorry end, dying in penury after drinking his way through at least three public houses. His efforts on behalf of his fellow professionals had been genuine enough; if only his private life had not been the stuff of which the average director's nightmares were made.

# 5

# *Revival – Meredith and Manchester* 1901–7

In the years between 1901 and the start of the First World War, the Football League strengthened its grip on the professional game, taking in popular Southern clubs such as Fulham, Chelsea, Tottenham and Bristol City. The Southern League, weakened by such defections, pressed for amalgamation but was turned away, although it would eventually come to an arrangement regarding transfers.

Meanwhile, the maximum wage and the transfer system seemed not to have had the desired effect where winners and losers were concerned – the hoped for 'equality' remaining a pipe-dream. The 'Super League' of the 1890s – Aston Villa, Sunderland, Newcastle United and Everton – was joined by Liverpool, Sheffield Wednesday and the two Manchester teams, City and United, and between them these eight teams won all the League titles up to the war. They also took fifty per cent of Cup wins, and between the years 1904 and 1914 there was not a Cup Final that did not feature either one or two of the 'Super Eight'.

The first Players' Union had drawn heavily upon such top teams for its leadership and inspiration. With the rise of new football centres the radical torch would be passed on. Just as Everton, Sunderland and Aston Villa players had come together in the late 1890s to produce the first Management Committee, so in 1907 Manchester and Newcastle players would also discover a close affinity where football politics were concerned, their powerful collective presence drawing in other like-minded men from a variety of clubs – though, curiously, not Aston Villa.

A variety of reasons have been put forward to explain why, in December 1907, the second attempt to form a Union was announced to the sporting press. On the wider political front, legislation such as the Trades Disputes Act 1906 made it easier for unions to operate, and the Workman's Compensation Act of the same year opened the door for players to gain compensation for accidents incurred while playing.

Within the more claustrophobic football world, the FA and Football League had continued to bicker, principally over finances and their respective responsibilities and roles. The FA was, in fact, rapidly moving to a position where it could relinquish all responsibility for financial arrangements between clubs and players.

Thus players perhaps saw an opportunity to reopen their case for economic freedom; a few may even have had before them the vision of an independent breakaway League composed of top League teams. These and other considerations must have contributed towards creating an atmosphere ripe for exploitation. But historical forces, no matter how powerful, have to work through individuals, and individuals often arrive at history's turning points via circuitous, sometimes even baffling, routes.

One of the main features of the first dozen or so years of the new century, where the Football League was concerned, was the rapid rise to fame of Manchester. Prior to 1900, neither Ardwick (which became Manchester City in 1894) nor Newton Heath (Manchester United in 1902) had made much of an impact (although Ardwick had once featured on the League's 'blacklist' for excessive poaching).

Although Newton Heath had been a member of the First Division since 1892, it was City which first found real success – promoted to the First Division in 1899, Cup winners in 1903, League runners-up in the same year, they set the pace for United to follow. By 1908 United were League champions and City were in third place. Belatedly, Manchester was now a force in football. Behind the bare facts, however, lay a more complicated, fascinating story, one with direct consequences for the Players' Union.

The maximum wage, imposed in 1901, was almost impossible to adhere to for ambitious big city clubs like Manchester City. The Manchester public, not to say businessmen and local worthies, were anxious for success. That one of the nation's largest cities, home of the industrial revolution, should be unable to produce a prestigious team seemed absurd, even insulting. Such expectations made for impatience, which in turn led to the bending of many rules.

When First Division status – painfully earned on a shoestring budget – was briefly lost in 1901, wholesale changes occurred at Hyde Road, Manchester City's original home. Backed by newspaper millionaire Edward Hulton's money, Scotsman Tom Maley rapidly bought and built a successful new side that swept back into the First Division and took the FA Cup to Manchester for the first time the following year.

Billy Meredith, for a decade the City team's star, explained the sudden success simply:

> What was the secret of the success of the Manchester City team? In my opinion, the fact that the club put aside the rule that no player should receive more than four pounds a week.... The team delivered the goods, the club paid for the goods delivered and both sides were satisfied.

The following season, however, City's strong challenge for the League title ended disappointingly: needing to beat Aston Villa in their last match (in the hope that Newcastle might drop a point at lowly Middlesborough), City tried hard but lost 3-2. The match was marred by fighting among the players both during and after the game and, following as it did some ugly incidents in an earlier City versus Everton match, the FA felt obliged to investigate.

The subsequent enquiry revealed startling and totally unexpected evidence of attempted bribery involving of Meredith and, despite his protestations of innocence, he was suspended for a year, banned from City's ground and fined.

More sensations were to follow as Meredith, angered by the attitude of Manchester's City's officials, pestered the club for financial recompense. This led to yet more official investigations with Meredith ultimately turning 'King's Evidence', admitting

illegal payments and thus bringing down the whole house of cards
City had so carefully constructed.

So outraged was the FA by what had been uncovered that it
virtually dismembered the club: the complete Cup-winning side of
1903 was suspended and banned from ever playing for City again;
directors (including Josh Parlby, one of the original Football
League founder members) were banned for life and the club was
fined to within an inch of survival.

Meredith, along with other key City players, was subsequently
snapped up by Manchester United, a club with just as much
ambition as City but with a rather more far-sighted management.
Within two years United were League champions, the following
year they took the Cup and in 1910 the whole organization moved
from east to west across the city to spacious Old Trafford, to a
stadium built for the twentieth century and a fitting stage for its
talented, attractive team.

Despite his successful move to United, however, Meredith was a
changed person. The traumatic events of 1905-6 had turned a
taciturn but essentially contented man into a bitterly aggressive
critic of a system he felt had robbed him, not just of his dignity, but
also of the financial rewards he considered were rightfully his.
Moreover, for a few horrific months he had been an outcast, with
no prospect of employment in football, facing bankruptcy: no
benefit, heavy fines to pay, his career in ruins.

A more cynical man might have shrugged his shoulders and
awaited developments. After all, it was a cynical game. But
Meredith had a touch of naïvety about him: he wanted justice. It
had been his pursuit of justice rather than vengeance that had all
but destroyed the City club and all but finished him as a player.
With a hefty suspension already imposed on him from the bribery
case, he might well have found himself banned from the game for
life, with yet more unsolicited revelations. Yet he went ahead and
told the FA everything. The subsequent year and a half's
suspension left him with time on his hands to contemplate exactly
what had happened to him.

With little direct evidence, it is difficult to know whether the
Union idea was entirely Meredith's or the result of discussions and
debates among his new Manchester United team-mates. In 1907,
the year the Union emerged, Meredith had been with Manchester
United for less than a year, yet he may well have known many of the

United men for much longer on a personal level. United's old ground at Clayton was no more than a mile or so from City's ground at Hyde Road. What cannot be denied, however, is the close affinity that swiftly grew up between the ex-City men and their new United colleagues – a sense of group solidarity that would prove crucial for the Union in the next few years.

Whether Meredith took any part in the old Players' Union is also hard to ascertain. It would have been difficult for him to have avoided hearing about it, however, for at least two of his close friends and playing partners during the early City days had been Union Management Committee members.

One, Joe Cassidy – who had played for Manchester United/ Newton Heath since 1895 – partnered Meredith for a year at City during the 1900-01 season before moving on to Middlesborough.

The second, however, had been none other than Jimmy Ross, ex-Preston Invicible, who had arrived at City in 1899 and stayed for three years.

Ross, as we have seen, had been something of a mixed blessing to the Union: his criticism of that body had provided hostile newspapers with useful anti-Union copy. But Ross had always stuck by the Union and his sudden death in 1902 came as a shock to everyone at Manchester City. His lack of provision for a wife and children after a career at the very top of the game suggested something fundamentally wrong at the heart of football.

Union 'influence', however, did not stop with Ross. Another City stalwart in the early years of the century had been 'Di' Jones, a fellow Welshman and close neighbour of Meredith's when both had been youngsters. He had come to City from Bolton where he still lived and where he had been part of a famous Wanderers defensive trio – Sutcliffe, Somerville and Jones.

Somerville, of course, had been a leading light in the old Union before becoming secretary of Bolton in 1899; he had played for the Players' Union team against the Scots in 1899.

Meredith and Jones were close friends, fellow Welsh internationals – in fact, Jones had tried to persuade Meredith to join Bolton in 1894 and so Meredith knew Bolton's Union men socially. When Di Jones also died suddenly, only a few months after Ross, from an infected injury incurred during a pre-season practice match, Meredith once again came face-to-face with the harsh realities of professional football.

The City club denied all liability for Jones, claiming he had not been 'working' at the time of the injury, even though the practice match had been watched by a paying crowd of 20,000. Jones's widow and children were left with no insurance cover and had to rely on the proceeds of a collection and a benefit match with Bolton. Little money was, in fact, raised.

A fourth Union man to play for City had been goalkeeper Jack Hillman, who had played for the Players' Union side in 1900.

Finally, there had been the sudden influx of Scottish players brought to the club in 1901-2 by Tom Maley – brother of Celtic manager Willie Maley. Celtic, of course, had long been a centre of 'radical' football politics and its players had been influential in founding the old Scottish Union. The new Scots' bargaining skills soon resulted in the wages and bonuses bill that had caused Clegg of the FA almost to weep. Meredith, too, must have shed a few private tears when it emerged that he had been paid less than one or two of the more recent Scottish arrivals....

Thus the City club between the years 1899 and 1903 probably saw more 'political' activity in footballing terms than many other clubs. Being an organization of rapid, not to say mercenary growth it could throw no veil of respectability over its boardroom activities with which to intimidate players – unlike Aston Villa, for instance, with its imposing Birmingham aldermen and 'Golden Era'.

To have played for such a club, as Meredith had done ever since its entry into League football, must have been an education in itself. And when he told a reporter in 1907 that 'the player of today realizes the serious side of football more than the player of five or six years ago', he was speaking from bitter personal experience: 'They congratulate me and give me caps but they will not give me a penny more than men are earning in reserve teams.'

Although he would always declare his love for football (and would continue playing at the highest level until he was fifty years of age) he was now impatient with 'sentimental' reasoning which resulted in regulations that punished and branded him an outlaw and forced him to sit in front of committees of 'gentlemen' who treated him no better than a common thief.

It was this impatience that led to the resurrection of the Players' Union in 1907 and which gave the new organization its distinctive character, so setting the tone for its confrontation with football's authorities in the years to come.

# 6

# *The New Union* 1907–8

The old Players' Union had appeared rather suddenly with little press warning or fanfares. Meredith's Union, by contrast, had been discussed at length for some months prior to its inaugural meeting in December 1907.

**THE RESURRECTION.**
*Willie Meredith is endeavouring to revive the Players' Union.*

Manchester Evening News *pocket cartoon, November 1907.*

Meredith appears to have been interviewed on three or four occasions and his views and aims met with little opposition – indeed, almost everyone seemed to be in favour of the Union.

John Lewis, stern, high-principled ex-referee and League committee member commented in his *Athletic News* column: 'It is the duty of all professional players to at least hear what can be said in favour of the Union,' while the newspaper itself, in an editorial, declared: 'We cannot conceive of any player with a grain of sense refusing to support the establishment of a body for the protection of his own interests.'

Doubts were nevertheless expressed elsewhere concerning the amount of support Meredith would receive:

> From past experience, though, of the apathy of the player towards anything of the kind we confess to being sceptical as to the success of the scheme. We may be wrong and if so we are sorry but at the same time we feel that we should not like the task of collecting the Union

NEW WELSH REVIVAL.

Meredith: Friends, countrymen, players, lend me your ears!

[Meredith has issued a circular advocating a Players' Union—an old scheme revived.]

*A reader's pocket cartoon,* Manchester Evening News *circa 1907* subs. We sincerely hope that the players will prove these views are pessimistic but we remember the last Players' Union meeting called at Birmingham when not a single player put in an appearance.

Meredith was enthusiastic, however, and from the outset placed his own experience at the forefront of his argument for the Union, particularly where wages were concerned:

> What is more reasonable than our plea that a footballer with his uncertain career should have the best money that he can earn? If I can earn £7 a week, why should I be debarred from receiving it? I have devoted my life to football and I have become a better player than most because I have denied myself much that men prize. A man who takes the care of himself that I have ever done and who fights the temptations of all that can injure the system surely deserves some recognition and reward!

Thus the wages question featured strongly on the new Union's agenda. As Meredith termed it, 'Free Trade' was wanted. Where the transfer system was concerned, opinions seemed to have softened. While still irked by the system, Meredith seemed keener to amend it to include the player in any possible benefits it might bring. It was a key difference between the old and new Unions reflecting the changed circumstances of the football industry.

One thing, however, had not changed. The new Union was also inclining to the FA for help:

> Meredith hopes to see the day when the players have direct representation on the ruling body. He says there are many matters that ought to be brought to the attention of the FA and he is convinced that the members of that body do not realize some of the conditions under which players labour.

The first meeting of the new body was held on 2 December at the Imperial Hotel, Manchester. Among those present were no less than seven Manchester United players: Meredith, Charlie Roberts, 'Sandy' Turnbull, Herbert Broomfield, Alec Downie, Charlie Sagar and Herbert Burgess. There were two City players – Johnny McMahon and Irvine Thornley – plus Andrew McCombie of Newcastle, C J Craig of Bradford City, A J Evans of West Brom, Harry Mainman from Notts County, Bert Lipsham of Sheffield United and Walter Bull of Spurs. Jack Bell, now of Preston, provided a link with the old Union, and application in writing was made for John Cameron's account books.

The country was divided into regions and representatives were appointed to each. Two weeks later, in London at the Charterhouse Hotel, Meredith chaired the Southern section meeting and an entrance fee of 5s plus subs of 6d a week were confirmed. A week later, a third meeting at the Maypole in Nottingham saw Herbert Broomfield officially appointed as secretary (replacing an accountant named Menzies who was asked to resign as he was not a player) and vice-presidents of the Union were appointed.

They made impressive reading: John Davies chairman of Manchester United, John Cameron of Newcastle United, and the chairmen of Spurs and Bradford City. Jimmy Catton, *Athletic News* editor, was also proposed and in the following weeks H G Norris of Fulham and John McKenna of the Football League Management Committee were also asked to join. A solicitor was taken on (who just happened to be Manchester City director Wilkinson) and a bank account opened. Finally, in January 1908, the first Management Committee met: Mainman, Bull, McCombie, Meredith, Roberts, Lipsham, Craig and Broomfield.

A request was made to the FA for a fund-raising match; the request was granted. It was a painless, one might almost say, euphoric beginning and within weeks of the Union's establishment it was claimed that the majority of players in League football had joined.

The Manchester United men had, ever since the start of the 1907-8 season, been assiduously spreading the message wherever they played: each visit to a rival club served as a recruiting drive and the team's successes on the field were evidently matched by their persuasiveness and popularity off it.

Manchester United were unquestionably the team of the moment. Massive crowds were turning out to watch this classic eleven as they swept all before them. By 1 January 1908 they had won 17 and drawn two of 21 League games, had scored 57 goals and conceded 24; they were top of the League and well on their way to bringing the League championship to Manchester for the first time.

They were a glamorous side at a time when the popular media – newspapers, particularly, but also cinema and music-halls – were successfully establishing and exploiting footballers as attractive entertainment figures.

Throughout the early part of 1908 Fred Karno's famous 'Football Match' sketch was playing to packed houses and featured on stage many famous footballers. The sketch itself centred around the bribery of a goalkeeper, played by Harry Wheldon, who boasted among his personal friends most of the Manchester players, to whom he would send telegrams of support prior to crucial matches.

Film companies were filming Cup and League matches which were shown in the new cinemas beginning to make their appearance up and down the country – or in music halls as part of the bill of entertainment, and the natural alliance between popular entertainers and famous sportsmen was being cemented.

The Manchester players had long been favourites of that most famous of music-hall comedians, George Robey, and in 1907 Meredith had played for a Robey Eleven at Stamford Bridge against Chelsea to raise money for charity. Three of Meredith's colleagues that day would later join him on the Players' Union executive. In December of the same year Meredith and Robey had arranged a spectacular charity match (just days after the launch of the Union) that involved the old City team versus the new side in aid of a George Robey bed at Manchester Royal Infirmary. The match was hugely successful (though hardly designed to please the FA).

There were political overtones, however, in the association with variety artists: 1907 had seen the Variety Artistes Federation fighting out an industrial dispute with theatre managers and agents for more freedom and higher wages. Prominent footballers had taken part in fund-raising events for the Federation's Benevolent Fund: Fred Kitchen, another of Meredith's friends, was on its executive. In time, the favours would be returned.

The United team's popularity (and that of Newcastle United who were storming to their third Cup Final in four years) cannot be over-estimated as a factor in the sudden strength and confidence of the new Union. Star players and winning teams could not be ignored in the new, more buoyant and thus more profitable era of professional Edwardian sports. Nor, it seemed, could the demands for wage freedom be long denied.

Here were men famous the length and breadth of the country, fêted and pursued by the aristocrats of the entertainment world, watched by hundreds of thousands of people week in and week out, the objects of veneration and admiration; yet the amount they could earn was limited to an arbitrary figure pulled out of the hat by a collection

## THE STEPPING STONE.

INTERNATIONAL ASSOCIATION PLAYER: Come along, boys; it's an easy jump from here.

Manchester Evening News, *circa 1908.*

of small-town football club directors some seven years previously. What is more, it was a figure that, if unofficial gossip is to be believed, almost no major club adhered to and which the majority of First Division clubs certainly wanted to see swept away altogether.

It would be intriguing to know just how influential such men as J H Davies and J J Bentley were at this stage in the Union's history. Bentley had become president of Manchester United in 1902, brought in by chairman Davies, a wealthy brewer, as part of his rescue package for the United club which was close to bankruptcy. Bentley was by 1907 president of the Football League and a vice-president of the FA – one of the most powerful men in football. His views on wages were unequivocal: he was against all restraints, as had been his old friend and co-founder of the League, William McGregor.

Bentley, though, was no enemy of the transfer system: indeed, he had played a major role in defeating the FA's attempt in 1900 to abolish the system. He was now leading a campaign to abolish the £4 ceiling on wages and at the same time was on very close personal terms with men at the helm of the Players' Union.

In the summer of 1908, Bentley accompanied the United team on their tour of Europe. He fell ill in Vienna and was left behind to recover along with the United centre-forward Jimmy Turnbull who nursed him back to health. Bentley was so grateful to Turnbull that he gave him a specially engraved gold watch on their return.

Davies was also on good terms with many of the United men. He it was who set Billy Meredith up in his ill-fated sports-equipment shop in St Peter's Square in 1906. The first Union offices were above the shop for a while, later moving a few doors down. Davies also paid the Manchester men's expenses for their trip to play Newcastle in the first Union benefit match in April 1908, and one cannot avoid the feeling that for such powerful men the Union might have looked a good investment in their campaign to sweep away wage restraints.

Subsequent events, however, would establish that the Union was no puppet organization: nor was it devoted to the interests of 'star' players, despite their inevitably high profile on management committees. Meredith's original title for the Union had been the 'Players' Union and Benefit Society' and although this soon became the 'Association Football Players Union' the purposes of the organization, as its rules and constitution suggest, where less fortunate players and their families were concerned, was clear.

Its first objective was 'to promote and protect the interests of the members by endeavouring to come to amicable arrangements with the governing football authorities with a view to abolishing all restrictions which affect the social and financial position of players and to safeguard their rights at all times'.

Other objectives were to provide members with legal advice and legal assistance, to help transfer-listed or disengaged players to find employment, to provide temporary financial assistance for members and their families if and when necessary, generally to regulate relations between professional football players and their employers, and to do all things necessary to help advance and promote the interests of members.

Within a few months of being established, the Union was pressing compensation claims for injured players and arranging money for families of men who had died leaving no adequate provision. The Sheffield United player Frank Levich had died in just such circumstances, whereupon the Union sent £20 to his mother and wrote to the Sheffield club to ask that the amount paid out would equal what his wages would have been for the remainder of the season. They also wrote to the FA to ask for a grant for Levich from the FA's own Benevolent Fund.

Thus began a series of investigations and case work that saw the new Union take on the role of Benevolent Society, secure in the knowledge that the Workman's Compensation Act provided a legal background for such activity. Ironically, it would be this work, rather than the potentially more divisive and explosive issues of wages and transfers, that would eventually bring the Union into a head-on collision with football's authorities.

Yet it was the question of wages that consumed most of the newsprint devoted to the Union in the second part of 1908; more specifically, how could the maximum wage be altered or amended, given that it was simply not being adhered to by many clubs?

At the 1908 FA Annual General Meeting, the maximum wage was once again reaffirmed; the bigger clubs could not persuade enough smaller ones to support a 'free-market'. Bonuses were therefore seen as the next best thing to aim for, and a variety of schemes were put forward, discussed and analysed. John Lewis, FA council member and League Management Committee member, had already devised a profit-sharing scheme and the League Management Committee in October 1908 presented a more comprehensive profit-sharing scheme, including elements of an idea first put forward by C E Sutcliffe, whereby players received 50 per cent of club profits at the end of the season, divided up on a 'talent – money' basis. This last scheme had been favoured by Players' Union vice-president Rinder and given support by the Union itself.

The Union, however, was reluctant to take part in the debate: as Colin Veitch of Newcastle explained, the Union was not represented on the FA council and felt that it should proceed with caution.

In May, with Manchester United still on the continent, the Union Management Committee met in Manchester at the Midland Hotel to discuss some of the schemes. Sutcliffe was present to outline his idea but, in truth, there was little prospect of any idea coming to fruition. The Southern League appeared to have set its face against the idea of bonuses and had indicated that it would block any such innovation. And so the Union, having waited patiently to see whether real change was a possibility, finally declared at its AGM in December that it was pressing for complete freedom:

> For the policy of limitations and restrictions that has failed after a trial of seven seasons, the Players' Union begs leave to offer a policy of mutual arrangements based on free bargaining in all matters

affecting the service of players and their clubs.

As for the transfer system, the Union suggested that 'clubs and players should be encouraged to enter into arrangements for periods of two seasons and upwards'.

The resolution was accompanied by this pointed observation: 'Free bargaining between clubs and players would do something more than merely bring to an end the generally admitted inequalities of remuneration; it would cause the scandal of suspensions to cease and save gentlemen of high social standing the humiliation of being pilloried in the public press.'

The Union's position appeared, just as it had been in 1899, to be consistent with that of the FA and, just to rub it in, the Union concluded its AGM resolution thus:

> The Players' Union cordially supports the Council of the FA in their efforts to procure the deletion of the wages rule and the hope is sincerely expressed that the excellent reasons that prompted the Council of the Association to their action may speedily become apparent to every club management.

This cool, detached approach reflected the confidence of the new Union: barely a year old, yet seeming to have learned a great deal from the old Union's failure.

In August 1908 new offices had been opened in St Peter's Square in Manchester, and secretary Herbert Broomfield – now having moved from Manchester United to Manchester City – had been granted a salary of £156 per annum plus an assistant at 30s a week. The Union rules had been printed on strong card and sent to members' clubs to be hung on dressing-room walls. A Union badge had been suggested and designs were being considered. And a Union journal was also being prepared – to secure a direct line of communication to members free from press interference.

Not that it was finding it difficult to find press outlets for its views. With the rapid growth of football papers – almost every town had at least one evening paper that carried football news and results and most local papers now produced 'specials' or carried pages devoted to the game – the opportunities to be interviewed or to contribute articles were numerous. One paper in particular, *Thomson's Weekly News*, a penny weekly appearing on a Thursday and selling at that stage well over 300,000 copies, announced in

Many Famous Players
are Writing Special

# FOOTBALL
# ARTICLES

FOR

# THOMSON'S
# WEEKLY NEWS

AMONG OTHERS

COLIN VEITCH
WILLIAM MEREDITH
JAMES LAWRENCE
BILLY HOGG
JACK RUTHERFORD
CHRIS DUFFY
TOM NIBLO

Look out for these
up-to-date articles
EVERY WEEK

On Sale Every Thursday.          Price 1d

*November 1908*

November 1908 that Colin Veitch, Billy Meredith, Jimmy Lawrence and many other 'popular, prominent players' would be writing special football articles.

From that point on, the *Weekly News* would continue to offer players – particularly Union members and officials – a regular platform from which to hold forth in unprecedented fashion. This freedom to voice their ideas and reactions, to criticize openly League and FA officials and actions, would significantly alter the nature and climate of the struggle between football's administrators and the men they sought to control.

Inevitably, Meredith's column, which would be a regular *Weekly News* feature for the next six years, was the most outspoken and he would use it to provide readers with an almost weekly update on Union affairs and activities.

He, or his co-writer, would often manage to work in a reference to the Union even when the issue at hand seemed unconnected, a perfect example being the piece he wrote in December 1908 under the heading: 'Should Players Receive Presents? Willie Meredith

Answers Mr Pickford and Gives His Views on the Point.'

Pickford, revered FA councillor, had declared that the occasional giving of presents to players (tradesmen offering overcoats, boxes of food, etc., for players scoring so many goals, etc.) was a 'vicious principle'.

Meredith confessed: 'I am inclined to laugh.' Pickford, he thought, was behaving like an old woman ('excellent gentleman though he is') and he went on to explain something of the psychology of the professional footballer at work and how players never allowed promises of gifts and money to affect their play. He continued:

> They (the players) are, as a whole, an over-generous careless race who do not heed the morrow or prepare for a rainy day as wise men would. This trait in the character of the players has been taken advantage of over and over again by club secretaries in England. Many a lad has been tricked into signing on by vague verbal promises deliberately made to be forgotten once the ink was dry on the form. It is only recently that with steady improvement in the class of men playing the game as professionals the players have seen the folly of the careless life and have realized that they have too long put up with indifferences and injustices of many kinds. The only way to alter this state of things was by united action hence the formation and success of the Players' Union with its 1300 paying members at the end of the first year.

As for Pickford's fears that the giving of presents 'opens the door to what is tantamount to indirect payments to players above the regulation limit', Meredith's reply was unequivocal:

> What opens the door to irregular payments is the rank injustice of the £4 per week limit and of the transfer system which gives a club £1000 for a player and allows the latter – one really ought to call him the goods – £10. If the £10 went to the club and the £1000 to the man whose ability it is the agreed value of, there would be more justice in it.

1908 had thus seen a new Union, confident and outspoken, establish itself once more at the heart of football's affairs. At the Ye Old Royal Restaurant in Birmingham, Broomfield declared that 'a trying ordeal has been pursued successfully' and that the Union had once again been successful in stirring the FA into action. Changes, Broomfield predicted, were on the horizon. He could not have known just how close those changes were.

# 7

# *Confrontation* 1909

The year 1909 would prove to be one of tremendous upheaval and anguish for both the Players' Union and football in general yet, even now, more than eighty years on, it is difficult to discern clear motives or to draw firm conclusions. And watching the various participants in the developing football 'crisis' as they stumbled from conference to confrontation and back again, one cannot help feeling they too were confused – even shocked – by what was happening to them.

Of course, football cannot be divorced from the world in which it exists; the anxieties and emotions of society at large feed into the game at all levels, distorting and sometimes corrupting it. 1909 would be no exception and 1909, if we are to believe the popular press, was a very strange year indeed.

From roller-skating crazes to new-fangled cinemas showing murders and orgies and dancing girls; from striking postmen, Variety Artistes and miners to policemen baton-charging unemployed marchers; from the menace of Germany building battleships and airships to the horror of bomb-throwing anarchists in the East End; from people dying of heart attacks as they crammed into post-offices to collect the first ever pensions to vivid reports of pit-disasters – whenever one turned a page it seemed the world was going crazy. 'Hysteria' was an over-used word; 'morals' seemed under threat from all sides.

The view was a partial one, of course; the eye of the mass circulation newspaper had suddenly become, thanks to 'wire' photography, a veritable kaleidoscope of confusing and sensational images – images that were manipulated to sell newspapers. The morals agonized over were usually those of the working class – dancing too wildly, spending too much money; the rapid social changes regarding pensions and unions were the result of a reforming Liberal Government.

But whether the sense of doom and dislocation, of impending social chaos or even outright revolution was shared by all classes or was simply the morbid preoccupation of the privileged few, it affected the way things happened and imbued even the most trivial incident with a sense of importance.

1908 had ended with the Players' Union declaring itself opposed to those twin demons, the maximum wage and the transfer system, yet prepared to welcome any modifications or reforms if such changes meant the chance for players to earn more money. The majority of observers in the sporting press had applauded the Union's moderate, cautious approach. Few perceived any inherent threat in the Union's

Manchester Evening News, *January 1909*

attitude. C E Sutcliffe, from his eyrie in Burnley, saw differently.

In an article he wrote in December 1908 for the *Athletic News*, Sutcliffe violently attacked the Players' Union's 'amazing proposals'. They were, he said, 'but the outward and visible sign of their inward greed....' The Union's resolutions were 'contemptible clap-trap'; 'immoderate and unreasonable', and to grant them would be 'suicide' for football, and would lead back to the days 'when such a spirit of selfishness was ruining the game and the clubs'.

Just why Sutcliffe should have responded in such a way appeared a mystery to many. A few months prior to his outburst he had personally presented his own bonus scheme to the Players' Union Management Committee and although he had subsequently expressed impatience with the Union for not having expressed an opinion on the matter, it had been made clear to him that this was not a condemnation of his ideas – simply that the Union had no appropriate platform, being unrepresented on the FA council, and would wait until its AGM before stating its opinion.

Furthermore, the Union's subsequent opposition to the maximum wage was shared by the FA and a majority of First Division clubs. Thus, in attacking the Union in such sneering and insulting terms, Sutcliffe was behaving, on the face of it, rather oddly.

But Sutcliffe had a clear vision, that of the Football League system as it then stood, sacrosanct and inviolate. The continual arguing, lobbying and pressure by the bigger clubs for wage reform clearly irked him. Talk of a Super-League was both unsettling and distasteful to him. His own club, Burnley, would not feature in such a breakaway; it was too small and vulnerable. At that very moment it was languishing in the lower half of the Second Division and struggling financially. The nationwide craze for roller-skating could only damage clubs like Burnley; it was said that the town had six roller-skating rinks taking over £1000 a week.

Thus the idea of players being free to demand more money for their services must have been genuinely disturbing. Add to the fact that famous club chairmen were helping the new Union and perhaps Sutcliffe's venom can be understood.

Response to his outburst, however, was at first muted. No official Union reply was forthcoming but within days, Colin Veitch, Newcastle captain and a future Union chairman, did take him to task in his *Weekly News* column – though politely and almost apologetically.

Veitch pointed out the obvious – that the Union was not alone in advocating abolition of the wage limit, that changes to the present system would be welcomed if that was all that could be expected. Indeed, Veitch wondered what exactly the Union could do, 'for to have suggested another scheme in its place would surely have placed it [the Union] in an illogical not to say farcical situation'.

But Veitch was more concerned to answer Sutcliffe's more serious charge – that professional players could not be trusted, that they were not to be regarded with the respect that professional men might automatically deserve. For this, one senses, was the real issue – the status of professional players and their right to stand as equals alongside administrators, managers, directors, etc. and to have a voice in their own affairs.

Sutcliffe clearly preferred to see the players as they had supposedly been in the 1880s – mercenaries, pirates, racing from club to club grabbing whatever they could. Veitch was adamant that those days had gone: 'The type of man in the professional ranks of today is of another stamp altogether to the professional of twenty years ago and you must not saddle the misdeeds of his predecessors upon his shoulders....'

Veitch concluded by pointing to where the Union could prove its value:

> The players are joined in brotherhood through the agency of the Players' Union and I am quite at one with him [Sutcliffe] that the Union should take strong measures with any member found guilty of offences detrimental to the true interests of the game and incidentally harmful to the rest of the professionals by the same process.... It is the duty of the present-day professional to vindicate himself in the eyes of everyone, even those whose prejudices prove a formidable barrier to understanding, and the Players' Union can help in the manner suggested.

Sutcliffe's prejudices, however, would prove formidable. Within days he had returned to the fray in an *Athletic News* article entitled: 'Who Shall Be the Masters – Players or Clubs?' He reiterated his opinion regarding the 'utter absurdity of the players' demands' but went even further, stating: 'It is now not a fight between one section of clubs and another but whether the players have to rule the clubs or the clubs the players.'

It is important to note here that it is Sutcliffe who introduces the words 'fight' and 'rule'. No one else at this stage on either side of the management–player divide in early 1909 saw the issues at stake in this light. Sutcliffe was banging a drum while the world looked on bemused. However, events were gradually moving his way.

In late January 1909 the Players' Union Management Committee decided to take Reading FC to court on behalf of one of its players seeking compensation under the Workman's Compensation Act.

The Union claimed that the club had been dragging its feet in settling the claim and that recourse to the court was a last resort. It was an innocuous enough case: the player had injured himself while playing cricket during pre-season training and had claimed that the club was liable. The judge disagreed and turned the claim down but the Union immediately announced that it would be taking more such cases to court.

Broomfield and his Management Committee were taking a calculated risk. It must have been in their minds that the old Union had been practically strangled at birth by the FA's insistence that recourse to the courts to settle disputes between clubs and players could only happen with their permission – and then only after the issue had been investigated thoroughly by the FA itself.

But that had been before the passing of the Workman's Compensation Act in 1906 – a piece of legislation that offered all working men the chance to obtain compensation for injury at work.

Once it had been established that a player was a working man (something that could only be decided upon in court, hence the Union's determination to push certain cases through in order to establish case-work) the clubs had decided to band together in an Insurance Federation. Therefore the Union was anxious to establish proper machinery to deal efficiently with claims. After all, this was one of the reasons it had come into existence.

The long-winded procedure of clubs referring individual cases to the FA and then waiting until the latter had come to a decision (and charging the player £1 for the privilege!) was, the Union felt, being exploited by the clubs as a delaying device. The Union committee decided, therefore, after waiting patiently for more than a year, to break the circle, to take someone to court and force everyone's hand. As Broomfield wrote to the Reading secretary:

I sincerely hope I may be of some help to your club in the future to make up for any little inconvenience your directors may have felt with regard to the action, but it is better both for clubs and players that these points should be settled; that is why we are bringing them forward for if we don't, no one else will. Our actions are not meant to be antagonistic. At the same time I am sorry to say they will cause a certain amount of friction but it seems clear to me that there will have to be friction before we get harmony.

It is clear from such Union correspondence that Broomfield was genuinely anxious to relieve the FA of what was rapidly becoming a technically involved process: new legislation inevitably meant leaving the old, leisurely gentlemanly system behind. Broomfield saw the possibility of a claims board being set up consisting of Union members and club representatives, perhaps with some FA representation as well.

But such good sense was far too progressive for the majority of clubs. The spectre of the law was already causing alarm bells to ring in boardrooms up and down the country and the FA, urged on by club directors peeved and resentful at the Union's 'litigious' approach, decided that it would not be pressured into anything.

*Manchester Evening News, March 1909*

In mid-February the Union was flatly told: 'All such disputes must be adjudicated by it [the FA] and not taken to a court of law.'

Broomfield responded: 'The Management Committee of the Association Football Players' Union are not convinced that they are expected to regard seriously the opinion that a football player forfeits a common legal right on entering a professional engagement with a football club.'

He referred to Union rules (which had been passed by the FA) that provided for legal assistance and insisted they would continue to provide that assistance.

The FA retorted that Broomfield was being 'bombastic' and a fortnight later, on 8 March, the FA abruptly withdrew its recognition of the Union.

This sudden 'crisis' had not, however, occurred in a legalistic vacuum. The court case at Reading and the moves by the Union to institute proceedings at Rotherham and Croyden county courts on behalf of more players had rapidly altered attitudes.

C E Sutcliffe was now no longer alone in criticizing the Union. In the *Athletic News*, slighting references to the Union being little more than a 'debt-collecting agency' and to its 'fighting, antagonistic attitude' were becoming more frequent, while elsewhere in the sporting press rumours were spreading that the Union was contemplating a strike.

This latter canard was to be cleverly exploited by Sutcliffe in an article written in early March to coincide with the FA's withdrawal of recognition of the Players' Union.

Billy Meredith had written an article some weeks earlier entitled 'If the Pros Struck' – a lighthearted account of a dream he had had. Sutcliffe wasted no time in separating fact from fantasy: 'When I read this wonderful dream I thought it was a rich joke but I was solemnly and publicly assured last Wednesday by a member of the PU that they are all laying their plans for a strike three years hence....'

It was typical of Sutcliffe that he would reveal no names; red-herrings were a speciality of his, and no amount of protest on behalf of the Union that such an idea was preposterous could remove the nagging doubts. Even J J Bentley was moved to protest. Referring to Meredith indirectly as 'a player whose fame is not altogether to be envied', he continued, 'The very suggestion of a strike of footballers shows the meanness of the motives behind it and in my judgement cannot be too strongly condemned.' The FA, he went on, 'would stand no nonsense of that sort.... The Union are making the pace too hot to last ... they seem to have the idea that they are the people and everybody else must take a back seat. But they will have their knuckles rapped.'

The rapid closing of ranks on behalf of large and small clubs in the face of a 'militant' union was just what Sutcliffe wanted. Anxious to close down all discussion concerning the removal of the maximum wage and changes in the transfer system, he and others succeeded in diverting attention to the dangerous threat posed by rapacious, greedy players.

The FA had been more than helpful in this respect. A year earlier in the summer of 1908, anxious to rid itself of involvement in the squabbles regarding club finances and the responsibility to prosecute clubs breaking the rules, it had offered the clubs an 'amnesty' whereby all past misdemeanours such as the paying of illegal wages and bonuses would be forgotten. The clubs would reaffirm their loyalty to the FA and its laws, and with the decks thus cleared, a final settlement regarding wages could be reached.

The clubs had not taken the offer up and had continued to discuss possible bonus schemes – as late as January 1909 the League was canvassing clubs with a possible scheme.

However, faced with the prospect of a strike-prone 'litigious' union threatening to drag clubs to court at the snap of a tendon, the League as a body swiftly changed tack. In February a majority voted to accept the 'amnesty' offer. According to Sutcliffe, this dramatically altered the 'balance of power'.

The clubs, he wrote, had previously been afraid of upsetting the players (and thus their Union) because of the danger of players 'turning King's Evidence' – as Meredith had done – and revealing all to the FA:

> But the FA offered a free pardon to the clubs if they would cease to be dictated to by the players; if they would refuse to pay players sums of money in violation of the rules. The clubs consented to be honest and started with a clean slate. The players have lost their power, they ceased to be the real master!

It must have come as quite a surprise to the majority of players to realize that they had, in fact, been 'the real masters'. It was typical, however, of Sutcliffe's mentality that he should have placed all the responsibility for financial misdemeanours at the feet of the players and that he should find nothing odd in penning a phrase like 'the clubs consented to be honest'.

But he was certainly correct in that a new alignment had emerged, one that suited him – the League clubs now united and blameless, standing firmly, loyally, behind the FA, happy to watch as the latter took on and, hopefully, defeated the Players' Union.

Useless for Broomfield to insist to his increasingly nervous members that he had sought no such confrontation. The end result was the Union suddenly out in the cold. And within a week of the refusal to recognize the Union, the FA demanded that every player sign a 'loyalty' pledge to the FA to be inserted in his agreement for the new season.

From that moment on, the Union was on the defensive, having to react to events rather than initiate them and, as the season's end approached and players prepared to scatter to the four corners of the kingdom and beyond, Broomfield and his Management Committee continued to play down talk of a confrontation or a strike. They insisted that face-to-face negotiations with the FA would sort out all 'misunderstandings' and they continued to work quietly to bring about such a meeting.

To those members unhappy with what they were reading in the press, Broomfield recommended that they trust the Union. Nothing drastic would be done, he assured them, and they would not suffer. To Greville Morris, who had written to complain of the 'unwise' moves of the Management Committee and the feelings of fear among members at being suspended and seeing their careers ruined, Broomfield wrote:

> With regard to professionals suffering, in my opinion, the suggestions appearing in the press regarding suspension of players are all bluff. The members of the Union need have no fear of suspension. If anyone were to suffer in that way it would be the management committee and myself, not the players. But there is little likelihood of even that. Everything will be done for the benefit of the professionals without jeopardizing their means of livelihood.

Through Jimmy Ashcroft, Broomfield did indeed meet John Lewis, FA committee member (as the latter walked between main stations in Manchester on his way south!) to talk over a possible arbitration meeting. According to Ashcroft, who had also talked at length to Lewis, the FA was 'sympathetic' to the Union's demands; it simply wanted to know what the Union required: 'He was much impressed by what I said and his personal opinion was that we shall be refused nothing by the FA.'

**DAILY SKETCH, SATURDAY, APRIL 3, 1909.**

## IMPORTANT FOOTBALL CONFERENCE

Mr. H. Broomfield, Manchester, secretary of the Players' Union, in conference with Alderman Gee, vice-president, and Mr. W. A. Appleton, secretary of the General Federation of Trade Unions, yesterday in London.
*Daily Sketch photos.*

Unfortunately, nothing of substance was agreed upon – certainly no invitation to the next important FA meeting on 2 April just prior to the England–Scotland international, a meeting that might have avoided much of the ensuing strife.

Towards the end of March, however, all this delicate behind-the-scenes diplomacy was replaced by some remarkable front-page drama, the popular press once again setting the pace with rumours that certain England players were thinking of refusing to play in the forthcoming international.

A *Daily Sketch* report claimed that the England selectors were 'haunted by the fear of a strike during their deliberations....' Who the players were and exactly why they were threatening to strike remained obscure and largely irrelevant – the 'strike' bogy was refusing to lie down.

Broomfield, however, at this crucial moment, took a decision that seemed to fly in the face of all the Union's denials that strikes were being contemplated. It was announced that on the Friday prior to the International, Broomfield would be meeting with officials of the General Federation of Trades Unions, as well as talking to the England players.

There had been no indication either in letters or in Union minutes that the Management Committee had contemplated involving the mainstream union movement. Unfortunately no one reading the caption 'The Crisis Over' beneath pictures of Broomfield in consultation with GFTU officials on the eve of the international, could be blamed for concluding that something drastic *had* been contemplated.

The role in the dispute of the GFTU was something of a puzzle. It was a body – independent of the TUC – which had been formed in 1899 to work for industrial peace and to seek to prevent strikes and lock-outs particularly involving smaller unions. The *Daily Sketch* reported that it had advised the Union to 'grin and bear it', that the 'smoother way out of the difficulty for the present was to lie low until the season proper starts.' One GFTU official was even quoted as saying: 'A strike at the fag end of the season would be suicidal for the great body of pro-footballers.'

Had the GFTU therefore persuaded the Union not to call a strike? Or had the Union called in the GFTU to persuade the England players not to take unilateral action? If a strike had not been contemplated, why the involvement of the GFTU?

What made matters worse was that there was no clear Union 'line'. Anonymous Union spokesmen were quoted setting a needlessly belligerent tone, like the 'well-known captain' quoted in the *Sketch* on the fateful Friday declaring that 'the climax had been reached … come when it may there is to be a war and the battle will eventually go to the players.'

As for the England players themselves, once again, confusion reigned. The *Athletic News* claimed that Broomfield had been turned away from the England hotel:

What did he want? The team had no need of any advice from him and we hear that they strongly resented his intrusion. An England eleven can surely battle their bravest for England without the emissary of a union to stimulate them?

The players were said to have drawn up a statement after the game (which the English won 2-0) stating that 'there was never the slightest doubt as to our determination to play our hardest and do our best to accomplish a victory for England against Scotland'. Suggestions to the contrary were dubbed 'an insult'.

Bob Crompton, England's captain, was said by the *Bolton Cricket and Football Field* to have used the traditional after-match dinner speech to 'expose the impudent assumption of the Players' Union' and that he 'gave voice to his indignation in no uncertain terms'.

Meredith later claimed in his *Weekly News* column that there was no truth at all in the assertion that Broomfield had been trying to bring the England players out. He blamed the London press for whipping the whole thing up. Whatever the truth, there can be little doubt that the incident was a publicity disaster for the Union, losing the organization a great deal of credibility in the eyes of players ambivalent towards the Union as well as shocking many of the Union's supporters among club directors. And it afforded the Union's enemies a field day as they poured scorn on Broomfield and the Union idea in general.

For the many 'loyalists' it was an opportunity to display the patriotism that had gradually entered the argument – the implication that unions and strikes were somehow 'un-English'. The England–Scotland match was then the pinnacle of the season, the blue riband match, the oldest such fixture in history – a royal occasion.

To be selected was akin to being 'called up' and certain players looked at it in such a light. Thus, when Billy Wedlock, Bristol City's captain and England centre-half had been asked if he would play: '… the little wonder turned abruptly and with withering scorn in his voice he said, "I am chosen, am I not?" '

Wedlock would in fact be regularly selected for England thereafter, despite the claims of Charlie Roberts, considered by many to be a finer player – but a staunch Union man.

The strike/non-strike affair proved to be a turning point in the life of the new Union. Affiliation to the mainstream union movement cut through all arguments concerning wages and bonuses and compensation cases. Clear evidence that the Union realized it had made a mistake was the decision a few days after the England international to 'defer the question of joining the GFTU until August' and to continue the original course of obtaining an audience with the FA.

Thus April was a nervous month. The Management Committee sought legal opinion on the rules of the FA and the so-called 'loyalty' clause to be inserted into each professional's contract. They also pressed on with a compensation case against Crystal Palace but in doing so they lost a valuable ally. The Union solicitor and Manchester City director Wilkinson decided he could no longer continue acting for the Union and resigned. It was an ill wind, however – the solicitor who took over the case, Thomas Hinchcliffe, was destined to become one of the Union's greatest friends.

From the FA's point of view, life continued as normal, the George Parsonage case being a perfect example of what Billy Meredith called the 'autocratic' nature of the governing body.

George Parsonage, a Fulham player, had been asked by his manager to talk to the manager of Chesterfield who was interested in signing him. Parsonage had no desire to leave Fulham but was prevailed upon to meet Mr Swift, who made the customary offer of a £10 signing-on fee and £4 a week. Parsonage reiterated the fact that he did not want to be transferred but, in his own words, 'I became tired of Mr Swift's endeavours to persuade me to transfer my services from Fulham to Chesterfield. I asked him, in what I regarded as jocular mood and only with the idea of getting rid of the matter, for £50....'

Swift promptly reported Parsonage to the FA. An enquiry followed and Parsonage found himself suspended from football for life.

Just why Chesterfield should have behaved in such a manner was a mystery, except that in 1909 they were engaged in a losing struggle to be re-elected to the League. The Parsonage case was perhaps a chance for them to prove their loyalty to the regulations and thus curry favour. Whatever their motives, they had succeeded in ruining Parsonage's football career.

No wonder, then, when the FA and the Union finally met at the end of April that Harry Mainman, Union chairman, could say to Clegg, 'We look upon the clubs as the enemies of the players.'

Clegg's apparent astonishment that such a statement could be made and his subsequent declaration that with such sentiments 'there was little hope of an understanding being reached', speaks volumes for the gulf that then existed between the two bodies.

The meeting had been the Union's main hope. Broomfield and Mainman for the Union, and Clegg, Wall and Davies for the FA talked over a number of Union proposals: a claims board with equal representation for the FA and Players' Union, to decide on player's claims against clubs; a national compensation fund with compulsory contributions jointly administered; plus the dropping of the £1 fee demanded of players who wished to make a claim against their clubs – all were rejected. It was a disaster.

The meeting over, the FA wasted no time in issuing another ultimatum stating that officials of the Union who did not give an undertaking before 17 May that they would in future act in accordance with the rules of the FA would be suspended from taking any part in football or football management.

The FA also claimed that AFPU members had not been fully consulted and called for a special general meeting at which Union members could express their opinions upon the policy of the committee. It was clear that the FA had decided that Broomfield and Mainman did not represent the bulk of the players and that they were responsible for much of the trouble that had occurred.

Finally, the FA pointed out that unless the AFPU complied with FA rules: 'It will be necessary for players to withdraw from membership of the Union if they desire to continue their connection with the FA.'

Events now moved swiftly towards total breakdown. On 7 May the Union Management Committee decided to resign except for Mainman and Broomfield who, being non-players, would not be affected by the threatened ban from football. Affiliation to the GFTU was raised again as a possible response; in May, Broomfield and Mainman were duly suspended.

Early in June came yet another ultimatum. In order to hasten the inevitable, the FA ordered all players to cease their membership of the Union, the deadline being 1 July. If they did not do so, their registrations as professionals would be cancelled.

On 1 July, as an opening shot in the coming hostilities, the Union officially affiliated to the GFTU.

# 8

# *Summer of the Outcasts* 1909

Once the Union Management Committee had resigned in early May and chairman Harry Mainman had left to spend the summer in his Reading home, Herbert Broomfield was very much alone in the Union office. Indeed, for all practical purposes, he was the Union: dealing with all correspondence, advising players on a range of problems, sending out information to the press, setting up meetings, paying bills as well as taking all the key strategic decisions in the propaganda war with the FA.

This might have been enough for any man, but Broomfield was also deeply involved in setting up his own manufacturing company to produce revolutionary rubberized footballs, a somewhat bizarre situation when the very future of the Union seemed to be hanging in the balance.

Broomfield had been a pro-footballer for some years, but by 1909 was on the verge of giving up the game. His career had been interrupted by injury although he was, in truth, more of a reserve player than a first team regular. He played a handful of games for Manchester United before transferring to Manchester City in 1908, where he managed no more than four first team appearances. Indeed, had Union affairs not sprung into such prominence in 1909, it is more than likely he would have left football to concentrate on his new business.

Intriguingly, his revolutionary football patent had been bought from Billy Meredith some two years earlier for a few hundred pounds. Meredith's own sports business went bankrupt in the summer of 1909 at the height of the 'strike' when a fire destroyed a great deal of stock, causing losses the business could not sustain.

It was said at Meredith's bankruptcy proceedings that the patent he had sold so cheaply was actually worth many thousands of pounds and could have saved him. Meredith, however, seemed to bear Broomfield no ill-will; in fact, he was one of Broomfield's greatest champions.

In July 1909, Meredith wrote a fulsome tribute in the *Weekly News* to Broomfield, congratulating him on the tremendous work he was doing for the Union, while also providing a vivid description of Broomfield's life-style:

If I were a wealthy man tomorrow I should spend my summer just as does Herbert Claude Broomfield.... In a lovely country spot on the edge of a pine forest in front of a large mere stands a little gaily painted building that no one can see from the road. It has two rooms, the kitchen has a fine range, the drawing room is pannelled and painted. There are four bunks and steps outside lead up to the roof which has a deck. It is the captain's cabin from a ship and is made into an ideal bungalow. There is a pretty garden and steps lead on to a fine tennis court. Here Broomfield and two chums live sleeping under the sky on warm nights, in the bunks when the air is colder. Tennis, golf, swimming, football and a punch-ball – all can be had on the spot. A gramophone sings the trio to sleep. They all cycle too and have created a sensation in their time in all three countries when touring on a triplet that bears motor-cycle tyres....

Broomfield was clearly not the typical professional footballer. Well-educated (having passed Civil Service exams) he was a part-time oil painter as well as the proprietor of his own painting and decorating business in Northwich where he lived.

He was a theatre-goer, a concert-lover and clearly destined to become a wealthy man. As Billy Meredith said, 'He is too clever and industrious a man to depend on football.'

However, Broomfield's lazy summer days were few and far between during the turbulent summer of 1909 and his Union activities were to prove a considerable emotional burden – nor did he receive a great deal of thanks or even support for shouldering it.

At one stage in late July he travelled down to London, back up to Newcastle and then across to Manchester in the course of three days to speak at three apparently crucial meetings, exhorting players to stand firm and not to resign from the Union.

In London he was simply rebuffed; in Newcastle he was at first supported, but no sooner had he returned to Manchester than the Newcastle players, led by Colin Veitch, had second thoughts and wrote to say they were resigning after all; only in Manchester did players declare their determination to hold on, although a few weeks later they, too, were writing in secret to say that if no one else came out to support them they would also have to throw in the towel.

Broomfield managed to persuade them to stick it out but one would have sympathized with him had he simply closed the office and settled down in London, for he was newly married.

Why then did he persist in the face of such odds? He was

certainly not using the struggle and the consequent publicity for self-promotion. In fact, where his football production company was concerned, it could have done him great harm for while he was engaged in orchestrating an acrimonious campaign against the FA, representatives for his new company were simultaneously trying to obtain the FA's blessing for his revolutionary football.

Nor was Broomfield cashing in directly. For instance, when *Truth* magazine offered him a fee of 2 guineas for an article on the dispute he only agreed if the fee was donated to the Fresh Air Fund, while he refused to supply a picture of himself.

He appears to have been driven by a genuine radical zeal, a belief in the fundamental principles of what the dispute appeared to be about. Exactly where he stood in conventional political terms would be difficult to determine. Like the majority of Players' Union representatives over the years, he gave little away. The only reference to politics as it affected the outside world came in a letter he wrote on 27 July to two non-footballing supporters of the Union struggle. He wrote:

> It is useless for members of the FA to go about lecturing on the purity of the game or its improvement whilst those men playing under its rules are relegated to the position of slaves.
>
> The despotism and tyranny of the Empire has been its downfall. If such methods are not approved of in Turkey I am quite sure they will not be tolerated in civilized England and for this reason I feel sure of victory.

For all his enthusiasm, however, there can be no doubt that the indifference, not to say downright hostility, of many of the rank and file players towards his campaign, took its toll. In a letter to Harry Mainman written in July he voiced some of his frustrations and anger.

Broomfield had been settling various Union debts and financial obligations out of his own pocket – things such as affiliation fees to the GFTU and solicitors' fees for work done on the Reading and Croyden compensation cases. Mainman had refused to pay for these items when Broomfield sent them to be settled, demanding instead more details. This response touched a raw nerve in Broomfield:

> I know you bear me no animosity and that you are to a certain extent justified in refusing to sign the cheques I enclosed. You say it is unbusinesslike. I quite agree with you but I should like you to tell

me how it is possible for me to carry along the work of the Union under present conditions in a strictly businesslike manner. If I had adhered strictly to business principles the Union would now have been a thing of the past. It is because I have never been afraid to find the money when urgently needed that we are in the position we are in today. I cannot for the life of me take your letter in any other way than as a reflection upon my integrity....

Broomfield appeared close to resigning:

I am more than ready to see the Union carried along on strict business lines and I suggest to you that the first thing that is done should be the selection of a new committee. I will not accept the responsibility of this work any longer and a committee must be formed immediately who are prepared to relieve me of the onerous duties which are thrust upon me. As soon as this is done I am quite willing to resign my position. The constant strain, the worry, the publicity and the criticism is not to my liking. I would much prefer to cultivate the social side of life which I have sadly neglected through my desire to obtain the emancipation of professional footballers.

He did not resign, of course, and Mainman apologized, as well he might. Without Broomfield's presence in Manchester, it is clear the Union would have collapsed. No one else would risk their careers by taking over his job; he was all the Union had.

His basic strategy was quite simple – to prevent the new football season commencing in August and thus pressurize the League clubs into leaning on the FA to back down in its threat to destroy the Union.

It was a propaganda war, the FA claiming that the Union had already been deserted by its members, the Union claiming that players would return in August and rejoin. Figures were regularly bandied about but only when pre-season training began would it be possible to draw firm conclusions.

Broomfield's day-to-day tactics, therefore, once he had secured affiliation to the GFTU and was certain of the defiance of the Manchester United men, was to broadcast these facts as loudly and as often as he could to anyone who might be interested; to emphasize in letters and at meetings that there was something to fight for, that the Union still existed and was not fighting alone; and to stress that the GFTU, not to mention the union movement in general, would ensure that men who stayed with the Union would not suffer financially if it came to an all-out strike.

The trade union movement did indeed appear to be genuinely sympathetic. Broomfield addressed numerous union meetings and received many individual letters of support from rank and file members.

By late August a number of union organizations had declared themselves solidly behind the Players' Union's struggle for recognition and in September the whole issue was debated at the TUC's Annual Conference in Ipswich. The Yorkshire and District Trades and Labour Council, the Lancashire and Cheshire Federation of Trades Unions, the National Union of Railwaymen, the Sheffield ILP – all wrote to offer support while the *Sheffield Guardian*, the *Railway Review* and the *Clarion*, among others, printed sympathetic articles.

It was noticeable, however, that players like Colin Veitch of Newcastle (later to become the chairman of the Union), although a declared socialist, viewed the progress of the dispute differently to Broomfield.

In June–July it had been Veitch's doubts and arguments that had seen the Newcastle players resign from the Union at a crucial point, when they had earlier told Broomfield to his face that they were prepared to stay out. Veitch had felt that such defiance was futile, that there was nothing to be gained in opposing the FA in 'militant' fashion.

There was thus reason to suppose that Broomfield's approach was not looked upon with favour by quite a number of players. This is not to say that they did not want the Union to survive; just that they felt, like Veitch, that 'confrontation' and wider union links were provocative and liable to be counter-productive. Fear was part of the reason for such timidity.

Many men were faced that summer with painful choices. Most simply resigned from the Union, signed a new contract with their clubs and went on holiday. Others however agonized over what to do and many wrote to Broomfield apologizing for resigning from the Union.

Some wrote defiantly one week, yet sent in their resignation the next. All of which made the Manchester United men's decision to stick by their Union membership all the more remarkable, their sacrifice all the more real.

Charlie Roberts had been the first to hear that he and his team were to be suspended for publicly stating that they would not resign from the Union: he had read about it in the evening papers delivered to his newsagent's shop:

> I had a benefit due with a guarantee of £500 at the time and if the sentence was not removed I would lose that also, besides my wages, so that it was quite a serious matter for me.

The club had told him nothing, however, so he and the rest of the United team turned up as usual at the ground the following Friday to see whether they would receive any pay. No one was prepared to talk to them except an office boy who told them there was no money.

> 'Well, something will have to be done,' said Sandy Turnbull as he took a picture off the wall and walked out of the office with it under his arm. The rest of the boys followed suit, and looking-glasses, hairbrushes and several other things were for sale a few minutes later at a little hostelry at the corner of the ground.
>
> I stayed behind a while with the office boy who was in a terrible state over the players taking things away and he was most anxious to get them back before the manager arrived. 'Come along with me and I will get them for you,' I said. 'It's only one of their little jokes.' I soon recovered the lost property for him. But it was funny to see those players walking off the ground with pictures, etc. under their arms.

Being barred from the ground, the Manchester men decided to continue their pre-season training at Fallowfield, the Manchester Athletic Club ground, secured for them by Broomfield. This turned out to be a publicity coup for the Union, as reporters and photographers arrived to interview and photograph the famous rebels. During one such session Roberts had the happy inspiration that helped create a legend:

> After training a day or two a photographer came along to take a photo of us and we willingly obliged him. Whilst the boys were being arranged I obtained a piece of wood and wrote on it, 'Outcasts Football Club 1909' and sat down with it in front of me to be photographed. The next day the photograph had a front page of a newspaper, much to our enjoyment, and the disgust of several of our enemies.

The Manchester men's defiance was admired by almost everyone, even J J Bentley, the Manchester United chairman, who made plain his disagreement with his players over the question of Unions and strikes (to the point of resigning from the club in late 1909) yet who still expressed admiration for their honesty. He reserved his harshest words for those he called 'cheats' – men who resigned from the Union in July in order to obtain their summer wages, yet who still intended to rejoin the Union in September and thus threaten the recommencement of the season.

As August began, however, and men started to drift back from their holidays to prepare for pre-season training, the growing uncertainty as to exactly how many men would refuse to abide by the FA's edict and rejoin the Union began to have the desired effect. On 4 August the FA suddenly requested a meeting with the GFTU in order, as it explained, to outline its own case.

It was reported in the *Manchester Evening News* that the meeting 'left a good deal to be desired. There was less frankness than there ought to have been. The federation will be quite unable to bring about a settlement unless both sides are ready to discuss all that is on their minds.'

The GFTU officials – Pete Curran MP, Alderman Allen Gee of Huddersfield and W A Appleton of the GFTU executive – then went back to the Union and began to work out a list of demands.

Broomfield travelled to Newcastle to talk to Veitch and Lawrence, and on 11 August it was announced that Newcastle United had come out in support of the Manchester United men. They were swiftly joined by players at Oldham, Liverpool, Everton and Sunderland.

As the pressure mounted, the FA took yet another significant step. On 18 August it met the Players' Union 'executive' for the first time since its 'abolition' to discuss the latter's demands.

Colin Veitch had now entered the picture as a Union spokesman and Broomfield's influence on events consequently began to diminish, though his campaign had succeeded in securing the key concession – recognition of the Union's existence. The three-hour meeting, which the GFTU attended as intermediary, was declared a success from the Union's point of view but a week later at a second meeting, the optimism was beginning to fade.

Putting aside relatively minor problems, such as finding an appropriately worded formula, the FA and the Union essentially reached agreement on four issues. First, the Union agreed to observe the FA's rules until they were changed in return for the FA agreeing to recognize the Union and lifting the suspension of the 'striking' players; second, the FA sanctioned the Union pursuing legal cases on behalf of its members against League clubs after the FA had first had a reasonable amount of time to resolve the dispute; third, the FA would pursue the abolition of the maximum wage and the retain and transfer system at future meetings; and fourth, the FA would continue to give its consent to an annual match to be played for the benefit of Union funds.

The issue on which the second meeting of 24 August ultimately foundered was the payment of the lost summer wages to the players who had refused to resign from the Union. The Union reps were adamant that the players should receive the £38 owing to them. The FA representatives voted by four votes to three against such payment and the conferences broke up, leaving the dispute unresolved.

According to Billy Meredith, the refusal to pay the back-pay gave the FA a way out of a deal it secretly disliked:

> As a matter of fact, I believe that the FA, believing that they would have the clubs with them ... did not want a settlement.... There is no doubt in my mind that the FA and the clubs believed that, if put to the test, the players would not fight. And it is not half a test that the players have to go through. The club officials are working for the FA all the time, the players are talked to unceasingly, invited to dinners, and all that kind of thing. It needs strong men to stand by the Union under such circumstances but I hope to see the players prove their worth to the public and earn the respect of all who like to see men fight.

Then began a process of intense lobbying, meetings, head-counts. On 27 August, the GFTU's Appleton strongly advised all professionals to refuse to attend any meeting or conference not officially arranged through their Union. The following day the FA met representatives of all the League clubs to ask for their unqualified support.

On the same day, at the Charterhouse Hotel in London, Alderman Gee addressed a meeting of 150 players who had decided to rejoin the Union. As a precaution, all players were advised to tell their clubs that they were willing to play, that they recognized the binding character of their contracts and that they were 'quite willing to fulfil their part and play football when and where directed'.

The clubs, of course, were obliged to suspend any players rejoining the Union. Sunderland announced it had had to suspend seventeen men; Manchester United had also suspended the majority of its professionals – and Meredith was keen to point out how little friction there was between management and players: 'The Manchester United officials think the world of their players and admire the pluck they have shown....' Davies was even reported to have been to see Appleton of the GFTU to see if there was anything he could do to help the situation.

However, the Aston Villa team – in fact, all twenty-eight professionals plus two trainers – signed a declaration that they had not rejoined the Players' Union and would not do so until it was sanctioned by the FA. They would, they declared, rely on the club's efforts to remove rules relating to wage restrictions. And such defections (Aston Villa were by no means the only club to come out against rejoining) served to encourage the FA in its obduracy.

Despite a last minute plea by the chairman of the Labour Party, Arthur Henderson, who offered to help settle the dispute via 'arbitration', the FA had determined on a course that appeared to mark a return to its earlier attempt to divide the Union members from those who led them. It announced that it was willing to assist the players in forming another organization to promote their affairs, advised and financed by the FA itself.

Clegg then announced a meeting between the FA and the rank and file players, i.e. non-Union players. He refused even to answer Henderson's letter.

Although attacked by almost everyone inside and outside the game (even in *The Times*) for their arrogance and their refusal to accept help from disinterested parties, the FA had a shrewd idea as to the nature of the men over whom it held such total sway. It had played a game of brinkmanship and now, with barely a day left before the season was scheduled to commence, it would gamble on its powers of persuasion combined with the overwhelming desire of most players to stop all the arguing and get back to playing, to achieve its desired end: to keep the world of football somehow divorced from the real world. The FA's gamble would pay off.

# 9

# *Settlement and Survival* 1909

The Birmingham meeting on 31 August 1909 must be regarded as a landmark in professional football politics. For the first time,

*Outside the Birmingham conference. Left: J T Jones (Municipal Employee's Association), Charlie Roberts, I Thornley and Mr Boswell (Assistant Secretary of the Players' Union); middle, J J Bentley; right, C Veitch, J Lawrence and A Bridgett.* Daily Dispatch, *September 1909.*

ordinary players had the opportunity to meet, talk to and even argue with the men who effectively ruled their lives.

It was a bizarre, sometimes farcical occasion, unstructured, confused and ending on a typically fudged note – ostensibly good cheer and fellowship but in reality a sad climbdown by the players, a literal turning of the back on an independent future.

The FA's insistence that the meeting was for non-Union players only was swiftly rendered null and void. Of the couple of hundred who turned up at the hall, at least 50 per cent were either members or ex-members of the Union.

Colin Veitch, now emerging as the 'conciliator', soon persuaded Clegg to let all arrivals into the hall – with the sole exception of Charlie Roberts, who was still technically suspended. Thus one of the founders of the Union had to stand outside the hall handing out leaflets while the Union's future was discussed inside. Billy Meredith, unsigned even with his club, remained in Manchester along with Broomfield. The GFTU had not been invited. The FA had secured just the sort of situation it had always wanted.

Clegg spoke first, the gist of his opening remarks being that the present trouble 'had arisen out of the action of certain parties who have been acting on behalf of the Players' Union'. The FA, he claimed, had been all in favour of the Union but the Union had broken its own rules by not trying to come to 'amicable' agreements with the governing bodies. 'A spirit of persistent and unremitting hostility had permeated the Players' Union's actions.' The FA had tried to reform financial regulations but the Players' Union had ruined such attempts by their actions.

Regarding the compensation claims, Clegg insisted that the FA had granted all that had been put forward; the FA was not, however, an employer. Neither he, Clegg, nor anyone else got anything out of football, only time and trouble.

Then, as if to emphasize the bonds that existed between the ordinary players and the FA, Clegg claimed that it had not been until 6 August that the FA had known what the Union had wanted. The FA had been 'in the dark along with the rest of the players'.

He then changed tack completely and warned that the players were 'ill-advised to think that because they had signed for their clubs that a court of law would uphold their claim to wages' (i.e. would override the FA's threat to suspend anyone rejoining the Union). 'I am not mentioning this at all with the idea of deterring you from doing anything that you want. I am just mentioning it....'

He then continued: 'Even if the courts did decide that you were entitled to this year's wages, what about next season? This is a serious question, is it not? It would be within the power of the FA to bring about that result ... of that there is no possibility of doubt because the rules provide that we may register only those players that we want.... Wouldn't you do the same if you had been flouted like we have? I don't say it at all harshly. I am only wanting to show you where you are likely to travel in order that you may avoid it.'

He went on to say that he hoped players would not place money too high on their agenda because that would be bad for the sport. 'We don't want the players to place remuneration too prominently on the programme....'

He finished by suggesting that the FA would like to fund an alternative union: 'We are not wanting you to form a Union that shall be under the finger of the Association but we don't want a Union in constant opposition to us. Surely we are entitled to ask for that?'

And he sat down to ringing applause.

He was followed immediately by Charles Crump, the main thrust of whose speech appeared to be that 'there is a desire in certain directions that the game be dominated by trade unions. He saw that Mr Veitch shook his head but he [Mr Crump] certainly thought there was a tendency in that direction.'

He went on to suggest that the clubs were not profit-making organizations, and that the players ought to realize this: 'There are a great many men whose interests in sport had led them to invest very considerable sums in the clubs. They were anxious that the game should go on. He asked the players to pause before they turned their back on those whose friendship they had tried....'

Thus the whole slant of the FA's argument was that football was not an industry, that too much emphasis on money threatened to ruin it as a 'sport', that unions had no part to play in the game and that the players had been led astray by certain elements on the Management Committee of the Union.

The players' response was revealing. Instead of talking in high-sounding generalities, those who spoke immediately got down to the realities of the FA's rule. Why had the Manchester United men been suspended? Why had George Parsonage been so abominably treated? Later on, Lyons, late of Manchester City and one of those punished by the FA during the Meredith scandal of 1905, took the opportunity to put his own case, claiming that he had been denied a personal hearing at the time of his suspension.

The key intervention was made by Colin Veitch, afterwards to be hailed as the 'diplomatist' and the 'peace-maker'. Whether through a pragmatic suspicion that open debate would soon degenerate into a slanging match, or because he believed that what had been gained at earlier conferences could be secured again with a little common sense, Veitch made two simple points: first, that the existing Union should continue, it being too much of a bother to create a new one, and second, that the Manchester United players should receive their back-pay and have their suspensions lifted. 'That is the chief trouble that is standing in our way. We all wish to conform to the rules of the FA but we also wish that this question of arrears of wages might be conceded by the Association.... The wages are the only bar.' He was loudly cheered as he sat down.

A fortnight earlier, when the FA had withdrawn from negotiations over the question of the wages, Veitch, unlike Meredith and others, had almost bent over backwards trying to work out why it had stuck on that point. He revealed in a newspaper article that it had taken him five days to work it out but that in his opinion the FA had merely wanted its position as supreme authority to be recognized. Thus, they expected the players themselves to come and *ask* for the wages, 'and then the FA might possibly have allowed the payment'. Failing that, the players could, with the FA's blessing, of course, have taken their case to court. Thus the FA would have lost nothing in terms of its prestige. Veitch had declared that he personally would try to secure a settlement along those lines.

Naturally, he was once again criticizing the tactics of the Players' Union Management Committee and those of Broomfield in particular. Clegg and Crump were not immediately receptive, however, to Veitch's suggestion. Could he guarantee that the suspended men would promise to abide by the rules of the FA?

Veitch said he would try to contact them that very day by telegraph. Before he could do so, however, Clegg returned to his earlier point concerning the Union issue. He suggested that all the trouble had been caused at earlier negotiations by the presence of a 'third party', i.e. the GFTU. He claimed that it would have been so much better if it had been left to themselves (the FA) and the players to sort things out.

Strangely, Colin Veitch said nothing to contradict him; instead, he went off to try to contact the suspended Union men. He failed, of course, but Clegg seized his opportunity. 'We cannot possibly get the thing in order to formally consider it and Mr Veitch has suggested the readiest way of getting at it. We had better conclude this conference and follow the matter up through Mr Veitch and his friends....'

There followed a string of platitudes: 'We must not expect to have it all our own way.' 'Life is a compromise.' 'Nobody gets his own way.' 'There must be give and take by both parties', etc., but when the final resolution was drafted, the FA had achieved exactly what it had set out to do. There was to be a 'truce'. Football would commence immediately. The Players' Union's proposals would 'be considered'.

DAILY DISPATCH, THURSDAY, SEPTEMBER 2, 1909.

THE KICK OFF!

The football season opened yesterday with every prospect of the dispute being finally settled.

The cartoon adorning the report of the conference that appeared in the *Daily Dispatch* had a player joyfully booting a football labelled 'discord' out of the ground; and for the majority of players, that appeared to sum everything up – the trouble was all over now and they could get back to playing football.

In a sense, they were right. The critical moment had passed; the possibility of halting the soccer season (the only way in which the powers-that-be would ever be brought to the negotiating table) had gone, and the unique combination of circumstances that had created such a situation would not occur again.

For Herbert Broomfield, architect of that supreme moment of truth, the 'victory' claimed by some was no victory at all. Congratulated by his business partner he wrote: 'Thank you very much for your congratulations. I scarcely know where I am today. I seem unable to breathe. I am not overjoyed, though everyone else seems satisfied ... because there is something sad about the whole business, to think that athletes should be so devoid of moral courage is not a pleasing thought and if you knew my experience the afternoon of the conference you would feel as I do.'

William Meredith, interviewed a day later in the *Clarion* newspaper, seemed equally adamant that no victory had been achieved. On being told by the reporter that the FA had recognized the Union, he replied: 'Yes, provided the players observe the rules and practice of the FA. What's the good of belonging to a Union if one fetters one's hands like that?'

Sam Hardy, writing in *Thomson's Weekly News*, was also unimpressed by what had been achieved: 'The conference at Birmingham is now ancient history. My anticipation that it would clear the air was rudely shattered.... It must not,' he declared, 'be peace at any price.'

Colin Veitch, on the other hand, was full of hope. 'Peace With Honour' was the headline above his article in which he claimed that the Birmingham conference had brought a complete settlement one step nearer. 'Step, did I say? ... A gigantic leap is more accurate in description of the space covered!'

The *Clarion* also interviewed him a week after Meredith and the contrast was telling. 'Is it peace?' the reporter asked. 'Yes,' Veitch replied, 'it is peace, and no, they were not "old-soldiered" into the negotiations, and yes their position was infinitely stronger.'

' "So the FA are in a more reasonable frame of mind?"

' "They might say the same of the Players' Union ... it's six and six I should say." '

Veitch's famous conciliatory nature, his determination to press on with negotiations, confident that the FA had the best of intentions, would, however, be sorely tried.

Putting a brave face on things, the Manchester United team, wearing their Players' Union arm-bands, ran out for their first match to resounding cheers. Within a month, the arm-bands would be prohibited by the League. Their back-wages would take almost six months to be paid; Charlie Roberts's benefit match against Newcastle would be refused; and it would take the intervention of both Veitch and Broomfield to persuade the United men not to go back on strike.

As the weeks passed into months, even with Colin Veitch taking a leading role in the discussions, the elusive settlement seemed further off than ever. With no deadline set, no ultimatum, the football authorities felt free to linger, to prevaricate, to change their grounds.

By October even Veitch was reporting back to the Union Management Committee that everything was back to square one. Meetings were useless and now the FA had introduced another element – a demand that the Union disaffiliate from the GFTU.

In a sense, the demand was perfectly consistent with everything the FA had done since August. Affiliation to the GFTU meant the players aligning themselves with the outside world; it meant accepting that football was an industry, that players were workmen. It was a gigantic leap that the FA was not prepared to make.

With relentless, unremitting determination, League and FA administrators, via their various newspaper columns and articles, kept up the pressure: strikes would disrupt forward planning in football; signing a contract implied a moral duty not to strike; the FA could sort out all the game's problems, etc. The simple fact that the law of the land guaranteed any man or woman the right to strike, whether affiliated to the GFTU or the TUC, for that matter, made no difference. The FA was seeking a declaration of principle from the players; an acknowledgement that they were different, that football was a special world governed by men possessing ancient and benevolent wisdom.

There were many prominent players who agreed with all this, of course: Bob Crompton, Ernest Needham, William Dunlop – English internationals and influential captains who had played a part in the Birmingham conference and who were against 'unionism'.

And finally, in mid-October, the Union relented. It agreed to hold a ballot of all members to decide whether to remain affiliated to the GFTU. The vote was decisively against: 470-172. The Union thus passed a resolution thanking the GFTU for all its help. The FA lifted its 'suspension' of the Manchester players and paid them their money.

Charlie Roberts, however, declared himself disgusted with the result:

> As far as I am concerned, I would have seen the FA in Jericho before I would have resigned membership of that body, because it was our strength and right arm, but I was only one member of the Players' Union. To the shame of the majority they voted the only power they had away from themselves and the FA knew it.

Meredith was equally despairing of his fellow-players: in his *Weekly News* column he wrote:

> The unfortunate thing is that so many players refuse to take things seriously but are content to live a kind of schoolboy life and to do just what they are told ... instead of thinking and acting for himself and his class ...

For Herbert Broomfield it was the final straw. In December he tendered his resignation; anxious as he was to turn his full attention to his business, he would remain close to the Union for some time and even resume the secretaryship for a period in 1913 when the position fell vacant.

Meredith, as usual, was fulsome in his praise:

> Herbert Broomfield is the first player who has pointed out to the players that they can protect themselves by unity and that if their cause was right they had no reason to fear saying so. He faced the power of the FA fearlessly, endured insult and abuse from his critics, worked night and day, travelled thousands of miles and spent at least £200 of his money because he would not touch Union funds until he had the consent of members to do so.... How many men would have dropped into the background as Broomfield has done, allowing others more popular with the FA than he is to voice his views in order that his presence should not hinder a settlement? Very few, I think. A grander, pluckier fight was never made than Broomfield has made!

And so the painful year 1909 ended, a year destined to remain etched on the memories of those who took part. As Charlie Roberts would write some years later: 'I shall never forget the summer of 1909 as long as I have breath in my body....'

# 10

# *Masters and Servants* 1910–11

The Union which emerged from the traumatic events of 1909 was no puppet organization, but its very independence merely highlighted what little power it possessed and how easy it was for football's authorities either to bully or ignore it.

For the next three years it would struggle along, tilting at the familiar windmills with high hopes but little success. There would be some small reform of wages and the Union would claim to have played a part in bringing them about, but in truth they were the handiwork of one man: C E Sutcliffe.

There would be some changes in the transfer system but, once again, Sutcliffe was the architect of these. The Union would be consulted, after a fashion, but its major initiatives would be rejected and its much contemplated legal assault on the transfer system would end in unlikely triumph for Sutcliffe and the League and bankruptcy for the Union.

Money would be the principle problem for the Union; where ready cash was concerned for administrative purposes, it would remain in the hands of the FA and to a lesser extent the League. The Benefit match had to be sanctioned by both bodies and, after a good start in 1910, this crucial fixture would be quite shamelessly manipulated by football's authorities in order to twist and bend the Union in whatever direction was required.

Yet the three years from 1910 and 1913 were still optimistic ones, years when men from the top League clubs continued to take a hand in running the Union organization and when membership would remain extremely healthy, although rarely more than 50–60 per cent of all professionals.

Although both Broomfield and Mainman stepped down from their respective posts as secretary and chairman, they remained close to Union affairs, Mainman continuing to serve on the Management Committee until the First World War, Broomfield eventually becoming a vice-chairman. Broomfield also continued to serve on special committees and even went along to meetings with the League Management Committee. His new football, meanwhile, made its appearance during 1910 under the trade name The Orb.

The replacements at the head of the Union – Syd Owen as secretary and Evelyn Lintott as chairman – were very much in the tradition of such post-holders: quasi-amateurs, men educated and trained in other professions.

Syd Owen was a chartered accountant and had served as the Union's membership auditor for some three years. He had played for both Stoke City and Leicester Fosse as an amateur, but by 1910 was with Northern Nomads; had represented England at amateur level and once been reserve to the full England side against Wales. Having played football in Russia, Sweden, Denmark, Holland and Germany, he would eventually go abroad as a coach. Owen would prove to be a perfect replacement for Broomfield – an energetic, enthusiastic organizer with a firm belief in principles – only his temper would eventually let him down.

Evelyn Lintott, a Bradford City player during his period as chairman, had also played for Queen's Park Rangers, Plymouth Argyle and Woking. Capped for England at both amateur and full level (versus Scotland in 1908 plus caps against Wales and Ireland) he was, by profession, a teacher. He beat Colin Veitch in the election for the post by six votes to three – a surprising result given Veitch's prominence in 1909, yet perhaps reflecting the links Lintott had with football in the south and west of England at a time when the Union remained a largely northern-dominated affair.

Although Lancashire and the north-east were heavily represented on the Management Committee, however, membership was by no means confined to men from the Manchester clubs and Newcastle, as was sometimes alleged.

In 1910, three Southern League players – Saul, Barnes and Piercy – were co-opted on to the committee and in 1911 Atterby of Plymouth Argyle was elected along with Bert Lipsham, once of Sheffield United but then of Millwall. McDowland of Chelsea and Collins of Fulham both served on the committee during 1909-10; for the rest, however, it was clubs such as Blackburn Rovers, Oldham, Preston, Middlesborough and Sunderland which supplied the bulk of committee-men. And in 1913, when Owen left to go abroad, his place was taken by Harry Newbould, ex-Manchester City manager.

The year 1910 would be dominated by the question of wages. The 1909 'strike' had proved to be the last straw for the FA and in January 1910 a spokesman wrote: 'It is incompatible with the position of the FA as the governing body of a national sport that it should be concerned in the financial arrangements between clubs and players other than seeing that the engagements which they enter into are observed.'

Because FA rules continued to refer to a maximum wage, League clubs could still only pay £4 a week. Whatever else they wished to offer was up to them, though, and early in the new year negotiations regarding talent money began between the Players' Union, the Southern League and the Football League.

The Union must have felt that radical change was close at hand. In January voting papers had been distributed by the FA to 74 clubs and to 1725 players to ascertain opinion regarding the abolition of the maximum wage. Although only 31 clubs bothered to reply (12 for abolition and 19 against) 1055 players did not return their papers, 795 voting in favour of abolition. This, Colin Veitch felt, quashed the 'absurd contention that the players themselves did not desire any change in the present conditions'.

In February, the Union Management Committee, after considering various wages schemes, declared that 'the only solution to the vexed question between clubs and players is the abolition of the wage limit'.

After some wrangling, however, the resolution was extended to read: 'but would willingly accept any scheme that tends to improve the now existing conditions'.

Eventually a wages conference was held on 25 February 1910 at the Grand Hotel, Manchester, the Union being represented by Evelyn Lintott, Jimmy Sharp, Broomfield and Owen. The Union scheme, drawn up by Owen, was given 'a courteous hearing', but C E Sutcliffe's eight-point plan was eventually adopted in full.

Owen's report back to the Union AGM in August was positive:

> The Union representatives cannot help feeling that they influenced the conference and convinced the various official bodies present that something more than the old hard and fast rules of payment was needed. We asked for more but feel that we did well under the circumstances in getting what was obtained. One thing is certain. Had there been no Union there would have been no conference, no discussion of schemes and no alteration.

The only straightforward changes, however, that players and club managements could easily understand and which looked automatic, were the talent money schemes. Bonuses could be paid by clubs finishing in the top five of any division. The top club could disperse £275 amongst its first team, the runners-up could disperse £220 and so on. These payments, however, were not compulsory.

The changes in actual weekly wages were designed to reward long-serving ('loyal') players. After two years, a player on the maximum wage might be offered an extra 10s a week for two years. After four more years' service, another 10s rise might be awarded. Thus it would take a player six years to move from £4 maximum a week to £5. Since the great majority of players was not on £4 a week anyway, this 'concession' had little effect on the bulk of pro-players.

Where players' benefits were concerned, the new proposals looked logical enough. After three years' service, a player could ask his club for a benefit to be awarded for five years' service. After that, he might ask for a ten-year benefit. But here the discretionary element played an even more crucial part. As Charlie Roberts wrote:

> I know that a player can make an agreement after three years service for a benefit, but how many clubs will allow him to make it? At the end of his third season, take it that a player asks for such an agreement, and the club refuses. What then? If the player refuses to sign on, what happens? The longer he delays signing, the more wages he continues to lose. He has no power to force the hands of the directors and he cannot go elsewhere owing to the stringent transfer rule.

The question of whether or not a player was in line for a benefit had a direct bearing on the next apparently radical change, this time to the transfer system. Once again, the new rule was clear enough to C E Sutcliffe:

> Where players are transferred by a club for financial reasons such a club may pay to the player a percentage of any transfer fee in lieu of accrued benefit, not exceeding the following scale: After one year's service – 10 per cent; after two years' service – 15 per cent; after three years' service – 25 per cent.

Charlie Roberts was once again scathing; in fact, no one seemed to know how the rule was supposed to work and the Union had to write to Sutcliffe for clarification in December 1910. At first it had seemed to grant a player a share in his transfer fee. Not so, Sutcliffe replied – the player *might* receive a share of the fee if the club had been forced to sell him to meet its debts. The share of the fee was calculated to compensate the player for any loss of accrued benefit. If no benefit had been promised, then there would be no share!

As Roberts commented, everything depended upon whether the club wanted to give something or not:

> I know a player who last April asked for a two-year engagement but was told that he could not have it, and was reported to the FA for refusing to sign on, a thing he had not done. When seen again in the first week of May he was told he had to sign or give up the game as they would not allow him to go anywhere else. Of course the player did sign on simply because by delay he was losing summer wages.

As if all this was not unsatisfactory enough, the conditions of service had been altered to allow clubs to insert into players' contracts a '14-day' rule whereby 'if a player proves palpably inefficient or is guilty of serious misconduct or a breach of disciplinary rules the club is allowed to terminate the player's contract. The player has right of appeal to the League Management Committee and a further right of appeal to the Appeal Committee on making a deposit of £5'.

With the closer working relationship now established between the Southern and Football Leagues, not to mention the Scottish League, a player accused of 'palpable inefficiency' would be unlikely to find a new club in senior football unless he went to Ireland. The club concerned, of course, still held his registration and could still put a fee on his head.

Roberts summed up the average professional footballer's true position: 'Certain provisions have been attached lately which many players have objected to but it is no use. If you don't sign you have to clear out of the game.'

**THE WEEKLY NEWS, SATURDAY, APRIL 8, 1911.**

*A historic event: a deputation from the Players' Union meets with English League officials at Liverpool to negotiate conditions. Left to right: C Roberts, A Bridgett, C Vetch and A S Owen (Secretary of the Players' Union).*

Colin Veitch, of course, had always taken an optimistic line: caution and patient plodding would eventually reap rewards. Thus he set about planning the Union's proposals for 1911, imagining that a process had begun that would simply accelerate. In April 1911, along with Charlie Roberts and Arthur Bridgett, he took his ideas along to the League for consideration.

The proposals were that players not offered a 'reasonable wage' should be given a free transfer; that players in service for five years should become exempt from the maximum wage (i.e., should attain freedom of contract); that players having, on 30 April, completed four years' service be granted a rise of £52 a year; those completing two years, £26 a year; plus a new set scale of talent money: £2 for a win, £1 for a draw with £3 for a first-round Cup win rising to £15 a man for the Final. Added to all this, it was proposed that a transferred player should receive a percentage of the fee.

According to the official League history, 'A long discussion took place in a very friendly spirit.' A few days later, the *Athletic News* commented that the proposals were 'not preposterous,' and that the players had a good case regarding 'freedom of contract'.

C E Sutcliffe, however, was in no doubt that the proposals were unreasonable. He was of the opinion that wages were already high, that talent money was already good and he dismissed the idea of a free transfer out of hand. Freedom of contract, he declared, was not a very inviting topic. Clubs would be 'harassed' by their players and higher wages would result.

In fact, he insisted that the present financial regulations would remain in place for some time, due to 'the financial havoc caused by the unwarranted and ill-advised actions of the Players' Union two years ago....'

In short, Sutcliffe dismissed the Players' Union proposals with contempt and almost loathing:

> It is no use mincing words, the clubs cannot stand the ever-increasing drain.... The club manager is often at his wits' end to pay his way. He is signing bank guarantees and finding money out of his private means to meet players' demands. Why should he be compelled to go further?

He even went as far as to say: 'I boldly assert that very few clubs had value for money spent in the season 1910-11 and I should say the majority of directors and managers are glad that the worry is at an end for another season.'

It was useless for Sydney Owen to write a week later wondering where exactly the money went when individual clubs were drawing 20,000–30,000 spectators every fortnight and still declaring losses. Useless also to point out that the Union's proposals for Cup bonuses would result, if implemented, in a total of £3431 being paid to players while the competition as a whole would earn £70,000. The consultations concerning wages were over.

The only concession Sutcliffe would allow in 1911 was the removal of the stipulation that only clubs in financial difficulties might pay players a share of their transfer fee. This absurd rule had thrown up so many anomalies that even Sutcliffe could see the error of his ways. But the idea that a player might automatically share in his transfer fee was flatly refused:

> To make the sharing of transfer fees compulsory would be to place the clubs at the mercy of the players; in other words to make the servants masters and the masters servants. We have had too much of that in the past.

Such bombastic, hostile reactions to what had been genuinely thought out and deeply pondered proposals saddened Colin Veitch. By 1911 he had succeeded Evelyn Lintott as chairman and his diplomatic moderate approach seemed to be paying no dividends at all. Fortunately for Veitch, he had a great deal with which to compensate himself.

The youngest of four sons of a Newcastle relieving officer, he was a talented actor and a musician and during the years 1911-13 he was chorus member of the Newcastle Amateur Operatic Society, as well as a member of the Clarion Dramatic Society (later the Newcastle People's Theatre). With the latter he performed in plays by Bernard Shaw and Shakespeare. Indeed, he was praised by Shaw himself for his performance as Old Malone in *Man and Superman*. Veitch was both chairman and producer with the Clarion, as well as a conductor of Gilbert and Sullivan with the Newcastle Operatic Society in which his wife was an accomplished performer.

A talented, versatile man, his socialism was not of the bureaucratic kind – in 1912 when the League Management Committee began to tinker yet again with the financial regulations (placing a limit on the amount a player could receive by way of benefit) he wrote:

The League Management Committee is out to equalize benefits. This means that benefits must be reduced in amount. In the matter of equality I believe the general impression amongst the mass of the people is that socialism aims at a similar equal distribution of wealth amongst the people. How would the League Management Committee fancy being called a body of Socialists? Yet with so many attempts to make everyone equal – a thing absolutely impossible in the minds of anyone with a grain of reasoning – it would appear that the mass of the people would be justified in applying that term according to the popular idea of the Socialist theory.

Apart from that, however, the amount of legislation which has been, and is, forthcoming would appear to suggest to me that a form of bureaucracy as what is being slowly but surely secured. Most people are heartily sick of legislation in football. In fact, everybody is tired of it except the legislators themselves and they seem to have got the idea that they must go on in order to justify their existence as ruling body. The thing becomes a mania for some people.

A mania indeed. Yet perhaps Veitch's knowledge of Gilbert and

Sullivan afforded him a wry perspective on the pretensions and pomposity of men such as Sutcliffe – veritable Pooh-Bahs. It is certain that the affair of the Union badges might well have been written by Sullivan.

As far back as November 1908, the Union had decided on a badge for members, issued free. In February 1910 the Management Committee voted on whether the badge should be a lapel badge or an arm-band. A vote of 8-2 saw the arm-band selected. In November Owen sent a circular to members explaining the motives behind the badge:

> ... the wearer of the badge ought to make it a point of always 'playing the game' in the way it should be played, in a clean, straightforward and sportsmanlike manner; otherwise he brings not only disgrace upon himself but the public ridicule of the Union as people will rightly say what is the good of a Union which cannot control its own members?

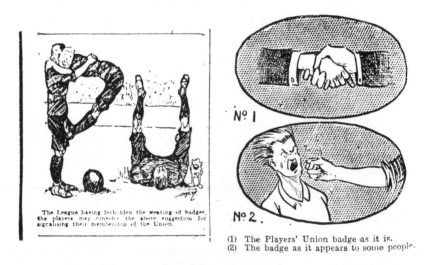

(1) The Players' Union badge as it is.
(2) The badge as it appears to some people.

*Cartoon comments on the badge issue*

The *Athletic News* commented: 'A circular with a better object and more aptly phrased could not have been issued.' However, two weeks later, every League club in the land received the following letter from Tom Charnley, League secretary:

Five prominent members of the Swindon Football Team—Jefferson, Kay, Tout, Silto and Bolland—with three docile (more or less) pet dogs.

*The cloth cap image of professional players.*

'Dear Sir,

It has been reported that players who are members of the Players' Union contemplate wearing Union badges during the matches in the coming season.

The League Management Committee have no desire to appear to deal unfairly with the players or unkindly towards the Union but consider that if they allowed the badges to be worn unpleasantness, both amongst players and a section of the spectators' might be caused.

The Management Committee have therefore decided that in the interests of the game and all concerned, the wearing of badges cannot be sanctioned and clubs must not in any case allow their players to do so.'

Manchester United, Newcastle United and Sunderland players decided to defy the League and wear their badges. An 'unfortunate incident' had thus occurred.

Lintott, Bridgett and Owen were duly summoned to the League headquarters in Preston to explain themselves. The League were affronted at having been bypassed but were apparently even more concerned that the badges would lead to victimization of non-Unionists. Thus, the League considered them to be a menace to good-will and good sportsmanship – the very opposite of everything Owen had said they were.

Indeed, the League Management Committee, in deciding to ban the badges, claimed that the whole affair had been 'calculated to cause unpleasantness'. The *Athletic News* went so far as to assert that crowds had booed the badge-wearers.

Meredith was predictably indignant. The badges had been a pet project of his, symbolic of the Union's *esprit de corps*. 'The Day Will Come' he thundered in his *Weekly News* column, 'when the players will wear the badge whether the League likes it or not!' and he claimed that the League were really afraid that the badge might lead to more Union recruits.

Two days later, C E Sutcliffe entered the debate. The League had apparently been lenient – it could have fined and suspended the men involved and, under the inevitable, wearying headline: 'The Clubs Must Be The Masters', he laid down the law:

There can be no misunderstanding the resolution; badges must not be worn. If they are, suspensions must follow immediately, and will not readily be removed.

# 11
## *Kingaby* 1912

The dispute of 1909 had been sparked off by the Players' Union insisting on its right to make up its own mind on whether to take to court cases which the football authorities either could or would not settle.

The case against Crystal Palace FC heard in late 1909 at Croydon Crown Court (for which the FA's permission had not been sought), had proved successful and was regarded as a vindication of the Union's stance, although it had subsequently agreed to temper its approach and give the FA a chance to solve particular cases first.

Nevertheless, it was becoming abundantly clear that contractual freedom – one of the major goals of the Players' Union – could only be secured through a court of law.

Justice, or the lack of it, was a persistent theme running through players' newspaper articles during the post-1909 years: whether it was the arbitrary treatment men received at the hands of FA disciplinary tribunals or the grossly unfair manipulation by clubs of the 'signing-on' process at the end of each season, there was always some *cause célèbre* to exercise the mind – and the Players' Union felt increasingly drawn to intervene.

The suspension of 'Ginger' Lyons in June 1910 and later of Dickie Bond in March 1911 were two instances where players had been punished respectively for foul play and swearing, on evidence supplied not by the referee but by an individual spectator in the stands. In Lyons's case, it happened to be an FA councillor; and considering that Lyons had spoken out vehemently during the FA–Union conference of 1909, complaining about his treatment during the Manchester City affair of 1905, one wonders whether he had been singled out for punishment again.

The Union requested the FA to reopen the case and allow Lyons to speak on his own behalf. The FA remained unmoved, however, and Lyons had to serve out his sentence.

Where Bond was concerned, a resolution was forwarded to the FA that went somewhat further:

> As the matter thus resolves itself into a question of one man's word against another's, the sentence imposed on Bond seems altogether out of proportion to the 'crime' which he states was never committed.

It was an 'unsatisfactory state of affairs' and the Union requested the FA to let it know about such cases in advance so that the players might have the chance to formulate some defence with the help of the Union's solicitor.

Bond had been suspended earlier in the season and put on the transfer list for allegedly fighting in a public house along with two other Bradford City players while on a motoring jaunt. Bond had written an article for the *Thomson's Weekly News* outlining the facts and his suspension had been lifted. He later thanked the newspaper for affording him the chance that his club had denied him – yet the club had behaved no worse than the FA in this respect.

Of equal concern to the Union was the continuing tendency of some clubs to refuse to honour contracts which involved financial obligations to players. One such case was that of Jimmy Buchan of Manchester City.

Buchan had first signed for City in March 1905. Thus, by 1910 he was eligible for a benefit. His claims to the latter rested on his contract for the 1909-10 season which had been accompanied by a letter from club chairman Wilkinson (ironically the Players' Union's ex-solicitor) promising Buchan a benefit of not less than £500.

The club, however, refused the benefit request for the 1910-11 season and had placed Buchan on the transfer list. The Union took

Buchan's case up and approached the FA, stating that it would like a decision from the FA, 'without prejudice to any further action the Union might take on the player's behalf'. The case had by then been in progress for some five months.

The Manchester City club's response to this move is revealing. Club manager Newbould (who, within two years would be the Union secretary) complained that this claim by the Players' Union not to be bound by the FA's decision was 'grossly unfair'. He continued; 'We are quite willing to leave the matter to the FA as final arbiters but we strongly object to the Players' Union exploiting the FA as a tribunal whose decision is to be regarded or disregarded according to its suiting their purposes or otherwise....'

City need not have feared. Buchan – who had been reluctant to go to court anyway – was transferred to the Scottish club Hibernian in June 1911 and accepted a settlement from the City club.

The law was therefore still seen as the bogy of both League clubs and football's authorities, there being more than a suspicion that rules and regulations regarding contracts and tribunals would not stand up to serious legal challenge.

For the Union the law was the great hope, and yet there were obvious risks involved. It was one thing to take cases to county courts under the Workman's Compensation Act in order to claim compensation for injury, loss of back-wages, etc. Already the Union had developed a system for such actions, many of which were settled out of court at little cost either to player or Union.

It was another thing entirely, however, to engage eminent KCs and to mount a major challenge in the High Court to question the legality of either the transfer system or the maximum wage. This would involve major expense, with no firm guarantee of eventual success. The Union, though, was plucking up courage. In a sense, it was the next logical step.

The Union had been established to bring about major reforms. It had survived a massive assault by football's rulers; it might not survive another. Meanwhile, the League was growing more and more powerful and the FA less and less inclined or able to help professional players. The Union had no power to change things from without – having cut itself off from the trade union movement, it had no real 'muscle'. Thus it had to change the ground rules, had to break the vicious circle. And it would be the transfer system that would be the target.

By mid-1910 the Union was consulting lawyers in London about
the legality or otherwise of the transfer system and by September it
had compiled a short-list from which it might select a test-case.

Among the names mentioned was Leslie Skene of Fulham,
involved in a six-month-long dispute with the club over various
payments claimed by him; Fulham were holding him down and
paying him no wages so that Skene was eventually forced to travel to
Ireland to obtain work in football to tide him over. Then there was
Jesse Pennington, an England International, later to become a Union
Management Committee member, who was also being prevented
from leaving his club, West Bromwich Albion, because of a wages
dispute.

In September 1910, however, the name Kingaby appears for the
first time in the Union minutes as a possible test-case.

Kingaby had had a colourful though not particularly untypical
career, complicated only by the fact that he worked for a woollen
manufacturer in London and thus was only free to play on Saturdays
and bank holidays. Until 1906 he had played for Clapton Orient at
outside right when Aston Villa noticed and bought him for £300,
paying him the maximum wage of £4 a week for his Saturday game.

After two months, however, Villa decided they no longer wanted
him and offered him back to the Orient for £150. Orient could not
pay the fee, so Kingaby went on to Villa's retained list with no
contract and no wages. He immediately decamped to Fulham, who
were then in the Southern League and thus not covered by the
League's regulations. Villa tried to lure him back, offering him £4 a
week, but Kingaby stayed at Fulham until 1908, when he went to
Leyton Orient. In 1910, following the agreement between the
Football League and the Southern League regarding registration and
transfers, he suddenly found himself once more on Villa's books –
now with a £350 price tag on his head! The fee was ridiculous, of
course, but the League Management Committee could only see its
way to reducing it to £300. Kingaby was, to all intents and purposes,
out of football for life. He asked for a free transfer from Villa, as a
club called Croydon Common was prepared to pay him £2 a week,
but Villa initially refused.

On paper, it looked like the perfect case. Kingaby, however, was
very much his own man and insisted on instituting legal proceedings
privately; only after the case had begun did he approach the Union
and ask for assistance.

The Union advised him to place the case in the hands of Hinchcliffe, the Union solicitor, but Kingaby refused. In December 1910, however, Harry Mainman was authorized by the Management Committee to go to London with £50 as a contribution towards Kingaby's costs – on the strict understanding that he press on with the case and not drop it.

Enquiries by the Union over the next few months revealed little progress, simply postponement after postponement. In April 1911, Billy Meredith wrote in the *Thomson's Weekly News* that the case was sure to come to court that June, but it transpired that Aston Villa had offered Kingaby the free transfer he had asked for and that the player, having obtained a contract with Peterborough City at 30s a week, was declaring himself satisfied.

Kingaby nevertheless announced that if the Union conceded certain terms to him he would continue with the action, presumably in the hope of winning damages, but Colin Veitch commented: 'To those terms no one on earth would have agreed.'

The Union, therefore, decided to look for another test-case, but somehow the Kingaby issue refused to go away. At one point, Veitch threatened to reveal in print Kingaby's demands in order to scotch rumours that it had been the Union that had got cold feet and dropped the case; indeed the Union magazine had already hinted at Kingaby's 'excessive demands' – which only brought the latter's solicitors into the argument, threatening to take the Union to court over possible libel of their client! The Union was now caught in a legal web, a situation that appears to have induced both parties to join forces once again. For in January 1912 the Kingaby action was back on course and on 30 March, before a special jury of the King's Bench Division, the case of Aston Villa versus Kingaby opened.

For such an apparently momentous step, this strange prelude was hardly the best preparation. But it had caused uneasiness among football's ruling bodies, for it was clear that informed legal opinion favoured the Union's position.

Union commentators were certainly confident. When C E Sutcliffe wrote an angry piece in June 1912 about the Union's 'bitter attack', Meredith coolly countered that it was a friendly action to test the system in law: 'I can't for the life of me see what Sutcliffe is driving at.'

Veitch, too, was confident and conciliatory: 'We bear no

animosity towards our employers in the matter at all ... we get on very well with the clubs but we don't get on well with the transfer system.'

Sutcliffe, however, had spent months preparing for the trial, arriving at the court laden with files and papers, eager for the moment when he would be called. After all, the retain and transfer system was the basis upon which his conception of the League rested: without it, chaos and Armageddon would result.

Acting for the defence was Montague Shearman KC, a man who a short time previously had given his opinion to the Union that the players' contract was 'contrary to law'. Years later, Sutcliffe would write that Shearman seemed initially not to have grasped the transfer system nor to have understood the law applying it. Sutcliffe had been obliged to explain it to him.

In court, Mr Rawlinson KC, acting for Kingaby, immediately made what was to be a fundamental error. He set out to attack Aston Villa's *motives* in setting a prohibitive fee on Kingaby's head, rather than attacking the transfer system itself.

The subsequent debate, therefore, took for granted the 'legality' of the system. Rawlinson made no attempt to prove that it was an unreasonable restraint of trade. Rather, he claimed that Aston Villa had acted 'maliciously' when using it.

The judge simply concluded that on the evidence, he could see no 'malice'. Indeed, he stated that 'when a man exercises an undoubted right the question of motive is not a sufficient cause of action'.

In response to Rawlinson's other main charge, that there had been a conspiracy between Villa and the League to restrict the field of Kingaby's employment, the judge simply repeated what Sutcliffe himself might have said: that the League used the system to prevent clubs filching players from one another. They had not been aiming to damage Kingaby personally.

The hearing lasted just two days and the judge ruled that there was no case for Aston Villa to answer.

That the verdict was an unmitigated disaster for the Union cannot be denied. So many unpleasant consequences flowed from it, not the least being the problem of paying the legal costs.

The Union was now almost bankrupt, owing money to its own solicitors and Kingaby's solicitors, plus costs to the League. Worse still, there was no immediate way it could raise that money.

By taking the plunge and pursuing the Kingaby case to the bitter end, the Union had incurred the deep displeasure of the FA. Ever since 1910, when the Kingaby case had first been mooted, ominous signals had come from FA headquarters – in particular, the refusal to allow the Union to hold its apparently automatic Benevolent Fund match in 1911.

The FA's reason for refusing had been that the Union already had enough money in its Benevolent Fund. Leaving aside the fact that this decision appeared to be a clear breach of the 1909 agreement between the FA and the Union, the refusal demonstrated two things. First, that the FA did not regard the Union as a truly 'independent' body, i.e. the FA had the right to inspect the Union's books whenever it felt so inclined, and to act upon what it found; and second, it would only allow it to raise money for 'benevolent' purposes. In fact, the FA's refusal to grant the match was caused by the Union borrowing money from its Benevolent Fund to pay back Broomfield for expenses he had incurred during the 1909 'strike', as well as to pay for Kingaby's costs.

The Union's assurances that it would repay the borrowed money as soon as possible had not satisfied the FA. It wanted the Union to promise never to use Benevolent Fund money for any other purpose than helping players in need.

The immediate aftermath of the Kingaby case thus saw the Union anxious to raise money; and the only sure way of doing that would be to hold a benefit match between the English Players' Union and the newly formed Scottish branch.

In March 1912, however, it was the League that raised objections, ostensibly because players were needed by clubs for important matches. According to Meredith, however, the League was really trying to twist the Union's arm:

> The League has been induced by the advice of certain people to try to stop the Union increasing their funds. Why? Because they are afraid, terribly afraid of an appeal in the transfer case action.

The proposed benefit match was thus shelved until the new season. By October 1912, the League had agreed to the release of various players – on condition that the Union pay all profits from the match to the League as repayment of legal costs.

Syd Owen had negotiated long and hard with the League over

this, assuring them that all would be acceptable to the FA. He was wrong.

Now it was the FA's turn to push the Union around. It immediately announced that it would not be giving permission for the match because the Union had still not satisfied it about the use of Benevolent Fund money. The League in turn accused Owen of deceit, an accusation that proved too much for him.

He penned an angry letter to the *Sporting Chronicle*, accusing the FA of breaking its word concerning the granting of the match:

> I venture to suggest that the Football Association have clearly shown that they are desirous of handicapping the Players' Union in every way they can....
>
> Of all the high-handed, intolerable things Mr Crump and his colleagues at the FA have ever done, this act of breaking faith with the players, of failing to keep a promise and of advancing for doing so the extraordinary reason that the Players' Management Committee refuse to allow the FA to dictate how the Union funds shall be spent, is the king of them all.
>
> It is regrettable because it is stupid, and because it is clear evidence of a vindictive spirit....

Owen's bitter letter reflected the anger and frustration that had been building up within the Union ever since the Kingaby case had ended.

The League, now financial overlords, were pressing on with endless restrictions and regulations, some defying logic. For instance, with the passing of the Insurance Act in 1911 a man in employment had to pay 4d a week which would guarantee him 10s a week if he were to fall ill and not be able to work. Clubs were told by the League that this payment could breach the maximum wage, thus the clubs were to take the 10s out of the players' wages.

Then there had been Sutcliffe's latest resolution regarding players' benefits, which he now insisted should be limited to £500. It seemed that wherever a player turned, there was yet another provocation. As Colin Veitch remarked in September 1912: 'The only limitations we seem able to arrive at are those of legislation and the players' patience. Patience is a virtue – and to change the old form we might add – to be imposed upon.'

Owen's outburst demonstrated that he for one was no longer willing to be patient. It was to cost him his job.

The FA decided to make an issue of the letter and demanded on apology. Owen refused to give it, nor would he give the FA the undertaking it required regarding the Benevolent Fund. If he had counted on the support of his colleagues on the Management Committee, however, he was to be mistaken.

In October Charlie Roberts, Jesse Pennington and Jimmy Fay were invited to see League officials after a League Management Committee meeting 'to have a chat over the trouble'. According to a journalist, 'Friendly advice was offered by the President of the League and others....'

Subsequently, the Management Committee decided that it could not endorse the contents of the letter which had been 'ill-conceived, hastily written, full of tactless remarks and random insults'.

The League, however, refused to let the matter rest there. It refused to recognize any communication from Owen as a representative of the Union – an incredible move when one considers that Owen was the legally appointed secretary. But the pressure paid off. In December Owen was formally censured by the committee which also assured the FA that all its conditions regarding the Benevolent Fund would be met. Owen had, by now, had enough. He announced in January that he had secured a job as a coach in Budapest. He resigned as secretary of the Union.

The Union had thus allowed its secretary to be hounded out of the game, a disgraceful episode and one that could do it no good in the eyes of its members, whatever their opinions on the matter. In fact, it could be said that Owen's departure marked the end of the first 'heroic' era of the Union's existence, begun in such style in 1908, now ending in virtual bankruptcy and impotence.

Although Herbert Broomfield returned as secretary pro tem, his main task was the mournful one of attempting to prevent the Scottish branch from withdrawing from the Union. He failed.

In March 1913, the Union appointed Harry Newbould, ex-Derby County, ex-Manchester City manager as secretary. No firebrand, he announced in the Union news-letter:

> I want every player to feel that I have accepted this position with the object of considering their requirements and with a firm intention to do my duty to the Union and to every individual member, at the same time using every possible means in my power to work amicably with the FA and the FL in the best interests of the Union.

I am sure that our members realize that we must have a governing body and that the rules and regulations of these authorities must be observed. This is absolutely necessary for the proper conducting of our great national winter pastime.

Within nine months the Union offices in St Peter's Square in the heart of Manchester had been removed to a room in Newbould's house at Longsight, in Manchester's south-eastern suburbs. The long years of hibernation had begun.

# 12

# *Edwardian High Summer* 1912–14

Ivan Sharpe, doyen of football writers of the inter-war period, once described the years 1900 to 1914 as football's Golden Age, claiming that the game was more attractive then, the great players more skilful and versatile – even the crowds somehow more likeable and less 'neurotic'.

Sharpe's vision of the game perhaps had more to do with a nostalgia for his own lost youth than with objective fact; but where the Players' Union was concerned, it would certainly be many years before the sense of positive self-esteem, of clarity of purpose, of sheer good-natured optimism that characterized much of what it did during those Edwardian years, would ever be recaptured.

For despite the defeats and miscalculations, the errors of judgement, not to mention the never-ending, losing battle to persuade the rank and file to part with their weekly sixpenny 'sub', the Union attempted and achieved a great deal, spurred on by an ideal of 'brotherhood' that today looks as out-of-date as leather toe-caps and lace-up footballs.

The summer sports festivals of 1911, 1912 and 1913 were ambitious, sometimes chaotically organized affairs run on shoestring budgets, relying on the endless energy of men like Syd Owen (who made himself ill organizing the Old Trafford festival of

105

ENTRIES CLOSE SATURDAY, AUGUST 2nd.

# Association Football Players' Union

FOUNDED DECEMBER, 1907

THIRD ANNUAL

# Athletic Festival

100 Yards Open Sprint (3 yards limit). Winner holds the "Athletic News" Cup (Value £25)

## SPRINTS, RELAY RACES, &c.

## On the LEEDS CITY F.C., GROUND, Elland Road, Leeds,

Saturday, August 9th, 1913.    Commencing 3 p.m.

*Professional Starter :  Mr. R. LANE, Manchester.*
*Professional Handicapper:  Mr. A. NICHOLLS, Manchester.*

SECRETARY:
H. J. NEWBOULD, 14, St. Peter's Square, Manchester.

## Admission Sixpence & One Shilling.

1911), Harry Newbould, Colin Veitch, plus scores of unpaid helpers, supporters from various clubs and players themselves.

Supporters came from all over the country to cheer their own men on – a crowd of 15,000 attended the 1911 Festival. There were place-kick competitions, dribbling competitions, sprints and half-mile runs (incredibly no five-a-side competitions because the FA refused to give its permission).

Prizes were small except for the magnificent cup presented by the *Athletic News*. In fact, it and *Thomson's Weekly News*, were the only sponsors the Union managed to attract, both the League and the FA holding themselves aloof. Harry Wright of Derby was the first winner of the *Athletic News* trophy – awarded for the fastest sprinter among pro-footballers.

In 1912 the Union became more ambitious and invited professional runners from all over the world to compete for prizes of up to £100 – although most money made by such pro-runners was via trackside bets and wagers.

Ostensibly to raise money for the Union's Benevolent Fund (and to help players get fit for the coming season), the sports were, in fact, a brave attempt to establish the Union as an independent organization capable of looking after itself. However, the hoped-for profits were not forthcoming – only the Old Trafford festival made any money (£150) and that had to be prised from the Manchester United club via a writ! Nevertheless, if the Great War had not intervened,

FOOTBALL PLAYERS' MAGAZINE.

# Hardships of the Transfer System
### By CHARLIE ROBERTS, Manchester United.

the sports festival might well have gone from strength to strength.

The Union magazine was a well-produced and generally well-written publication appearing between 1910 and 1913. Edited by Stacey Lintott and later by Harry Newbould, it devoted its pages to discussions of standards of conduct on the field, reminiscences, Union news and advice, opening its pages to referees and club managers – even to C E Sutcliffe.

How many copies it sold per week is impossible to say; likewise, its

FOOTBALL PLAYERS' MAGAZINE.

(H. J. NEWBOULD).

profitability. It probably lost money but there was no other publication of its kind attempting, as it did, to draw together all clubs and players in dialogue. Neither the FA nor the League, with their more considerable financial means, attempted such an enterprise – the FA being too aloof for such a 'popular' measure, the League too motivated by sectional greed to contemplate such altruism.

However, it was the day-to-day benevolent work that was the Union's most solid achievement. Throughout all the high-profile disputes and arguments with the authorities, the business of distributing sums of money to players in need, players fallen on hard times, families and dependants of players who had died, continued.

This, along with the determination to alter the legal framework in which players operated, was the reason the Union had been founded, and between 1908 and 1914 the numbers of men and women the Union assisted ran into hundreds, the amount of money disbursed into thousands. Widows automatically received a £10 grant (raised by a levy of all members) plus any other expenses deemed necessary. Management Committee members, and the secretary in particular, spent a great deal of their free time travelling up and down the country looking into individual cases, investigating appeals, handing out small but crucial sums, paying funeral expenses, removal costs, bailing men out of prison, replacing furniture, paying hospital fees – the cases were endless.

In the *Thomson's Weekly News* of February 1913, an article written by Billy Meredith entitled: 'Ever Heard of the Benevolent Fund?' took the FA's own fund to task: 'Billy Meredith wonders what it is and what it does for the players.... Judging by the constant applications to the Players' Union for assistance from players suffering from misfortune, the FA Benevolent Fund, whatever else it does, does very little for players....'

It was a constant criticism made of the FA – that it allowed its Benevolent Fund to accumulate massive amounts, yet rarely paid anything out. The FA's answer was that it rarely received any requests for money. In truth, destitute players and their families had no way of approaching the FA, whose procedures and attitudes smacked more of Poor Law Guardians than of dispensers of desperately needed money (most of it accumulated through the efforts of professional players and clubs).

The Players' Union, down to earth, prepared to knock on people's doors and make on-the-spot assessments, not to mention immediate payments, filled a pressing need.

Even with the advent of the Workman's Compensation Act and the establishment by the League of the Football Mutual Insurance Federation, the legal case-work of the Union increased dramatically. Cases concerning clubs failing to pay arrears of wages, clubs not paying wages in full, clubs refusing to honour agreements or even not offering players agreements at all – year by year the work of Thomas Hinchcliffe, Union solicitor, became more and more an integral part of Union affairs.

It was during these early years that the Union also established itself as an unofficial employment agency, a clearing-house for players desperate to find a new club but possessing no knowledge of possible openings or opportunities.

Clubs often put men on their retaining list but failed to circulate the information to other clubs. In fact, the vast pool of retained labour – men unable to leave the club which held their registration – became such a scandal in 1910 that the League, urged on by the Players' Union, issued an instruction to clubs to release players after a certain period if they had no more use for them.

But in general, information – even the price the club had placed on a man's head – was hard to come by, and the Union served a useful purpose by bringing players and clubs together.

Yet, despite all the efforts, not to say sacrifices, of men such as Broomfield, Owen, Bradshaw and Veitch, professional players as a whole remained apathetic towards the Union. Such attitudes appalled Charlie Roberts. 'Shame on you!' he cried in an article in the Players' Union magazine in March 1914, pointing out the fact that, of an estimated 4740 professional players engaged by some 158 clubs in England and Wales, only 700-odd were members of the Union.

FOOTBALL PLAYERS' MAGAZINE.

# A Straight Talk to Non-members.
### By CHARLES ROBERTS.

Prestigious clubs such as Aston Villa, Tottenham, Chelsea, Blackburn Rovers, Sheffield Wednesday and Middlesborough were among those without a single member. As Roberts pointed out, all players would have benefited from a successful outcome to the Kingaby case. As it was, a small minority would have to settle costs of up to £1000. No wonder he could write:

> I know no class of working people who are less able to look after themselves than footballers; they are like a lot of sheep.... They cannot think for themselves and as for taking care for themselves, it makes me smile.

And one could well understand him declaring:

> ... the work has been left to a handful of us but I am telling you now that I have just about had enough of trying to raise the status of the professional footballer. It takes up time that I now cannot afford to spare and unless the players next season take a greater interest in the Union I for one am going to leave them to it....

Roberts could not have known that the 1914-15 season would be the last for some time. Yet his warning, 'If you allow the Players' Union to die through indifference so sure am I that you will live to regret it', was eerily prophetic.

War was declared a few months later in August 1914, throwing almost every aspect of day-to-day life into confusion. With thousands of men volunteering for the forces, with industrial production rapidly having to adjust itself to wartime needs, with transport systems disrupted and all open spaces (such as football grounds) being commandeered, the Football League competition was initially thrown into disarray.

Some clubs experienced dramatic slumps in attendances (up to 50 per cent in certain cases); for one or two badly placed clubs, bankruptcy loomed within weeks of the start of the competition.

It was thought at first that the League competition would have to be abandoned – a fierce debate took place concerning the morality of some men playing football while others died in the trenches. But once it became clear that the game had a part to play as entertainment for the masses – not to mention in the recruitment drives – the League Management Committee felt obliged to devise a plan to ensure that no individual club suffered or went under.

By the end of September 1914, C E Sutcliffe had devised just such a plan. The Football League would preserve its physical integrity by cutting the wages of professional footballers.

As was traditional, the last to hear of the scheme and the last to be consulted were the players themselves. The first official communication the Union received was a letter from the Southern League's secretary requesting a meeting to discuss implementation of the scheme. A few days later, still not having spoken to the players, Sutcliffe unveiled the scheme in all its intricate detail in the *Athletic News*, the nub of which was that wages would be reduced on a sliding scale. Those men on £5 a week would lose 15 per cent of their wage (15s), down to men on £2 a week who would lose 5 per cent of wages. The money would be taken by club secretaries and put into a central fund from which sums could be drawn by clubs in debt. There was also to be a percentage levied on gate money, but this had not yet been sorted out.

Sutcliffe's justification for the scheme was that if no one came to the aid of clubs facing losses, then those clubs would cease to exist. He estimated (using figures nobody else was ever shown) that almost 500 players would lose their jobs. There was, he declared, no alternative to his scheme. Even if clubs did manage to struggle along, some players would have to take cuts in wages while others would take home their full pay. That, he declared, would be unjust: 'Every penny contributed by players would go to players,' he had printed in bold type.

The *Thomson's Weekly News* interviewed a number of players soon after the scheme was outlined, and the response was generally hostile. There was anger at the speed with which it was being rushed through and there was disquiet at the disproportionate amount players, as against clubs, were contributing.

Why, it was asked by Jimmy Lawrence, a Union committee member, if the League clubs were suddenly so keen to help one another out did they not simply pool gate money and share the money out according to need?

# THE FOOTBALL ASSOCIATION

## COMES IN FOR A SLASHING CRITICISM

### FROM CHARLIE ROBERTS, OF MANCHESTER UNITED.

Thompson's Weekly News *headline, 1914*

Another player wondered what the FA was doing with its Benevolent Fund money. Why could it not use the money to help players facing pay cuts?

Then there was the question of the players' contracts, usually so binding when looked at from the clubs' point of view, now apparently to be torn up.

And what of the large profits made by some clubs during the previous season? Some larger clubs did, in fact, state that they would not join the scheme, feeling that they ought to be allowed to arrange matters with their own players independently. Southern League clubs were doing just that.

In the meantime, the Union met the League Management Committee in Birmingham. Its stance was simple: if the scheme was indeed the only one possible (which it doubted, expressing scepticism of some clubs' cries of poverty) then it would recommend its members to accept the scheme if the money taken from players was regarded as 'deferred pay', to be repaid at a later date.

This the League representatives rejected out of hand. When the players tried to rephrase their resolution suggesting that clubs which took money out of the fund should repay it later 'for the purpose of refunding to the players the money contributed to the fund', this too was rejected. (As the *Athletic News* reported, 'Many intricate objections were urged to this course....')

Not only were the Union's suggestions thrown out, but the League Management Committee announced that the scheme would start, like it or not, the very next week. Consultations were over.

At a League General Meeting an hour after the meeting with the Players' Union, the scheme was adopted unanimously, leaving Sutcliffe ecstatic. The decision he later described as being, 'like a refreshing breeze from the moors ... the finest tonic imaginable to the depressed mind'. The unanimity the clubs had shown (in agreeing to reduce players' wages) had been 'the practical exemplification of the true League spirit in noble fashion'. If only the players had been present, he mused, they might have caught the 'spirit of generosity and self-sacrificing'. Questions of trade union principles were irrelevant, he wrote; the continuance of the game was of far greater importance.

The players, he felt, were being offered a great opportunity: 'I am satisfied the players will accept their share of responsibility and contribute to the fund – a special fund for the relief of players. In doing so they will have the everlasting joy attendant on the knowledge that they did their share to keep the wolf of poverty and the sad havoc from the door of other less fortunate players.'

And just in case this sanctimonious nonsense proved unsuccessful in persuading the men 'to do their duty', he revealed the familiar iron fist beneath the velvet glove:

> In view of the spirit of the clubs, the only alternatives to my mind are to end the season or – well, the other is a secret but it might bear the imprint of a threat, and these are not the days for force in civil life.... The first contribution by players is due from this week's wages. Players may well pay up and be thankful that they can do their share and that things are not worse....

The Union was not to be bullied, however, and persisted in pressing what it felt was a reasonable point – that men with legal contracts ought not to tear them up for the sake of a scheme that was being steamrollered through, the mechanics of which were still vague and the need for which still unproved.

They drew up a letter for players to use with their clubs that safeguarded their rights:

> Please take notice that I accept the reduction in my wages as a
> Football Player 'without prejudice' to my rights, under the existing
> agreement for service, to sue for the amount so deducted should
> occasion arise.

With that, the Union Management Committee declared that it
was up to individual players to decide what action to take, but the
advice was not to sign one of the new contracts.

With intense pressure coming from all sides – sections of the
press calling players 'mercenaries' for continuing to play anyway;
club managements understandably eager to collect the 'contributions'; the heightened sense of drama the war was giving to
everything – most players felt they had little choice but to accept
Sutcliffe's scheme. Most signed new contracts within the week; few
dared to present the covering letter.

Players at one or two clubs, however, decided that they were not
going to play ball, and demanded their wages in full. Manchester
United men, inevitably, were among the 'rebels'.

The *Athletic News* wasted no time in condemning them:

> It is evident that these men are without any feeling for their brothers
> on the field and do not care a farthing about anybody but
> themselves. They have contracts. They want their pound of flesh
> under their bond. The public of Manchester will know what to think
> of them ... they are birds of prey ... they are so-called men who will
> not lift a finger to help their fellows ... they once called themselves
> The Outcasts. They deserve to be....

The Manchester United men were not alone. The following week
it was reported that Bradford City, Tottenham Hotspur, Sheffield
United and Wednesday plus Aston Villa were all refusing to sign
the new contracts, while Newcastle and Sunderland had insisted on
the Union letter being inserted, safeguarding their rights to sue
later on.

The Union, in the persons of Colin Veitch, Tim Robinson and
Harry Newbould, once again met the League, but John McKenna,
before storming out of the room, simply insisted that the Union
withdraw the letter.

The *Athletic News* reported:

The meeting at Bradford was, we hear, the best proof that a Players' Union can never prosper until there is a great change in the tone and temper of the players. Never a player ought to have murmured.

Even when allowances are made for the heightened atmosphere of wartime – the jingoism then prevalent, the possible lack of perspective – the hysterical reactions of men like Sutcliffe and McKenna when faced with the mildest of opposition to their scheme is hard to credit, let alone excuse. Because it was not untypical. The refusal even to discuss the pooling of gate money, the reluctance to reveal any substantial figures to back up their claim, the scorn with which they responded to the idea of paying back money taken from men who would never be able to retrieve it, while the clubs would always be able to recoup their losses, was all too characteristic of their general approach to players, whether in peace or war.

The war simply offered them the perfect opportunity to bully and threaten players who dared question their version of reality, because the scheme was designed primarily to ensure the survival of forty limited companies, not to feed players and their families. The following season, just before the League competition was finally abandoned in its traditional form, plans were drawn up to scrap summer wages entirely and pay men no more than £2 a week.

In October 1915 the Union Management Committee held its last Annual General Meeting of the 'pre-War' period at the Old Swan Hotel, Pool Street, Manchester.

Its liabilities over its assets were £478, with a bank overdraft of £48. Secretary Newbould had by then resigned but had continued to act in a voluntary capacity while not demanding rent for the Union offices.

The Union, in fact, was almost non-existent. In April, in the minutes, the sense of gloom was put into words:

Expressions of regret were made at the lack of interest shown by the majority of players in their own welfare and the hope expressed that they would come forward and support the Union in its endeavours to right matters ere the position of the professional players becomes hopeless.

# 13
# *Roberts Revives the Union* 1918–19

Between October 1915 and 1919 the Players' Union ceased to exist; so, indeed, did professional footballers, even though the League carried on as if nothing had happened. Competitions continued, referees, club officials and managers were paid, while many clubs made reasonable profits.

C E Sutcliffe later declared that his efforts during the war to keep everything going brought him more satisfaction than anything else he did in football. However, if Sutcliffe had a 'good war', football in general hardly improved its image in the eyes of respectable society. Indeed, the professional game was so heavily criticized in the first six months of the war that nothing it subsequently did – either in collective or individual terms – could ever quite remove the stigma that it had 'dragged its feet' and that football folk had been reluctant to 'do their bit'.

If the jingoists had had their way, professional football would simply have closed up shop in August 1914 and all players enlisted *en masse*, as many rugby players (amateur, of course) had done.

But the majority of players had not been able simply to hang up their boots and enlist. Most were married men with wives and children to support – in 1914 and 1915 it was single men who were expected to drop everything and join the colours. There was also a great deal of confusion about fitness. Football players were regarded as being fine physical specimens and thus perfect for the army, but to

116

# THE QUESTION OF THE MOMENT.

*Humorous suggestions for cutting costs at clubs during the war.* Athletic News,
*November 1914*

those who knew anything about the game this was nonsense. Many
players suffered from a variety of occupational injuries that rendered
them useless for the regular army.

On top of this was the fact that clubs, as employers, were by no
means consistent in their attitude to men leaving and joining the
forces. Officially the line was that all men must be encouraged to join
up – this was Union policy too. Some clubs at first offered men full
pay if they went, or promised to look after their wives and children.
Aston Villa sent out a circular to their players in December 1914
making just such an offer. Manchester City also said that they would
continue paying wages to men joining up 'provided we have the

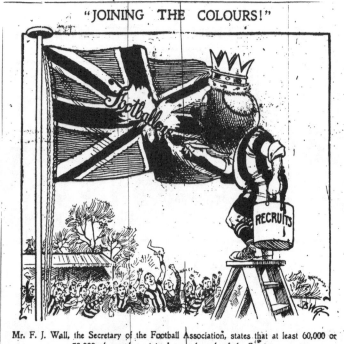

"JOINING THE COLOURS!"

Mr. F. J. Wall, the Secretary of the Football Association, states that at least 60,000 or 70,000 players have joined some branch of the Services.

Athletic News, *October 1914*

money at the gate'.

According to the *Athletic News* of 15 April, however, 'the attitude of the clubs has been that they wished to keep their players until the

THE BRIGHTON AND HOVE ALBION TEAM AT DRILL.
The First Club to Commence Military Duty.

end of the season and that there had been no real encouragement given to the men to join such as has been given by the average employer of the country'.

Early on in the war, some League clubs attempted to put a more acceptable gloss on things by insisting that their players train for both military and sporting duties. Clapton Orient, with the cooperation of Hackney Borough Council, had a rifle range at their disposal and the players were expected to put in regular practice; Tottenham, Everton and Liverpool offered the same facilities. Aston Villa actually issued a distinctive 'uniform' to its players for drill, bought thirty rifles for shooting practice and engaged a number of ex-army sergeant-majors to organize things.

Whether players were obliged to engage in these various activities is not known; however, players were certainly used in recruitment drives. With a captive audience inside a League ground, the army would try to persuade players to join up before the game and thus encourage men on the terraces to follow suit.

Lieut. EVELYN H. LINTOTT.
The Holder of the First Commission Given to
a Professional Footballer.
(Photo by the Bradford "Telegraph.")          Athletic News, *28 December 1914*

Of course, individual players joined up in great numbers, many ex-Players' Union men among them. In fact, it was an ex-chairman of the Union who was the first pro-footballer to earn a commission – Evelyn Lintott. Colin Veitch – despite pacifist leanings – joined the RGA as a private, eventually applied for a commission and became a lieutenant. Other ex-Union men to join up were Tim Coleman (who joined the Footballers' Regiment, along with Joe Mercer's father), plus Sandy Turnbull. Charlie Roberts made repeated attempts to join but was refused on medical grounds, while Billy Meredith, being well into his forties, was ineligible. Meredith continued to turn out regularly for Manchester City, making almost 100 appearances for little more than basic expenses – joining thousands of other players in providing probably the most consistent form of relaxing, cheap entertainment (apart from the cinema) available for men and women during a time of great national stress.

> " We must all do our part, and I shall not be satisfied until we have two or three Footballers' Battalions fighting in Flanders."
> —Joynson Hicks, M.P.

Players were not quiescent, however, regarding their position. It is difficult to know how many of them agreed with the two Liverpool men who, late in 1916, tried to present a petition to F J Wall of the FA asking that players be paid £1 a match, but the *Thomson's Weekly News* reporter wrote: 'You can take my word for it that from what I know the petition that was presented echoes the sentiment of every player with whom I've come in contact.'

Charlie Roberts, writing in the *Saturday Post* in August 1916, was typically forthright:

The players have now put in a full season without pay and are being asked to do the same for the forthcoming season. We can but admire those who are anxious to help another make ends meet but if he keeps helping until he himself cannot make ends meet then he must be classed as a fool. I'm strongly of the opinion that players should receive pay for playing. If a player is ineligible for the army or working on munitions he should not be debarred from picking up a few shillings extra because one or two members of the FA (who are very comfortable thank you) think that professionalism in war-time is 'all wrong'. The hypocrisy of the whole thing stinks in the nostrils ...

I hear the clubs are saying 'We won't forget you.' I've been at the game too long to take any notice of such piffle and I hope others will take the same view of it. We've had some!

I do feel that the player has been the MUG too long. Some are only earning now about 3s a week instead of their £4/£5 a week. Food too is twice as dear and yet the FA ask the footballer to give them more 'thankyou football'....

Players, come along and show your British pluck – for heavens sake, stick up for your rights!

Hostilities ceased in November 1918 – and within days arguments were raging as to when professional football should recommence. On 23 November the League announced that players could now receive £1 a week for playing – consisting of 2/6d for training twice a week and 15s expenses per game. Sutcliffe explained:

> Before clubs can pay normal wages they must get back to normal gates and normal players and until they arrive at something like normal conditions it is impossible to get back to the old order of things when they paid what one could regard as generous wages to players ...
>
> At the same time they were bound to remember they had a number of players who had been loyal to the clubs and played the game, and they must not forget they had a large number of players who had been loyal to the country and played the 'Greater Game'.

Thus the clubs could not pay wages, he announced. And they would not hark back to the rules as they stood before the war: 'It would mean they would revert to contracts and agreements between players and clubs that were then in existence.' The Management Committee felt that this would not be fair to the clubs. Nevertheless, he promised players that the clubs 'would not run away from their pledges'.

The decision clearly disappointed the vast majority of players. They had agreed to the suspension of their contracts for the duration of the hostilities; the war had now ended but the emergency regulations were to continue. More worrying was the suspicion that many clubs were quite happy to let players continue playing as semi-pros (or rather, poorly paid amateurs) indefinitely. It was this that finally sparked off the first rebellious move on behalf of the players.

On 16 December the *Sporting Chronicle* reported that a meeting had been held at the Memorial Hall, Farringdon, in London.

Topical Times, November 8, 1919

# THE DELINQUENT.

## By ALFRED LEETE.

*Hasher Smith, of the Dare-Devil Rovers, appears before the F. A. for rough and ungentlemanly conduct on the field.*

*Humorous comment on the all too serious predicament for players.*

H W T Hardinge, the Arsenal and England international, had presided over a meeting of 'former professionals' (sixty in all, representing the majority of clubs in the London Football Combination) who had decided to form a union to be known as 'The Professional Football Players' and Trainers' Union'.

Among those present had been 'old' Union men Frank Bradshaw, Tommy Elliot and Harold Halse, plus Charlie Rance of Spurs, Danny Shea of Fulham and eight Spurs and Arsenal men. The 'niggardliness' of the £1 allowance was mentioned, but what was distinctive about the meeting was the presence of bona-fide Union officials: W Wells, London District Secretary of the Electrical Trade Union; S Bradley, London District Secretary of the ASE; and Mr Mulhearn of the Boilermakers Union, he being elected secretary of the new organization.

Wells declared that there was only one way in which pro-footballers could ensure their livelihood and that was by becoming members of a trade union.

Bradley, who said he had helped Colin Veitch draw up the constitution of the 'late Players' Union', assured players of trade union support in the case of a dispute, while on a more traditional note Frank Bradshaw suggested a meeting with the London Combination to urge that body to ask the FA to increase allowances.

Hardinge then bitterly attacked the transfer system, and the meeting closed after arranging a future session when a constitution would be drawn up.

The move had clearly taken the 'old' Players' Union by surprise. With Colin Veitch still abroad in France, and purportedly having resigned as chairman (being out of touch with football affairs and unlikely to return for a while); with Charlie Roberts out of the game through injury and contemplating retirement; with the rest of the old Management Committee scattered either in the forces or out of football entirely – a coherent response to the League's proposals had been impossible.

The new Union, however, certainly galvanized the League into action. When a series of demands was drawn up, including a £6 a week minimum wage, yearly contracts and an end to the transfer system, the League Management Committee responded by convening a meeting in the second week of January to which it invited a representative of every League club plus two players per club. As Sutcliffe put it: 'This is an innovation in football but the needs of the time demand the change.'

Of course, it was no innovation, although it had been ten years since players and football officials had last met in such extraordinary circumstances to discuss an impending crisis. Much had changed during those ten years but a great deal else remained the same, as the meeting would demonstrate.

Just as in 1909, the main issue would be the recognition of the Players' Union. However, in 1909 it had been the FA with whom the players had been arguing – now it would be the League.

Strangest of all would be the position of Charlie Roberts. In 1909 Roberts had been the radical locked outside while declaring his allegiance to the Union movement; now he would be very much on the inside, the moderate, declaring that the Players' Union should be run on constitutional lines, i.e. with League and FA approval.

In fact, when the meeting began there was no Union official speaking for all the players. Roberts – present as one of Oldham Athletic's players – had been elected as 'spokesman' for the players, but the League was still responding to the London Union's proposals, Sutcliffe spending a great deal of time juggling charts, statistics and bank-balances to demonstrate that the demand for £6 a week was an 'impossibility', that most clubs were deep in debt and that, if pushed, only a third of them could afford even £3 a week. Nevertheless there was definite feeling that more money could be paid. Henry Norris, director of Fulham FC, announced that his club could pay its men more and would be asking the League for permission to do so.

Roberts, replying to Sutcliffe, accepted his analysis as far as it went (there was little else he could do without figures of his own) but insisted that many players 'were at a low ebb' and that something would have to be done.

It was at this crucial point in the proceedings that Jesse Pennington rose to ask whether, if there was an amalgamation of the two unions – the old and the new – the League would meet their representative and negotiate accordingly. John McKenna, League president replied:

> So long as you are organizing along Trade Union lines the League cannot meet your representatives. We never refused to meet the representatives of the old Players' Union but there was a vast difference between football players and trade unionists (hear hear). We will not accept a players' union on trade union principles and whose strength lies in the strike clause.

Sutcliffe went further, stating that what the League objected to was 'men who were officials of trade unions and who knew nothing at all about the management of football coming to interfere with those who had managed football all their lives'.

It was the old issue – 'men outside football seeking to drag the players into conflict with the clubs'.

Roberts then declared that the old Union was still in existence and would be prepared to deal with the League on proper constitutional lines – i.e. renunciating traditional union methods and links with the wider union movement. There followed a hurried meeting between both players' organizations before Hardinge returned to announce that the players concerned who represented the London clubs 'had unanimously decided to join hands with the Old Players' Union and by doing so had dropped forthwith the old trade-union influence in the London movement.'

McKenna was delighted (and possibly mightily relieved): 'Well, if there was no other good to come out of this meeting it has done good because in my opinion you have taken the right action and one that will commend itself to every well thinking man.'

Whether this strategy had been devised beforehand by the Union is impossible to tell. Roberts wrote later that it had taken the London men a mere ten minutes to decide to give up their organization and hand over their books to him. With everything happening so quickly, the two Union sides had clearly not had time to meet prior to the conference and, knowing what would please the League officials and judging that strike threats were simply not on, Roberts had decided to bargain away what he had once called, 'our strength and right arm' in order to break the deadlock.

For along with the announcement that 'Trade Unions' had been discarded, he made a request for a doubling of the £1 allowance. The response was swift. Players and press were asked to leave the room while the clubs talked it over (or rather, while Sutcliffe told the clubs what they were going to do).

Within half an hour, the players were called back. The £2 was theirs. For Charlie Roberts it was a moment to savour: 'Nothing I have done has pleased me better,' he wrote afterwards, adding that he had surprised even himself at how persuasive he had proved to be, especially with the London men whom he said had been 'seething with discontent'.

He returned to Manchester, assumed the mantle of chairman in

Veitch's absence and set about formulating plans for the election of a new management committee and a request to the FA for a benefit match.

For C E Sutcliffe, the conference had also been something of a triumph. Once again, he had appeared single-handedly to have fought off a dangerous challenge to the League's authority, for it had been his figures and arguments that had persuaded the players not only to moderate their demands but indirectly to return to the fold in familiar guise, meek and relatively toothless (although Charlie Roberts would certainly not have seen things in that way).

More significantly, however, Sutcliffe had won a tactical battle with certain larger League clubs, some of whom had appeared close to breaking ranks. Intriguingly, the rise of the London Union had coincided with a threat – never more than that, but worrying nonetheless – by some London clubs to form a London League based on the successful wartime London Combination League.

There had been considerable sympathy expressed by individual London club directors for union wage and contract demands (for instance, Sutcliffe had crossed swords with an Arsenal director named Hall regarding the idea of freedom of contract which Sutcliffe had called, 'contrary to the laws of civilized society').

By persuading all clubs to accept a limited scheme of pooling gate receipts to help the poorer clubs find the £2 a week 'allowance' deal awarded to the players, Sutcliffe had succeeded in drawing all clubs tightly together again. Larger clubs had always resisted the idea of pooling gate receipts, but Sutcliffe had presented it to them as the most efficient way to buy off the militant player threat. As gate receipts rose dramatically, week by week, the bigger clubs no doubt calculated that, even with the levy, with wages pegged at £2 a week, they could make substantial profits for the time being.

For Sutcliffe, however, the principle of pooling gates meant much more than short-term expediency. To him, it was a small but significant step towards the ultimate 'equalization of income and expenditure' that he saw as the true League ideal – an ideal that was to cost professional players so much in the years ahead.

# 14
## *Good Times* 1920–22

Where the football industry was concerned, the gloom and depression of the war years were shaken off with almost indecent haste. Within two years of the Armistice, the League had expanded to four divisions – and by 1923 the pre-war complement of forty teams had risen to eighty-eight.

The bulk of the Southern League had been 'lifted' to form the Third Division South – along with that League's key administrators – thus the Football League reigned supreme in England and Wales, and for a year or so made more money than it knew what to do with.

Inflation played its part, of course (admission fees went up from 6d to 1/-) but 'gates' were now massive as men flocked back into 'civvy street', repossessing the factories and the towns they had temporarily handed over to their women-folk. Football was the immediate beneficiary of this return to normal, although within a year or so other entertainments would begin to compete with a vengeance.

For professional footballers, the 'boom' receipts took some time to filter through into their wage-packets but when they did it must have seemed the dawn of a new age. Alas, the dawn was a false one.

For Charlie Roberts, chairman of the Union between 1919 and 1922, it was a period of great hope: Union membership grew rapidly; funds swiftly moved into the black, and the status of professional players looked set to rise. Roberts himself worked tirelessly during his period in charge, travelling the country speaking at numerous meetings. His was a blunt, no-nonsense approach, as suggested by his various writings exhorting men to join the Union for their own good. He did not attempt to persuade, but tried to shame players into working for their own benefit.

As a captain, first of Manchester United and then of Oldham Athletic, he had always succeeded in earning the loyalty of his men. He was a 'player's player', leading by example. Intriguingly nick-named 'Jack Johnson' during his heyday because of his power, domination and fearlessness (not to mention his almost bald, close-cropped hairstyle), by the 1920s he was no longer a player and would soon step up into management.

As we have seen, Roberts's early radical days – when he had seemed to be more aggressive and overtly political than the genuine socialist Colin Veitch – were now over. Indeed, by the late 1920s he was standing as a Conservative in local Manchester by-elections.

Yet in comparison to many of the men who would serve on the Management Committee during the inter-war years, Roberts would always appear a firebrand – outspoken, given to impatience, a genuine product of the more optimistic, hearty Edwardian days.

His colleagues on the Management Committee in these early days were by no means overawed by him. In fact, in terms of intelligence and administrative calibre, men the equal of Jimmy Lawrence, Jesse Pennington, Harold Henshall, Edward Holdsworth and Joe Shaw would be hard to find in the ranks of professional footballers.

Lawrence had been a Union member since 1907 and had first served on the Management Committee in 1909. Glasgow born, he had made his début in goal for Newcastle United in 1904, facing the then rampant Manchester City and Billy Meredith. A fine journalist, he would contribute some telling rejoinders to C E Sutcliffe. By now in his thirties, and approaching the end of his playing career, he would soon move into management – first with South Shields and then with Preston North End in 1923.

Jesse Pennington had also been on the pre-war Management Committee. Considered the finest full-back of his generation, he had won twenty-five England caps and had appeared against Scotland on eight consecutive occasions. By the 1920s he had already established himself as a successful businessman and in the 1930s he would become a coach at Malvern College.

Joe Shaw was another long-serving player, having been at Arsenal since 1908. He would eventually become a key member of the famous Arsenal back-room staff as assistant manager to both Herbert Chapman and George Allison.

Harold Henshall of Notts County had been a Villa player before the war and would take over the running of Notts County later in the 1920s, while Edward Holdsworth had been a player for Preston since 1908, clocking up over 200 appearances. Add to these Jimmy Fay, who would become the mainstay of the Union until well after the Second World War, plus vice-president Herbert Broomfield, still playing an important role in Union affairs, and it can be seen that the Union under Roberts could not complain of weak leadership.

In administrative terms, the Union swiftly organized itself although its offices were to remain for some time a room in Newbould's house in Longsight (just a short stroll from Billy Meredith's successful public house, the Church Hotel). In March 1919 its bank-balance stood at less than £50 and membership under 300. In May a benefit match was played at South Shields – the Players' Union versus South Shields and District. Men such as Charles Buchan, Billy McCracken, Clem Stephenson, Fanny Walden, Ted Vizard, Eli Fletcher and Sam Hardy took part and the match raised over £500.

At the Ninth Annual General Meeting in Manchester in August 1919, the entrance fee to the Union was raised to 1s and Harry Newbould, secretary, was given a rise to £7 a week, plus £1 a week rental. He was also granted £100 for his war work and for the financial sacrifices he had made on the Union's behalf.

By August 1920, at the tenth AGM, the general account had soared to over £2000 and membership had risen to the highest ever figure – well over 1000. In November, to cope with the flood of correspondence at the office, a typist was taken on at £2.50 a week. By September 1921, Union funds had risen to such an extent that the Management Committee was able to invest £2500 in Corporation Stock – the start of a sensible policy of salting away assets.

Such a buoyant financial situation, unheard of in the Union's short history, merely reflected the sudden relative prosperity of professional footballers in general. With clubs earning massive

4                                                    Topical Times, October 8, 1919.

Herbert Lock, the famous Glasgow Rangers Goalkeeper, with his wife and family.

Tommy Broad, of Manchester City, with his wife looking after their poultry.

Famous Footballers at Home

W. Mayo, late of Swansea Town, now of Newport County, and Mrs Mayo.

Tom Miller, of Liverpool, and Mrs Miller.

A happy group, showing F. Potts, Bradford City, with his wife and boy.

Howard Matthews, Oldham Athletics, having a game with Baby Matthews.

PRINTED AND PUBLISHED BY D. C. THOMSON 12 FETTER LANE, FLEET STREET, E.C.

4 OCT 19

amounts, the League could hardly continue paying men just £2 a match. Wages, however, were still pegged back during the 1919-20 season, and despite Union demands for increases reflecting the inflation that had occurred since 1915 (anything up to 75 per cent on pre-war prices), the League awarded them only a 50 per cent increase on the pre-war maximum (and this to be paid only during the playing season).

Thus, the year-round weekly pay of professional players went up to £4.50 a week, not much of a reward for men who had made so many financial sacrifices for so many years – and nowhere near the extravagant promises made by League Management Committee men when they had cut wages in 1914.

By 1920, however, even C E Sutcliffe had to concede that clubs could afford more. In March he wrote:

> The arguments for better wages are unanswerable. In view of the decreased value of the pound, players must have more and in view of the increased popularity of the game and increased gates, the bulk of the clubs can pay more.

Just a month earlier, in February, the third round of the FA Cup had drawn over half a million spectators paying over £33,000 in gross receipts.

Grounds were groaning – spectators literally so. At Chelsea there were scores of injuries when a roof upon which people were standing collapsed on to spectators below. Even teams with nothing tangible to play for were reporting record takings: Bradford City finished the season in mid-table and were knocked out of the Cup in the second round, yet they registered gross takings of over £35,000, and profits after all expenses and taxes of £22,000.

C E Sutcliffe's team, Burnley, were another small club reaping a financial harvest, though in their case it was as much due to success on the field as general euphoria off it. Burnley were League runners-up in 1920, champions in 1921 and third in 1922 – and during their championship season they made a clear profit of £13,000. No wonder Sutcliffe could afford to sound magnanimous and to encourage other clubs, despite 'certain difficulties', to 'act favourably towards the players ... it is evident that further concessions must be cheerfully made to them....'

He had, by the time he made those statements, already announced that for the season 1920-21 wages would double – the maximum rising from £4.50 to £9.00 a week – to be paid all the year round. In addition to this, there would also be the possibility of 'talent money' consisting of £2 a win and £1 a draw, as well as various FA Cup bonuses.

The Union would claim credit for the pay rises, and Sutcliffe would comment:

> The arguments of the deputation from the Union were lucidly placed before the League committee with a reasonableness yet earnestness and sincerity we all admired.

Players' representatives, however, were still in the position of being supplicants rather than equal negotiators. The Union had called for freedom of contract but this was as far away as ever. Sutcliffe wrote:

> The Football League is not yet ripe for freedom of contract and until the true League spirit of mutual respect and help has permeated every club and its management I am bound to regard freedom of contract as mischievous and a misfortune to the game.

This is a clear reference to the pooling of gates which was to continue after the war, 'away' clubs receiving 20 per cent of the gate money. The Union was bold enough to enter this debate in early 1920, suggesting that away clubs should be given at least a third of the gate money. The *Athletic News* politely told the Union to mind its own business.

The demand that players should receive a larger share of a transfer fee was also flatly turned down. In fact, with fees rising dramatically and some fortunate players actually receiving over £1000 as their portion, the League Management Committee decided to place a limit on what a player could receive. Thus it announced that a player could be awarded no more than he might have received from a benefit – and they were placing a ceiling on benefits too! Not surprisingly, such arbitrary decisions caused great bitterness and anger among players.

Nevertheless, the new wage structure satisfied some men at the very top of the profession – indeed, players with four or five years' continuous service in a First Division first team could expect to take home up to £10 a week. Inevitably, such sums attracted most attention, and it was extremely hard for the Union to convince

24        Topical Times, May 22, 1920

# FAMOUS FOOTBALLERS AT WORK

Jim Goodchild, Manchester City, is an Engineer's Machinist.

Charlie Rance, of the 'Spurs, is a draughtsman at Walthamstow.

George Jarvis, of Stoke and Glasgow Celtic, is an electrician.

Andy Watson, Bolton, drives a motor.

PRINTED AND PUBLISHED BY D. C. THOMSON & CO., LTD., 12 FETTER LANE, FLEET STREET, LONDON, E.C.4.

people outside the game that professionals in general were by no means living in clover, particularly when men like Sutcliffe insisted on talking about £9 maximums and benefits of £650 etc. as though they were the norm for all players. It was rarely spelled out that such figures, as well as talent money and shares in transfer fees, were all *possible* rather than *mandatory* – that clubs could implement all or none of them just as they saw fit. Jimmy Lawrence was adamant:

> No rules regarding the rewarding of players are compulsory. Increase in wage benefits and shares of transfers are optional. Indeed, in all – but particularly in regard to benefits – the amount a player receives is generally arrived at by a – shall we call it – dignified process of haggling? It isn't always a gift, a reward for meritorious and continued service in the real sporting sense; it is an arrangement generally.

Such an arrangement was arrived at with the club possessing the power ultimately to keep the player 'strung up' if he did not accept the deal offered.

It was at the harsher end of the game, where the unglamorous 'haggling' was endlessly going on, that the Union was now doing its best, most effective work. Legal case-work had begun before the First World War but with bureaucracy increasing in day-to-day post-war life, with Insurance Acts, income tax on benefits, plus the massive increase in membership due to the expansion of professional football, the Union found itself called upon to do more and more.

The Union's solicitors fought scores of cases where the sums of money involved ranged from £40 to £300. Teams such as Leadgate FC, Aberdare, Pontypridd and Newport Association FC, where rules and regulations regarding contracts often went largely unrecognized but where men were still attempting to make a living by playing football, were chased, badgered and harried into paying money involved that might otherwise have been refused.

And it was not just small clubs that were involved: Sheffield Wednesday, Norwich, Crystal Palace, Manchester City – all found themselves fighting compensation claims, injury claims, insurance claims – or being forced by the Union to recognize decisions taken by the League Management Committee that they would rather have ignored.

Just occasionally, too, directors of clubs discovered that, with the

Union's help, a lowly player might actually bite back, as in the case of Spottiswood versus Crystal Palace, its chairman Bourne and the publishers of the *Daily Mail*.

Spottiswood, a Crystal Palace player, had been suspended for life for a certain offence. The suspension had, however, been lifted and Spottiswood had been engaged by Clapton Orient. Some time afterwards an article appeared in the *Daily Mail* publication called *Answers* under the title 'A Glazier's Gossip', in which director Bourne had mentioned Spottiswood's 'ruination by betting' and his suspension for life.

Spottiswood objected to the article and through the Union began an action claiming damages for libel against both Bourne and the publishers of *Answers*. Not long after the trial had commenced, an out-of-court settlement was negotiated which resulted in Spottiswood receiving over £50 in damages from both Bourne and *Answers* plus costs. As the Union solicitor Hinchcliffe commented:

> I was immensely pleased with the result which goes to show that even wealthy newspapers cannot libel with impunity (and get off scot-free) those who are in less fortunate circumstances and trying to earn an honest living.

Charlie Roberts was even more pleased:

> Do you think for one moment that Spottiswood would have ever taken action on his own? It would have been impossible for him to fight a powerful body like the *Daily Mail*....

There was a certain poignancy, however, about the Spottiswood case. By 1921, the FA had decided that players' freedom to contribute to the press should be drastically curbed. Anything construed as 'damaging to the game' was prohibited. Players could lend their names to innocuous match reports or write (or have ghosted) tame life-stories, but anything critical of the FA, the League or individual clubs was not allowed. The days when Meredith Lawrence and Veitch could use their *Thomson's Weekly News* columns to present their ideas and those of the Union with freedom and sometimes uncomfortable candour were over.

Press coverage of football in general was, in any event, rapidly becoming more 'popular': even the *Athletic News*, once the *Times* of the football world, seemed to be turning away from the 'politics' of the game and concentrating more on the action. It was thus ironic that with such a virtual explosion of coverage, space should be filled with pictures, large headlines and gossip.

The restrictions, though, did not appear to apply to League Management Committee members; Sutcliffe would continue to earn a hefty supplement to his income via articles in publications such as *Topical Times, Answers, Sports Pictures,* etc. – and would continue to attack the Players' Union with impunity.

With no regular outlet of its own, the Union found it hard to respond effectively and Sutcliffe could get away with making claims such as 'criticism of the practice and policy of the Management Committee and the Football League is almost dead. The old cry for a free transfer for the player who has no offer of re-engagement is now seldom heard,' when only days previously the Union had been arguing with the League over just such an issue.

In December 1920, a few days before the FA ban came into force, Jimmy Lawrence, in a rare *Athletic News* article, commented on Sutcliffe's methods. While complimenting him on his efforts to uphold the interests of the clubs, Lawrence nevertheless found fault when Sutcliffe attempted to 'enlighten the public as to the position of players.... Personally I have a fault to find when he does the latter. It is that he omits much, and to one who knows what takes place, Mr Sutcliffe's omissions are of more importance than his statements.'

Yet that, of course, was the point. Much of Sutcliffe's writing was tailored to suit his cause. He was a one-man propaganda machine on behalf of the League and his influential and prominent articles in popular magazines helped shape the outlook of the average fan and thus, in turn, the attitude of the general public towards the professional player.

And it was an attitude that the Union was powerless to influence or educate. To the casual observer, the professional footballer was a lucky fellow, as was alleged by *Cupid and Football Answers* of 14 February 1920:

> The footballer is usually a presentable fellow, clean, manly, good-tempered. Also he is a bit of a catch as a sweetheart. As a bachelor at least, he has money to burn on chocolates, picture palaces and the like....
> If he is worth having as a sweetheart, he is equally so as a husband

 Alex Kane, the Portsmouth goalkeeper, giving
Arthur Wood, who keeps goal for Clapton
Orient, a run round in his side-car. Wood lives
with his father at Portsmouth.

*In the mid-1920s many players were banned from riding motor bikes. However Union*
*man Arthur Wood decided to ignore the ruling.* Sports Pictures, *14 March 1925.*

– a healthy life, good, regular wages, a benefit to look forward to and a good chance of starting a business of his own or well-paid employment as a manager, coach or trainer when he retires ... Undoubtedly the average footballer is a bit of a matrimonial catch these days....

Nothing the Union did could alter this cosy but generally misleading image – an image hard to square with the treatment players were receiving from their ruling bodies: gagged where talking to the press was concerned; not allowed a representative on the National War Fund, set up to disburse money among relatives of players killed during the war; prevented from being elected on to boards of football clubs (as the FA commented, 'There must be no sinister motive or ulterior reason for seeking to assist in the governing of clubs....'); not to mention being restrained and restricted in ways that could hardly be conceived by workers in other walks of life.

Within a couple of seasons, too, even the 'new deal' on wages would turn sour. In 1921, as if to make sure the Union did not get too carried away by the League's earlier 'generosity' or with the idea that it could expect more in the way of 'concessions', almost everything put forward for discussion by the Union regarding wages, transfers, etc. was rejected.

The Union had, in fact, referred to its members' 'extreme discontent' with the way the sliding pay scale system was working. They demanded its abolition and called for the institution of a maximum wage of £10 week with freedom of contract up to that amount. They also drew the League Management Committee's attention to the fact that 'there is a more serious state of unrest than is generally realized' among the players, particularly concerning the way the committee had been cutting the shares of transfers awarded to certain players by their clubs.

The League nevertheless turned its back on all but the most minor of adjustments. The sliding pay scale would remain: making maximum pay awards compulsory, it was said, would be 'unjust' to the clubs. Shares of transfer fees would be pegged to £650, as would benefits. To the suggestion that the cost of living was rising, the League retorted that it was rising for clubs, too. What was more, the public was now demanding all sorts of improvements in facilities which would cost money to provide. Thus, the players were being told to get to the back of the queue once again.

As it was put at the League's Annual General Meeting in July 1921, beneath the chandeliers of the commodious Connaught Rooms: 'We have gone quite far enough where wages are concerned!'

For Charlie Roberts, presiding over his last AGM in September of that year, the solution was simple:

> If you will tell me how players are going to get anything unless they organize I would like to meet that man. You must all appreciate that the day has arrived for collective bargaining.

Yet how to bring such a situation about without recourse to traditional Union methods? It was a conundrum to which Roberts had no solution, except to berate and exhort his fellow players:

> Some of you boys no doubt do not fully recognize the difficulty we have in trying to get the smallest concession for you. The League and the FA are very funny people to deal with and we shall never be able to get much for you unless you stand loyally by us.

As Newbould added, that loyalty was not always forthcoming:

> I hope there will be far more real enthusiasm next year. Further, I regret to say that there was a great lack of interest by members even in their own Benevolent Fund match. They let us down shamefully at South Shields. The same regrettable apathy occurred in connection with the revival of the Union Athletics Festival. Gentlemen, this is not worthy of the players, and I feel sure you will agree with me. Surely he is a strange man who cannot help himself?

For Charlie Roberts, however, such considerations were now over. Having been appointed manager of Oldham Athletic, he was obliged to retire from the Union, and to mark his passing, the Management Committee presented him with £53, a gold watch and an illuminated address.

Robert was clearly moved ('You don't know how I feel here today....'). For fourteen years he had been at the centre of the players' struggle, had more than once put his financial future on the line, had most certainly sacrificed his international career through his outspoken support for the Union.

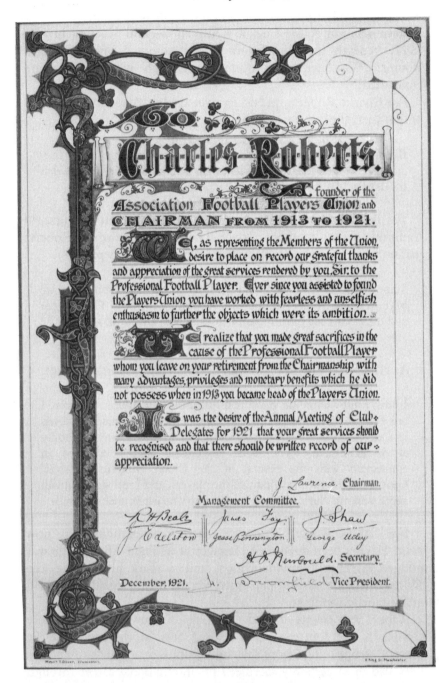

*Commemorative scroll presented to Charlie Roberts on his retirement in 1921.*

Roberts had been guided by simple straightforward notions of justice and fair play and his departure marked the end of an important chapter in the Union's history. His final words as chairman summed up the man and his achievements:

> I like to think to myself that in the future I can say, 'Charlie, you have done your duty to your fellow players....'

# 15

# *The Leddy Case* 1923

Charlie Roberts's departure in December 1922 was a severe blow to the Players' Union. His qualities of tough leadership were sorely missed in the six months following his resignation when the Union found itself in the midst of a crisis that would lose it much of its new found prestige, not to mention its precious membership.

The damage might have been repaired had he not been followed into retirement by certain other senior members of the Union, in particular Joe Shaw, Jimmy Lawrence and Jesse Pennington.

Their replacements – Harry Matthews of Oldham, Moses Russell of Plymouth Argyle, George Utley of Sheffield United and Charles Buchan of Sunderland – were by no means raw youngsters. All but Buchan were close to retirement and all had careers straddling the war. Yet none could claim Union experience.

The only man who could – Jimmy Fay – thus took over the chairmanship and provided some continuity, although he too, was close to giving up the game and taking his benefit.

Fay, in fact, could claim to be one of the Union 'originals', having joined in 1907 and been elected to the Management Committee in 1912. His career had stretched across twenty years since he had made his professional début in 1903 for Chorley at the age of nineteen, earning just 10s a week.

In 1905 he was signed by Oldham and played 100 consecutive games for the club, missing only one game in six years, during which time Oldham rose from Lancashire Combination level to the First Division of the League. Upon asking for a rise to 30s a week, he was promptly sold for £750 to Bolton Wanderers, where he stayed for ten years, eventually moving to Southport General in 1921.

A halfback and sometimes inside-forward (he scored 21 goals in 26 games in the latter position for Oldham in 1909-10), he was a cultured, intelligent player, never a 'hard man', earning for himself the nickname 'Gentleman Jim'.

Nevertheless, the days when the Union could boast leaders who were instantly recognizable to the average supporter were passing. In fact, the only man who could be described as a 'star' player at the zenith of his career was Charlie Buchan, the independent-minded goal-scoring inside-forward for Sunderland. He would remain on the committee until 1925, taking over as chairman whenever Fay was absent – before Herbert Chapman lured him south to Arsenal.

All this is not to suggest that men like Utley and Russell were not good players nor unsuitable as Management Committee members – quite the opposite. Star men were not 'typical' professional players, and to attract a mass membership the Union had to be concerned with the preoccupations of the average professional. Thus, knowledge of life at the lower end of the football scale was crucial.

Russell, for instance, spent the whole of his career in non-League or lower-League football. A fearless, rugged defender, born in New Tredegar and a player for Merthyr in his youth, he signed for Plymouth in 1914 when they were still in the Southern League and was with them when they made their full League début in 1920.

In fact, he captained them for six consecutive seasons when they were runners-up (thus just missing promotion.) When at last they were promoted, he was no longer a regular first-team player.

His true glory days came when playing for Wales for whom he won 23 caps as a fullback helping them to two Championship titles in 1920 and 1924. (In the last, he scored a decisive penalty in Belfast to help Wales to a soccer 'Grand Slam'.)

In his early international days he had played with Billy Meredith – one of the reasons why he joined the Union Management Committee.

Harry Matthews joined the Committee the year Oldham slipped out of the First Division and the year Charlie Roberts took over as manager. Perhaps it was Roberts's influence that persuaded Matthews to join the committee. The Oldham presence was certainly a significant one: ex-player Fay was chairman, manager Roberts had been chairman, Matthews would serve as chairman in 1929 while yet another Oldham player – Harry Grundy – would be players' auditor in the 1930s.

Utley had been a prominent player for Sheffield United since 1913 when the club had bought him for a record £2000 from Barnsley. His bargaining skills had secured him a five-year contract, the team captaincy, the tenancy of a sports-goods shop in Bramall Lane that supplied the club itself, plus the promise of a lucrative benefit. The benefit was to cause some friction within the Sheffield United players' ranks and would reveal the tensions and anxieties existing just beneath the surface of the 'cigarette-card' image. In 1913 Utley had been offered £800 or a benefit match; he had chosen the match. However, the League subsequently decided that benefits should be limited to a maximum of £650. Utley's agreement predated this, but his team-mates were unhappy and in 1922 certain senior men wrote the following letter to the club's directors:

> We the undersigned beg to ask the reason of this exceptional procedure. We had been given to understand that no player was to have a definite match set apart for his benefit; but that a fixed sum as has been given in the case of other players was to be guaranteed.
>
> This has naturally caused some dissatisfaction among the players in general, for why should Utley have preferential treatment seeing that in regard to service he is less entitled to a benefit than some of the undersigned?
>
> We remain Sirs, your obedient servants,
>
> (signed) W Gillespie, W Cook, J E Kitchen, H H Pantling, W H Brelsford, J Simmons, H Gough, A Sturgess, S Fazakerly.

Some of the eight appeared before the board and were satisfied by an offer of benefits to the players who had requested them. Each of these benefits was £500 while Utley's match raised over £1000.

Utley could not be blamed for securing terms so much better than many of his team-mates but what struck him most forcibly was the apparent arbitrary nature of individual men's agreements – the way in which preferential treatment, exacerbated by the non-binding nature of the League's sliding wage scale and benefit structure, made for lack of solidarity among players.

The varying fortunes of some of Utley's team-mates following the benefits argument also impressed upon him the necessity for change that only a Union might bring.

Fazakerly, having been refused a benefit, eventually forced the club to sell him after dodging training and intentionally playing badly, angering fellow players and supporters alike.

When the veteran international, Gough, took a pub to provide for his imminent retirement, the Sheffield United directors summoned him and informed him that he had broken his contract (Sheffield players were expressly forbidden to become publicans while under contract). Gough replied that he was prepared to take the consequences and the directors resolved that 'the player was to be informed he would be held liable to make good any damage or loss which the club might sustain in consequence of his breach of the agreement'.

He was eventually forced to pay back wages he had received under the 'broken' agreement and was reported to the FA, who suspended him.

The club thereafter refused to release him unless another club paid a prohibitively large transfer fee of £2000 – for a man of Gough's age and lengthy career, such a fee meant that his football career was finished. The Players' Union decided that it could not help him.

It can be no coincidence that when Utley left the Management Committee in 1924, Harry Pantling, one of the original 'protesters', immediately took his place.

Men like Utley and Pantling were knowledgeable and experienced, and had valuable contributions to make. But as the committee became less 'attractive' in terms of star men, it necessarily lost much of the influence that comes with Cups and League Championships. Significantly, men playing for teams such as Sheffield Wednesday, Huddersfield and Arsenal – the inter-war 'super-teams' – would not lend their names to the Union cause.

Anyone who had been on the committee in 1922, however, would have been in difficulties. For some months there had been rumours that clubs were facing yet another crisis. The massive increases in attendance that had occurred so suddenly after 1919 now went into reverse. Clubs which had planned, indeed committed themselves to expensive extensions and improvements found themselves running into large debt as gate money declined. Large and small clubs faced losses ranging from hundreds to many thousands of pounds. Clubs situated in areas particularly hard hit by the trade recession – the apparent key to it all – suffered most: Durham City registered a loss in 1922 of almost £2000, Grimsby of £3000, Bristol City approaching £4000.

The first straw in the wind for the Union had come in late 1921 in a letter from League secretary Tom Charnley refusing the Union permission to organize a benefit match '... in view of the bad times generally caused by the trade recession....'

Nevertheless, the unilateral decision to cut wages, taken in April 1922 at an emergency meeting of the League Management Committee, came as a bolt out of the blue. Although the committee had been called in to a meeting just prior to the decision being taken by the clubs, the room for meaningful consultation was nil.

When asked by John McKenna, League president, for alternative suggestions to help the poorer clubs, the Union members were nonplussed. They had been given no time to prepare proposals, and were also unconvinced that such a drastic move was justified – after all, Spurs had just made a profit of some £17000 and Liverpool of £6000.

Jimmy Lawrence suggested that there was, in fact, no crisis at all. Gates were still well above what they had been in 1914, and it simply looked to him as though players were once again being asked (or rather told) to rescue clubs that had got themselves into trouble by sheer mismanagement.

When asked for the figures upon which the proposed need for wage cuts had been based, McKenna replied that he did not have them. In fact, where the question of hard facts was concerned, the League officials would remain vague. This simply fuelled the Union's suspicion that the calculations had been based upon a crude maximum wage multiplied by the number of first-team players.

The truth was that only a certain percentage of men received the maximum: most were either below it or only on it when in the first team. What the Union called for was a calculation based on an average wage – a more exact guide as to what clubs were spending on wages.

Arguments over figures, however, were irrelevant. The League had decided on a crude, across the board cut to £8 a week maximum in season, £6 week during the summer. For some men it meant a loss of wages of up to £80 a year. McKenna's argument that men below the maximum would not be affected merely demonstrated the man's ignorance. The Union pointed to cases where men were cut from £6 a week to £5; not only that, men on the point of moving up the scale were pegged. Thus it was a combined wage cut cum wage freeze.

For the Union, however, the question was not so much that of the fine details of how much and whom, but of what their response should be. Sadly, it was confused, contradictory and ultimately irrelevant.

At the first meeting called by the Union to discuss the cuts, representatives from some sixty-nine clubs attended – a ground-swell of indignation that could have been harvested to some effect.

Instead, the Union Management Committee decided it would obtain legal opinion concerning men who had signed contracts before the cut was announced; surely, it was argued, there was a chance here for victory in the courts. Also, it was decided to

My Impression of Jesse Pennington, West Bromwich. By Fred May.

*Caricature of the long-serving committee man, Jesse Pennington,* Topical Times, *8 May 1920.*

circularize the clubs in an attempt to persuade them to reconsider the cuts at their Annual General Meeting in May – there had, after all, been plenty of evidence that some clubs had not wanted to cut wages but had been dragooned into agreeing by C E Sutcliffe's persuasive tongue. And finally, Union members were advised to hold off signing new contracts until the League clubs' meeting in May.

But it was the old question of persuading men to gamble with their summer wages – and many men were not Union members anyway. As one delegate put it:

> They all know that often players get two or three days in which to make up their minds about signing. A man was probably approached at some railway station and asked if he was going to sign the form or not. The man would sign and the Union would be beaten by their own members.

In fact, Jesse Pennington, Management Committee member, advised anyone who asked him, to sign and thus secure their summer pay. His reasoning was simply that League clubs were certainly not going to reverse their earlier decision; in fact, clubs had been told not to discuss the matter. And seeing Everton and Liverpool players signing new contracts after being spoken to by John McKenna, Pennington felt that the issue had been settled.

Charles Buchan nevertheless called for a motion of censure of Pennington at the next Management meeting – many Union members had thought that Pennington's advice had been the official Union line.

Pennington, however, was simply being realistic. In May, the clubs confirmed the cuts and, despite some defiant words (the Huddersfield Town side declared they would stand out if asked to, and one delegate declared that it was not so much a question of wages but an attempt to smash the Union), the Management Committee ultimately decided to advise members to sign 'under protest'.

In a sense, the Union could not win. If it called a strike, as some men demanded, it would have been destroyed. Even by May a majority of men were thought to have signed on and were already away on their vacations. If it failed to call for radical action, then those looking for a lead would (and indeed did) feel that the Union had nothing to offer.

Instead, the Union decided that its only constructive move would

*William C 'Billy' Rose, pioneering professional with Swifts, Small Heath, Preston North End and Wolves. The man who first proposed a Players' Union in 1893.*

*John Cameron*

*John Devey*

*Stalwarts of the 'old' Union.*

*Dan Doyle*

*Jack Bell*

William Meredith

Charlie Roberts

Harry L Mainman

Evelyn Lintott (William Powell)

Founders of the new order.

*The famous 'Outcasts' team of 1909. Back row, left to right: H Moger, J Picken, W Corbett, R Holden, H Burgess, J Clough, W Meredith, G Boswell (PU Asst Sec); Front row: G Wall, A Turnbull, C Roberts (capt), T Coleman, R Duckworth; Inset: H Broomfield.*

*Herbert 'Rabbit' Kingaby. Subject of a law suit that almost wrecked the Players' Union.*

*Alfred Sydney Owen, Players' Union Secretary 1910–13.*

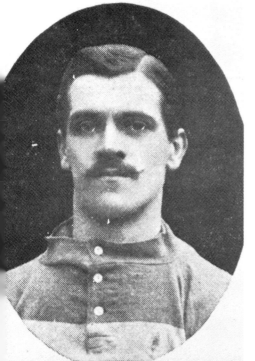

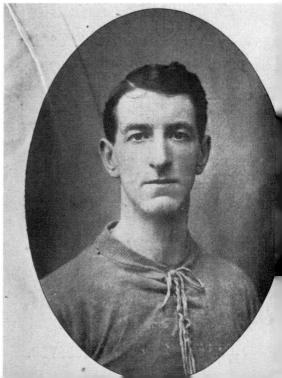

*Colin Veitch, Newcastle United. Writer, conductor, composer, actor and PU Chairman 1911–18.*

*Harry Wright, Derby County. First winner of the* Athletic News *Cup, awarded to the fastest sprinter among professional players, 1911.*

*Thomas H Hinchcliffe Esq. PU solicitor 1909–39.*

*Charlie Roberts and Jimmy Fay enjoy a joke during the Union sports, 1911.*

*Charlie Rance, Tottenham Hotspur and Derby County. Co-founder of the London 'breakaway' Players' Union, 1919.*

*Charlie Roberts (Chairman of the Union 1919–21) with wife Mary and children William, Hilda and Chris.*

*Howard Matthews, Oldham Athletic. PU Chairman 1929–31. (Stuart Beckett)*

*Dave Robbie, Bury. PU Chairman 1931–6.*

Jimmy Lawrence

*J Lawrence*

*C Buchan*

*J Shaw*

*M Russell*

*F Womack*

*J Pennington*

*C Stephenson*

*E Fletcher*

*E Beecham*

*Management Committee members, 1920s.*

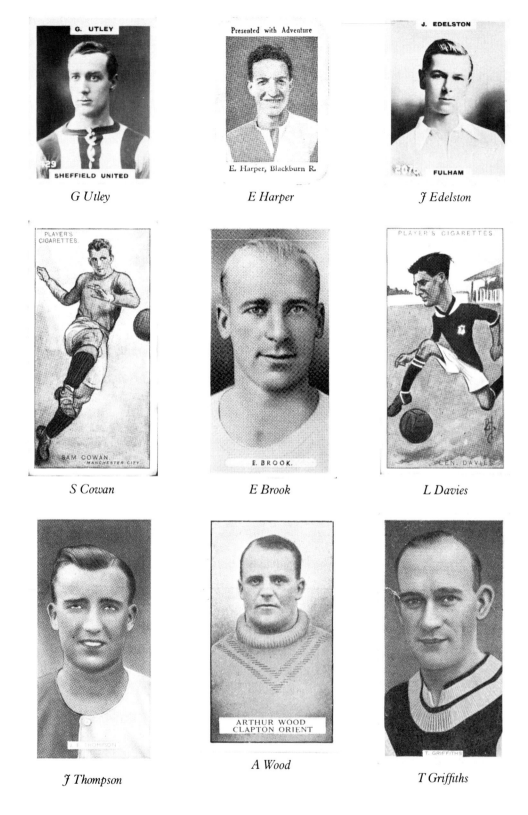

G Utley

E Harper

J Edelston

S Cowan

E Brook

L Davies

J Thompson

A Wood

T Griffiths

*Management Committee members, 1930s.*

be to mount a test case in law to question the legality of the League's decision. The Union solicitor felt that the League, in altering Rule 7 to introduce a new maximum wage, had forced clubs into breaching a number of contracts.

As Harry Newbould said in a letter to *Athletic News*:

> It is common knowledge that this rule was practically forced on the clubs, that they had no opportunity to consider it and that many of them voted for it only under strong pressure and with great reluctance.
>
> It is also common knowledge that the rule was introduced on the eve of signing-on time. In other words it was a pistol levelled at the players' heads without reasonable consideration by the clubs or players.

*Henry Leddy in action*, Topical Times, *3 September 1921.*

The case eventually chosen was that of one Henry Leddy, a Dubliner, centre-half and captain of Chesterfield, who had previously played for Tranmere Rovers and Everton in the First Division. Leddy had signed his contract in March 1922, guaranteeing him £9 a week all year round until May 1923. The League resolution had come a month later, thus Leddy had refused to sign a new contract and had 'brought his action to contest the right of the club or the Football League to break his contract under the common law of the land'.

Although considered a 'Union' action, the truth was that the Union had had to ask the FA for permission to help Leddy take the case to court. As the *Athletic News* put it:

> It was obvious that the FA would not be prepared to give the Union as a Union such consent because that would be the full recognition of the Union as an agent for the player and that the FA has always rigidly avoided.

The application therefore had to come from Leddy. Actually he had asked for permission in mid September 1922, so that it took the FA a month or more before deciding to let him proceed. As usual, much confusing publicity surrounded the case. It was alleged that Leddy had in fact settled with the club and that the action was over ('Someone seems to be anxious to abandon it for him'), and Leddy would write to the Union declaring his disgust with the various conflicting reports. Chesterfield, he revealed, had offered him his wages under the new agreement. He had, at first, refused, but had subsequently agreed to accept 'on account and without prejudice'. The player and the club, Newbould insisted, were on friendly terms.

The Leddy case dealt with the question of whether the League had the power retrospectively to alter contracts already agreed and signed between a player and a club. In signing a contract, both parties bound themselves to abide by the rules of the League, the League in effect being a third party to the contract.

A section of League Rule 12 stated that the League had power 'to cancel agreements with players which are contrary to the rules of the League'. The nub of the argument was, which rules? Those in force when the contract was signed, or the new rules as amended in April by the League to cut the maximum wage?

The judge in Chesterfield Crown Court appeared unwilling to accept that the contract between Leddy and Chesterfield could not be subsequently altered, because, he felt, both parties had agreed to abide by 'the current rules, or the rules from time to time existing … of the Football League'.

As things stood, therefore, no contract could remain inviolable. The League could change the terms at any point. Judgement was for Chesterfield, with costs. It seemed the Players' Union had suffered yet another legal body-blow.

Unlike in 1912, however, when the Union had no money to proceed with an appeal, this time, with several thousand pounds in stocks to draw upon, Hinchcliffe urged an appeal. It was set for May.

Much damage, though, had already been done to the Union. The Leddy case seemed to sum up the Union's feeble response to the wage cuts. Membership was plummeting: in August 1923, from 1900 the previous year it was down to 500. And in the troubled period after the Leddy case, C E Sutcliffe appeared to feel that it was time to deliver the coup de grâce.

On 10 February 1923 two articles appeared under his name – one in *Sports Pictures* entitled 'Will Football Wages Be Reduced?', the second in *Topical Times* entitled, 'Is the Players' Union a Useless Body?'

The former article was concerned, once again, with the threat of 'bankruptcy' facing many clubs and the possibility of cutting wages:

> Will the League propose a further reduction? This is a difficult question to answer at the present moment, for the League has never acted prematurely or on insufficient information, notwithstanding what the Players' Union said last April.

Once again the sorry state of club finances was all the players' fault:

> The clubs made the mistake of signing up players at excessive wages. It will not be done again. The players who are not amenable to reason will soon find that it is hard to kick against the pricks. It is the mercenary spirit of some players which makes the maximum necessary.

However, the League Management Committee would not stand by 'and see the clubs oppressed'. Compulsion, he claimed, was the last resort:

> If players are reasonable, the clubs can go on; but either compulsorily or voluntarily, wages must came down and in many cases not merely for next season, but to the end of this....

Quite clearly, Sutcliffe felt that the Leddy case justified tampering with players' contracts almost at will. Incredibly, a little later on in the same article he defended the unlimited transfer fees – in terms of free-market economics!

> The price is regulated by the law of supply and demand ... we are told professional football is commercialized sport. Then what business is it of yours or mine what fee Everton paid Dundee for Alec Troup? The clubs are limited liability companies....

None of this, though breathtaking in its hypocrisy, was particularly new. The *Topical Times* article, however, certainly marked out new ground. Sutcliffe made his attitude quite clear – belittling the benevolent work the Union did, attacking players in general ('You may tell me I have a bad opinion of them. No, I have a poor opinion of human nature....') and suggesting that it was time the players ditched their organization once and for all:

> I am not going to say that the Players' Union in unnecessary ... but it is a useless institution on present lines.... The policy of the Players' Union has been to get all you can, hold fast to all you have got and, lest the clubs may threaten to cut down wages, always be Shylock and Oliver Twist rolled into one.

He went on to predict again that wages were too high and that they would have to come down:

> We shall have trouble in the future ... some players will kick. The Players' Union will be dictated to by the few, some of whose players are in the sere and yellow. Then will come the struggle. It will be the last as far as I am concerned.

Apart from reviling the Union and insulting its officers, there was another theme running through this and subsequent articles – Sutcliffe's apparent unrivalled knowledge of the law. Clearly, Leddy was going to be another Kingaby in his eyes, and he wheeled out that historic case in order to belabour the Union once again:

> The Players' Union, which has always been impressed with the necessity of doing something to justify its existence, attacked the Football League and challenged its right to retain a player on offering reasonable wages.

Sutcliffe's account of the Kingaby trial was by now beginning to sound like a chapter in an heroic drama, with himself set firmly in the role of hero. The lawyer acting for the League had turned to Sutcliffe and said, 'Please teach me', after which he had declared, 'Mr Sutcliffe, you are the first man who dared to tell me I did not know the law.' Later, as the judge rose to sum up the case and pronounce in Sutcliffe's favour, 'His fine, manly athletic form seemed to overwhelm me....' And though proud, Sutcliffe admitted, 'In a sense, I was terribly disappointed. I did want to get back into the witness box. I wanted to get my own back....'

Clearly the Leddy case was going to provide him with that lost chance – to get his own back. In March 1923 he returned to the subject in his *Topical Times* column, anticipating the verdict in a most unlegalistic way:

> ... they knew that by their action they were creating a very embittered feeling and were forcing the Football League to treat them very differently in the future than they have been treated in the past. They were warned against their senseless action but persisted and now Leddy v Chesterfield looks like being another monument to their folly. If the players had been content to leave themselves in the hands of the Management Committee of the Football League they would have saved quite a lot of money and much loss of prestige and reputation.
>
> I have previously told you there will be another fight. Until the present spirit has died away and the hot-heads have left football for the good of the game there will always be trouble ahead.... If the players would scrap their Union they would lose nothing but gain a lot.

The Union's response to all this was an open letter to the *Sporting Chronicle*, published on 20 February and subsequently reprinted in booklet form for circulation among players and the public. It was a mild, diplomatic document, for the most part simply stating facts, outlining all the things the Union had done, pointing to the thousands of letters the Union received from players asking for help, the many replies of thanks for assistance, and stating quite clearly why there was a need for a union and why it had been founded:

> It evolved out of much injustice and hardship experienced by professional players who, with neither funds nor organization, were at the mercy of clubs and the Football League.

It also expressed surprise that Sutcliffe could make such allegations when he, of all people, being the League solicitor dealing with the multitude of Union cases through the Football League Insurance Federation, would have known more than anyone else.

Perhaps Sutcliffe realized, in a moment of clarity, that he was going too far. In a subsequent article while describing the early days of establishing the Burnley club, he wrote:

> In those days I contracted a complaint which no doctor has ever yet diagnosed, and which I describe in my own language as 'a mad brain'. There is no remedy for it and so I suffer on.

It could have been added – and so does everyone else suffer on.

Sutcliffe's ultimate triumph, however, was not to be. On 8 May 1923 (just a few weeks after Wembley staged its first chaotic Cup Final) at the Royal Courts of Justice in the Strand, Mr Justice Lush and Mr Justice Salter allowed the Union's appeal and awarded Leddy his back pay and costs for both hearings. The League declined to take the matter further and abandoned the action. Leddy, and the Players' Union, had won. As Newbould declared:

> The result of this case has far-reaching importance to your association and the members thereof, and was indeed a great victory which, as you are aware, was proclaimed in the press throughout the land. It was, of course, a fight for principle and it proved that the courts will not allow the breaking of players' agreements either by clubs, Leagues or Associations.

Looking back, the Leddy case could be described as a turning point in the Players' Union's thus far troubled history. While it did nothing to stem the outward flow of members and while it had no effect on men's immediate financial situations, it marked a halt in the relentless grinding down of players in the legal sense.

Had the case gone the other way, there might well have been no real point in the players' body attempting to stand independently. The League could have continued to act with total impunity, making a mockery of the professionals' legal rights.

Now at least there was a pause, a time for reflection. There were no more across the board wage cuts in 1923, nor in the following seasons. In August, the second most significant event of the year

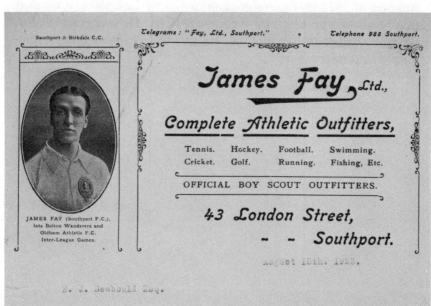

Southport & Birkdale C.C.

Telegrams: "Fay, Ltd., Southport."

Telephone 988 Southport.

# James Fay, Ltd.,

## Complete Athletic Outfitters,

| Tennis. | Hockey. | Football. | Swimming. |
| Cricket. | Golf. | Running. | Fishing, Etc. |

OFFICIAL BOY SCOUT OUTFITTERS.

### 43 London Street,
### - - Southport.

JAMES FAY (Southport F.C.),
late Bolton Wanderers and
Oldham Athletic F.C.
Inter-League Games.

August 15th, 1923.

H. J. Newbould Esq.

Dear Harry,

In reply to your letter of the 14th inst. you will
cheque enclosed, duly signed.

With reference to my position as Chairman of the
Players Union, I have given this serious consideration since
your visit here, and I have decided to resign the position, or
not to stand at the coming election of Officers, I will explain
reasons when I see you.

Kindest regards,

I remain,

Yours faithfully,

James Fay

occurred. Jimmy Fay, who had taken over the chairmanship in the summer of 1922 on the resignation of Jimmy Lawrence, intimated that he wished to resign for business reasons. He was persuaded to stay for another twelve months. He was to remain with the Union for the next thirty years.

# 16
## *Hard Times* 1923–28

The years following the successful outcome of the Leddy case were desperate ones for the Union. Membership fell to pitiful levels (the 1925 Annual General Meeting was attended by just eight delegates representing little over 100 members). Yet the Union was by no means the moribund organization some historians have suggested.

Income and investment were to remain healthy and the Union solicitors were to continue fighting case after case for individual members, winning in the process many thousands of pounds in compensation and providing a ready source of upbeat news to boost the morale of those men still keen enough to persist in the soul-destroying work of seeking out and collecting subscriptions from indifferent colleagues.

Wage negotiations were by now very much a matter for individuals. There would be no nationwide negotiated increases for decades to come. It was every man for himself, bargaining face to face with directors and managers, trading personal skills and reputations for a hodge-podge of bonuses and benefits.

Players at the highest level were, as usual, generally well-paid, but whether all men – or even the majority of men – were, as Sutcliffe put it in his article in *Topical Times* in 1924, '... by comparison with men engaged in skilled trades on velvet' is debatable.

To men of Sutcliffe's jaundiced outlook, pro-players were still to be treated as though they were careless children. Although no longer, 'pot-walloping, whisky-swiping', they were still their own worst enemies where money was concerned:

'Thrift is a word unknown ... where I should walk, they ride and where I should go by tram, they engage a taxi. Money is round and round it goes....'

But as the 1920s progressed, the sheer size of the professional football industry and the vast amounts of money that it generated convinced more and more objective observers that pro-players should be regarded as highly skilled entertainers. Herbert Chapman, Arsenal manager, wrote:

> We live in an age of specialization. We find it carried to a fine art in industry. The same applies to the man who takes up football in a professional capacity. He makes it his speciality and works at it consistently until he has reached as near perfection as his abilities will permit. He has to live, therefore, he devotes all his time to training and the game; he must be paid.

However, as players became more and more regimented in terms of their everyday freedoms, and their daily lives become ever more cribbed, cabined and confined as the era of the professional coach slowly dawned, the opportunities to earn more money were also gradually restricted.

With each succeeding slump in general trade there were calls from various clubs to reduce wages across the board. And although no such reductions were made, the freedom clubs had to squeeze down the wage bills was exercised with ever more ingenuity.

The sliding scale was the principal method employed. In the 1920s it was still being hotly debated, its potential for reducing overall wage bills gradually being grasped by managements.

Briefly, it might work as follows: a player in the first team received the maximum £8 a week; if in the second team, £6 a week; if unable to secure a place even in the 'stiffs', his pay might drop to £4 a week. Once out of the first and second teams, the extra bonuses for wins and draws went as well.

In an industry where 'form' was often a matter of tactics, of individual judgement or perhaps of just plain fate, such a system of payment engendered insecurity, anxiety and often discontent among playing colleagues.

Thus, although the average football fan considered players well-paid, referring always to the 'maximum wage' etc., there were, in fact, wide variations not only between clubs and divisions but within clubs where a definite hierarchy existed. At the bottom were the majority of lower-paid players; above them, players earning more or less the maximum; and above them an elite of 'stars' who could expect to supplement the maximum wage by other earnings directly or indirectly derived from their status.

There was a constant movement up and down this hierarchy as players' fortunes fluctuated with their age, fitness and expectations.

| | *Players' Weekly Wages 1934-5, Sheffield United FC* | | | |
|---|---|---|---|---|
| *Player* | *Playing Season Wage* £ | *Close Season Wage* £ | *Bonus for for 1st XI Appearances* £ | *Bonus for for 2nd XI Appearances* £ |
| Barclay | 8 | 6 | – | – |
| Barker | 5 | 3 | 3 | – |
| Boyd | 8 | 6 | – | – |
| Hall | 5 | 3 | 3 | – |
| Hobson | 3 | 2 | 1 | – |
| Holmes | 8 | 6 | – | – |
| Jackson | 5 | 3 | 3 | – |
| Killourhy | 6 | 4/10/- | 2 | – |
| Pickering | 8 | 6 | – | – |
| Williams | 6 | 6 | 2 | – |
| Anderson | 5 | 3 | 3 | – |
| Coward | 2/10/- | – | 2 | 1 |
| Earnshaw | 2/10/- | – | 2 | 1 |
| Goodison | 2/10/- | – | 2 | 1 |
| Gooney | 6 | 6 | 2 | – |
| Hooper | 5 | 5 | 3 | – |
| Johnson | 5 | 3 | 3 | – |
| Smith | 5 | 5 | 3 | – |
| Stacey | 6 | 6 | 2 | – |
| Wildsmith | 1 | – | 2 | 1 |
| Wilkinson | 5 | 5 | 3 | – |

With acknowledgements to Nick Fishwick

From the table showing the different terms offered to various Sheffield United players in 1934-35, it can be seen that only four players were guaranteed the maximum wage, though other players received it if they played in the first team.

In 1935 Sheffield United applied the sliding scale to every player, and their records show the type of movements that occurred within the players' hierarchy. Several of the players in the table were no longer wanted. Holmes's basic wage was cut to £5 a week and Smith's to £4, although both could receive the maximum if they played in the first team.

Hobson's wage was increased to £4 a week while Jack Dodds was offered a basic £4 per week plus £3 first team bonus when he signed on in 1934 – but his ability saw his basic wage increased to £5 in 1935.

Between the years 1935 and 1939, no player at Sheffield United was offered the maximum wage unconditionally – thus even at big clubs only players of first-team standard received top money. In fact, only ten per cent of full-time players were said to receive the maximum in the 1930s, although the actual number may have been higher as more men received it than were guaranteed it by contract.

Not surprisingly, players disliked the system as it made competition for first-team places even more intense; and it cannot have helped foster strong bonds of feeling at certain clubs where the sliding scale was insensitively applied. Indeed, suspicion, resentment and a sense of injustice were almost natural products of this system that players had no say in formulating or applying.

With the Union effectively locked out of wage negotiations on any level, its role was thus increasingly that of watchdog for those players sensible or aware enough to use the Union solicitor when in trouble.

The Union was also to take on broader issues that would be advantageous to all players (Union members or not), such as the taxation of benefits, an unwelcome development that undermined a principal source of many players' post-career security plans.

But where the vexed question of the retain and transfer system was concerned, no move could be contemplated with membership so low; although in a period when transfer fees were to rise to previously unheard of levels, the injustices of the system as it applied to men much lower down the scale continued to sour relations between players and clubs.

Little publicity was given to the plight of men who had been 'strung-up'. Occasionally, however, a story would appear, especially if it concerned a prominent player.

One such was Tommy Hamilton of Preston North End – a club notorious for its high spending in the 1920s. Hamilton was a fullback who had been with the club four seasons and played over 120 matches. In 1924, Preston were strapped for cash:

> At the close of the season I was asked to make arrangements to be photographed as I was going on the tour to Belgium and a photo would be required for my passport. But a few days later that was all knocked on the head. I found my name on the open-to-transfer list! And the fee opposite my name was £4000! Who can afford to pay that these days?

The fee was reduced on appeal to £2000, but it was still too much for a player like Hamilton and, though Everton expressed an interest, he remained on the list throughout the close season, receiving no pay.

> I continued to wait but when the season opened and I was still idle I decided to take whatever came my way. When Dick Kerr's – a Lancashire Combination club – made their offer I accepted at once. I am employed in the shop and I shall play for the team every week.

Preston thus lost him, albeit for a short time. Later that season they offered him another contract and Hamilton resumed his career with them, playing another five seasons – during much of that time in the same team as Alex James, for whom Preston had paid £3000 (one of a group of men the club paid over £13,000 for in all).

The Preston Club had therefore saved money on Hamilton – money it was quite happy to spend in abundance on 'star' players. Hamilton's story at least had a relatively 'happy' ending, but every April and May the signing-on period produced its crop of private tragedies, the scramble for scarce places, the tense moments waiting to enter the manager's office, the close scrutiny of the 'retained' list.

It was a hard, not to say cruel world. As one manager was quoted as saying in April 1927:

> It is unfortunate but seeding has to be done each year; clubs have to

protect their own interests. Again, clubs who have had bad seasons
have to try and save a bit of money in summer wages to make up the
deficiencies....

The smaller fry would always suffer, of course:

The pitiful part of the business concerns those players who have
been professionals only one or two seasons and have failed 'to make
good'. In many cases they will be thrown on to the trade market and
the situation becomes worse when it is realized that in certain
circumstances these men have no handicraft at their finger-ends.
They become casual labourers. Unskilled workmen, they are
handicapped and may have to seek the dole.

The Players' Union would make great efforts in years to come to
provide a safety-net for such men – clearly the 'industry' had no
interest in such rejects, the discarded chaff produced in the search
of the genuine article.

Men like Jimmy Fay realized, however, that only when it could
offer such men something tangible would the Union become a real
force – only when these and others clinging tenuously onto a career
in the game could see that the Union might make a difference to
their lives would they bother to pay their 1/- a week. But for now,
insurance schemes, provident funds, etc. were pipe-dreams – all
that the Union could contemplate in the mid-1920s was an
improved death levy of £100....

The football world in general, however, was expanding. The
1920s saw the international game making great strides and for a
time Great Britain was part of that process. Between 1924 and 1928
the FA was a member of FIFA, although the insular attitude of the
Home Associations made wholehearted cooperation difficult.

New countries brought new ideas – and the British football
establishment during the inter-war period regarded new ideas as
anathema. In 1924, for instance, the USA and Holland put forward
the suggestion at FIFA's Paris conference that one, perhaps two
substitutes, be used in case of injuries. Jimmy Catton, doyen of
football writers and semi-official voice of the establishment
considered the idea 'so amazing as to stagger those who uphold the
rigour of the game in this country'.

The USA was to provide the British game with more food for
thought in the next few years. The economic slump in the early

1920s saw mass emigration from Britain to the USA and the Commonwealth; inevitably, footballers, particularly those with industrial skills, were tempted to try their hand abroad (particularly if there was a chance of obtaining a good job as well as earning money playing).

American professional soccer 'took off' in the 1920s after a Scots eleven toured the Eastern seaboard in 1921. An American Soccer League was established soon after, and by 1923 US soccer scouts were busy in Scotland and, to a lesser extent, England, seeking out prominent players.

In practical terms, the sport was never to establish itself firmly in the States; it had failed on a couple of occasions before the First World War and would do so again after the Second, US sports fans

Page 16

December 27, 1924.

# SPORTS PICTURES
## and
## FOOTBALL MIRROR

### THE PIONEERS.

*Ideal Xmas Gift.*
RUGBY FOOTBALL
By W. J. A. DAVIES.
Booksellers, **10/6** net.

*Gift that Delights.*
EDUCATED EVANS
By EDGAR WALLACE.
Booksellers **3/6** Bookstalls.

(T)    Scottish football circles were much perturbed when some of its best-known players succumbed to the blandishments of agents of the Almighty Dollar, and went off to join Boston, U.S.A. Any English or Scottish League club would be pleased to have this trio for their half-back line (left to right): Jock M'Intyre (late Greenock Morton), Mick Hamil (Irish international and once of both Manchester League clubs) and Tom Muirhead (Scottish international and late of Glasgow Rangers). These players are the pioneers of a movement which looks like rivalling baseball in the States.

*Scottish players in the USA.*

remaining stubbornly true to their own pro-sports of baseball and later grid-iron.

For a time, however, the lure of the Yankee dollar unsettled the football rulers in Britain – particularly when the threat to decamp to the US was used as a bargaining counter at signing-on time.

There was the expected official criticism – men who chose to break free from their contracts being dubbed 'freebooters'. And predictions were made that they would all rue the day, particularly as the FA announced that anyone who left without his club's permission would be banned from football in the UK for life.

Yet enough men of quality made the break to cause some startling headlines: 'Is American Football Menace Real?': 'US Agents On The Prowl'; 'Menace of American Football', etc.

Menace, of course, was the key word. Because, as the USA was not bound by 'international' agreements regarding contracts and transfers, men could sign for American clubs without asking or needing permission from their home club – thus valued transfer fees were lost.

Scottish clubs, in particular, suffered most. Men from Aberdeen, Partick Thistle, even Rangers left for clubs in Boston, Brooklyn and New York. Tom Muirhead, Scots international, signed for Brooklyn for two years; McIntyre of Morton joined Boston for a good job and $2400 a year; Mick Hamill, Irish international, spent some years with Boston. But English clubs lost players too: Gillespie from Preston, Mitchell from Notts County and Sam Chedgzoy of Everton were prominent captures, while Harper, Arsenal's Scottish international goalkeeper, also fled to the USA for a number of years.

It was known that Jack Hill, Burnley captain and England centre-half, had threatened to go to the US if his terms were not substantially improved (a slap in the face for C E Sutcliffe, Burnley chairman) while Joe Cassidy of Celtic played cat-and-mouse for some weeks before finally resigning from the Glasgow club.

The culmination in this process came in 1928 when it was announced that the New York Giants, a baseball club which also ran a soccer team, had offered Dixie Dean £25 a week to play for them.

Dean had just completed his record 60-goal season to bring Everton the title. He was Britain's most famous player at that stage and being sought by Arsenal. Whether he seriously considered the

US offer is not known. His biographer states that Dixie would never have left his beloved Liverpool, just as he turned down the chance to go to Arsenal. But the choice was never offered to him in any realistic fashion. Oddly enough, Dean – a good baseball player himself – was to meet his American equivalent in terms of fame though certainly not fortune: Babe Ruth.

Ruth, who had scored a record 60 home runs in the same year that Dean had scored his record 60 goals, had come to the Everton dressing-room one afternoon in 1930 to meet the famous Dixie and confessed himself staggered that Dean was only earning £8 a week. He expected a star of Dean's magnitude to have been receiving at least a cut of the gate money!

The possibilities offered by the American clubs were predictably derided by administrators such as Sutcliffe who could see, probably with some relief, that there was no 'crock of gold' on the other side of the Atlantic. There was certainly no more freedom for pro-players – after all, it had been A G Spalding, the father of US baseball, who, before the turn of the century, had established a system of club controls over pro-players very similar to those operated by British soccer clubs.

But the sense of frustration felt by star players, indeed by all first division players, at the financial conditions under which they laboured – the endless restriction, the laughable wages they received when compared with other 'entertainers' – had been given an outlet by the American offers. The American experience seemed to suggest there was another way of doing things, one that seemed more equitable, that rewarded celebrity and skill and entertainment value.

And while the tedious, unchanging repetitive justifications of League officials, allied with the constant cries of poverty from club directors, could not, on the face of it, be contradicted, the idea that this was the inevitable order of things was being challenged.

Not, unfortunately, by the Players' Union, and not by men in a good position to do so, such as Dixie Dean. During the later 1920s, the Union was still struggling, in modern football parlance, to 'keep its shape'. Harry Newbould, speaking to delegates at the 1924 Annual General Meeting, expressed his frustration by giving delegates a run-through of the Union's history since 1909. He concluded:

The player today is reaping the benefit of that history and until such times as he needs the help and assistance of the Union is prepared to let others bear the burden. Shame, I say.

The Management Committee, though losing men like Charles Buchan, Moses Russell and George Utley, gained such long-serving stalwarts as Len Davies of Cardiff and Bangor, Robert Hughes of Bristol City, Arthur Wood of Clapton Orient and Frank Hilton of Notts County – all of whom would sit on the committee well into the 1930s, providing continuity and dedicated service.

Arthur Wood, Clapton Orient's goalkeeper, admiring his father's international cap. Harry Wood, the old Wolverhampton player, represented England on three occasions between 1890-96.

*Father and son: Union men from different generations.* Sports Pictures, *5 December 1925.*

Wood's promotion to the committee was not without its poignant aspect. His father Harry had been a Management Committee member on the old Players' Union at the turn of the century before leaving Wolves for Southampton.

1925 also saw the arrival on to the committee of Dave Robbie, dashing Bury right-winger, Motherwell-born Scot, who would later become chairman of the Union. Thus while short of members, the Union was never short of willing men to put in time – even though for some years it seemed such a thankless task.

For there has probably never been a time, before or since, when the Union had such a low profile. Its affairs were rarely reported in the national press. Its magazine, though competently produced, was poorly distributed and made a loss. Its very existence posed no threat at all to the League. Indeed, Sutcliffe, writing in *Topical Times* in September 1927, could even mention it without resorting to insults, although he could not resist the temptation to make a dig of sorts:

> The annual meeting of the Players' Union passed with little notice or comment. The Union is in a very healthy position financially but I sometimes wonder when I see games played and players rushing in regardless of the limbs of the opponents what some members of the Union think of some others ... I keep looking for and hoping for some public pronouncement by the organization which will help cleanse the game from foul and unfair tactics in vain and until we have it I confess that the Union to my mind is failing in its greatest mission.

The middle to late Twenties certainly saw a great deal of breast-beating in the press and at FA level concerning the 'levelling-off' of football in terms in individual skill, of increasing defensiveness, a general dourness inhibiting talented ball-players of ever more dash and speed and ever decreasing subtlety.

But it was no use complaining, as the *Athletic News* did season after season, about 'frenzy', 'frantic football', 'mechanical play', 'hurried and thoughtless', etc.; no use tampering with the rules, as the authorities had done in 1925 when changing the offside law in an attempt to encourage goal-scorers. The League system, lumbering Behemoth, would simply devise ways around such tinkering and eventually produce, in the shape of Herbert Chapman's Arsenal, the epitome of inter-war football – the third-back game, a foolproof defensive system that would reap the Highbury club such enormous dividends in succeeding decades, and which would gradually stifle adventurous, innovative play.

The doubling in size of the League, from two to four divisions, the increase in the number of games played each season, the increased 'fear' of relegation in financial terms – these were now the imperatives moulding the shape of English football.

Initiative and independence were now at a premium, engendered by a wage system that placed first-team men under increasing pressure to stay in the team, come what may, especially with clubs carrying complements of players of forty-plus and a veritable sea of unemployed young men clamouring to take their place.

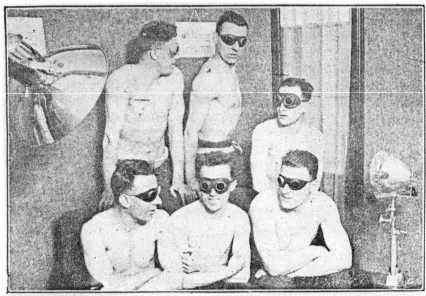

Northampton players undergoing a course of the now fashionable ultra-violet ray treatment in preparation for their Cup-tie with Millwall. From left to right the players (who are unrecognisable in their protective goggles) are (standing) E. Bowen, R. Malone and J. Weston ; (seated) S. W. Odell, W. Shaw and T. Smith.

Individual players could hardly be held responsible for such momentous developments. Players were increasingly being asked to perform restrictive roles on the field of play. Systems were more and more the vogue, with fitness, strength and stamina the essential requirements, while off the field, restrictions on players' personal lives increased: where they could live, how they travelled, where they went at night – all such decisions were abrogated by Club officials.

The Players' Union could only reflect these developments, both in its inability to convince men that it was worthwhile joining and in its relative helplessness to influence the progress of the game.

Yet, gradually, changes *were* occurring. Harry Newbould's sad death in April 1928 after a long debilitating illness resulted in Jimmy Fay being appointed secretary. For so long a reluctant chairman, he was now unanimously chosen in a contest with a Harry Matthews – and immediately asked for a rise in salary. He felt that £416 per annum plus expenses was poor recompense for a job which he had, for a year or more, virtually been doing for free, travelling regularly from Southport where he had an outfitters' shop, to Newbould's house in Longsight, where the Union office was situated.

Charlie Roberts, however, Union vice-president, felt that the salary was sufficient until such time as Fay produced 'results'. Fay thus set about organizing a membership recruitment drive and moving the Union office back into the centre of Manchester.

It was a symbolic step – and for the next fifty years the Old Corn Exchange Buildings at Hanging Ditch would be the Union's home.

# 17

## *Jimmy Fay Takes Over 1929–34*

Jimmy Fay's membership drive, which began in earnest in 1929, was based on the belief that pro-footballers, like union members in general, need chasing before they will pay their membership subs. The fact that during the inter-war years the union movement in general lost members, expecially after the 1926 General Strike, could only have had a peripheral bearing on Players' Union activities.

During the mid-Twenties and early Thirties, unemployment was to reach previously unheard of levels, and in such circumstances membership of trade unions in general would fall. But throughout the same period no football club of note folded and few footballers were thrown permanently on to the unemployment scrapheap.

If a club even looked like getting into difficulties there were at least half a dozen others waiting to take its place in the League; and club rosters remained extremely large. While there was certainly a great deal of cost-cutting at the edges, and wages in general were squeezed, most clubs had on their books the equivalent of three full sides. Some even had more; thus as a labour market pro-football remained relatively unaffected by general industrial trends.

This conviction of Fay's was further fuelled by the fact that Union membership at certain clubs was often wildly erratic. One season, upwards of forty men would be signed on, paying subs; the next, absolutely no one. The problem was that a season's good work could be wiped out at one fell swoop with the untimely transfer of a good collector; the constant movement of men from club to club created an unsettling, ever-changing pattern that made long-term planning extremely difficult.

The key, however, was to find sufficient men of ability and tenacity to make the effort; and that was where management men like Len Davies of Cardiff were worth their weight in gold.

From 1922 until the early 1930s, Cardiff's membership total was more than healthy. When Davies left to become player-manager of Bangor, the tradition was carried on for a season or so by E Jenkins, but ultimately fell away. Meanwhile, Davies actually succeeding in unionizing little Bangor.

Bury was another unlikely team regularly turning in membership figures in excess of thirty per season, all of which was due to their captain, Dave Robbie, who had built up the numbers almost from scratch.

Even Clapton Orient, one of the few clubs in the League to face closure during this period and which survived largely through the efforts of the local community and much luck, turned in good Union figures due to the presence of Arthur Wood – though it was often a struggle.

The pattern was repeated at a score or more 'unfashionable' clubs: Archie Rawlings at Preston North End; Jack Hacking at Oldham; Henry Leddy at Grimsby; Goslin at Bristol City; Joe Edelston at Fulham – collectors and delegates who built up membership rolls that would put to shame some of their larger club contemporaries.

Where the bigger League clubs were concerned, the pattern of membership was not always either consistent or logical. The two clubs with the greatest traditions in Union terms – Manchester United and City – were almost always unionized. City, with the continued presence of Meredith as player and later as coach well into the 1920s, were a Union bulwark right through the inter-war period, men like Sam Sharp, Eli Fletcher, Sam Cowan and Eric Brook proving valuable servants.

Manchester United, although never experiencing a season without members, dipped perilously low in 1923-4 when membership totalled a mere six, but gradually built their way back through the 1930s.

The north-eastern giants, Newcastle United and Sunderland,

were generally solid, with just the occasional year when membership slumped. J Low and Jesse Carver, at either end of the inter-war period, proved worthy successors to Veitch and Lawrence at Newcastle, but Sunderland proved more erratic, missing the years 1935-8 totally for some unexplained reason.

More difficult to explain, however, was the poor record of the Merseyside clubs, Everton and Liverpool. From being pioneers at the turn of the century, these proud clubs were completely non-unionized when Fay took over as secretary in 1929 and remained so for four years before McPherson, Hansen and later Matt Busby took on the role of collectors and returned Liverpool to full strength.

Everton, however, remained a non-Union club until the 1937-8 season when Joe Mercer, Cliff Britton and Charlie Sagar picked up the banner. It has been said that the Everton board discouraged players from involving themselves in Union activities. It is, perhaps, no coincidence that the club chairman throughout the inter-war period was Will Cuff, a dictatorial, 'hard as nails' character who would become League vice-president in 1936 and president in 1938. Cuff was known to enter the dressing-room on occasions and tell the team how to play. He was also prone to silence League Management Committee members if they were saying something that irked him. Perhaps his influence was significant, but there is little hard evidence.

Jimmy Fay's missionary work was to take him to every club in the League, and within a remarkably short time, membership rose to above the thousand mark – well short of 100 per cent, but approaching respectability. It was clear, however, that without the larger clubs and the prestigious players, the Union would remain unsung and largely unnoticed.

The top teams of the 1920s were not, in fact, anti-Union. Huddersfield, triple champions under Chapman and Clem Stephenson between 1923 and 1926, always had at least twenty-five men signed on, while Sheffield Wednesday, champions in 1929 and 1930, were also strongly unionized – although neither team supplied any Management Committee men. However, with the rise of Everton and Arsenal (who would take five of the remaining nine League titles and appear in two Cup Finals before the war) there began a disturbing tendency for the 'glamour' clubs to turn their backs on the Union altogether.

Fay's strategy, once he had managed to hoist membership back into respectable figures, was to confront the problem head on: he took to naming the 'guilty' clubs in his AGM report, even releasing such information to the press. Thus Arsenal, Everton and Chelsea were regularly upbraided while in 1933 he added Leeds United, Middlesborough, Sunderland, Sheffield Wednesday, Sheffield United and nine other Second and Third Division teams to the sorry list of clubs which could boast of no members at all. At the same AGM the following resolution was passed:

> The delegates of the AFPTU assembled here today representing the majority of the professional players throughout the country strongly protest against you and your colleagues for not supporting the Union at the same time receiving the benefits that have been secured for you in the past.

In the Union Management Committee minutes of February 1933, the attitude towards such clubs was made somewhat plainer:

> There are still a number of professional footballers connected chiefly with the richer clubs who take a very selfish view and have no consideration for their brother professionals.

The absence of Arsenal was particularly galling. Here was the country's (not to say the world's) glamour club, containing great stars like David Jack, Alex James, Cliff Bastin, etc.; and yet, since 1924, apart from a brief period in 1931 (when Alex James paid his Union subs for the first and only time in his career), the club had been almost completely non-Union.

It was not as if Arsenal had no pedigree in Union terms. In 1919 Hardinge had been more radical than Charlie Roberts and in the 1920s Joe Shaw, closely followed by Tom Whittaker, had seen to it that Arsenal never had less than twenty members per season. Charlie Buchan, of course, a Management Committee member in the early 1920s, had joined them in 1925: yet apart from the occasional lone sub payer, Arsenal remained outside the fold until 1936 when Wilf Copping and George Swinden joined the club. (Wilf Copping had been a vigilant and successful collector and delegate while at Leeds United.)

It was suggested that Herbert Chapman's influence had something to do with Arsenal's lack of involvement; yet when

Chapman had been at Huddersfield, there had been no shortage of Union members. A curious twist in this tale came in 1933 when Jimmy Fay wrote to the club captain, Tom Parker, to ask why the Arsenal men were refusing to join. He received a reply from Parker that had been dictated by 'H C' – clearly Herbert Chapman. Unfortunately, the contents of the letter were never revealed.

The obvious answer, of course, as to why the Arsenal men (and their expensive neighbours Chelsea) could not be bothered was that they were quite well off, thank you, their future secure. But in Alex James, England's premier team had a man who spent most of his career at the top fighting quite openly and controversially against the system which the Union was dedicated to dismantling.

In 1931 James effectively went on strike, refusing to re-sign for Arsenal at the season's end and thus deliberately forfeiting his summer wages. Arsenal had no intention of putting him on the transfer list and James appeared uninterested in playing for anyone else. He simply wanted the chance, so he told readers of his newspaper column, to consider various money-spinning offers he had received from organizations and individuals outside of football.

Alec James, the brilliant Scottish International, whose transfer to the Arsenal was first announced in "Sports Pictures," in his new job at Selfridge's, where, besides persuading customers to buy the new "Alec James football," he will teach the youngsters all the tricks of the skilful player.

He knew that Arsenal could offer him no more than the
stipulated maximum wage – thus he was not attempting to twist the
club's arm. Even had Arsenal been prepared to pay him
'under-the-counter' money, James's high-profile, headline-hitting
campaign made such tactics suicidal.

In the event, James re-signed at the start of the 1931-2 season,
having secured for himself an extension of his famous Selfridge's
demonstrator's job and a new newspaper column. But his one-man
campaign had been more of a cry of frustration at the absurd
position in which a man of his talent and entertainment value found
himself.

James, unlike almost all of his Arsenal colleagues (who were
generally aspiring middle-class, careful savers and abstemious),
enjoyed the company of jazz musicians, film-stars, boxers and
golfers. He was their equal in terms of reputation, talent and
box-office appeal – yet he was earning a mere pittance compared to
their lavish salaries.

James was never content, as Dixie Dean had been, to remain
dutiful, thankful and respectful of his 'betters'. In a sense, James
did not 'know his place'. Rather, he saw himself as an essential cog
in a vast new entertainment industry. Just like Herbert Chapman,
Arsenal's innovatory manager, James knew that Arsenal were in a
different league entirely:

> It seems that some people outside the game are beginning to realize
> there is big money in football. They have perhaps seen an Arsenal
> balance sheet and it's no use telling them to read Wigan's....

He saw signs of development in world football that could pose
both as opportunities and serious problems to the insular, parochial
British:

> One of these days a syndicate with the necessary capital to
> command, composed of men who haven't the faintest regard for the
> game as a game or the smallest respect for the football laws of these
> islands will hoist the jolly roger and sail off on an adventure which
> will make the soccer world gasp. On board will be the best
> twenty-two players in British football. They will base their scheme
> on the indisputable fact that every footballer – perhaps I had better
> say professional footballer – has his price.

James's Packer-style pirate tour, though not a new idea, was certainly inspired by the startling suggestions of boxing promoter Jeff Dickson who revealed that he was considering buying up, lock, stock and barrel, a couple of football clubs and transplanting them to the Continent. There was also the idea floated by the Greyhound Racing Association (a sport making great inroads into the traditional soccer heartlands) of staging a lucrative World Championship Club tournament at Wembley Stadium.

James's view of the game and his own position in it was thus unashamedly commercial. As he stated during his 'strike':

> I haven't the slightest intention of posing either as a martyr or as a crusader fighting to right the wrongs of the oppressed brothers of my profession. In football – off the field, of course – it must always be each man for himself. And professional footballers didn't invent that rule.

James's stance, though couched in such overtly selfish terms, had more relevance for the Union than he knew. The commercial possibilities of football were expanding fast, yet they would be held back and almost choked at birth by football's administrators, whose

*One player's attempt to cash in.*

sentiments and outlook had been formed in Edwardian, even Victorian England. Just as Britain's involvement with the Continent, in purely football terms, would be stifled and restricted, so would the game's involvement with the newer commercial forces be spurned. Thus the money that might have made footballers' lives more secure, their profession more certain, would never arrive.

Fay may well have been frustrated in his attempt to involve star men such as Alex James, Alex Jackson, Hughie Gallacher, etc., but he gradually succeeded in broadening the Union's activities and slowly began to build a secure platform from which an attack on the old restrictive controls could be mounted. His 'gradualist' approach, however, led to a minor power-struggle within the Union.

In the minutes of the Management Committee meeting of 27 July 1931, Charlie Roberts, Union vice-president, is reported to have been pressing for a discussion on Rule 10 which involved granting vice-presidents a vote at Management Committee meetings, plus a permanent seat on the committee, 'as a safeguard to the Union in future'.

Roberts was ruled out of order and it was suggested that the AGM was the correct place for such proposals. However, in August, at the Union's twenty-first AGM (only fourteen delegates attending), Roberts was prevented from speaking by chairman Robbie. In fact, Robbie threatened to adjourn the meeting if Roberts did not cease interrupting him.

Roberts evidently did not stop and the meeting was adjourned. The rule changes were never considered although Roberts remained as vice-president. A resolution was subsequently passed, clearly aimed at him, stating that in future only Management Committee members be informed of meetings.

Roberts appears to have been angered by the lack of effort made by the Union to challenge the retain and transfer system. In November 1929 the Union Management Committee had requested a meeting with the League Management Committee 'to discuss the adjustment of certain rules which are considered not to be in keeping with the times'. i.e. the retain and transfer system.

The committee then spent some months working on various proposals to put to the proposed meeting. However, in April 1930 a letter was received from League secretary Tom Charnley stating that, 'after careful consideration of the suggestions made, the Management Committee were not prepared to suggest to the clubs that any alterations of rules and regulations be made. It would, therefore, be useless to arrange for any deputation....'

At the Union AGM of that year, a resolution was sent to the FA protesting at the 'harsh and unfair treatment which many of its members are made to suffer each year under Rule 31 (Retaining Fee)', but this too resulted in nothing but a blank wall. In November the League Management Committee once again refused a request to meet and talk – the pointless cycle of supplication and rejection seemed set to go on forever.

Charlie Roberts was obviously urging the Union to take a more aggressive line: the safeguard of permanent seats for himself and vice-president Broomfield clearly designed for a period of outright confrontation *à la* 1909. But Jimmy Fay was not going to lead the Union into a strike.

His strategy was to build on small victories, to pressurize, to publicize where possible, to win members over by convincing them there was something tangible to be gained by joining the Union. And in fact there were plenty of areas where Union action was becoming essential – particularly as the Depression started to bite and clubs began to feel the financial pinch.

By 1932, the number of players being forced to seek unemployment benefit had dramatically increased, not because there were fewer positions for them at clubs, but because clubs were holding more and more men on their retain and transfer lists, determined to make something from their departure, and at the same time keeping a pool of free labour at their disposal. With many clubs unable to afford big fees, the men retained remained out of work, and thus had to sign on the 'dole'.

The Union had already expanded its unemployment bureau considerably – circulating clubs with lists of available players, their names, positions, and vice versa. Now it took upon itself the job of collating information regarding the newly professionalized French clubs where opportunities for British players were becoming available.

Thus, while the headlines of the popular press blared out yet another 'menace' to British football and while Sutcliffe was predictably threatening and sneering ('players may burn their fingers ... better be careful or there will soon be empty pockets,

Daily Mail, *20 April 1922.*

sore heads and sore feet....') the Union was arranging for its members to travel to France for trials on good financial terms – many of these men still being registered in Britain.

At the same time, the Union approached the Ministry of Labour to complain about 'alien' players coming to Britain and taking British players' jobs.

The sudden increase of players on the dole, however, soon caused another headache for Fay – and another opportunity for action. The Department of Labour suddenly ruled that professional footballers were 'seasonal workers' and thus not entitled to dole. Fay therefore arranged a meeting with the relevant government officials in order that he might mount an appeal on their behalf.

As Fay explained in the Report to the 1932 AGM:

> After correspondence with the Parliamentary Secretary to the Ministry of Labour I was advised to send in writing a full statement of the case of Professional Footballers to the Umpire for his consideration in connection with the appeals now before him.

In July Fay, accompanied by F J Wall of the FA, went to see the Umpire and answered detailed questions. Fay impressed the Umpire and some time afterwards he learned that his efforts had been successful – players could now receive their dole.

Fay was quick to point out how membership of the Union enabled members to appeal successfully against such decisions and his efforts received good coverage in the press. As the 1930s progressed, Fay would find himself increasingly involved with government departments and civil servants, taking on problems basic to the interests of members – members who were now joining in ever-increasing numbers.

Times were quite definitely changing and players were gradually emerging from a nether-world of subservience and dependence. In 1929, for instance, an important resolution was passed at the FA's Annual General Meeting – despite opposition from both William Pickford and C E Sutcliffe – regarding a player's right to attend an enquiry into his own conduct. Not only could a player attend; he could now cross-examine witnesses and call for rebutting evidence. As E J Scott of Herts FA put it:

> I am quite aware your rules permit a player to ask permission to be

heard in person but what is the good if you decline to see him? The most democratic game in the world should not be governed by the autocratic system now in force.

When Pickford claimed that such a rule-change would cost a lot of money in expenses, H P Cordell of Essex remarked: 'I cannot get the words justice and expense to go together'; and when Sutcliffe tried to protest that the idea was 'offensive to referees' and that the resolution would 'kill' refereeing, he was interrupted by angry protests.

In 1929 Union members also began a concerted campaign to protect themselves from unfair, libellous criticism in the press. It started in May when a Southport player, Harry Beadles, complained that local newspapers had reported him having signed for Workington Town FC after having been released from Southport. The Union solicitor took the case up, the paper apologized and printed a correction.

# NOTICES TO WHOLE OF CITY PLAYERS.

## TWELVE MEN ONLY WILL HAVE THEM WITHDRAWN.

## LEN DAVIES TO GO?

## ASTON VILLA MAKE INQUIRIES.

LEN DAVIES.

South Wales Evening Express, *11 March 1929*.

About the same time, the Western Mail Ltd was being pursued by Cardiff City players and management for a misleading report in the *South Wales Evening Express* that announced the whole of the Cardiff playing staff up for sale. Len Davies, Union Management Committee member, was pictured in the report and the Union was about to enter the fray on his behalf when the newspaper settled, paying £100 to be shared among team members.

The Union solicitor remarked: 'This would have been a fine opportunity for the Union to prove its real worth to their playing members but as all persons were satisfied with the settlement the free advertisement was unfortunately denied you.'

Having been given the nod, however, Union members were on the lookout for reports that could be construed as libellous, and within six months the Union had a perfect test case: Joseph Bowman of Doncaster Rovers complained that an article written in the *Daily News and Westminster Gazette* reporting a cup tie between his team and Stoke City was clearly going too far.

The reporter had called the Doncaster team, among other things, 'absolutely hopeless, inept, deplorable, laughable and an insult to English football'.

The case was taken up, damages for alleged libel claimed and by the end of the year substantial costs had been agreed, each Doncaster player receiving £41! The Union duly printed a small pamphlet outlining the case for distribution among clubs, Fay declaring:

> The professional footballer who has to earn his daily bread by his play does not, as a sport, object to fair criticism or comment ... and one would almost regret the day when fair comment in newspapers should be stifled from publication, but at the same time writers of articles cannot be allowed to go out of their way to overstep the bounds of fair comment and libel individual players, otherwise they must expect to pay and pay heavily for their folly....

In the next few years a score or so of libel actions were pursued against papers ranging from the *Thames Valley Times* and the *Midland Daily Telegraph* to the *People*, the *Express* and the *Mail*, alleging inaccurate and damaging descriptions of players (one being called a veteran when he was only twenty-three, one being sent off when he had in fact been carried off, etc.), journalistic 'jokes' not appreciated by players, fictitious incidents that could never have occurred, and so forth.

Players were suddenly very touchy, and occasionally their touchiness was rewarded with cash – more often the paper agreed to print an apology. But the libel actions, amusing as some of them were, were yet more evidence that players were slowly starting to assert themselves, take themselves and their professional position

140     \*\*\*     Topical Times, July 29, 1933.

# The Folks at Home

## WELL-KNOWN ANGLO-SCOTS AND THEIR FAMILIES

"The Day We Packed The Hamper—" featuring JIMMY DUNN of Everton, along with Mrs Dunn and Jimmy junior.

Mrs JIMMY BROWN, wife of the Manchester United outside-right.

Just a quiet cup—DAVE ROBBIE, the Bury outside-right and his mother.

more seriously and, through their Union, claim some of the privileges of 'ordinary' citizens.

Thus Charlie Roberts's impatience with Fay, and his demand for more aggressive tactics – well meaning though it was – were seen by Fay and his Management Committee as a path that was not only incorrect but also unpractical, although, as will be seen, the committee would not shrink from threatening 'drastic action' when the occasion arose.

Fay had joined the Union just a year or so after Roberts and his experience matched that of his predecessor. Fay's judgement and work during these years was to be respected. He was also working on a committee that could draw on long experience.

Dave Robbie, the chairman, had joined the Union in 1921 and had been a Management Committee member since 1925. A bachelor, he dedicated himself to Union work for more than ten years before retiring from playing to become a coach at Plymouth.

Len Davies, now player-manager at Bangor, had also been on the Committee since the mid-1920s and would serve for almost ten years.

And with the departure of men like Moses Russell, Harry Pantling and Arthur Wood, the committee gained men such as Ted Harper, Joe Tate and Harry Grundy.

Harper was one of the finest centre-forwards of the inter-war

Topical Times, June 30, 1934.                                      887

# "GET A MOUTHFUL OF THIS!"

### SAYS TED HARPER DOWN ON THE POULTRY FARM

The Blackburn centre-forward and his brother-in-law perform a tricky operation at their poultry farm at Ewood.

period, setting goal-scoring records at three different clubs and scoring an incredible 328 goals in a career of 266 games. His League record of 43 goals while playing for Blackburn Rovers in 1925-6 was only broken by Dixie Dean scoring 60 in 1928.

Harper brought to the Management Committee a definite glamour. He was also a good businessman, running a successful poultry farm, and thus a good advertisement for the Union.

Joe Tate was a rarity for the period – an Aston Villa Union member. Captain of the club, an England international, he was also trained as an accountant and put in almost 200 appearances for Villa before leaving the game in 1936 to concentrate on his tobacconist business.

Harry Grundy, Oldham captain, was another quiet, intelligent player who took over as members' auditor, thus continuing Oldham's proud tradition of supplying office-serving members.

And in 1932 Sammy Crooks arrived, dashing, outgoing England winger, a true contemporary 'star' and destined to become one of the Union's most valuable, long-serving committee members.

The committee on which Fay sat as secretary was therefore a fine mix of experience and talent – men representing all levels of the profession. In October 1934, Herbert Broomfield attended a Management Committee meeting in his capacity as vice-president. For some of the committee it was like meeting a living legend – even Robbie had never met him before. Broomfield gave a short talk on the early days and the committee listened respectfully. It must have been an eerie experience: so much had changed since the 1909 strike when he had been a young man fighting a lonely battle for the Union's survival. Now the Union had a modern office, duplicators, a salaried secretary and typist, more than £10,000 invested and close on 1500 members.

Yet so much remained the same: C E Sutcliffe's word still seemed the law; the transfer system appeared even more unjust than before the war; the maximum wage had not been raised for a decade. Even Billy Meredith remained on the door, as he would continue to do for the next twenty years, checking members in, keeping strangers out.

# 18
# *Lost Opportunities 1934–36*

The Depression of the early 1920s and the problems it caused professional football mark a definite turning point in the relations between professional players and the Football League. The stresses and strains of the period revealed the essential inadequacy of the game's rulers and administrators – their inability to cope with the demands of a huge labour-intensive industry; their unwillingness to accept inevitable changes; their incapacity to adapt and grow.

Men such as McKenna and Sutcliffe based their claims to power on the fact that they had been involved in pro-football ever since its inception. Unfortunately, their very longevity was to become a millstone round the neck of the game. They were men from another era entirely (in itself, no bad thing) but they persisted in treating the pro-grame as though times had hardly changed at all. Their solution to so many of football's problems was to suggest the clock be turned back.

In C E Sutcliffe's case, when reading through his various articles written during the Thirties, one gets the distinct impression that he had lost the desire to see pro-football develop at all. Once a visionary who had plotted and planned the League's expansion and domination, now nothing pleased him: BBC broadcasting was a foolish idea; foreign tours were a waste of time and his thinking seemed ever more obsessed with telling people how to run a club on a shoestring: players should either be amateurs or semi-professionals; managers were a luxury; bonuses and incentives were wasteful; benefits should be cut back to the bare minimum, etc. All of which was innocent enough, except that Sutcliffe was still the most powerful man in the nation's – indeed the world's – most prestigious professional sport.

It is hardly surprising, then, that the Players' Union found itself taking on ever-more responsible roles: no one else appeared either sufficiently capable or aware to deal with the real human problems that pro-football had almost unwittingly created.

No sooner had Fay dealt with the problem of unemployed players being listed as 'seasonal' workers, than he was faced with the question of whether players were still classed as 'manual workers'. At stake were various benefits under Health and Insurance Acts passed since the war.

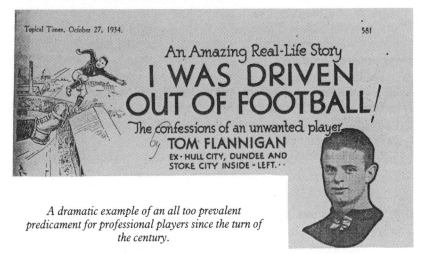

Topical Times, October 27, 1934. 581

An Amazing Real-Life Story

**I WAS DRIVEN OUT OF FOOTBALL!**

The confessions of an unwanted player

by **TOM FLANNIGAN**

EX-HULL CITY, DUNDEE AND STOKE CITY INSIDE-LEFT..

*A dramatic example of an all too prevalent predicament for professional players since the turn of the century.*

The Union was asked by the Ministry of Health if it wished to take a test case to court, and on 23 April 1934 Justice Roach in the Law Courts decided that pro-players could, in fact, no longer be considered 'manual workers', if earning more than £250 per annum.

As this affected players' insurance cover, it caused a great deal of worry, not helped by the attitude of the League.

At first the League Mutual Insurance Federation (effectively run by Sutcliffe as the League's solicitor) let it be known that it would continue to treat all players, no matter how much they earned, in similar fashion when it came to the question of compensation.

Within a few months however, Sutcliffe was to suggest changes to the basic player/club contract that made such an assurance sound extremely hollow. In fact, his new contract clause, if adopted, would have threatened the financial security of any badly injured player.

For some time Sutcliffe's journalistic pieces in *Topical Times* had been harping on a predictable theme, i.e. how heavy a burden professional footballers were on football clubs, how they did not actually earn their summer pay, and how clubs were saddled with a player once a contract was signed, whether that player turned out to be any good or not. It was all, he seemed to be saying, so one-sided:

> Some players are engaged at absurdly high wages and out of all proportion for the services which can be rendered to the club. That is the club's lookout and they must be prepared to carry out their share of the bargain – and I write the word emphatically – yet although the club is compelled to keep its part of the bargain, some players fail lamentably yet continue like a financial millstone round the necks of the clubs.
>
> The powers at present given to clubs to terminate contracts are inadequate for it is extremely difficult for a club to prove 'palpable inefficiency', and unless there is flagrant and wilful breach of training rules and regulations of the club, the latter must continue to pay the wages to the useless player.
>
> Would any ordinary employer of labour do it or agree to enter into such a contract?

But Sutcliffe went further. Inefficiency was one thing – injury another entirely. Clubs, he complained, had to fulfil their part of the contract even when a player was so seriously injured he was of no further use to them:

> No such responsibility is placed on an ordinary employer of labour for immediately a workman is injured his wages cease and he is put on 'compensation'.
>
> The financial strain on the clubs has become so severe that they cannot afford to pay full wages and if they carry out the obligations under the Workman's Compensation Act they must be relieved of the responsibility to pay wages.

In order to justify this startling suggestion, Sutcliffe went on to assert (as he had done on a number of previous occasions with particular reference to the Players' Union) that many injuries were due to players' own recklessness and thus were the players' own fault.

Furthermore, '... so long as the injured player receives the same wages as he would receive if playing there is not the full reason for carefulness in play and the strong desire to return to the game at the earliest possible moment.'

Sutcliffe declared that he had no desire to deprive the players of anything; he just wanted to 'bring to an end the trickery of any instinct to be unscrupulous or to sham injury as a means of getting something in lieu of wages until signed on....'

Sutcliffe's concern over the cost of injuries appears doubly ironic when one considers the Football League's ever-increasing predilection for speed, strength and toughness. The off-side rule change of 1925 was credited with creating the distinctively English 'biff-bang' style of play, all thrills and spills and long passing, in which the need for speed meant ever more relentless training for stamina – lapping and sprinting and jumping. Not surprising, therefore, that the injury toll should rise; Jimmy Fay, in fact, lamented that compared to the pre-war days a footballer's career seemed to be getting shorter and shorter.

Sutcliffe, however, seemed blissfully unconscious of such considerations: all he saw was the increase in doctors' bills, and his inevitable target was the player.

He had been attacking players in print for some time – the headlines alone of some of his *Topical Times* pieces between 1932 and 1934 make clear his feelings: 'Sack the Lot and It Will Serve Them Right!'; 'The Lazy Player Must Go!'; 'How Unscrupulous Players can "Do" Clubs'; 'Players I Want to See Thrown Out'; 'A Straight Talk to Conceited Players', etc. – all of which made for lively journalism; turning such sentiments into football legislation was a different matter entirely.

At the Players' Union AGM in August 1934, Jimmy Fay announced that the meeting had before it 'a question of a more serious nature than the Union has dealt with for many years'. Sutcliffe had proposed an addition to players' agreements that read as follows:

That if at any time during the period of agreement the player shall be prevented by illness or accident from performing his duties he shall receive during the first month, fortnight or any shorter period of such incapacity the salary mentioned in the agreement and during the second consecutive period at the option of the club, one half of the same salary.

If he shall be so incapacitated during a longer period then the salary shall at the like option cease to be payable during such longer period without prejudice either to the club's right to transfer fee or to the player's right to compensation (if any) under the Workman's Compensation Act.

The outrageousness of such a proposal brought from the Union a swift determined response. With the press present, the Union Management Committee issued the following statement:

That the Football League Management Committee, for reasons best known to themselves, seem to be intent upon making the position of the players as difficult as possible; that the attempts to impose upon players such conditions of employment are tantamount to slavery; that should players have the misfortune to be stricken with illness or crippled physically they also wish to cripple them financially ...'

The meeting then carried the following resolution:

That this meeting of delegates of the AFPTU strongly condemns the proposed addition to players' agreements ... this proposed addition is a serious matter to all players (and the game) and we demand that it be withdrawn. If it is accepted by the clubs the Union will take drastic action and fight the matter to the end....

In truth, the Union was not alone in its condemnation of the proposed alteration. Fay revealed that many clubs were willing to support the Union in whatever steps it decided to take.

In the event, no action was required. Sutcliffe's resolution (although he considered his arguments 'unanswerable and unassailable') was withdrawn – on the face of it, a most satisfying victory for the Union.

Yet the situation remained both confusing and unsettling, and, where Fay and his committee were concerned, increasingly bitter. For in August 1934, in the midst of the bickering over injury insurance, a solicitor from Liverpool had come up with a startling suggestion that could have lifted professional football and footballers on to a different financial plane of existence entirely.

Watson Hartley's scheme was based on the fact that since the start of the 1930s the football pools had rapidly grown to become a multi-million pound industry earning almost everyone untold riches: the Government received millions in taxes, punters regularly struck lucky, the pools companies themselves made healthy profits. Unfortunately, the game upon which it all rested received not a penny.

Watson Hartley's idea was for the League to patent the fixture list and then charge the pools companies for the use of it. With the money they received, football's multiple problems could be solved at a stroke.

However, as Hartley explained to Jimmy Fay in a letter in August 1934:

> You will scarcely credit me when I say that a scheme ... with such potentialities for the players, who after all should be the prime consideration, since without them there would be no game at all, did not even get a hearing by the Football League Committee; they refused point-blank to consider it even though they were committed to nothing if they investigated it and then turned it down, the investigation costing them nothing; and even though they were assured that the provision of the necessary funds was as certain as that two and two make four. No, they simply didn't want to hear anything about it.

Difficult to credit indeed. And for Jimmy Fay – who would soon be facing an about-turn by Sutcliffe on the question of injury compensation for men earning more than £350 a year, thus involving the threat of more test cases and expensive legal action – the League's attitude must have seemed bordering on the criminally insane.

Hartley had turned to the Union for help in putting pressure back on to the League and the FA to think about his scheme. The potential advantages to be gained by players, as he explained, were the stuff of which Jimmy Fay's dreams had long been made: a pension fund for players of five or more years' service on retirement; centres for training young players in football skills; official hostels for injured and sick players paid for by private insurance; assistance for clubs in financial difficulties; and increased pay for players.

Hartley calculated that these ideas could easily be afforded from the £200,000 he saw as being the League's potential income from the pools. After all, the pools companies were earning well over £2 million from football at that point.

Why had the League turned the idea down? Initially because the pools were a form of gambling. As the League stated: 'There can be no connection, however vague, between the League and betting.'

This was not the first time the Football League had stood on its principles and turned down a potentially lucrative idea because of its connection with gambling. In the early 1930s, dog-racing had caught the nation's imagination and had become immensely popular – so popular that it was even claimed to be denting football attendances.

Various clubs had sought permission from the League to install race-tracks at their grounds in order to tap some of the resulting income. But the League had banned such moves.

Gambling, of course, had been a source of much practical and moral concern to both the League and the FA ever since football had become popular back in the nineteenth century, and there can be no doubting the sincerity of men such as Sutcliffe in their antipathy towards it.

But the pools posed no threat to football. To organize a series of fixed matches in order to scoop a jackpot was well-nigh impossible – and League officials knew it. And where ethics were concerned, Jimmy Fay could claim that the League now had a more pressing moral responsibility towards the many hundreds of players who were being impoverished as the football industry itself grew larger and larger.

Watson Hartley corresponded with Fay during August and September 1934; they held clandestine meetings and Fay proceeded to help Hartley with small sums of money in order that the latter could continue working on his scheme. Hartley used Union headed notepaper to circulate League club directors, pressurizing them to approach the League – and eventually the League Management Committee decided to reopen the issue.

Hartley was interviewed in December 1935 and appears to have impressed the committee with his plans, for in January 1936 the League at last met the pools promoters – who were themselves busily manoeuvring in order to gain the best possible deal for themselves.

Shut out of the proceedings and powerless to influence events, Fay, his Management Committee and Hartley himself could only watch in dismay as the League proceeded to stumble into an outright and ultimately humiliating confrontation with the pools companies.

Unsure, perhaps, of their ability to win an expensive court case over their right to control the use of their own fixture list, split down the middle over the ethical question of accepting 'tainted' money, daunted no doubt by the prospect of handling such vast sums of money, the League Management Committee eventually swung from accepting a deal to attempting to destroy the pools industry itself!

Sutcliffe 'masterminded' a farcical strategy of withholding each week's fixtures until the day before they were to be played. It took just three weeks for the campaign to be utterly discredited, after which the League backed down, having in the process contrived to make itself look utterly foolish, to lose vast sums of potential gate money as crowds stayed away either in confusion or resentment, and, ultimately, to squander for some time any chance of earning money from their own priceless asset.

Not content with that, Sutcliffe and Howarth appear subsequently to have tampered with League Management Committee minutes in order to conceal from the world at large exactly what the committee's motives had been during certain critical stages of the abortive negotiations with the pools companies, when it had been cash rather than ethics that had been at stake.

In early 1936, helped by Fay and the Players' Union, Hartley tried once again to drum up support for his meticulously worked-out scheme by publishing it in various newspapers; but the League had now turned its back on any plan to raise money via its fixture list, whether or not associated with gambling.

Sadly, the Union then had to drop its support for Hartley, despite a last-minute plea by Billy Meredith who had become Hartley's firm friend. In later years Meredith and Hartley would collaborate on smaller schemes selling pools forecasts and Hartley would keep in touch with Fay. In fact, on 6 February 1939, after the League had once again turned down an offer of pools money for its Jubilee Fund to help old players, he wrote:

It is a tragedy that all our work of three years ago should have ended up in smoke. They had the opportunity to get anything they wanted at that time and on subsequent occasions. And the players are the sufferers all the time.

The pools 'war' confirmed, if confirmation was needed, that football's governing bodies had fallen shamefully behind the times, both in attitude and practice.

The never-ending pleas of poverty and the need for cheeseparing economies were now no longer to be accepted at face value. If football clubs were poor, it was because they were individually or collectively unable or unwilling to grasp the financial opportunities presently open to them. Thus they could not expect their employees either to understand or accept such a situation indefinitely.

Nor were professional footballers in the mood to accept any longer without comment each and every edict issued by football's authorities relating to players' rights and freedoms.

In June 1936, in the wake of the pools fiasco, the FA passed a resolution drawing members' attention to 'the growing practice of players contributing signed articles, reports containing criticism of their colleagues and opponents and giving interviews in the press ... also forecasting the results of matches, etc.'

The FA declared that it was 'of the opinion that such criticism and forecasting must cease', and clubs were requested to 'take the necessary steps to secure this end'.

Fay told the 1936 AGM delegates that this was a yet further curtailment of players' liberties, not to mention yet another curb on their ability to earn extra money. He demanded from the FA a 'definite meaning' of the resolution. In a rather chastened-sounding reply, the FA explained that the resolution 'did not preclude players writing for the press – only that criticism of colleagues must not be included....'

With more than £12,000 in the bank, with membership approaching 1500 and with signs that both the League and the FA were finding their grip on things faltering somewhat, Jimmy Fay's Union was clearly moving into a position where it could start to influence events rather than simply react to them. As Hinchcliffe, the Union solicitor, put it in 1936:

It is of the utmost importance, more so today than ever in the history of professional football that every player, for so many reasons, should become a member of the Union if he has to maintain and force (should necessity arise) his legal rights....

Topical Times, July 15, 1939.                                            5

A STAR TELLS HOW HE WOULD TACKLE—

# PROBLEMS A PLAYER HAS TO SOLVE FOR HIMSELF

"SHALL I SIGN — OR NOT?"

Sparetime Study

LOST FORM

The Snag of Swopping Positions

NO SMOKING?

"Reduced Wages— What Can I Do?"

by TOMMY LYON.
Chesterfield inside-forward

# 19

# *Approaching Storm 1936–39*

1936 saw important personnel changes at the top of both the League and the Players' Union. John McKenna, president of the League since 1910 and a Management Committee member since 1902, died in March 1936 at the age of eighty-one.

'Honest John' had been a powerful figure in the founding and development of Liverpool FC, and during the term of his record presidency had become truly popular. Thus his death was genuinely mourned by administrators and players alike. It opened the way, at last, for C E Sutcliffe to assume the mantle of president – something he had long coveted. Yet it was a sign of how much his reputation had been dented by recent events that his election was by no means unanimous.

Where the Players' Union was concerned, August 1936 saw the departure of chairman Dave Robbie, who obtained a coaching position at Plymouth Argyle and, feeling he could no longer devote sufficient time to the Union, tendered his resignation.

Sammy Crooks declared that Robbie's departure would be a serious loss to the Union: he had been chairman since 1931 and a committee member since 1925 – thus giving valuable service during a crucial rebuilding period. It was decided to buy him a suitable memento and £10 was set aside for a gold watch.

Within a year, however, Sammy Crooks himself would take over from Robbie's immediate successor, Albert Barrett of Fulham, and would remain chairman until 1946.

Crooks – genial, self-effacing ex-miner from County Durham – had been a player with Durham City until 1927 when, as he put it, 'I stepped off a coal lorry one Thursday and George Jobey, Derby County manager, was waiting to sign me up.'

As a young miner, Crooks had suffered severely from rheumatism contracted while working in wet conditions below ground, an affliction doctors warned would leave him crippled for life. But Sammy Crooks had battled his way to fitness and with Derby became one of England's fastest and most effective wingers – indeed, only Eddie Hapgood would earn more England caps between the wars.

A happy-go-lucky man, with a shock of blond spiky hair, he would, it was said, give you his last ha'penny if he thought you needed it, and he saw his Union role in simple common-sense terms. He had no discernible political bias: the Union was there to help players do the best for themselves, to assist them when times were hard. He felt he was putting something back into the game that had given him a great deal. Always on the maximum wage and able to supplement his income with regular England appearances, he was sufficiently well-off to send both his sons to private school and to afford a car when cars were generally owned only by members of a considerably higher class.

With his young wife, Sammy would motor up to Manchester to Management Committee meetings, a man at the top of his career, skilful, gregarious, a perfect ambassador for the professional game and for the Union he was to lead for almost a decade.

The Union Management Committee in general was starting to exhibit a more high-profile image. Along with Crooks there was Sammy Cowans, a popular, powerful Manchester City centre-half, and Eric Brook, another City man at outside left. Both men were England internationals. Cowans was a versatile wing-half who played in three Cup Finals for City, captained the side when they took the trophy in 1934, and made over 400 appearances for the club in twelve years. Brook was an irrepressible player – 'every team's bright spark' as Ivan Sharpe called him – who made over 500 appearances and gained eighteen England caps, but had the bad luck to be in competition with Arsenal's Cliff Bastin.

These two flamboyant and intelligent men would, along with Crooks, become firm friends and provide the Union with a solid England international base. In fact, during the mid-to-late 1930s a number of 'characters' served on the committee, all of them bringing something new and lively to the proceedings.

Norman Mackay from Plymouth Argyle was a Scot who had previously been with Hibernian and Aston Villa. He played in Ireland with Bohemians, gaining an All-Ireland Cup medal and then moved to Lovell's Athletic in Wales with whom he won a Welsh Amateur Cup medal. At Plymouth his terrier-like tackling soon established him as a great favourite at Home Park.

Tom Farquarson, an Irishman who gained caps for both Eire and Northern Ireland, was Cardiff City's keeper on 445 occasions and in two Cup Finals. His novel method of facing a penalty – standing inside the goal and advancing to the goal line as the taker of the penalty stepped forward – led to the FA ruling that keepers should remain motionless on the goal-line until the ball is struck.

Yet another Celt was Tom Griffiths, Middlesborough's Welsh keeper (twenty caps for Wales between 1927 and 1936) who had seen service with Everton during Dixie Dean's heyday.

Other less celebrated men who would serve on the committee during the crucial few years before the war included Harry Wass, who served Chesterfield at fullback and halfback between 1924 and 1937, playing over 400 times for the Saltergate Club; Syd Gibbons, Fulham player with almost 300 appearances; and Andy Beattie, Scotland International and Preston captain during the old club's 1938 FA Cup triumph.

1937 saw the Union bracing itself for a struggle. At the AGM it was announced that only eleven clubs in all four divisions were now non-Union, and that membership figures, approaching 2000, were the best since 1920.

Along with increasing popularity and membership came confidence. There were now also one or two small 'perks' accompanying membership – a discount scheme offered to Union members on purchases from a large London warehouse company; and a subscription withdrawal scheme whereby retired members could claim three-quarters of their subs paid during membership.

Meanwhile the Union office dealt with over 2000 letters and circulars in the course of 1936 while the Union solicitor continued to squeeze out of the League Insurance Federation cash for members injured but not covered by the Workman's Compensation Act.

In 1937 there had been a small increase in bonuses offered by the League for wins, etc. but this only threw into starker relief the fact that there had been wage stagnation since the early 1920s.

As befitted a man who had done so much to hammer home the reality of the low levels of footballers' pay, Jimmy Fay decided to begin his campaign for improvements by attacking the 'retaining fee' – the amount offered to players by clubs desiring to retain them.

The suggested minimum that a club could offer was £208 – anything lower than that should have resulted in the automatic free transfer of the player – and yet clubs were offering men considerably less than that amount and still placing them on the retained list if they refused terms.

When cases such as this were referred to Fred Howarth, the League secretary, he replied that the stipulation was merely 'a reasonable wage'. This 'serious injustice' was pointed out to the FA – but the Players' Union AGM went further and decided to press for an official retaining fee of £260 (in other words, a new minimum wage).

With 'gates' now recovering and clubs earning regular profits, the Union declared it was 'time for a deputation to be met by the League in order that "better terms and more equity be obtained" for players'.

The request, sent following the August AGM, took the usual season to come to fruition. March 1938 saw the League finally consent to a meeting – the first for a decade.

The Players' Union/Football League meeting of 1938 was noteworthy for the fact that it was the last time Charles Sutcliffe would come face to face with the organization upon which he had poured such scorn and insult, and which he had generally dismissed with contempt throughout his many years of involvement in football politics. Within a year he would be dead.

Now, however, on 21 April 1938, the 'negotiations' were taking place against the backdrop of the League's 75th anniversary – its Jubilee Year, and Sutcliffe's apogee. As President he was orchestrating an orgy of self-congratulation, preparations for which had been under way ever since the previous summer. The climax was a grand banquet in May 1938 attended by 650 special guests,

Topical Times, March 25, 1939.

# THE BEST DRESSED PLAYERS

TED CATLIN (Sheff. Wednesday) —Likes his materials hefty and very much built to order.

BERRY NIEUWENHYS (Liverpool) —Subdued good quality materials. Always looks well cared for and well turned out.

HARRY HOLDCROFT (Preston North End)—Always spruce but conventional.

GEORGE AINSLEY (Leeds Utd.) — Unconventional, comfortable and colourful.

FRANK SWIFT (Manchester City) —Has a good eye for blending the colours.

PERCY GROSVENOR (Leicester City)—Sophisticated taste.

LEN BUTT (Blackburn Rovers)— Bright dresser, likes light, colourful effects.

BOB STUART (Middlesbrough)— Crisp and dapper.

described as the largest single gathering ever witnessed in British football with a guest list 'a veritable who's who of football'.

Needless to say, the Players' Union received no formal invitation; individual players did attend as club guests, including Union chairman Sammy Crooks. By the time he sat down, the outright rejection by the League of all the Union's requests had to be digested along with the eight-course meal, vintage wines, port and ancient brandy.

Sutcliffe, aware perhaps that history was watching him, had opened the negotiations in curious fashion, lamenting the fact that although the League Management Committee had received several requests from the Union for meetings over the years, 'unfortunately they always arrived too late for our meeting which had already been fixed'.

While Jimmy Fay and his negotiating team were scratching their heads over this, Sutcliffe went on to declare that the League Management Committee was 'prepared to listen to all they [the Union] had to say and that Fay and his committee should 'not be afraid of voicing their opinions on the requests and grievances which had been put forward'.

After two hours, during which the Union had pressed for a maximum wage increase of £1, insisted on a fixed retaining fee of £260 per annum (or else a free transfer) and emphasized the unreasonableness of the amount players received as a percentage of any transfer fee, Sutcliffe closed the meeting with yet more platitudes concerning frankness, candour, calm and courtesy.

Of course, nothing was subsequently granted, nothing conceded. Thus at the 1938 AGM held in August, delegates were angry and bitter. There were now demands for another meeting with 'drastic action' being threatened unless something concrete emerged.

Early in 1939, Fay organized two special 'extraordinary delegate meetings' – one in London and one in Manchester – in order to gain maximum backing for action should the League once again turn a deaf ear. These meetings, both in their size and the determination expressed by the delegates to stand for no more prevarication from the League, demonstrated the serious nature of the rift between employers and employees.

By their continuous, almost logic-defying, refusal of each and every request made by the Union, the League had created such pent-up anger and frustration that the only possible result of further stone-walling would have been an all-out strike – had not the Second world War intervened.

At the London delegate meeting attended by fifty-nine club delegates representing over 300 members, the 'outdated, one-sided' regulations were attacked and demands voiced for representation on the governing bodies of football; for 'modern' employer/employee relationships; and for the truth to be told about exactly how much pro-players received by way of pay.

At Manchester the press were called in to hear the comprehensive demands of both meetings:
- an immediate pay rise;
- a minimum wage of £4 a week;
- two weeks' pre-season training to be paid at playing season rates;
- contracts to run from the beginning of August to the end of July, to prevent clubs saving money by keeping men out-of-contract during the summer;
- larger shares of transfer fees;
- 100 per cent increase in bonus payments;
- compensation/injury payments to be fixed and compulsory;
- representation on the Jubilee Fund.

All delegates gave the Management Committee their full backing, pledging to 'stand by the Union whatever action it may be deemed necessary to take in the future'.

Acting President Will Cuff (Sutcliffe having died in January 1939) thus came face to face with probably the most determined Management Committee of the inter-war years – certainly the most confident and, in terms of cash and membership backing, the strongest.

Moreover, some kind of confrontation seemed inevitable from the moment Cuff demanded to know the exact membership figures of the Union before discussions had even started – only to be told by Fay that membership stood at approximately 1850, 'and eighty or so non-League members, many of these having been forced out of League football to try to earn a living owing to excessive transfer fees placed upon them....'

Cuff was no conciliator. He was very much a man in the Sutcliffe mould, a 'master' (as Dixie Dean approvingly called him), though unlike Sutcliffe, who was small and frail, Cuff was stocky and tough. One senses that a fight with the Union would have suited him perfectly in order to demonstrate his fitness for the job of president.

In fact, all demands by the Union were once more turned down at the League AGM a few months later. The Union's response was to prepare for 'drastic action' at the commencement of the 1939-40 season. However, within days of the resolution, football was suspended as war was declared: the antagonists were thus to remain frozen in mutually threatening poses until 1945.

In one significant respect, however, both organizations had been momentarily united – in joint mourning at the passing in 1939 of two men who had come to symbolize the aims and hopes of their respective organizations – Charles Sutcliffe and Charlie Roberts.

Roberts's death had occurred a few days before the 1939 AGM; fulsome tributes were paid to his memory by veterans Fay and Meredith and a minute's silence observed.

Sadly, few other founder members of the Players' Union received such well-deserved farewell salutes. John Cameron had died in 1935, Colin Veitch in 1938 and Herbert Broomfield was to die a month after Roberts. Strangely, where Broomfield was concerned, even though he was still a vice-president of the Union, no one seemed to know where he lived; thus the Union was unable to send either a wreath or condolences to his family.

On a wider front, of course, 1939 was a chaotic time. The declaration of war came as no real surprise – daily life in Great Britain had been subtly shaped by the growing threat of hostilities for quite some time. But the sudden ending of 'normal' life saw people rushing in all directions: sending children away to the countryside, hurrying to various call-up points, digging shelters and preparing for the worst.

Football ended just a week into the new season, so that many footballers found themselves stranded and were involved in dashes back to distant homes in search of jobs and somewhere to live.

In contrast to 1914, there was no delay in halting professional soccer: little alternative either, given the demands that 'total' war made on essential supplies, not to mention the draconian restrictions on assembly and movement. The transport system was thrown into turmoil, men were plucked into various branches of the services almost immediately. Within months of the declaration, some clubs had virtually no players at all to call upon, even had there been games for them to play in.

Topical Times, September 23, 1939.

SOME SOCCER STARS ACTIVE IN OTHER "FIELDS"

For the Players' Union – Jimmy Fay and Sammy Crooks in particular – the first few months of the war brought a flood of enquiries: the sudden cancellation of agreements and the abrupt stoppage of wages meant there were many men without a penny, especially those who had just finished a summer on the retained list and had thus received no cash for some months.

There were anxious requests concerning how much money clubs were obliged to pay regarding contracts already signed. The League eventually announced that those players who had been 'on call' to play on 8 September – the second Saturday of the season – were entitled to that week's pay. Inevitably, various clubs did not respond and the Union had to do a great deal of chasing up. One such case would result in Jimmy Guthrie entering the Union on behalf of his playing colleagues at Portsmouth – and staying in.

The healthy state of the Union's finances meant that it was an ideal position to help men suffering hardship. As Fay remarked at the 1940 AGM, 'My main object during the past twelve years in spite of strong criticism was to build up the funds of the Union to enable it to function through any crisis that might arise.'

Although the crisis this time was a war rather than an industrial dispute, Fay could allow himself a feeling of vindication.

Membership subscriptions more or less ceased when the season did (though Jimmy Guthrie was to collect the Portsmouth men's subs and send them in). Indeed, many men took advantage of a relaxation in the Union's rules relating to Rule 7 (whereby a retiring member could claim back most of the subs he had paid in during the course of his membership – usually a sum of about £20) which proved extremely popular, helping many men out at a tricky moment.

Above and beyond that, the Union found itself paying out to men for travel, rail-fares and removal costs; there was extra money paid to families who had recently lost bread-winners, while the Union was also bracing itself for huge expenses relating to the test cases then going through the courts about claims by the Inland Revenue for tax on benefits – cases the Union would eventually lose.

The Union's own running costs were cut to the bone. The office was removed to Fay's home above the shop in Southport, thus saving on travel, wages and rent, while application was made to the Chief Registrar of Friendly Societies for a relaxation in the Union's rules. Clearly the Management Committee meetings, not to mention the

Charlton devote a morning each week to A.R.P. work under Inspector Clark (left), of the local brigade. How many of these players can you identify ?— HOLLIDAY, ALLEN, GASCALL, BRIDDON, POYSER, LANGDON, and W. SCOTT.

AGMs, would be disrupted and all concerned were adamant that the Union should continue in operation, no matter how intermittent. As Crooks put it in 1940: 'The Union must endeavour to retain the membership, keep them in benefit and assist them in every possible way.'

Although battening down, therefore, the Union would remain *in situ*: the lesson of 1914 had clearly been learned.

Most importantly, at the AGM in 1940, a new trustee was introduced to take the place of Charlie Roberts – Mr S Sanderson, JP, secretary to the Card and Blowing Room Operatives Association. Sanderson was also provincial secretary of the National Association of Trades Union Approved Societies – thus he could speak for over one and a half million trade-unionists. Even in 1940, he could see the germ of coming changes:

The first step is to win the war. That in the midst of peace wise men prepare for war is without doubt a profundity. Equally so is the truism that in the turmoil of war wise men prepare for peace ...

Jimmy Fay echoed the sentiment, and made a prediction:

The administration must go on, we must keep in touch with the members so that when this terrible struggle is ended we may be in a position to represent the members in an endeavour to make the livelihood of the professional footballer more secure and much more equitable than it has been in the past. When that time arrives, great leadership will be necessary and I feel sure that your Management Committee will not be lacking in efforts on your behalf.

# 20

# *Post-war Militancy* 1946–47

Unlike 1914, when so much criticism had been heaped upon players and clubs for continuing to play once hostilities had commenced, 1939 saw swift, decisive action taken that left no one in any doubt as to what the priorities were. The League programme was immediately halted and, when football recommenced in the form of a reorganized competition in late 1939, it was clear that what was being provided was considered as essential entertainment.

In addition to this, many ex-professionals were given special tasks (related to fitness training) within the armed forces and their contribution was immense. The men at the very top of the profession were entertainers in their own right and their privileges – the freedom to leave units in order to play in 'internationals' and representative matches – appear not to have been resented. After all, vast amounts of money were raised in this way for charity and morale was considered as important as weapons.

Thus professional football in general could be said to have had a 'good' war.

Just as during the First World War, however, professional footballers ceased to exist as legal entities; their contracts were cancelled and they were no longer covered for injury under the Workman's Compensation Act. The clubs continued to operate, though, and, as in 1914-18, retained their hold on players whose contracts they were no longer obliged to honour (and which, in many cases, they had no intention of honouring).

Nevertheless, certain League rules regarding registration were relaxed. With the resumption of organized competition in 1940 and especially in 1941, players were permitted to play for different teams, sometimes even in the same competition. Disruption was so great that some clubs could not count on having eleven men available on match day and many a supporter found his dreams coming true as he stepped from the terrace on to the pitch to play alongside his heroes.

The League system was split into two in 1941 when the London clubs unilaterally formed the London War League. For a time, matters were desperate for those clubs situated in areas where bombing was a regular fact of life.

By 1943, however, enemy bombing raids were much reduced, crowds began to flock back to football and the professional game started to generate vast sums of money for a variety of wartime charities while many clubs also began to make healthy profits once again.

For players, the rise in gates and the return to relative prosperity meant very little. Throughout the first four years of the war, players were granted just 30s a game. In 1943, upon application to the League by Jimmy Fay, this was raised to £2 a match.

Many men, however, were seeing the best years of their playing lives being gradually whittled away. Six years is a large slice to take from anyone's career but considering that a professional footballer's 'life' generally lasts no more than ten years, the Second World War ruined the hopes and dreams of hundreds of players. Those not in the forces – working in factories, munitions or reserved occupations – continued to turn out each weekend but it was a twilight, part-time career and as a letter to Jimmy Fay from Jimmy Guthrie, Portsmouth captain and future chairman of the Union, written in early 1943, demonstrates, there was a certain amount of resentment building up:

> The football player has been hard hit and I am sure no one will deny that 30/- is a very meagre sum. Many players are having a very hard time making ends meet. Why not make a limit of £3 and a minimum of 30/- and allow clubs to pay for time lost? Take my own case, for

instance. We play every Saturday for 30/- but by doing so we deprive ourselves of earning more money over the weekend, but what can we do? Football is our life and we must play to keep in the game ... play or else get out of the game.... All we ask for is a square deal. I don't think we are getting one.

The consolation for men such as Guthrie and many others watching how the country was gradually changing was that, with the end of the war in sight, the future looked brighter than ever before. The expectation was that society would be rationally organized and planned: a Health Service, slum clearance and municipal housing, new towns, educational overhaul. In short, a planned society that would sweep away all the old worn-out relics of the past and replace them with new, vibrant, dynamic structures. As Jimmy Fay wrote to Ernie Thompson (ex-Management Committee man but now a CSM in the Glider Pilot Regiment):

I can visualize a great opportunity for the player to demand a thorough overhauling of the out-of-date rules, particularly those affecting agreements, wages, benefits, transfer fees, retaining fees, compensation, insurance, etc. There is something to work upon, such as the Beveridge Report and the Atlantic Charter.

But he added ominously:

These appear to cover everybody except the professional footballer....

Given the traditionally bleak and selfish attitude of most League clubs, Jimmy Fay, though he might have had high hopes for society in general, was wise to assume that grim times and hard battles lay ahead before players could reap the benefits of wider social changes.

The Players' Union Management Committee had begun to look forward as early as 1943. At the AGM in August in Derby, attended by members Cann, Beattie, Crooks, plus Jimmy Hagan, 'Dally' Duncan, Stan Cullis and Jimmie Guthrie, attention was drawn to the need to 'give security to all players when they retire from the game to live comfortably and to enable them to start a professional, commercial or business career'.

By then Fay had already made representations to the League regarding the future. In June he had written to Fred Howarth asking whether the League had considered any plans for reorganizing football after the war. In his letter Fay had emphasized the 'hopeless' condition of many men who would be too old to resume their careers through no fault of their own, and wondered if the clubs might give the players their eight-month agreements, which had been taken from them at the start of the war: 'It would enable those players who may not be re-engaged to live for a time whilst they are seeking a new club or searching for employment.'

Howarth had replied in typically non-committal terms: 'The interests of the players had not been lost sight of,' he wrote. But in fact the League AGM of that year concerned itself with the routine details of the existing wartime competition, its only concession to players being an additional 10/- per match, and that only after heated discussion.

By the 1944 AGM Fay was warning:

> In my opinion, unless the players make a definite stand as soon as hostilities in Europe cease, the position of the majority of players will be little better than pre-war days, when many players had only a bare existence.

By then, of course, Fay and Crooks – who had been ever present throughout the war, despite the fact that their respective sports goods' shops had been rendered defunct by wartime restrictions on goods and general trade – could count on radical support.

Jimmy Guthrie, Portsmouth's pre-war captain, had first approached Fay in 1939 concerning back-pay the Portsmouth club was withholding from several players. That issue satisfactorily settled, Guthrie had continued to correspond with Fay, pouring out his anger and frustration at the conditions under which footballers laboured.

From the very start he urged the necessity of strong determined action once the game restarted; and he was soon offering Fay help in dealing with Union problems in the south. His letters to Fay reveal, even then, an impatient, restless character, full of missionary zeal:

> The footballer, like the people, have the making or breaking of all their conditions but they are too damned stupid, lazy and selfish to bother about them. They need leaders who are willing to give their time to drive sense into them.

The Union, he said on a number of occasions, was faced with the greatest chance in the history of the game to make radical changes; it would be criminal to miss that chance.

By 1943 he was serving on the Management Committee, a much-needed shot of adrenalin into the Union at a time when both Fay and Crooks – despite their undoubted commitment and record of services – were looking to hand the torch on to others.

By 1944, however, it was not only Guthrie who was angry. The post-war planning committee of the Football League had reported its recommendations. There would be, prior to League football's recommencement proper, a 'transition period' during which all players would remain part-time (thus remain in their jobs wherever possible) and be paid a maximum of £4 a week, with no bonuses.

The Players' Union was quick to react: 'It is an insult to offer such terms and will meet with great opposition from the players,' it declared at the Union AGM.

There had already been complaints concerning the niggardly amounts of money the League's Insurance Federation had been paying out to men injured during wartime games. And while there were no reliable gate-figures available, it seemed to the naked eye that crowds at football matches had never been higher.

A demand, quoted in the AGM report, was made immediately that the £2 match fee be doubled as 'it was generally agreed that the majority of clubs last season made fairly large profits and are sounder financially than they have ever been in the past'.

The demand was ignored and by mid-1945, with the war rapidly approaching its end, the Union was pressing for immediate action.

In June, with members of the old committee still away in the forces, three new men were co-opted; Jimmy Guthrie, who had been acting unofficially for some years already; Frank Broome, the ex-England and Aston Villa player/winger; and 'Dally' Duncan of Derby and Scotland.

The value of having remained organized and ready, prepared with various contingency plans, was to be swiftly demonstrated. With the 'transitional' season of 1945-6 about to start, the Union put out an immediate demand for an £8 match fee maximum. It would, they declared, 'be an opportunity for clubs to show their appreciation of and recognition to the experienced players for their splendid services during the war. The majority of clubs can well afford an increase and would willingly approve.'

Guthrie, who had already been working assiduously in London, drumming up press support and sounding out various club directors, knew that there was disagreement among the clubs regarding the new wage rates. He was equally certain as to what the Union's stance should be: to decide upon a figure and stick to it.

By August, when the Union delegates met in Manchester for their 35th AGM, the League had already met – and seemed confused. According to Jimmy Fay, the League's AGM had ended 'in a state of chaos and bewilderment and it appeared that it was left to the clubs to solve the question'.

The wages issue, however, was just one aspect of the League's confusion. Fay had harder words of criticism where the question of suspended agreements were concerned, not to mention the various schemes to provide insurance and security for older pros. As he told delegates:

> We have suggested schemes to the League to provide for players in the future at the end of their playing days. Schemes by two of the League clubs to end all financial troubles were circulated to the whole of the League members and wonderful schemes they were. They appeared to be received with jubilation by many of the clubs, but not a word was raised about them at the AGM of the League. No doubt you will be wondering why this unprogressive spirit, why no effort to bring the game up to date with the changed times.... The answer is that there is sufficient money in the game to provide security for all. It is big business and should be in the hands of big businessmen....

Fay's indignation at the League was surpassed by the anger of many of the delegates. Calling the meeting to order with a great deal of difficulty, Sammy Crooks summed up. There were two possible courses to take. The first was simply to refuse to restart the football competitions. As no one was reliant for a living on football at that point, all still being part-timers or in the forces, this course of action would be relatively painless to members. (It would, however, threaten the pools. As Guthrie had written to Fay some weeks earlier: 'Think, no Pools! What will the man in the street think?') The second course would be to demand an immediate meeting with League officials while commencing the season 'under protest'.

The split represented by these alternatives reflected the changes that had occurred on the Management Committee. In addition to

Guthrie and Crooks, five new men had been elected: Frank Broome; Joe Mercer, Everton and England wing-half; Bob Stuart of Middlesborough; Norman Low of Newport; Alan Brown of Huddersfield and Joe Wilson of Reading. If one can make a crude distinction between 'radicals' and 'moderates' then Guthrie, Wilson and Brown were the former, while Mercer, Broome, Low and Stuart were the latter, with chairman Sammy Crooks prepared to accept a majority verdict. As will be demonstrated, this basic split would work against the Union's initial strategy and ultimately its interests.

At this point, however, it seemed unreasonable not to compromise and accept the moderates' suggestion – a meeting with the League. That the Union was well organized and clearly expressing the moods and opinions of the bulk of the players could not be denied. With men now flocking back to their clubs as demobilization began, and factories ceasing to produce weapons, there was clearly a sense of impending confrontation.

There was also the complication for the clubs that a Labour Government had been elected and legislation – in particular the Reinstatement of Civil Employment Act, which made it compulsory for a company to re-employ those who had worked for it in September 1939 – was preventing the football industry from slipping back into its old, unregulated, semi-feudal state. The Union thus appeared to be a particularly unwelcome nettle that had to be grasped.

The new committee moved swiftly. Having notified the League that a meeting was essential, it proceeded to draw up new demands. The transitional period was clearly a dead letter: football would have to be placed on proper terms immediately, and that meant a new wages deal.

Thus at 2 pm on 29 August, at the Midland Hotel, Manchester, Union officials Crooks, Mercer, Brown, Guthrie Low and Dearson met a sub-committee of the League Management Committee.

League president Cuff welcomed the delegates and immediately attempted some mild intimidation by announcing that he did not like the tone of the letter calling for the meeting. 'It is not necessary to use the word *demand*,' he said. The League was always prepared to meet the Union.

Thus admonished, the Union delegation put their case: £12 a week maximum and £5 minimum, plus a long list of additional demands relating to agreements and accident insurance. The Union also referred to yet another rumoured offer from the pools companies (reputedly £¼ million 'for the benefit of the game'). Understandably it wanted to know if an offer had, in fact, been made for it had some suggestions as to how such money might be spent.

Cuff's incredible response was that pools' initiative 'was and wasn't an offer'. Topic closed! (In fact, the League was once again engaged in spurning offers from the pools companies, while at the same time crying poverty to the players....)

The meeting concluded with the usual caveat that everything would have to be decided by the clubs themselves 'at the earliest opportunity'. In fact, it would be another two months before the clubs finally met, and then to pass a motion that wages return to pre-war levels!

Perhaps the clubs had expected the players to respond in the traditional way: complain but comply. If it was a game of bluff, however, their hand would immediately be called by the Union. The League's terms were rejected and the membership balloted on strike action. On 5 November the result was announced: 62 clubs had voted for a strike, only two against, the rest having failed to reply. The stoppage was set for a fortnight thence, 19 November. It was now up to the League.

Cuff was almost indecently swift in responding, announcing that 'the Management Committee will meet representatives of the Union at the earliest possible moment'. His willingness to talk was praised in the press, and contrasted with various League managers who had rushed into print boasting that they would defeat any strike by using amateurs and non-Union men (Stanley Matthews, it was pointed out, was one such non-Unionist).

The press was generally well-disposed towards the Union and some journalists had by now grasped the realities of the players' wages. Clifford Webb in the *Daily Herald* wrote:

> The players are not asking for the moon. They are not suggesting for a moment that every player should be paid £12 a week or, while still in the forces or on essential work, £8 a match. These figures are suggested maximums. The players are equally concerned with fixing a minimum figure which they suggest should be £5 a week. Could anybody regard that as an outrageous proposal?

A week later, at 10 am on 12 November, at the Midland Hotel, the Union committee gathered for a meeting prior to facing the

League Management Committee again. They had a shrewd idea as to what might be offered and they were determined to hold out for the maximum. They then entered the negotiating room, perhaps a trifle nervously, with a sense that history was being made. For the first time players' wages were, in theory at least, open to round-the-table negotiation.

The usual *Alice in Wonderland* logic applied, however, Cuff welcoming the Union delegation and asking them what they wanted. Crooks reminded Cuff that the Union delegates had come to hear what the League had decided to offer.

Cuff then proceeded, inevitably, to outline the problems the clubs were facing: their heavy liabilities, their financial obligations plus the latest League 'bogy', the 'unjust' Entertainment Tax (though he barely mentioned the fact that admission charges had increased from 1/- to 1/6d).

The special pleading over, however, Cuff announced that he would deal with the Union's demands in reverse order of importance, building up to the climactic matter of the wage question.

Thus, agreements for men who could play full-time: conceded, but no agreements for men who could not devote their time to the game full-time (a potential loophole here for the clubs to exploit); August to August agreements: deferred; a formula regarding injury compensation: accepted for the present; regular meetings between the League and the Union: agreed; wartime service to count towards accrued share of benefit: 'impossible'.

And so, at last, to wages. The £12 a week maximum and £5 a week minimum Cuff dismissed as impossible. The League Management Committee had recommended that a maximum of £9 a week be offered and a £5 match fee for men still in the services or engaged on essential work. Thus the League, faced with a Union that had almost unanimous backing for an all-out strike, was prepared to offer a wage rise of just £1 a week on 1939 levels.

As the Union delegation began to protest, Cuff tossed in a sweetener: bonuses would be introduced at the rate of £2 a win and £1 a draw. The 'negotiations' now began; unfortunately, the Union delegates did most of the arguing among themselves.

Having retired to another room, they began to discuss the offer. Guthrie and Wilson were for strike action if the £12 demand was not met. The clubs, they asserted, could afford it and the successful strategy of no concessions should continue. Joe Mercer, on the other hand, felt that the offer should be accepted. It was a fair one but, more importantly, he was convinced that the membership would not hold solid. Some would accept the offer and the Union would thus be split.

Others on the committee agreed with him and the argument continued for some time until a compromise was arrived at. They would ask for £10 a week and the £5 minimum – and no bonuses.

Crooks returned to Cuff, but Cuff would not budge. It was a take it or leave it offer. After one more attempt at compromise, the Union delegates decided to accept the League offer.

Cuff was jubilant, declaring, 'We have arrived at another landmark in the history of League football. We fully recognize the part you play in this great game and whilst you have not got all the points you ask you have got some portion of them.'

Thus was sown the seed of great bitterness among the majority of players as they resumed their full-time status – those, that is, who could obtain contracts. For a score of clubs immediately began to search for ways of exploiting the inevitable existing confusion as men either returned to the game from the army and industry, or were recruited as apprentices from school.

With no minimum wage established, men were offered employment on a match by match basis; others were signed on and put into the reserves to play in Combination leagues where the new rates of pay did not apply, thus enabling the clubs to sign men on for £3 and £4 a week. The ruses employed were without number; the motive, simple greed.

For the Union, the negotiations had revealed traditional splits and this resulted in a certain amount of backbiting. Jimmy Guthrie had already complained in private about Joe Mercer. He claimed that at the August meeting with League officials Mercer had 'soft-soaped the management'. Guthrie wrote to Fay, 'There is nothing so cheap as flattery, Jimmy'; to which Fay replied that he, too, had been surprised by Mercer's attitude, which he felt had not accurately reflected the feelings of the delegates.

Guthrie had also criticized Joe Wilson – a man as radical as himself – for getting the originally demanded figures wrong, i.e. he had told the League Management Committee that the Union wanted a minimum of £5 when it should have been £6.

Wilson himself had been critical of Mercer: even up to the last minute, before the crucial negotiations with Cuff, he had been urging Fay to drop Mercer from the committee because the latter was still in the forces and thus unable to strike even if he had wanted to: 'I object strongly to Mercer's ideas and feel his opinion is self alone. I imagine many of our members would rather have someone in his place with a little more fight.'

Mercer himself was always adamant that he was doing what he thought best for the players and his assessment of the unlikelihood of a solid strike cannot be dismissed.

While many delegates expressed anger and determination to hold out, they could not really be sure what the average player might do, confronted with an offer of £9 a week, particularly as there was no 'average' player at that stage. Many young men coming into the game for the first time had been recruited during the war and had no experience of playing as full-time professionals with a proper contract. What did the Players' Union mean to them?

Many more men, too, were unsure of where they stood *vis-à-vis* contracts that had been terminated at the start of the war and benefits they might yet reap that had also been frozen. Some had moved home since 1939. It was a chaotic time, filled with uncertainty, not to mention the fact that the maximum wage meant little to the bulk of players; many would be lucky to receive £5 a match, and many more would receive even less – a headache for Jimmy Fay as most men in trouble would eventually turn to him for advice and help.

In fact, Fay's workload must have been enormous during this period and the pressures on him relentless. On the one hand he had Jimmy Guthrie urging for action on all fronts, convinced that the clubs had been let off lightly and that the next time the Union should stand firm. Guthrie was, in fact, already preparing plans for the next wage round in April, meeting with journalists and MPs, and as he freely admitted, using Jimmy Fay as a 'sounding board' ('My head is full of lots of ideas!').

Then there was Joe Wilson, in the throes of being transferred from Reading to Barnsley yet still finding time to write long letters, urging Fay to reform the Union: 'The silly weak-kneed way it is being handled now,' he declared, had to stop. Fay, insisted Wilson, needed full-time helpers, paid staff – what was he doing about it! A closed shop was crucial, area organizers necessary – and what was Fay doing about the pools?

In fact, Jimmy Fay was conducting negotiations with various

pools companies all through 1945 and well into 1946: Strangs, Zetters, Empire Pools and ITP were all approached by him for contributions towards a Benevolent Fund he was attempting to set up. All expressed tantalizing interest, but all would eventually be frightened off by the attitude of the League and the FA. Yet even on this topic there existed fundamental differences within the committee.

Unlike Joe Wilson, Guthrie had always been sceptical of the pools and their offers of money. What, he wondered, was the catch? Far better, he suggested, to make contact with radical MPs such as J P Mallalieu from Huddersfield and talk about nationalizing the Pools 'for the benefit of sport' – an idea hardly likely to appeal to the Pools companies.

To top all this, Fay still found time to help the Scottish players form a Union of their own. Contacted in December 1945 by Alex Miller just prior to the threatened New Year's Day strike by Scots professionals, Fay wrote long letters of advice and encouragement regarding insurance claims, constitutions and even collectors' cards. In January 1946 he travelled to Glasgow to talk to the men concerned, lending his experience, his calm, sensible know-how, so that within six months the Scottish Union was well under way – the first such organization since the abortive split with the English Union in 1913.

In February 1946, Sammy Crooks indicated that he would soon have to step down as chairman. Fay's right-hand man for so long, friend and confidant, he had secured a job as chief scout at Derby and was clearly unable to devote much more time to the Union. Joe Wilson took over as chairman until the next AGM; Crooks promised to continue attending until then, for already preparations were well under way for the next round of pay negotiations with the League.

Once again, the £12 maximum and £5 minimum were the cornerstones of the demand but, once again, Cuff indicated that such claims were impossible to meet. The Entertainment Tax, though now reduced, was still being used as an excuse. (The reduction, apparently, could not be passed on to the players because clubs were committed to reducing prices to the public as part of a deal they had made with the Government. However, so many clubs would shamefully try and evade this that the League chairman would be called into the Treasury to be roundly told off.)

This time, Cuff indicated, there would be no negotiations. The

Management Committee would recommend a £10 maximum to the clubs (£7.10s in the summer). The Union took little time in rejecting this and restated their original demand.

Two weeks later, the clubs threw out every Union demand and endorsed Cuff's recommendations.

It was clear that such a farcical routine could not continue. The Union Committee Management met in May and expressed its dissatisfaction, not only with the offer, but with the way the League Management Committee had presented the Union's case to the clubs. The wage offer was thus accepted 'under protest' and strike action now seemed inevitable.

But not before the Union had bade farewell to Sammy Crooks. In his letter of resignation, Crooks wrote:

> As you are all aware I am a players' man and shall continue to be no matter what my position in football and shall advise the younger generation that it is essential to join the Players' Union to fight for their rights....

Jimmy Fay told the Management Committee:

> When I look back over the long years I well remember my visit to the Derby FC ground in March 1930, twelve months after taking over the position as secretary.
>
> I knew none of the players and after I had addressed them I was amazed to see what appeared to be a boy come across and converse about the Union and then said, 'Leave it to me, I'll get them to join. Send me all the particulars.'
>
> I feel, gentlemen, that today we are losing one of the staunchest Union members we have ever had and I think that, whilst he is going over to the other side, he will always be with us in spirit....
>
> In conclusion I would like to say, Sammy, do well to the players in your charge, treat them as humans and they will do well for you.... Gentlemen, he can leave the Union knowing he has done his duty for his fellow professionals....

# 21

# *Chairman Guthrie* 1947–51

There could have been no other candidate for chairman on Sammy Crooks's retirement than Jimmy Guthrie. Ever since he had first made contact with Jimmy Fay back in 1939, asking advice as to how to claim a week's back pay for himself and his Portsmouth colleagues, Guthrie had demonstrated a determination and commitment to the cause of the pro-player unsurpassed by anyone else in the Union's chequered history.

Guthrie was a Scot from Luncarty. His father, originally the village blacksmith before becoming the proprietor of a bicycle-shop, died in debt when Jimmy was just thirteen.

The boy progressed through Junior Scottish football and eventually, at the age of seventeen, was signed by Dundee, the club's chairman handing him £100 in an envelope to take home to his mother.

In 1936-7 Guthrie, then twenty-three years old, after deliberately asking for a stiff pay-rise, was transferred to Portsmouth, a team more often than not in the lower half of the First Division. Nevertheless, he succeeded in leading Portsmouth to the FA Cup Final of 1939 where they faced Major Buckley's young high-flying Wolves side – hot favourites after finishing runners-up in the First Division for the second successive season.

The Wolves players were clearly nervous, however, and Guthrie – a tough-tackling wing-half – soon 'sorted out' the skilful Wolves winger McGuire:

> Then the ball went out to young Mr McGuire. I timed the tackle well and he went down hard. I picked him up and muttered, 'Next time you'll finish in the Queen's lap'.... We were not troubled again by McGuire and began to knock the ball around....

Portsmouth went on to win the Cup and Guthrie's lifting of the famous trophy proved to be his last significant moment as a player. Within a few months of the start of the 1939-40 season he was injured in a car crash. His sojourn in hospital, he later claimed, allowed him time to ponder on things and he resolved to enter the Union and battle for change.

His impatience to get to grips with the game's problems (not to mention its rulers) would be both gratifying to and problematic for Jimmy Fay: gratifying because Guthrie undoubtedly took on a great deal of physically demanding work – meeting MPs and lawyers, briefing the press, travelling to clubs to talk to players and directors; problematic because he also generated a great deal of controversy which often made matters unnecessarily difficult, when Fay would be required to pick up the pieces.

They made an unlikely duo: Fay the white-haired, immensely experienced, cautious Lancastrian; Guthrie the restless, sometimes bombastic 'radical' Scot. Just how much control Fay was able to exercise over Guthrie is difficult to say. From the moment Guthrie assumed the chairmanship, the latent possibilities of the position were unleashed. Until then, the chairman had been a man of responsibility without a great deal of influence. Fay, with his decades of experience, his knowledge and above all his permanency, had actually run the Union. Sammy Crooks had been his willing partner but, like Robbie before him, had been essentially an ambassador.

Guthrie saw the chairman's role as more important and crucial than that. He had been elected by the membership and was thus 'head' of the Union. This is not to say that he attempted to downgrade Fay – that would have been impossible not to say inadvisable. But from the very start Guthrie went his own way – a tendency made much easier because he based himself in London and made no secret of the fact that he thought that was where the Union's permanent offices ought to be.

Guthrie placed a great deal of store in 'influential people': he cultivated friendships with MPs such as J P Mallalieu and Ellis Smith, and lawyers like Terence Donovan and Walter Moncton, who would prove to be good friends to the Union.

On one level such lobbying was practical:

> For the price of a round of drinks I got the best legal advice and my friendships meant that when work was required for the Courts we were represented at the lowest possible fees.

But the increased contact with lawyers, MPs and trade union officials had a more serious purpose. Guthrie wanted the Players' Union to become more 'political'. He agreed with Joe Wilson who had criticized the Union set-up as 'weak-kneed' and inadequate, and he was soon to challenge the traditional Players' Union idea that only the secretary should be paid and thus be full-time.

Only in such a way, he felt, could players break out of the closed football world in which they had always been at the mercy of the League and the FA. That was the main struggle: whereas the latter organizations strove mightily to keep the world in general – government, trade unions, the pools, the public, the press – at bay, the Union were determined to win their cooperation.

From late 1946 onwards, therefore, the Union agenda would be set by Jimmy Guthrie. Ideas, reforms, campaigns were unleashed at almost break-neck speed. Never in the history of the Union had so much been attempted in so short a time: wage increases, Provident Fund, Players' Charter, a magazine, joint committees, new contracts, not to mention a complete overhaul of the structure of the Union itself. Guthrie truly caught the spirit of the time; with a Labour Government pushing through a massive programme of economic and social reform, he had a perfect example to guide him.

The danger was that he would move too fast for his Management Committee colleagues – perhaps even the membership at large; that he would lose contact with the realities of the game and thus cut himself adrift. For now, however, everyone seemed prepared to go along for the ride – and an exciting one it proved to be.

The Union, during these post-war years, could draw upon a fund of goodwill, not simply because the game itself was so immensely popular but because the clubs seemed intent on behaving so badly, with such disregard for public opinion.

At times their flouting of agreements – even political directives – bordered on the breathtaking. Their meanness regarding the payment of players (and their ingenuity in breaching both the letter and spirit of agreements) was thrown into stark contrast by their continued, often rude, refusal to accept offers of help from the pools firms.

This, combined with their apparently bottomless purse where transfer fees were concerned, caused widespread bafflement. To many observers, it seemed incredible that clubs could plead collective poverty and cry out for government assistance while at the same time spending tens of thousands on star players.

Not surprisingly, the press during this period appeared keen to support and publicize the players' arguments, and here Jimmy Guthrie's assiduous lobbying and lunchtime Fleet Street briefings could be said to have paid off handsomely.

Indeed, a journalist such as Alan Hoby in the *People* ('The Man Who Knows') could almost have been Guthrie's mouthpiece at times, his outspoken column providing evidence and examples to back up Union claims and campaigns, his criticism of the League scathing if a little melodramatic at times ('I Accuse Football's Führers'.)

Hoby's articles often concentrated on the harsher aspects of professional football and helped underline both Guthrie's and Fay's insistence that their battle was on behalf of the majority of hard-pressed working professionals rather than the men at the very top of the profession:

> Behind the clamour and glamour of the world's greatest game is often a bed-rock of loneliness and fear. Behind the current cascades of cash into the League clubs' bursting tills and Pools promoters' bulging pockets is a seamier side to an entertainment industry which still ranks amongst the poorest paid on the earth....

In November 1946, just after the first Union–League confrontation, Hoby dealt with a problem then widespread in Britain: homelessness. He interviewed Queen's Park Rangers manager Dave Mangnall who revealed the plight of a number of his players: 'Seven of my boys are either separated from their wives and families or have no homes at all.' And he cited the case of Ivor

Powell, a Welsh international who was on the maximum wage of
£10 a week: 'He cannot find a home in London. His wife lives in
Blackpool with her parents while Ivor lodges in a restaurant in
Shepherds Bush. On his salary he has to send about £6 10s home,
feed and clothe himself as well as pay tax with the rest and also
spend nearly £3 every weekend on the rail-fare to Blackpool....'

There were others: Danny Boxshall ('six years in the army and
proud owner of a military medal') who lived in one room with his
wife and family in Harrow; John Barr, ex-POW, Scottish
centre-half reserve with a wife and baby up in Lanark who could
not afford even a pre-fab.

It was easy, then, to point to the hypocrisy of League clubs who
claimed they could not afford to pay men more, yet who were using
new houses as bait for top stars: Jimmy Seed was reported to be
standing (in vain as it turned out) with an estate agent, house keys
and papers in hand, waiting for Tommy Walker of Chelsea to
appear and sign on for Charlton.

However, public anger and a sympathetic press – welcome though
they were – could not alone produce results. The clubs proved
themselves immune to public criticism, convinced that no one
outside soccer could possibly comprehend the complexities and
problems of the game – certainly not the paying public and
particularly not the press.

The Union thus needed powerful allies and in late 1946 it found
one in the unlikely shape of the Ministry of Labour.

The 1946 Annual General meeting of the Union had given the
Management Committee a mandate to go back to the League
regarding the wage settlement of the previous April. Great
dissatisfaction was expressed and impatience voiced at the fact that
the committee had not called for a strike, that it had accepted the
wage deal 'under protest'.

Soundings suggested that there was not a club in the League
whose players would not support action and when the League
Management Committee refused a meeting, the press were
informed that a complete stoppage of football was now the Union's
only alternative.

Just how aware the Union Management Committee was of the
wider political implications of such a decision is unclear. Members
seemed genuinely taken aback, however, when, a few days later,
they were contacted by the Industrial Relations Office of the

Ministry of Labour which had read about the proposed action in the newspapers.

It urged the two sides to get back together again as soon as possible, stressing that under the War Emergency Act – then still in force – a strike was technically illegal. (The Labour Government, desperate to keep production up at a critical period of reconstruction, was doing all it could, with TUC cooperation, to prevent industrial stoppages.)

Nevertheless, if after further talks either side was to ask for arbitration, voluntary or compulsory, and if the Ministry felt that it could not grant such arbitration within twenty-one days, the strike action could commence. Whether they liked it or not, both the Union and the League were now deeply entangled in the intricate web of industrial relations.

The League and Union thus met once more, on 19 September 1946, at the Midland Hotel, but it was clear from the outset that Will Cuff was not amused. Why, he demanded, had the Union called the meeting? The pay bargaining procedure for 1946-7 had been concluded in April and 'he could not see any reason why the clubs should be called together to consider the same requests'.

He suggested the Union come back in March, but Jimmy Guthrie refused. Cuff then repeated that the clubs simply would not negotiate, and suggested the Union go back to its members and consult them again! Guthrie explained that there was no need – the Union Management Committee had a mandate to settle there and then. But it was clear that Cuff was stonewalling, clear that the meeting was a waste of time and clear that he and the League Management Committee were indignant that the Ministry of Labour had been involved at all.

Eventually Guthrie suggested voluntary arbitration, which Cuff contemptuously refused. Guthrie had no alternative, therefore, and informed Cuff that the Union would be seeking compulsory arbitration. The meeting ended abruptly.

The Ministry of Labour thus had until 15 October to intervene but as the days passed it seemed no official action was forthcoming. On 14 October the Union Management Committee met in Manchester and settled on a strike date of 23 October; indeed, the information was just being issued to the press when, with a fine sense of theatrical timing, the phone rang. It was the Relations Officer suggesting that the two sides re-enter negotiations with a Ministry man as 'referee'.

DOHERTY ATTACKS FOOTBALL AS CAREER Page 7

**SOCCER**

BRAY-WAY TRAINING PICTURES AND STORY Centre Pages

Vol. 1, No. 2      January, 1948      Price Sixpence

## *Why Are So Many Footballers Unsettled?*

# PRESS FLAY THE TRANSFER SYSTEM FARCE

*WALKER (Chelsea) looks as if he is booting Aston (Manchester United) in the pants—and enjoying it!— but the camera lied.*

BRITAIN'S National and Provincial Press seems stoking up for a storm to sweep away football's antiquated transfer system. About time, too. For years, sports writers have murmured about this buying and selling footballers, discussed in guarded language its abuses, referred often to its unfairnesses.

In private and in print, many writers have urged the game's legislators to do something or the whole crazy edifice would come tumbling about their ears.

Nothing has been done to show those warnings have been heeded. Now the black storm clouds gather over the heads of football's leaders. "Daily Express" Columnist, Frank Butler, blasts:

"*Stan Matthews, Tom Lawton, Wilf Mannion, Peter Doherty, Bob Langton, Jock Dodds and now Uncle Stan Mortensen and all . . . practically every footballer with a name is, or has been, unsettled since the war.*

"*What does he (Mortensen) mean by saying he is unsettled? Why was Tommy Lawton unsettled? Why are so many footballers unsettled? That is a question for the F.A. and the Football League to look into because the transfer system is becoming a farce . . .*"

Geoffrey Simpson, the "Daily Mail's" Sports Editor, noted for his cool outlook on any vexed sports question, was moved by the Mortensen transfer request to comment:

"*He is the sixth Blackpool player to ask for a transfer this season, but this sort of thing is going on all over the country. It is typical of the unrest among footballers to-day.*"

Anyone makes a grievous mistake who believes the system can remain if ways and means continue to be found of making the "stars" content. Let the "stars" look after themselves (as they seem well able).

The transfer system is rotten chiefly because it is unfair to the other 99 per cent. of professional players who are not graded as "star" class.

**OFFICIAL JOURNAL OF THE FOOTBALL PLAYERS UNION**

On 17 October, at the Ministry offices in London, Jimmy Guthrie, Frank Broome, Bob Stuart and Jimmy Fay sat down opposite the League Management Committee with Mr Stillman, the relations officer, in attendance.

It must have been a chastening experience for Stillman. After three hours of acrimonious argument, he called a halt and asked to talk in private with the Union men. He complained that the discussions could go on for hours; new questions were being raised all the time and it had become far too complicated for him. In fact, he would be able to make no recommendations at all to the Minister.

Guthrie was angry and impatient; time was being wasted and the League was clearly not negotiating in any recognized fashion. However, Stillman managed to persuade both sides to form yet another joint sub-committee to meet as soon as possible to thrash out a basis for a possible settlement.

Two weeks later, at the League's offices in Preston, the two sides faced one another again, Cuff setting the tone of the meeting by announcing that, in his opinion, the whole process was unnecessary especially as the War-Time Emergency Powers Act only applied to industry, not football, and that any arbitration award would be challenged by the League in the courts.

That small pleasantry over with, the two sides proceeded to work out a possible agreement covering all aspects of pay, injury compensation, benefits, minimum wages and shares of transfer-fees. Cuff emphasized that the agreement had to be acceptable both to the League Management Committee *and* the clubs and that a decision would have to wait until at least the end of February.

Three months later, on 24 February, the League clubs met in closed session and, without offering any explanation, proceeded to throw the whole 'agreement' out.

On 25 February Jimmy Fay wrote to the Ministry of Labour to request that the issue go to compulsory arbitration and on 10 March at an extraordinary meeting of Union delegates in Manchester, the Union committee was roundly criticized by delegates for allowing the League constantly to play for time, so much so that almost a whole year had now passed since the dispute had begun.

Strike action was once again set for 21 March but, mercifully, the Ministry of Labour at last decided to refer the whole dispute to the National Arbitration Tribunal under the chairmanship of Lord Terrington.

It took the tribunal just two weeks to come to a decision – and the Union appeared to have been granted most of what it wanted. The claim for a £12 maximum during the playing season (£10 in summer) was granted; and a minimum wage of £7 playing season and £5 summer was secured for all full-time players over the age of twenty, plus August to August agreements. On the question of the transfer system, the tribunal made no recommendations but felt that there was a need for an authoritative joint negotiating committee along the lines of the Whitley Councils operating in other industries: this, it was felt, could deal with transfers and benefits, as well as 'stabilize amicable relations between clubs and players'.

The Union Management Committee was understandably overjoyed – it was a significant, albeit limited, victory although critics were quick to point to its shortcomings. The tribunal had only dealt with full-time players, for example, which left the clubs plenty of scope for manipulation; and, of course, little had changed where the basic contract was concerned – the transfer system remained in place along with the maximum wage.

But for Guthrie and the Management Committee, the award of 1947 was seen as only a beginning. Having got their foot in the door, they now wanted permanent access – and the tribunal's recommendation that a joint negotiating machinery be set up was taken by the Union as an imperative.

Thus, in the teeth of League opposition (but with invaluable support from Stanley Rous at the FA) a committee would eventually be successfully established with a definite set of rules of engagement.

At the same time, the process of establishing some kind of insurance-cum-pension scheme was also set in motion. These twin objectives, plus Guthrie's push to reform the Union itself, would dominate matters for almost the next three years.

The pension idea – which would soon become known as the Provident Fund – had long been a dream of Jimmy Fay's. The Second World War had halted his plans to establish a joint League/Union endowment policy covering all players, which was designed to ensure a professional player could count on a substantial sum of money at the end of his career in order to build a new life.

Fay had seen this idea as complementary to his efforts to set up a training scheme for men approaching the end of their careers, and thus in need of skills for business or a trade.

The philosophy behind all this was simple enough: footballers were taken into the game at a very early age and rarely had time to prepare themselves for the end of their playing career. Football as an industry demanded such total dedication; surely it owed it to its employees to see that they did not suffer, that they were not simply discarded after use.

The haphazard and arbitrary 'benefit' system seemed to Fay an unfair, not to say pernicious influence in the game. It was insecurity on the player's side that led to so much contractual strife. To be dropped from the first team, for instance, meant not just a possible cut in wages and a loss in personal esteem; it also meant a potential lowering of the player's 'value' in market terms. This could pose a threat to his future earnings: his claim to benefit could suffer, and the potential size of any transfer fee that might be paid for him would be reduced, and with it his own possible cut.

A player – particularly one at the top of the profession – tended to put in a swift transfer request if dropped. Time was always short in a player's career, opportunities few and far between.

Fay was certain that if every player was guaranteed a substantial sum at career's end, much of the anxiety that led to such strife would cease.

By early 1949, lengthy negotiations involving various insurance companies had resulted in two rival schemes, one favoured by the League, the other by the Union and the FA.

The Union scheme guaranteed every professional player a lump sum on retirement equivalent to 25 per cent of his gross career earnings; the benefit system would thus cease and the scheme would be back-dated to season 1945-6. It would cost some £350,000 but the Union considered the industry could well afford it. After all, gates were now reaching record levels and clubs were reaping healthy profits. In 1948 alone, Everton made £25,000, Tottenham £20,000, Burnley £19,000 and Manchester City £16,000. Transfer spending was reaching incredible levels: Len Shackleton had just been purchased by Sunderland for £20,000 and Tommy Lawton had gone to Notts County in 1947 for £20,000, while it was estimated that Newcastle United – a Second Division side in 1946 – had wheeled and dealed to the tune of £156,000 over the last two seasons in order to secure promotion.

The League, inevitably, saw things differently. Its scheme would cost almost £130,000, representing a 4 per cent levy on League gates. It would guarantee every player a sum equivalent to 10 per cent of his total career earnings – something like £130 per player. What is more, the scheme would be back-dated only to 1948, it would exclude all non-League professionals and would only pay out when a man reached thirty-five years of age.

Guthrie was particularly angry about the exclusion of non-League men, pointing out that many such players had been forced out of League football by the retain and transfer system, while Jimmy Fay was saddened at the exclusion of so many players who were still in the game just after the war.

Understandably, with two such dissimilar schemes on the table, deadlock was inevitable. In February 1949, joint meetings on the subject were terminated, so acrimonious had they become.

Once again, it had been the League's unwillingness to countenance any changes to its proposals that had led to the impasse. A strike threat brought the Ministry of Labour on to the scene, and on 14 March 1949, at the Ministry of Labour offices under the chairmanship of George Isaacs MP, the three sides – FA, League and Union – gathered to attempt a solution.

In the end, it was Union that gave way, its own broker suggesting that, although imperfect, the scheme was a beginning and better than nothing. And thus the Provident Fund was born and though initially hailed as yet another breakthrough for the Union, it would ultimately be the cause of much controversy and heartache.

Even the celebratory banquet thrown by the Prudential Insurance Company proved to be a source of bitterness for Jimmy Fay. He was prevented from speaking by Fred Howarth, League secretary, who insisted that only chairmen of the organizations concerned address the gathering. As Jimmy Fay told the 1950 Union AGM:

> You can imagine my feelings, gentlemen, after the thought and time
> I had given this project.... I told the League secretary that my name
> should be associated with this scheme for all time....

As it was, just about everybody involved claimed credit for it; Guthrie, Stanley Rous, Arthur Oakley, the League president. But whether it would have proved a true monument to Jimmy Fay is questionable.

Its sights set deliberately low from the very start, the Fund gradually declined in significance over the years, based as it was on the shifting sands of League attendances. To administer it, however, the League headquarters had been compelled to take on another member of staff: such extra expenditure must have caused League secretary Fred Howarth many a sleepless night and only further increased the League's determination to use the Provident Fund as an excuse for keeping wage-levels down in the future.

The wider political fall-out hoped for from the establishment of the Fund was also moderate. Trainers were not included in the scheme and many indicated that they would now withdraw from the Union; there were also many bitter complaints from men whose careers had ended just prior to 1948.

The tortured conception and gestation of the Fund, however, only served to increase Jimmy Guthrie's determination to overhaul the Union's structure. Unless his proposed changes were introduced, he argued, the Union would never be able to push through real, substantial changes and it would always be dictated to by the League and the FA.

He began his drive in earnest in early 1948, but soon ran into stiff resistance. Briefly, Guthrie suggested that there should be three paid Union officials who would not be players, as well as five playing members of the Management Committee. The paid men would be empowered to make decisions.

He also felt that the Union office should be moved to London. Jimmy Fay immediately made it known that when and if the office moved, it ought to return to its roots, to Manchester.

In May 1948, Guthrie was granted regular weekly remuneration of £12 so that he could continue his work in London where he was responsible for looking after the Union's Block Accident Scheme, in addition to keeping up contacts with MPs and lawyers during what was considered to be a crucial period.

In August 1948 the Management Committee extended Guthrie's payment period until the next AGM – a decision that appears to have angered George Swindin, the Arsenal goalkeeper who had joined the Management Committee in October 1947 and who had always opposed the regular payment of Guthrie. Indeed, Swindin was so upset, he threatened to resign.

At the AGM, however, Guthrie's remuneration was confirmed for another year and he made a forceful speech, emphasizing the reasons why he felt the Union should re-organize:

> So long as we have playing members taking a leading part on the
> Management Committee we will have the danger of victimization. It
> is for you to consider whether or not the time has arrived when your
> Union spokesmen should be able to sit around the conference table
> and 'say their piece' without fear of their livelihood being
> endangered....

He pointed to other unions with full-time officials and insisted
that Players' Union men had been victimized:

> Do you think that our present set-up is the best one in view of the
> fight which is yet to come and which may well turn out to be more
> bitter than anything that has gone before?

The Union, he claimed, had achieved nothing up until 1939.
Thus, by implication, much of what had been achieved since then
was due to him.

The 'bitter fight to come' was, of course, the struggle to obtain
the new contract which formed the central feature of Guthrie's
Players' Charter (see page 262).

By the 1949 AGM, with the standing committee more or less
established and the Provident Fund agreed, Guthrie was more than
ever concerned that fundamental changes be wrought. The FA and
the League were composed of men who could devote their energies
full-time to their organizations, while the Union, established on a
part-time basis, was considerably handicapped.

But suspicion of Guthrie's ideas among Management Committee
members persisted. It would not be until 1950 that he would be
allowed money to rent an office in London, while the official office
would remain in Southport. There had always been a deeply held
conviction that those men who ran the Union should be playing
members. Even Charlie Roberts, one of the founder members, had
seen his effort to establish paid officials solidly rebuffed. And the
man who had rebuffed those ideas – Jimmy Fay – remained in
office.

Fay never spoke openly in opposition to Guthrie's plans, other
than to insist that the office must remain in the north, but he was
instrumental in persuading, on more than one occasion, George
Swindin to drop his resignation threat(s) and he quietly and

January, **1948** SOCCER 3

Editor: JOHN BATSON,
Editorial Offices:
41, Kensington Place, London, W.8.

### Editorial

**T**HE Football Association have made a grave error of judgment and shown lack of knowledge of psychology in publishing a " Black List " of 87 professional footballers against whom cautions were recorded during the period August 23-December 13.

No good can come of it. On the other hand, a great deal of harm can be done.

There *are* certain players whose general behaviour is not above reproach. They are so few, however, they could be numbered almost on the fingers of one hand.

*Yet the F.A. in one swoop attaches the stigma of unsporting conduct to 87 men, most of whom got into trouble, because their love for football made them over-keen.*

There is no appeal against a F.A. judgment, although players and clubs are often convinced men are sometimes reported unjustly. This is no attack on the present standard of refereeing. Still, who has not seen free-kicks awarded for fouls to the wrong team?

Public "Black-listing" excellently illustrates "giving a dog a bad name, etc." Does the F.A. *really* believe it will make the real Bad Lad better? Of course, it won't. He will probably become defiant. Not sorry.

*As for the player who believes he was innocent or committed a minor offence when worse offenders got off scot free, who can blame him if he becomes resentful?*

Even if clubs and players do disapprove of the " Black List," they may be influenced when they come up against a man who figures on it. Referees, consciously or subconsciously, may also react against a player, not to mention spectators.

There are the makings of broken careers in every " Black List."

**The F.A. would have displayed better judgement if they had "Black Listed" clubs not giving professionals a square deal with regard to pay and conditions.**

### George Swindin's Column

# FOOTBALL'S BROKEN MEN ASK FOR AID

**F**OOTBALL has more than its fair share of hardship cases. Some were considered at the recent meeting of the Football Players' Union Management Committee in Manchester. Members of our Union as well as the general public should know some of the pitiful details, although I have no intention, of course, of revealing anything which would identify a fellow footballer " down on his luck."

One case concerned a loan a player wanted from the Union to aid him over a difficult period. Injury has not only finished his playing career, but also caused an internal complaint for which he must have an operation before even being able to take up light work.

His income amounts to £3 2s. 6d. a week. Out of that he pays £1 14s. weekly for rent, rates, coal, light, etc. (he is searching for a cheaper house in order to curtail his living costs). Obviously, out of what remains he cannot afford the extra nutrition necessary to maintain his health even in its present poor state.

#### BOMBED OUT

Another case the Union have asked me to investigate concerns a player asking for a small loan with which to start a little business.

**There are eight in the family, which lives in a Nissen hut.**

The man was not injured while playing football. He and his family were bombed out during the war, he himself suffering injuries which left him completely broken in health.

In this case, previous grants have been made by the Football Association, Football League, and the player's old club as well as the Union. The player's wife thinks that the little business they would like to buy would provide an income sufficient to keep the family going, and would give her husband the stimulus necessary to restore him to something like reasonable health.

My job is to visit the family, and the person from whom it is proposed to buy the business. The Union Management Committee will then consider my report, and consider what action is necessary.

#### JUBILEE FUND'S JOB

Union funds are extremely limited. This broken player did, after all, play in those matches whose " gate " money went to swell the Jubilee Fund. I

*GEORGE SWINDIN, Arsenal goalkeeper and a new member of the Football Players' Union Management Committee, has been one of the big reasons for the League leaders' great run of success.*

feel that all hardship cases should be helped by that Fund.

As a Union, we feel very keenly when we hear of old colleagues broken in health and penniless. Invariably, we do our best to help.

But the Union funds, strictly speaking, are not for charity. The Union has a job to do. The fight for better wages and conditions and raising the players' status is costly.

**I suggest that the Jubilee Fund should deal with all cases of hardship. A visiting committee (including, if necessary, members of the Union Management Committee) should be appointed to look into cases on the spot, and to recommend grants.**

There is a huge sum of money available. Who has better claim than men whose playing efforts helped to raise it and who are now in dire need?

diplomatically kept the Management Committee intact when it might well have collapsed under the strain.

Guthrie's claims of victimization and his outspoken attacks on both the League Management Committee and the FA, both in print and in committee, were disliked by men like Swindin and Norman Low. Just as Joe Mercer before them (who was now with Arsenal and no longer a committee member) they saw no mileage in what they considered bombast and insult. It is in this light that the sad tale of the Union magazine – which rose and fell between 1947 and 1950 – must be viewed.

Guthrie had put forward the idea of a Union publication of some kind in mid-1947, announcing that 'a leading sportswriter' had offered to publish a magazine for the Union. The committee was interested, having been impressed by the Scottish Union's own paper-cum-magazine, the *Football and Sports Survey*.

By December 1947 the magazine, entitled *Soccer*, was on the news-stands; edited by John Batson, a sports columnist, and largely financed by him with some help from the Union, it was initially well-received.

Its first issue contained articles by Jimmy Fay, Guthrie and George Swindin, plus goodwill messages from Stanley Rous, Fred Howarth, the FA of Wales and FIFA. It was well supported by Fleet Street (which would produce the bulk of the copy in the succeeding years), in particular by Bernard Joy and Bernard McElwaine, and by managers such as Don Welsh and Dave Mangnall.

Gradually, however, the tone of the monthly magazine changed. After the first three issues, George Swindin ceased to contribute. In fact, Guthrie would be the only Management Committee member to write for it after its first season.

Guthrie used his column, understandably enough, to explain policies and outline ideas but the language that he and, increasingly, the editor began to use seemed calculated to cause the maximum offence both to the League and the FA.

In March 1949, with the League stalling on the question of the establishment of the Provident Fund and the Joint Committee, and with the Union having to approach the Ministry of Labour for help, Guthrie wrote:

> We cannot go on any longer under this football dictatorship. I personally believe that we would fare much better under state

control, with a Minister for Sport, a role which would be well-filled by Sir Stanley Rous, Secretary of the FA, who has progressive ideas and whom we, the players, trust and respect. One thing is certain – we are fed up to the back teeth with the League Dictatorship. We are tired of the humiliations and the planned procrastinations of this body. Professional football today is a stinking racket and the time has come for drastic action.

Editor John Batson went further: 'The Dictatorial League, like any other dictatorship, understands only one thing – force. Right. Let's give them force.'

In August 1949, however, editor Batson wrote an article which even Jimmy Guthrie must have considered 'over the top'. Commenting on a move by the FA to invite a German team to Great Britain, Batson launched into an hysterical diatribe against the Germans that bordered on the pathological: '... personally I think there are millions and millions of good Germans – all tucked up nice and cosy with six-foot-blankets on top ...'

Suggesting that Germans smelt, he continued by describing them as 'a racial stew of cissified bullies and spiritual pimps....'

The question of restoring sporting links with Germany was bound to cause deep pain and understandable anger among people who (like Batson) had lost loved ones in the war, only three years ended.

But Batson's article (which Stanley Rous described as 'sacrilege' and which led to George Swindin throwing bundles of the magazine on to the fire) had been written in a publication carrying the imprint of the Players' Union. And though Guthrie claimed Batson was expressing personal opinions, the Union's image was clearly suffering by association.

From that point on, however, even Guthrie ceased to write signed articles for the magazine. He did not, though, end the disastrous association of the Union with a man clearly suffering from a persecution complex and who continued to pour out criticisms and verbal assaults that were both embarrassing and insulting (describing one report of the Joint Standing Committee of the FA/League and Union as 'a squelchy dollop of high-smelling propaganda ... puerile, amateurish ... fit only for the waste-paper basket').

*Soccer* not only cost the Union many friends and members – it also cost it a lot of money. Editor Batson borrowed £350 in order to continue producing the magazine, but in vain. It folded in March 1950 through declining readership.

In 1953 the Union tracked Batson down and asked for the money back – only to receive an angry reply blaming the Union for ruining both his career and his marriage. Wisely, the Union wrote the loan off as a bad debt.

Although Jimmy Guthrie's energy and reforming zeal had won the Union significant gains in the years since the war, by 1950 his tactics and style were beginning to cause many within the Union to have serious doubts.

The political climate was changing: within a year, the Labour Government would have fallen and the days of crusaders and social revolutions would be replaced by a desire for consolidation.

The Cold War mentality rendered calls for nationalization, closed shops and strikes (plus the abrasive language of confrontation) suspicious; Guthrie's nickname, the 'Ball Game Bulganin', essentially frivolous, nevertheless had the effect of making him look a little out of step, even out of date.

Moreover, his protests in 1951 that he was 'no red' indicated his difficulty. The Players' Union had rarely, if ever, associated itself with party politics or ideology, and Guthrie's drive towards trade-unionism proper during a period when the rest of the country was settling down for a period of cosy prosperity looked increasingly unattractive to members of a profession who, by and large, liked to see themselves as 'upwardly mobile'. From now on, Guthrie would find himself battling against a tide.

# 22
# *Troubled Times* 1951–57

The Joint Committee of the Players' Union, the Football League and the Football Association would prove a constant source of disappointment, frustration and bitterness for Guthrie and his negotiating team. It was clear that the League, in particular, regarded it as a necessary nuisance – certainly not a true negotiating body.

As Guthrie ruefully remarked when assuming the chairmanship of the Joint Committee in July 1951: 'The past two years have been spent in exploration and whilst we have not made the progress expected it has been the means of getting to know each other better.' (Unfortunately for Jimmy Guthrie this was not necessarily to his advantage.)

Ideas would be exchanged, some argument would take place, but the real decisions would be taken, as ever, at the League AGM and then presented, as ever, on a take-it-or-leave-it basis.

Thus at regular intervals in the early 1950s the Union would find it necessary to turn to the Ministry of Labour, register a dispute and embark on a long, expensive legal process. Recommendations would be produced, published and then it would be back to the Joint Committee once more for yet more acrimonious and frustrating 'discussions'.

For instance, the September 1950 meeting of the Joint

# ALL FOOTBALL 2d

Incorporating "Greyhound Outlook & Sports Pictures"

No. 1100 • [Registered as a Newspaper] • • NOVEMBER 29, 1950

## Powell Defends Over-30's
### Page Five

*GUTHRIE alleges he has been subject to a "smear campaign."*

### Political 'witch hunt' looms in Big Football

# 'I'M NO RED,' SAYS UNION CHAIRMAN

## APPEAL TO MONTY

*GUTHRIE asks LORD MONTGOMERY President of Portsmouth F.C. and an honorary Vice-president of the Football Association, "really to investigate the present football system."*

### Hits at 'smear campaign'

#### (ALL FOOTBALL exclusive news)

LATEST move in Big Football's bitter, underground, no-hold-barred battle is a bid to begin a political "witch hunt" with the passing to a high Government official of "information" that Jimmy Guthrie, Chairman of the Football Players' Union, is a Communist.

This crowns what Guthrie describes as a "smear campaign to get me out of the way, and possibly cause a change of Union leadership more to the liking of a certain coterie."

#### "I loathe dictatorship"

He refutes the allegation he is Communist. "I believe a man's politics should be his private affair," he declares. "In this instance and because I loathe Communism and all forms of dictatorships, however, I deny I have ever had anything to do with such a political creed."

He went on: "I stress I detest all dictatorships—and what goes on, in professional football verges on dictatorship.

"In what democratic country can an employee be held by employers after he had served his contracted time and, in fact, be prevented from earning a living if he does not re-engage on any terms offered? Only in Britain, democracy's home, where the Big Football Industry shackles men in what is really slavery."

Guthrie recalled that last year, after questions had been asked in the House of Commons about players' pay and conditions, an undertaking was demanded of the Union not to seek the aid again of Members of Parliament. He refused to give it.

Guthrie pointed out that men of the highest national standing who have strong ideals about liberty, allow their great names to be linked with football in honorary capacities (Football Association honorary vice-presidents include Viscount Alexander, Admiral Sir Robert L. Burnett, Marshall of the R.A.F. Lord Douglas, Field-Marshall Viscount

*Continued on Page* 8

## SCOTS WANT TO KEEP THEIR AIN BAWBEES

NOTICE that to-day's Inter-League match is being played at Ibrox Stadium and not at Hampden Park?

Because Glasgow has already shown 100,000-plus crowds for mid-week quality matches can be accommodated, there has been speculation about why Ibrox has been preferred to the famous Hampden enclosure, which has room for 50,000 more than Rangers' 100,000 capacity.

Ten per cent. is the answer.

An old agreement gave Queen's Park a 20-per-cent. rental for these "big" matches. Nowadays, Inter-League ruling is that not more than 10 per cent. can be paid.

### Good deal for Erin

There is a growing feeling among Scotland football higher-ups that the respective Leagues should each retain the "gate" cash when staging Inter-League matches. Reason may be traced in cash figures for the match with the Irish League. Scotland's "cut" was, perhaps, enough to pay the team's expenses—though the previous season the Irish took £2,800 from Ibrox.

The match with the League of Ireland, in Dublin, resulted in Scotland's share being £400—at Ibrox again, Eire got £2,800.

Even with England's Football League, Scots have not fared much better. At Newcastle in 1947, Scots got £2,800, and last season, at Middlesbrough, their share was £1,700. In 1948, however, the Saxons took £5,000 from Ibrox.

### Crossword next week

ALL FOOTBALL'S recent invitation to readers to state which new features they would like in the paper resulted in widespread demand for a crossword puzzle.

Beginning next week, therefore, ALL FOOTBALL will have its own crossword. It will test your knowledge of football, its laws, personalities, feats and so on.

Other new and interesting features are being planned in response to readers' suggestions.

ALL FOOTBALL'S invitation still stands; write to the Editor about anything you think might improve the paper, and form an even closer link with readers.

## OUCH!

BARLOW, West Bromwich forward, registers anguish when the goalkeeper falls on his legs.

Committee was opened and then closed within minutes, the FA and League protesting that the Union had 'bypassed' them by referring certain issues to the Ministry of Labour. Similar protests followed in 1951 when, once again, the Ministry was called in at the Union's behest, this time to set up a far-reaching enquiry by a committee led by John Forster; and in 1953 yet another appeal for arbitration by the Union followed further League intransigence.

In 1952 and 1953 the Union did manage to obtain wage increases, taking the maximum wage from £12 a week in the playing season and £7.50 in summer to £15 and £12 respectively; but the cost, both financially and in terms of progress towards contractual freedom, was high.

The Forster Committee Report, in fact, was a substantial setback in the battle to achieve the Players' Charter and could be said to have marked the beginning of the slow decline in Guthrie's fortunes.

In April 1951, the Union had presented to the Joint Committee its proposed new agreement, coupled with far-reaching reforms involving the abolition of the maximum wage, the dismantling of the transfer system, legal and Union representation at FA and League disciplinary hearings, increases in international fees, compulsory bonuses, etc.

The League clubs, at a special meeting, threw out all the demands with one or two minor exceptions: in fact, without consulting the Union they actually *altered* the existing contract, reverting to July-to-July signing-on dates rather than August-to-August (which had been granted by the 1947 arbitration award) – thus enabling clubs to save money when men refused to sign on or when they were placed on the transfer list.

The carrot of an increase in the maximum wage was not enough to prevent an angry Union approaching the Ministry of Labour. However, after lengthy consultations, the Forster Report endorsed almost every League argument, from the need for the maximum wage to the essential nature of the retain and transfer system.

It merely recommended that certain obvious anomalies be changed, such as the non-payment of men on the retain and transfer list, legal representation for men appearing before League/FA commissions or enquiries, match bonuses and talent money to be obligatory rather than at the discretion of the club, and increases to be made in international fees – important changes but peripheral to the main thrust of the Players' Union's demands.

For Guthrie the Forster Report was particularly galling as the Minister of Labour who had set it up was none other than his good friend, Walter Moncton QC, now a member of the Conservative Government.

Moncton had told Guthrie back in 1947 that the existing players' contract would be unsustainable in a court of law; yet here he was suggesting that the Forster Committee's recommendations represented real progress for the Union. His reminder that if the Union still had trouble with the League and FA in implementing any of the proposals, it could register yet another dispute, was of little consolation.

But the Forster Report was more than just a personal disappointment to Guthrie. It threatened to undermine the Union in similar fashion to the Kingaby case in 1912.

The lengthy legal submissions, the lawyers' fees, etc. (despite the discounts Guthrie often claimed he won via numerous 'liquid lunches' in Fleet Street pubs) cost the Union some £1500 at a time when subscriptions were starting to fall away. Thus 1952 saw the Union sustain an overall loss on the year for the second time. In fact, the cost of bringing cases to the Ministry of Labour was becoming a constant drain on funds, added to which was the necessity, according to Guthrie, of maintaining an office in London and paying himself to continue the essential lobbying and entertaining.

The question of the financial integrity of the Union was central to Jimmy Fay's philosophy. He could recall the sorry condition into which the Union had descended following the Kingaby case, when finances had been in such a parlous state that the Union had had to be bailed out by the League and thus had almost ceased to be an independent body.

Fay's struggle ever since 1919 had been to build up Union funds so that it could remain independent – and his patient, plodding approach had paid off. Yet now, when money seemed so plentiful in the game and the possibilities so exciting, the Union was facing a financial crisis.

This had serious implications, not least for the ability of the Union to continue to provide crucial items such as accident insurance for members.

Where money was concerned, Guthrie's attitude was simple – it was there to spend. In 1954, after the Union had reported its fourth consecutive loss, Guthrie told the delegates at the AGM: 'We would never have achieved success if the system had not been attacked and if we had not used our accumulated profits. Surely it is better to use capital for the purpose of improving conditions in the profession than to accumulate it and suffer such conditions?'

Unfortunately, due to the League's continued intransigence, the tactic of spending vast sums of money to drag the League into endless arbitration disputes was not reaping much in the way of tangible reward. In fact, Guthrie's grand plans – his vision of transforming the Union into a 'proper' union, with full-time officials, etc., announced with such optimism in 1949 – were gradually collapsing as the financial squeeze took its toll.

In truth, Jimmy Fay had never really believed in the idea. In 1952 – his last AGM as full-time secretary – he told delegates: 'The suggested set-up has not been implemented; the chief reason, I would suggest, is that [the Players' Union] is not an industrial union and also it could not afford the necessary officials for financial reasons.'

The principal casualty of the subsequent financial cutbacks imposed in 1953 was Guthrie's London office, the importance of which to his personal image and that of the Union he led, cannot be over-stated.

He had obtained permission for the office in controversial circumstances. Calling a Management Committee meeting in London (which proved to be inquorate), he simply co-opted three men and pushed through his proposals, overturning an earlier decision to allow him to rent an office at the Union's solicitors for £100 a year and substituting another plan – to rent an office from none other than John Batson, editor of the controversial *Soccer* magazine, for £250!

Jimmy Fay had been unhappy about the meeting's ability to make such a decision (as well as to rubber-stamp Guthrie's pay and expenses) but Guthrie had simply produced a rather ambiguous letter from the Union solicitor and forged ahead.

His actions, whether unconstitutional or not, were highly unpopular, particularly with George Swindin and Billy Elliott, ex-committee members who immediately persuaded their collea-gues at Arsenal and West Brom respectively to withhold their subs, a move followed by a number of other clubs, Everton included.

It was a serious matter for the Union, especially when George

Swindin wrote a letter accusing Fay of underhand if not outright illegal tactics. Guthrie responded with threats of a libel action.

At a special Union meeting with Swindin present, however, Guthrie prevailed; and with an official London base, he was increasingly able to ignore his Management Committee colleagues if he felt the need. With the Law Courts, Fleet Street and Westminster just a taxi-ride away, he could spend his days and nights rubbing shoulders with men and women more to his liking, people who had power: 'top' people.

His attitude to the Union in general is summed up in his book *Soccer Rebel* (Davis/Foster, 1976):

> Most of the action in those vital days was centred on London where I was in constant contact with MPs, solicitors, barristers and insurance brokers, whilst Fay and his two girl typists looked after the day-to-day administration. Most of their time was spent in receiving and acknowledging subscriptions because players had begun to contact me directly instead of going through channels whenever they had a grievance to air....

When Management Committee members had a grievance to air, i.e. to complain about Guthrie's predilection for taxis rather than public transport, or for sending out memos to be typed to expensive agencies rather than doing it himself, one senses in Guthrie's dismissive replies a certain disdain for such 'provincials', little people meddling in affairs they could not possibly understand:

> Oscar Hold [a Management Committee member and Queens Park Rangers representative] was always visiting our London office at odd times and I had to tell him that if he needed information or direction about Union affairs he should telephone for an appointment. As it was, he was taking up unnecessarily the time of the typist and causing a hold-up in essential work.

This approach was to lead him into serious trouble in 1954 – trouble that stemmed directly from his own deliberate flouting of Management Committee wishes and his growing sense of being almost a Union in himself.

One of his responsibilities in London had been to deal with the Union's Block Accident Insurance policy – something Jimmy Fay had been extremely proud of establishing immediately after the war. Men were guaranteed sums of up to £500 in the event of disability leading to retirement. The premium was high but for a number of years the policy continued without trouble.

The problem was that the firm involved made little by way of profit: when there was a large increase in claims, the premium paid by the Union only covered some 25 per cent of that paid out.

By 1950, the amount guaranteed had been reduced to £300 and the premium was eating up over £6000 per annum – clearly a worrying trend which, added to the increasing cost of litigation cum arbitration was eating into the Union's investments.

By 1952-3, therefore, there was a move among members on the committee – especially Frank Walton who was himself an insurance broker – to find a better deal. There had been problems with some players not receiving payments which had led one committee member (the afore-mentioned Oscar Hold) to do some investigating for himself, visiting the insurance company without telling Guthrie, for which he was roundly criticized by the whole committee.

Eventually, the committee decided to place the insurance with another firm – Hammonds – but in August 1953 the firm contacted Jimmy Fay, claiming that Guthrie had informed them that their terms were not good enough and that he had placed the insurance business with someone else.

Confusion reigned for some days until Guthrie was finally tracked down and asked what he was doing. His answer was that he considered the terms that he had obtained (for which there was, however, no evidence on paper) more advantageous to the Union's membership, and that the Management Committee should 'leave well alone'.

Nevertheless, he was instructed to do as the committee had originally told him and was unanimously criticized. After all, men's claims were being held up and even put at risk by the confusion, with two or three different firms now involved.

The situation was made worse by the fact that Hold and Walton were pressing for the London office to be closed because they felt that its retention, not to mention the payment of Guthrie himself, was a waste of money. Thus, personalities were beginning to play as much a part as policies.

With the imminent retirement of Jimmy Fay and the need to find new premises for the Union offices (the old one was over Fay's Southport shop, which he was selling) there was a tug-of-war

**ALL FOOTBALL 2d**

Incorporating "Greyhound Outlook & Sports Pictures"

No. 1122   · · ·  [*Registered as a Newspaper*]  · ; ;  MAY 1, 1951

## 'ANALYST' HITS AUSSIE POOLS

*Cameraman's joy*

Red-headed SAM BARTRAM, Charlton's goalkeeper, cannot help being spectacular—witness this shot of the gallant Sam caught splay-footed as the ball streaked between his legs. Not many beat him that way.

### Union Chairman calling all players

# REFUSE TO RE-SIGN UNTIL DISPUTE IS SETTLED

**Meet Miss Football of 1950-51**

★

**Readers elect Aldershot girl**

THE Management Committee of the Football Players' Union urge members to refuse to re-sign for the 1951-52 season until the present dispute with the employers has been settled by the Ministry of Labour.

I want this message to go out to you through the medium of ALL FOOTBALL in order that the general public, upon whom we depend for our livelihood, will be "in the picture" and know what the trouble is about.

**by JAMES GUTHRIE**
Chairman of the Players' Union

We players have nothing to hide. Whether the employers have, remains to be seen. Let the Government decide between us. We will abide by the decisions of an impartial Tribunal.

After two years of negotiations for a new form of agreement now, at the end of the 1950-51 season, we are no nearer a solution than we have ever been.

We want to be freed from a system of slavery. Like any other worker, we want the right to move or seek new employers after we have served our contracted time.

**HINDERED**

Like any other worker, we want the right to earn as much as we can without being restricted by a maximum wage which limits to £12 a week even the topmost stars.

Every device has been used by the rulers to hinder our efforts to get British justice. High time the football fans knew about what has been going on behind the Big Football scenes.

We professional footballers first put forward one pro-

(Continued on page 2)

*GUTHRIE*

### REPORT THIS AT ONCE

IT is possible during the next weeks (says Guthrie) unfair pressure will be put on some players to induce them to re-sign their contracts against their Union's advice.

Instances of this should be reported at once to Union headquarters.

*MISS JEAN MARGARET JEFFORD*

### Close contest

ALL FOOTBALL readers have elected Miss Jean Margaret Jefford, 107, York-rd., Aldershot, Hampshire, as "Miss Football of 1950-51." The poll for the title was so close that the last post for votes decided the winner.

An early lead was taken by Miss Olga Williams, 47, Rydal-ave., Billingham, County Durham. There was a surge of votes on Friday, however, for Miss Jefford which took her to almost level pegging with the Tees-side

(Continued on page 5)

## We'll meet again in August

● This is the last issue of ALL FOOTBALL for the 1950-51 season. Publication will be resumed in August.

● Many hard-fought battles during the past nine months have resulted in ALL FOOTBALL being recognised as the champion of players' and supporters.

● New ideas will be worked out during the summer to make ALL FOOTBALL even better. Plans now "Top Secret" will make readers anxious not to miss a single issue during 1951-52.

● Warning: the newsprint situation worsens. There will be a rush for ALL FOOTBALL when publication is resumed. Make sure of your copy by giving an order to your newsagent.

● To our readers, the support and inspiration of ALL FOOTBALL in the season now finishing, we wish happy close-season days.

**THE EDITOR.**

*The last issue of* All Football, *successor to* Soccer.

between Guthrie and the rest of the Management Committee as to where the new offices should be – Manchester or London.

Guthrie insisted on London; Fay on Manchester. And Fay won. He moved quickly in early 1953 to secure two rooms in the Corn Exchange Building, Hanging Ditch (the same building in which the Union had had offices before the war), describing them to the rest of the committee as perfect. 'It would be impossible to find offices in London to compete with them.'

Guthrie continued to insist that the committee view premises in London – in Wardour Street and Tottenham Court Road – but they were considered totally unsuitable. Undaunted, in June 1953, Guthrie went so far as to suggest that the Union *buy* an office block in London for £12,000, claiming that by renting some of the rooms they could make a profit. But he had no support on the committee. Indeed, his tactics were almost designed to lose him friends. To pay for the office block he suggested that Cliff Lloyd, then on the point of taking over from Fay as secretary, be appointed part-time, while he, Guthrie, remain the only full-time Union official.

By early 1954, the London office had been closed at last, after much prevarication and ill-feeling, and Guthrie was having to work through Manchester. He was clearly disillusioned by the situation, while personnel changes on the committee had introduced yet more vocal critics of his role and method. However, it was over the vexed question of insurance that matters would come to a head – and Guthrie would be suspended.

Once again, for the 1953-4 season, insurance was placed with Hammonds. Once again, Guthrie could not be contacted to attend the decisive meeting and thus had to be told after the event. Still protesting that he could do better, he was directed to contact the insurers, accept their terms and circulate the membership with the information.

Guthrie did this, but included in the letter his *own* quotation for insurance and asked each member to vote on the one they preferred. Confusion reigned once again with players anxiously ringing the office to demand what was going on. Needless to say, Guthrie was rarely on hand to answer the calls and, with Cliff Lloyd taking a two-week holiday, it was yet more bad publicity for the Union.

Eventually, Guthrie wrote to Hammonds telling them that their offer was unacceptable to the members and that he had been instructed to place the insurance elsewhere. The insurers then contacted Lloyd who assured them Guthrie had no power to do such a thing, and persuaded them to take on the policy again. That settled, the committee turned its attention to Guthrie, this time with serious intent.

An Emergency Meeting of the Management Committee was held on 8 August 1954 at the Charing Cross Hotel, 'for the purpose of considering the chairman's action with regard to matters relating to insurance'.

Criticism of Guthrie, however, ranged much wider to include his loss of office furniture when the London office closed; poorly worded, sometimes inaccurate circulars sent out to the membership; the constant trouble at Joint Committee meetings regarding his forays into print and radio comments which antagonized almost everyone and which were alleged to prevent progress; his lack of accurate record-keeping and documentation, especially regarding his expenses; his inactivity regarding club visits – on and on went the complaints.

Finally he was asked to leave the room and the committee unanimously agreed to suspend him for a fortnight. Guthrie claimed in his autobiography that a delegate conference a week later overturned the committee's decision after hearing a speech from himself. The Union minutes, however, state quite clearly that the delegates backed the committee.

However, the crisis caused by Jimmy Guthrie's fall-out with the Management Committee cannot be laid entirely at his feet. There was clearly some confusion as to exactly what his role was or should be, due no doubt to the ad hoc way in which it had evolved.

Walton suggested that Guthrie would be better advised to concentrate more on the essential work of the Union, less on chasing these 'airy-fairy schemes' of his. And yet, the complete transformation of the legal and financial status of the professional footballer (as embodied in his Players' Charter) was Guthrie's *raison d'être*. If he was not to concentrate on this, then why pay him? The essential work of the Union was surely the business of the secretary. But therein lay another of the Union's problems.

Jimmy Fay had been hankering after retirement ever since the war, but with so much happening there had been neither the time nor the appropriate opportunity to install a successor.

In 1950 he indicated a definite desire to step down (he was now sixty-six and had been serving the Union for almost forty years) and suggested the 1951 AGM as a suitable date. Ray Minshull, the Liverpool player, actually went so far as to put in an application for the job but with the crucial date approaching it was clear no decision would be made, and he left football for a job in accountancy.

In March 1952, Fay announced once again that he was anxious to retire but that he would help out until a successor was appointed. Therefore a pension plan was swiftly agreed and implemented by April of that year.

Yet it was not until April 1953 that Cliff Lloyd was nominated for Fay's post, and although he was installed in June it was not until mid-1954 that he was settled into new offices in Manchester. Thus for at least three years the Union was guided by a 'caretaker' secretary while his successor would work for almost another year as an apprentice alongside him.

Jimmy Fay had never been an authoritarian figure; he preferred to work quietly, by consensus. A modest, moderate man, he was perhaps not best qualified to keep someone like Guthrie in check. Fay had always paid fulsome tributes to Guthrie's energy, commitment and achievements; but when events began to get out of hand, he faded into the background, leaving the Management Committee to shoulder much of the burden of bringing Guthrie into line. That was the committee's job, of course, but a secretary can wield great influence if he wishes, and as part-timers the committee members might have expected more help from Fay.

There was also the question of the Management Committee itself. Its composition had inevitably come to reflect a gradual lack of interest by top players in the Union itself. From the early post-war days, when international stars such as Frank Broome, Joe Mercer, Sammy Crooks, George Swindin and top First Division professionals like Alan Brown of Huddersfield and Elliot of West Brom had been at the heart of Union affairs, the committee had come to consist of men representing clubs in the lower reaches of the League and, increasingly, non-League clubs.

There had also been a worrying tendency to fill gaps on the committee by co-opting men. Danny Winter, Reg Halton, Arthur Banner and Len Stephens had all been invited by Guthrie to make up the number when a committee meeting had been inquorate, and because most committee members were held in London co-opted men inevitably represented London clubs. In fact, by the early 1950s there was hardly a committee member not with a southern club: Cliff Lloyd, though a Cheshireman, had been with Fulham and Bristol Rovers; Parker was with Newport; Oscar Hold was from Queens Park Rangers (though previously with Everton). Only Reg Halton of Chesterfield and Leicester could claim to represent anyone north of Watford – not a healthy situation for a Union with the bulk of its membership playing outside London.

**UNION LEADER**

REG HALTON, who was transferred from Bury to Chesterfield, is a member of the Football Players' Union Management Committee.

Although good committee men all, such an unrepresentative, not to say low-profile committee was suspected of having little influence at Joint Committee meetings (Guthrie's sarcastic comment about Banner holding up a Joint Committee meeting by going round the table collecting the autographs of the famous men present suggests he felt this was the case.)

At the 1953 AGM delegates demanded that the committee be strengthened, that players from non-League clubs should not be allowed to sit on it; the problem was that no one else was anxious to take their places – only one nomination had been received that year.

The committee's lack of 'star' quality was certainly a factor contributing to Guthrie's dismissive attitude towards them, and they were certainly conscious of his low esteem for them. Walton's comments during the delegate meeting that resulted in Guthrie's suspension suggested a reason:

> They had just heard Mr Guthrie give the usual list of post-war achievements of the Union, the main credit for which apparently he feels is due to him. There, in my opinion, lies the whole trouble – he is still living in the immediate post-war period when the big spectacular issues were being fought. Those times have gone but Mr Guthrie seems unable or unwilling to adjust himself to present-day conditions.

Thus, with his secretary poised for retirement, a Management Committee for which he had little respect, and general confusion on everyone's part as to exactly what he ought to be doing, it is little wonder Guthrie tended to set his own agenda and define his own terms of employment.

But perhaps the biggest of all problems during these troubled years was the lack of real commitment on behalf of the mass of the membership, a definite doubt as to the correct way ahead, the exact goals in view.

There had always been a trend among soccer professionals to look for an individual solution to general problems – particularly among those men considered most valuable to the system. Even so-called 'rebels', from Alex James onwards, had rarely if ever turned to the Union to help solve their problems. Instead the tendency had been to escape, trick or cheat the system – never to confront it.

The post-war years had seen familiar paths retrodden: in 1946, once again, the USA had seemed to offer, in the shape of the North American Professional Soccer League, the proverbial crock of gold; a year or two later, Italy had emerged as a financial force in the European game, offering men such as Wilf Mannion and Tom Finney lucrative contracts – failing, until the later 1950s, to attract any big names, but succeeding with lesser men like Paddy Sloan of Arsenal who went to Milan for £10,000, Jordan of Spurs who went to Torino, and Tommy Jones of Everton who went to Roma.

These had at least been legitimate moves. In 1950, however,

came the scandal caused by the Colombian club Bogota reputedly luring England centre-half Neil Franklyn into breaking his contract with Stoke City. It led to his ultimate suspension for a year and indefinite banishment from the England team.

The Colombian experience involved many more top players, of course, than Franklyn – George Mountford, Bobby Flavell, Billy Hogg, Charlie Mitten, Roy Paul and Trevor Ford. Some went so far as to sign contracts; most simply paid visits out of curiosity before hurrying back home, frightened off by the tales of horror recounted by Franklyn ('Maybe it is hard to believe but it took us a couple of weeks to teach them how to cook bacon and eggs and can you imagine an Englishman without his bacon and eggs? Every time we asked for soup we were brought porridge').

Yet although these and other headline stories concerning players unhappy with their clubs were clearly signs of a system under stress, the men involved appeared either uncertain as to what the issues really were or what they themselves should actually *do*.

Neil Franklyn concluded his autobiography, *Soccer at Home and Abroad*, by opining: 'I do not think that any player has a legitimate grievance over money,' and went on to say that he was against freedom of contract, against players sharing in transfer fees and against the abolition of the maximum wage!

Trevor Ford (a man regularly at odds with his clubs), on the other hand, was adamant: the Bogota fiasco was a shame, he felt, because, if it had succeeded, 'the League bosses would be forced to plug the leak in the only fair way possible – by offering the players better terms'. Yet Ford concluded his book thus: 'I have always fought my own battles in soccer. I have never asked the Union to help me. And I never intend to.' (Ford, however, had a personal grudge against Jimmy Guthrie. The latter had publicly rebuked him for refusing to play out of position at Cardiff. Ford commented: 'The insignia of the Players' Union shows two hands clasped in friendship with a soccer ball in the background. To me, it is the most ironic insignia of all the trade unions in the country.')

Even Len Shackleton, the celebrated outspoken 'rebel' whose biography, *Clown Prince of Soccer*, created such a stir – not least because it included an early chapter describing the footballer's contract as an 'evil document', outlining in admirable detail arguments against the maximum wage, the restrictions on players' lives, the transfer system, etc. – appeared to feel the Union, while 'working on the right lines', could achieve nothing until 'the staid gentry of Preston and Lancaster Gate are superseded by younger, more realistically minded men'.

Thus, if the so-called rebels could not see their way to supporting the Union unambiguously in its drive for total freedom, there was little chance that the majority of ordinary professionals would feel confident enough to do so. Particularly when Billy Wright, the most famous player in Great Britain – Footballer of the Year in 1952, record-breaking England cap-holder and the apple of the FA's eye – could write in his best-selling autobiography of 1953, after ridiculing the claim that players were poorly paid: 'Let's hear a little more about what players are prepared to put into the game and less about what they are prepared to take out of it.'

Had the membership been as determined and as clear-sighted – even as radical – as Guthrie, perhaps more might have been achieved.

As it was, his exasperation and impatience at the lack of progress and urgency led him into committing foolish, ill-judged actions and outbursts. As he said himself: 'Perhaps I was over-dedicated.'

# 23

# *The Fall of Guthrie* 1957

Cliff Lloyd confessed to feeling 'a bit disappointed' with the friction that existed on the Management Committee when he first took his place in April 1950, an understatement typical of the man who during the course of the next thirty years would play a crucial, not to say seminal, role in transforming the Union into the influential body it was to become.

Lacking the rhetorical power of a Guthrie, the charisma of a Joe Mercer, Lloyd made little impact in the early years. His was a trying apprenticeship: as assistant to Jimmy Fay in the early 1950s, he could only watch with dismay as Guthrie and the Management Committee argued and wrangled while Fay shook his white-haired head in despair.

Yet as he gradually took up the reins and began to grapple with the administrative and financial mess into which the Union was rapidly descending, Lloyd demonstrated that he was no mere cipher. The apparently inoffensive, genial exterior concealed a determinedly realistic, not to say unforgiving individual.

He was a football man through and through: 'Nothing else really interested me,' he confessed, although the hills and valleys around Helsby in Cheshire where he was born and to which he always returned undoubtedly came a close second.

Born in November 1916, the fourth of six sons, his childhood was happy if predictably hard: his father was a keen footballer, a useful fullback for Flint Town, his footballing skills earning him employment at BICC Cables. Cliff was to follow in his footsteps. Thus football was a part of Lloyd's heritage and pedigree.

Signed as an amateur by Liverpool, the Anfield club showed little subsequent interest in him until Bolton Wanderers – who had already given his elder brother a trial – expressed a desire to sign him professionally. This provoked Liverpool into giving Cliff a trial. He impressed and was signed on as a full professional in 1937.

At Liverpool he rubbed shoulders with Willie Fagan, 'Tiny' Bradshaw, Billy Liddell, Tommy Cooper and Matt Busby – but war broke out before Cliff was able to make the breakthrough into the Liverpool First team.

At the end of war he would be approaching twenty-nine years of age, with the best years of his football career taken from him.

Typically, however, he dwells only on the good fortune during those twilight years. Like many ex-professionals, he was soon in the Army Physical Training Corps and, stationed at Queen Mary's Hospital, Sidcup, he was perfectly placed to guest for London clubs. He turned out for Brentford, but principally for Fulham. He was selected for numerous representative matches, amongst them a Combined Services match at Wembley in front of 70,000 spectators, playing alongside Joe Mercer and Cliff Bastin. 'Things,' he said, 'were going so well.'

And they continued to do so after the war. He spent five happy years with Fulham along with Joe Bacuzzi, Pat Beasley and Len Quested; he coached in Norway (and could have had the job of coaching the national side had not Fulham needed him back at Craven Cottage); and finally he went to Bristol Rovers for a season. By then he was having fitness problems. Having broken his right leg playing for Fulham in a Cup match, he had, by his own admission, hurried back into action too soon. A series of niggling injuries convinced him that it was time to hang up his boots and take his benefit.

By then he was on the Management Committee, having taken on the job as delegate and collector for Fulham because no one else wanted to do it. His politics were always 'middle of the road' and though he attended every AGM and was convinced that the players needed a strong organization, he never pushed himself forward, never admitted to having ambitions where Union work was concerned.

His close friend George Wardle (Chelsea and QPR) proposed him for the Management Committee in 1950 but his nomination for secretary in April 1953 came 'as a bolt out of the blue ... no one was more shocked and surprised than me,' he admitted.

Danny Winter (another Chelsea man) had simply said, 'In my view there's only one man for the job and that's Cliff....' There were no competitors; the job was his for the asking.

Lloyd was the quintessential player's man. His career had been solid and respectable with a touch of wartime glamour to suggest what might have been. He was a talented coach with experience abroad; and he had suffered the anguish of severe injury, the dread of every professional footballer. Thus, he understood the profession – its unique blend of heartbreak and exhilaration – and those who approached him could feel confident not only that he appreciated their problem but that he could do something about it.

He was very much a 'hands-on' administrator, personally involved in everything, travelling to hearings, to meetings, to clubs up and down the country, day after day (but always returning every night to his home in Helsby). He was a 'worrier', a man who had no choice but to expend his nervous energy on each and every case, large or small. It is no wonder that he took only a couple of days' holiday in the quarter of a decade when he was in charge of the Union. (Those two weeks in mid-1954 when he had left the office to Jimmy Guthrie's tender mercies had been a salutary warning!)

And for the next couple of years – from 1954 to the beginning of 1957 – it would be Jimmy Guthrie who would present most of the problems, who would stand in the way of the essential financial and administrative shake-up Lloyd saw as essential if the Union was to move forward with any confidence.

On the face of it, progress had come to a halt where the grand reforms were concerned, ironically, just at the moment when Jimmy Guthrie was reaching his personal apogee – the entry of the Players' Union into the ranks of the TUC and his famous Blackpool 'slaves' speech.

When one thinks back to 1909 and the outrage caused by the Players' Union's decision to affiliate to the GFTU, the decision to join the TUC in 1955 would seem to have been greeted relatively calmly – although both the FA and the League representatives at the Joint Negotiating Committee 'expressed concern' at the Union's action, and appeared affronted that they had not been consulted first. (A trifle rich on the League's part as in the very same year it had taken a unilateral decision to cut the players' entitlement under the Provident Scheme from 10 to 9 per cent – and would cut it again over the next couple of years to 7.5 per cent.)

The publicity gained by Guthrie's speech, though extensive, appears to have caused some confusion in the professional ranks. While acknowledging the truth of what Guthrie had to say, there was a definite undercurrent of resentment that they, professional footballers, should be presented in such a sorry light.

Guthrie was quick to spot the reaction: 'The press headlines all carried the word "slavery", a designation that was not appreciated by all of my colleagues.'

Jimmy Fay, now retired, was moved to pen an article that appeared to wish to temper some of Guthrie's fire: 'No, the players are not so badly off,' was the headline beneath which Fay explained that whether a player could be called a 'soccer slave' depended on so many things – ability, club and opportunity. He went on, 'There's no suggestion that lesser known players should be given bank-managers' salaries and coddled as if they were too delicate to handle.' The Union was merely striving further to improve the general status of football as a profession.

Even Guthrie's celebrated speech reflected some of the contradictions inherent in such a diverse body of men appealing to such a solidly industrial organization for help. His description of the iniquities of the transfer system was skilful and could only result in indignation. Yet when he compared the relative fortunes of a top British player (Jackie Sewell) with those of a British player bought by an Italian club (Eddie Firmani), the assembled representatives of miners, factory-workers, railwaymen and unskilled labourers must have felt distinctly puzzled.

Sewell, Guthrie explained, though sold for £35,000 would receive just £10 as a signing-on fee, plus up to £15 a week in wages; Firmani, sold for the same amount, received a lump sum of £5000 plus £100 a week, a luxury flat plus his freedom to sign for someone else after two years. From 'slave' to 'capitalist' in one bound? Is that what the TUC was being asked to deliver?

No use explaining, as Guthrie did, that only 20 per cent of players received the maximum wage; that the average wage of a professional player was £8 a week, £2 less than the average industrial wage – it was the 'star' who dominated the headlines and shaped the popular perceptions.

And although Guthrie's speech was undoubtedly a fine one, topped and tailed by headline-catching phrases ('I stand here as a representative of the last bonded men in Britain.... We have had enough of Human Bondage – we seek your assistance to unfetter the chains and set us free!'), yet still it seemed oddly inappropriate.

Indeed, just how uncomfortable many players were with the TUC connection was demonstrated a year later over the related question of the closed shop.

Guthrie had argued for this for some years – on both practical and ideological grounds. When shown a Union balance sheet with its regular losses he would retort that the surest route to solvency was to have 100 per cent membership.

Players' Union membership was not automatic: there was no 'contracting-in' system and with a closed shop many practical problems would be solved. No need to chase collectors, no need to travel the length and breadth of the country exhorting men to part with their shillings – work traditionally shouldered by the chairman. Nor was it ever pleasant work; Guthrie was banned from many grounds, threatened at others, notably Manchester City where he had been told that he would be 'run out of the game'.

But Guthrie was adamant that a closed shop should be instituted for reasons of principle. All the struggles – for the Provident Fund, for the wage increases, for the improvements in players' contracts – were fought on behalf of the *whole* membership. Yet a substantial proportion paid no subs and thus contributed nothing to the cause. As Guthrie commented a little optimistically, 'This would not be tolerated in any other union, where a union card must be produced before the individual is allowed to start work.'

The problem with a closed shop was that it could only work efficiently with the employer's consent – clearly not forthcoming. And suggestions that Unionists should not play with or against non-Unionists as a way of pressurizing men to join posed obvious difficulties for a team competition. Guthrie, however, at the 1954 AGM, was adamant:

> In your own interests you must take drastic action against non-members as they are undermining your livelihood ... a united effort can defeat non-Union members who are in the minority.

Inevitably the question divided the Management Committee. Jimmy Fay had always said how good it would be to have 100 per cent membership but had baulked at the idea of compulsion. People, footballers in particular, had to be persuaded.

In 1955, however, in the wake of Guthrie's Blackpool speech and the prospect of the TUC taking up the case of the players in respect of the Players' Charter, an additional rule was proposed by Jimmy Hill as follows:

> No member of the Union shall be allowed to play with or against professional players who are registered with the Football League who are not members of the Union.

There was some heated debate among AGM delegates concerning this resolution, with Reagan of Norwich declaring that the Canaries were against a closed shop in principle. As a delaying tactic, an amendment was drafted setting a date for the implementation of the rule (30 June 1956), and this was adopted. However, it remained unclear as to whether the rule itself had been passed.

The following April, with the Union and the League locked in crucial negotiations regarding extra payments for floodlit matches and TV appearances, the League – president Arthur Oakley in particular – suddenly announced that it had discovered (via an interview in a Scottish newspapers with Guthrie) that it was Union policy not to play against non-Unionists. 'If this was so, there did not seem to be any point in continuing the discussion.'

---

**Do you know of a Non- Unionist employed in the Football League?**

**– IF SO, SEEK HIM OUT –**

**He should be inside the Association Football Players' & Trainers' Union**

---

The Union representatives (J Campbell, Walton and Guthrie) plus Cliff Lloyd appeared confused. Denying that Guthrie had said any such thing, they claimed that there had been a rule in existence for some five years relating to the closed shop, but that it had never been approved by the Friendly Societies Registrar. They declared, however, that under no circumstances would any Union member refuse to play with non-Unionists. They had simply been trying to encourage men to join.

Sensing that they had the Union in a quandary, the League representatives pressed home their advantage. No further talks could take place until the Union Management Committee had consulted its members and had the rule rescinded. The 'friendly atmosphere' in which the negotiations had hitherto continued could not be resumed until the matter had been settled. The Union committee put up no fight; it simply did as it was told.

Clubs were circulated with a recommendation that the 'rule' be rescinded so that negotiations could continue. Twenty-six clubs replied: twenty were against the rule. This was duly reported to the League Management Committee in May and negotiations continued.

In July, however, Cliff Lloyd disclosed that there had, in fact, been no rule at all! There had only been Hill's proposal at the last AGM which had not as yet been put to a vote.

Leaving aside the Union's strange confusion as to its own policy, it had been another miscalculation on Guthrie's part in boasting to a Scottish reporter that the closed shop had been implemented when nothing of the kind had occurred.

But the swiftness with which the idea had been dropped by the membership and the clear unpopularity of the idea at the grass-roots suggested that the proposed link-up with the TUC was viewed with mixed feelings by professional players. No wonder Jimmy Guthrie could complain at the 1955 AGM that the Union was no longer a militant one.

Nevertheless, members were by no means quiescent and, given a firm clear lead they were quite prepared to take action if need be. Proof of this came in March 1956 when a decision was taken by the Management Committee not to participate in televised or floodlit games unless the League negotiated in a constructive manner.

The confrontation had been brewing for some time, the League having clearly decided that the Joint Negotiating Committee was becoming a bore.

Its attitude appeared to be that once an issue had been decided upon there was no point in raising it again. By 1955, the question of the maximum wage and the players' contract were issues the League considered closed.

In February 1955, when the transfer system had been raised by the Union, Arthur Drewry of the FA, then chairing the JNC, had declared the idea of dividing the fee as suggested by the Arbitration Report of 1952 'was just nonsense', and he closed the discussion.

In April 1955, Fred Howarth, League Secretary, wrote to Lloyd: 'With regard to the agenda, I am to inform you that the League has decided to take no part in any discussion with regard to item 5, namely, Contract of Service, if the points to be raised are such as have already been dealt with.'

Upon receiving the Union's suggestions for discussion, he wrote back to say that many of the items had been discussed, 'in some cases more than once. I am therefore to ask you that, in regard to these items, you set out any NEW matters which you wish to be discussed....'

Subsequently, if the Union raised such issues for discussion, Drewry as chairman simply ruled the discussion closed. And there were further 'spoiling' tactics: the League calling meetings with the FA without informing the Union, changing the times of meetings to inconvenience players' representatives and refusing point blank to change them back again.

By early 1956, relations were further soured when the League once again reduced the Provident Fund entitlement without consulting anyone.

The League was clearly unhappy about the suggestion that the TUC chairman, Ted Hill, speak to the FA and the League regarding the players' contract of employment. It was also suspicious, not to say jealous, of the apparent agreement between the Union and the FA regarding a new Insurance Scheme. Thus it came as no surprise when the League announced in February that it would take no further part in Joint Committee meetings.

The Union response was immediate: on 5 March a circular was sent out to all members announcing a ban on members' participation in floodlit or televised matches. Exasperation was expressed in the circular regarding the lack of progress on almost all fronts and the threat of stronger action to come was made clear: 'The committee has resisted strong pressure to take more drastic action in the interests of the game and its public.'

In the face of such determined action, the League wasted no time in climbing down. Quite simply, there was too much at stake. Floodlit matches, a rarity in the early 1950s, had now become an important factor in many a club's financial balance sheet. As League gates in general declined, attractive mid-week fixtures against exotic opposition were reaping healthy profits. Where TV was concerned, the potential – especially with the advent of commercial TV in 1954 – was enormous. Clearly, this was no time for a showdown.

Just one week after the imposition of the ban, the League called a truce. On 12 March both Management Committees were in London holding separate emergency meetings, when the ritual eleventh-hour telephone call was made by Howarth proposing a deal. Howarth wanted an immediate withdrawal of the ban and a statement by the Union that it accepted the principles of the retain and transfer system plus the maximum wage. If it did that, the League would talk about money.

Lloyd replied that they wanted a proper negotiating machinery set up, as well as negotiations on the Arbitration Report of 1952 as a whole. The Union then sat tight.

Half an hour later, as they were preparing to leave their hotel room, the League phoned again, offering to meet the Union reps in person. The Union agreed; negotiations resumed, and the ban was called off.

Though it was hailed at the time as a triumph for the Union, it would be difficult to claim as much with the benefit of hindsight. After five meetings during the second half of 1956, the eventual results were anything but earth-shattering – particularly when one considers what the Union had conceded.

Match fees for 'additional matches' were set at a maximum of £3 and £2 minimum; match bonuses in general were increased to £3 for a win; the Provident Fund was increased from 7.5 to 8 per cent. On TV fees, negotiations were to continue. Where the maximum wage was concerned, an increase was conceded but delayed.

Howarth declared that it was 'the start of a new relationship between the League and the Union'. Guthrie considered it another 'sell-out' – though he claimed that even these small concessions had been wrung from the League because of the support expressed for the players by the TUC. The 'Doubting Thomases', as he called his Management Committee colleagues had now seen the value of wider trade-union contacts. Unfortunately for Guthrie, the Management Committee was increasingly doubtful as to the wisdom of maintaining contact with *him*.

Since his suspension and censure in 1954, matters had hardly improved. If the Management Committee had hoped that the closure of the London office might have curbed his tendency to go it alone, they were disappointed. If anything, his personal expenses increased – indeed, at the 1955 AGM, Boyle of Rochdale calculated that Guthrie was costing the Union some £1204.10s per annum in wages and expenses. Cliff Lloyd as secretary was only receiving £520 per annum – and Lloyd himself chipped in to point out that the meetings called to deal with Guthrie's suspension had cost £550.

In Management Committee meetings, Guthrie was increasingly isolated, supported only by Jimmy Hill. For instance, in January 1956 Guthrie had put in claims for £74 expenses covering October through to the middle of January, with no receipts to back them up.

It was decided, therefore, not to pay him the money and to restrict him to £2 a week expenses. When Jimmy Hill tried to have the £2 back-dated to October, no one would second the motion, despite an appeal by Guthrie to Arthur Banner.

Guthrie was also finding himself edged out of crucial decisions. The negotiations regarding the new Joint Insurance Policy (whereby the FA put in some £4000 from TV fees towards the premium) were carried out between Cliff Lloyd, Stanley Rous and Jimmy Hill. Guthrie at first complained that Rous was acting unconstitutionally in arranging 'secret' meetings with the Union, but Lloyd defended himself by pointing out that there had been nothing underhand about the meetings, that Guthrie had known all about them.

Guthrie then turned to the League without consulting the committee and suggested that it contribute £2000 to a scheme of his own – an action for which he was once again roundly criticized by the Management Committee.

Lloyd appeared to be building a good relationship with Rous – much to the irritation of the League – and Guthrie's suspicions and angry letters clearly jeopardized such bridge-building. A parting of the ways thus looked increasingly imminent, but it was Guthrie who finally set the tumbrels in motion, and once again it would be insurance that would prove his undoing.

In November, complaints regarding the Management Com-

## ASSOCIATION FOOTBALL PLAYERS' & TRAINERS' UNION

# BULLETIN

*Registered Office:*
504-6-8 Corn Exchange Buildings,
Manchester 4, Lancs.
Telephone : Blackfriars 7554

*Chairman's Address:*
12 Westbourne Road,
Croydon, Surrey
Telephone : Addiscome 3514

*Management Committee:*
J. GUTHRIE (Chairman)

C. LLOYD (Secretary)    O. HOLD    G. WARDLE    F. WALTON
A. BANNER               G. FOX     J. HILL      J. CAMPBELL

No. 1                        VOLUME 2                    September, 1956

## Union Charter

1. **A Standing Joint Committee for all employed in Association Football.**

2. **A Provident Fund for all employed in Association Football.**

3. **A New Form of Agreement for all employed in Association Football.**

4. **A Coaching, Physical Training and Educational Scheme for the purpose of employing ex-members full time.**

5. **A training Scheme for Referees for the purpose of employing ex-members full time.**

6. **Allocation of Cup Final Tickets.**

7. **Link up or closer contact with Football Supporters' Clubs.**

8. **World Federation of Association Football Players.**

9. **Accident Insurance Scheme for all employed in Association Football.**

10. **Television Match Fees for all employed in Association Football.**

11. **Fees for all Matches other than the normal cup programme for all employed in Association Football.**

1

mittee's handling of a number of issues were voiced by Ken Armstrong, delegate from Chelsea. Chelsea members in general were said to want the whole committee to resign to be replaced by men who were with full League clubs. Specific items were referred to: the failure to secure fees for TV appearances; the failure to secure tax-free benefits; the failure to organize a proper insurance scheme. This last seemed particularly odd in view of the fact that the new FA/Union scheme had been signed in October and was considered by the Management Committee to be a major achievement.

Guthrie, as the man supposed to be responsible for all insurance matters, was told to write to the Chelsea members and explain exactly what the new scheme entailed – although even then there was some suspicion that Guthrie was keen on an insurance scheme devised by Armstrong himself, who was an insurance broker. (In fact, Armstrong's scheme had been considered by the FA and the Union earlier in the year and rejected.)

At the same time as the Chelsea protests had arisen, there came complaints from Tottenham Hotspur, from delegate Tony Marchi who appeared to be of the opinion that Guthrie was not receiving sufficient support from the committee. Even Cliff Lloyd was mentioned as being 'opposed' to Guthrie.

Although no one said as much, it looked as though Guthrie was attempting some kind of coup. At the very least he was undermining his own committee's authority and even appeared to be misrepresenting official Union policy.

By January, with the AGM about to take place, swift decisive action had clearly been planned. If Guthrie had been attempting to remove the Management Committee by calling into question its credentials, then he had made a fundamental error.

First, the letters he had been asked to write were produced at a Management Committee meeting held just prior to the commencement of the AGM proper.

The letters were criticized, not just because they were inaccurate, but because they contained 'many grammatical errors'.

Then the Union accountant was ushered in. He stated that 'there are several points regarding the legality of the position of several members of the committee of management and the chairman'.

Only signed members of clubs could be members of the Union, the committee had to be elected from amongst them, and the chairman had to be a member of the committee. Thus, a number of committee members – Frank Walton, for instance – were disqualified.

In the case of the chairman, the situation was worse. Guthrie had ceased paying his subs from the moment his playing days had ended. The moment of truth had arrived. According to Guthrie, Walton simply stated that as Guthrie was no longer a member of the Union he could no longer hold a position in the organization. As from that moment, the chair was vacant:

> I was flabbergasted, breathless and the other committeemen – Jimmy Hill, Oscar Hold, Arthur Banner and Secretary Cliff Lloyd sat like ventriloquists' dolls saying not a word....

Guthrie insisted, however, that he be allowed to open the AGM, which he did, and immediately announced that the members of the present Management Committee, including himself, were not eligible to serve and that the delegates must decide whether or not to elect a new committee there and then.

It was decided to let the committee continue – but without Guthrie. He was not a member of the Union; he could not serve it. With that, Jimmy Guthrie left the hall; Jimmy Hill took over the chair.

Interviewed immediately afterwards, Guthrie appeared shocked and subdued. 'I did not expect this to happen after all this time. But it is one of those things – you can't have the luck of the draw all the time.' Asked whether he thought his sacking was pre-arranged, he replied, 'I don't think so. This is what the members wanted. That is all there is to it.' He had no grudges, he insisted, though he cut a sorry figure, 'almost in tears as he stood alone in the meeting-room while the delegates hurried to catch trains'.

It was not long before he was hitting back, however, declaring that he had been the victim of, among other things, a whispering campaign embracing the Union committee 'as well as the top boys of the Football League and the FA'. Chief target for abuse was Frank Walton, whom he accused of trying to get him replaced. But ultimately, he blamed himself for not insisting on a legal arrangement granting himself tenure.

And though he was missing the main point (that it had been his personal style and tactics that had led to his dismissal) he was closer to the truth than perhaps he knew.

During the next few months, Guthrie took legal advice as to his true position in relation to the Union: whether he *could* be sacked and whether he was entitled to some financial settlement.

It emerged that, strictly speaking, he still was a member of the Union but that the payment of a chairman was not provided for in Union rules. The Union might pay individuals to carry out specific tasks but the chair was an honorary position. There was a suggestion in the wake of Guthrie's departure that the Union recruit a paid organizer and that Guthrie would be in the running for such a job. But he quickly ruled that out:

> The job would have made me nothing more than a messenger-boy. I can imagine the procedure for Guthrie, paid organizer – 'Oh, Jimmy, wait outside while we talk business with the League, will you?' I will never take such a job with the Union.

Guthrie had always avoided being included in the 'staff' pension scheme, probably because he sensed that someone like Walton was trying to pin him down, trying to establish exactly what his relationship with the Management Committee should be.

But Guthrie wanted to run the Union like a union boss. He would not or could not compromise, and although the Union was heavily criticized for having 'ditched' Guthrie, it was really only trying, albeit clumsily, to untangle a situation that had become intolerable. As Cliff Lloyd commented much later, 'Jimmy was a fool to himself and only had himself to blame.'

Guthrie remained on the football scene for many more years as a columnist with the *Sunday People* and he continued to lead the Saturday night choir of expatriate Scots at such celebrated Fleet Street watering-holes as the Cheddar Cheese and the Clachan.

Few people ever had a bad word for Guthrie; all admired his undoubted dedication to the players' cause and, for those who knew him well, his personal kindness – particularly to the many young players arriving in London from Scotland in need of advice and a helping hand, just as he had once been.

But his departure from the Union shocked almost everyone – even those who had helped to engineer it. As the *Daily Herald* columnist Steve Richards wrote: 'The Players' Union ... without big, bold blustering Jimmy Guthrie. Unbelievable!'

# 24

# *Enter Jimmy Hill* 1957–61

The departure of Jimmy Guthrie might well have hung like a cloud over the Players' Union; fortunately, events moved so rapidly in the football world there was little time for reflection.

A few weeks before Guthrie left, Fred Howarth, *éminence grise* of the League, had also been eased out to make way for Alan Hardaker – a fresh face at last and though no more sympathetic to the Union, at least aware of the changes occurring in the football world.

In July 1957, Joe Richards replaced the ageing Oakley as League president. Clearly the League seemed ready to embark on some long overdue modernization.

Closer to home, in March 1957, Jimmy Fay died; after fifty years of struggling for the Players' Union, his long contemplated retirement had proved all too short. Sadly, by the time his death was announced to members at the 1958 AGM, the Munich air crash had occurred, an event of such significance in the football world that Fay's passing was, perhaps understandably, overshadowed.

So too was the death, at the age of eighty-three, of Billy Meredith, who had been ill and virtually destitute for some time. Billy had always been loyal to the Union he had helped to build and thankfully the Union never deserted him. Indeed, it had been helping him financially ever since the war and in 1956 had written off a substantial outstanding loan to him.

Cliff Lloyd visited Meredith a few weeks before he died and saw the great Welshman's unique collection of medals heaped in a box under the bed. (They would later end up in a pawn-broker's.) Lloyd was now the Union's elder statesman; and a great deal rested on his shoulders. Fortunately, a group of men were gathering about him who would provide crucial, often inspired, support over the next few turbulent years.

The most significant addition to the Union's ranks – not, in fact, a member at all – was a Manchester solicitor, George Davies. Invited to give advice during the final days of Jimmy Guthrie, he would remain to serve the Union for the next thirty years or more.

Davies and Lloyd were ultimately to form as close a working relationship as Jimmy Fay and Thomas Hinchcliffe had done in the inter-war years, because Davies shared Hinchcliffe's radical zeal for human rights and thus the players' battle for freedom. In addition to his official function, he was Lloyd's confidant, strategist and morale booster all in one – a source of reassurance and intellectual strength who would play an important part in winning the many legal and political battles ahead.

Within weeks of the 1957 AGM, the Management Committee confirmed Jimmy Hill as their new chairman – unpaid, it was emphasized. He was to prove the perfect choice: young, enthusiastic and not a little ambitious.

Hill had been proposed by Frank Walton who ironically, had previously held him largely responsible for keeping Guthrie in office on a number of occasions. Indeed, Walton had insisted on Hill's recounting Guthrie's various misdemeanors at the fateful AGM, suggesting perhaps that he shoulder some of the blame for the trouble Guthrie had caused. Hill later claimed that he had backed Guthrie simply because to have attacked him would have given ammunition to the Union's enemies.

Walton himself soon stepped down from the committee to become a club manager at Southend. His departure signalled that the Management Committee had virtually been transformed.

Now serving were Harry Hough of Bradford (who had stood for the chairmanship against Hill); Jack Campbell of Blackburn Rovers; Ian Dargie of Brentford, Tony Ingham of Queen's Park Rangers, Bill Roost of Bristol Rovers, Tommy Cummings of Burnley and Royston Wood of Leeds.

Quite suddenly, the dislocations and dissensions of the Guthrie years seemed like a bad dream, helped by the fact that men like Campbell, Hough, Ingham and Roost were of the same generation as Lloyd. Furthermore, having shared the same experiences, they could see things from the same point of view – that of the solid if unspectacular professional who spends much of his career with one club – the bread and butter player who is the essence of the professional game.

Campbell and Hough, in particular, would play active roles on the committee: outspoken and determined, they, along with Tony Ingham, would press the case of the ordinary player as against the 'star'; and in this respect they would regularly disagree with Jimmy Hill. However, as Jack Campbell says, 'We could argue but we were always good pals; we had some very good meetings and there was never any animosity.'

Personal friendships, in fact, were a key factor in the success of the new committee. Campbell, for instance, came from the same part of the country as Lloyd, had started at the same club, Liverpool, had seen his career interrupted by the war and had begun peace-time football with a club destined to spend most of its time in the Second Division.

In 1944 he had been transferred to Blackburn Rovers for £5000 but had received nothing by way of a 'cut' – the League having decided that wartime service could not count towards accrued share of benefit.

Campbell claimed that, had he known this, he would have refused to move as he had been unhappy at the prospect of playing in Blackburn ('a bigger dump than Bootle'). In fact, he spent twelve happy years with the club, eventually being susperseded by Ronnie Clayton at wing-half.

For Campbell, the years on the Management Committee were 'a great experience'. He would pick Cliff Lloyd up from his home near Warrington and together they would travel down by car (Campbell's not Lloyd's – it would be another ten years before the Union could afford such a luxury!) to London on Saturday night, invariably staying at a bed-and-breakfast in Earls Court: 'Cliff was always keeping an eye on the expenses and he'd insist we stayed in some right bloody dumps! Rats and all. I'd say, "I know we're only Second Division, Cliff, but this is ridiculous...." '

Harry Hough was also on good personal terms with Cliff Lloyd and, like Campbell, had suffered financial disappointment during his career. A miner during the war, he spent much of his career with Second Division Barnsley, whose chairman was none other than Joe Richards, League president.

Hough claims that in all the twelve years he spent at the club, Richards spoke to him just twice – the second time to block a proposed transfer of Hough to Walsall with the words: 'You'll go where I tell you.'

Hough eventually moved to Bradford Park Avenue, losing, he claimed, almost £1200 which the Walsall deal would have guaranteed him.

Hough, Campbell and the rest of the Management Committee were thus much more of a 'team' than previous groups had been. With Lloyd's administrative shake-up ensuring that lines of communications were simplified and decisions were taken rapidly and confidently, there was a general sense of involvement, while the old-fashioned virtues of thrift and accountability so dear to Jimmy Fay were reasserted.

Ever since he had become secretary, Cliff Lloyd had been coaxing the Union back to living within its means. Administrative costs had been reduced from £1363 in 1955 to £586 in 1958; and in 1959, with Jimmy Guthrie's expenses and London base gone, the Union actually began making regular surpluses, although, as the Union auditor commented in 1959, 'it will be many more years before damage inflicted in the last decade has been repaired'.

In 1960, despite Union subs being increased from 2/- to 2/6d (still a low figure when compared to other unions), membership began to show a gradual increase, although Aston Villa as if by some perverse tradition, still stubbornly refused to join.

Lloyd's internal financial and administrative reforms, plus the parallel overhaul by George Davies of the Union's rules and regulations, would nevertheless be the work of years. On the day-to-day political front, activity would soon become frenetic, with Jimmy Hill thrust into the spotlight within weeks of taking office.

Much has been made of Hill's grasp of public relations, his youthful persuasion (although he was by now well into his thirties) and the new 'positive' image he brought to the Union. His knack of catching good publicity did not start, however, with the Union. When he took over as chairman, his famous beard had already launched a thousand journalistic clichés ('the bold buccaneer', the 'plundering pirate', the 'beatnik with a ball') – much to Hill's surprise and delight:

> It was not done as a publicity stunt, although it has brought publicity. In two weeks I turned from being just Fulham's inside right to a personality plus. I became the only footballer with a beard and had changed myself from being the ordinary to the extraordinary. Advertisers became interested in me. The beard photographed well on television. People wanted to hear what I had to say about things....

Hill's understanding of the importance of publicity – of efficient, clear and simple presentation of ideas, particularly where TV was concerned – would prove an important bonus to the Union, especially when placed alongside the Football League's continued contempt for 'public relations'.

To make any real impact, however, it was essential that the Union be seen at the heart of things, influencing events rather than simply reacting to them. Thus, the Sunderland 'affair', which broke in April 1957, turned out to be a gift from the gods, a perfect, if shaky start for the new committee.

The investigations into the affairs of Sunderland in early 1957 revealed little new about the murky world of football finance: irregular and illegal payments to players, amounting to many thousands of pounds, stretching back many years.

Internal jealousies and rivalries, as well as some amateur sleuthing on the part of Alan Hardaker, had resulted in accusations and confessions that had, in turn, led to the setting up of a Joint FA/League Commission of Enquiry. This suspended certain directors for life and fined the club heavily.

The Players' Union became involved directly when five Sunderland players were named as having accepted illegal signing-on fees, and were thus summoned by the commission.

They asked the Union for help and, for the first time, Union representatives were allowed to be present as observers at such a hearing. The FA must have rued the day, however; the Union decided, on George Davies's advice, to take a bold course.

The men were instructed to say nothing at all when asked any questions by the members of the commission in order not to incriminate themselves. The Union would be making the point that British justice insisted that guilt, not innocence, be proved. In this way, the Union intended using the Sunderland enquiry as a means of challenging the supra-legal powers of both the League and the FA. Men faced with the possibility of losing their livelihood should be allowed – indeed, had the right to – a proper legal defence, a long-running issue ever since the 1952 Arbitration Tribunal.

They would also use the affair to highlight the absurdities created by the maximum wage, the hypocrisy (as they saw it) of 'trying' five men for offences they would claim were being committed in every club in the land. How little things had changed since 1907, when Meredith had founded the Union, citing just such sentiments.

Whatever their original strategy, however, the immediate outcome of the commission on 25 April came as a complete shock – even to George Davies.

Faced with five silent men refusing to answer any questions, the commission simply suspended them all, *sine die*.

The Union was suddenly thrust into the driving seat. Its members had been suspended (and were none too happy about the situation even though the Union had pledged financial support). What, then, was it going to do?

Hill's immediate response was to announce, at a press briefing some three days later, that the Union was calling on the League and the FA to hold an enquiry into the whole question of illegal payments. The Union, he said, would cooperate if three conditions were met: 'that no action would be taken against any player who gave evidence freely concerning illegal payments; that the five suspended players have their suspensions lifted immediately and reconsidered at a later date if necessary; and on the speedy implementation of any necessary changes agreed upon.'

The key element in the Union's approach to the football authorities was its declared intention to collect as many signatures as possible (a thousand was the projected figure) of men who admitted to having received illegal payments.

A special form had been produced for men to sign; such overwhelming weight of evidence, it was suggested, could not fail to force the FA and League to respond.

The petition idea, said to be the brain-child of a sports writer on Jimmy Guthrie's favourite Sunday paper, *The People*, was the factor that turned the Sunderland affair into something more than just another wages scandal.

Although not intended to be frivolous, it was, in essence, a stunt – and for that very reason perfect material for sports writers to seize upon and dramatize. But for Hill it rapidly became a personal nightmare.

Having committed the Union to securing a thousand signatures, the task now was to produce them – no easy job at the end of the football season with players disappearing on holiday. As Hill admitted in his 1961 autobiography, *Striking for Soccer*, 'We soon found we had taken on an impossible task.'

Driving up and down the country in his car, he claimed remarkable success but would not reveal the figures to the press – who were thus free to speculate. As a consequence, the campaign was dubbed a mess, a flop, a disaster: players were said to have refused to take the risk while others had simply laughed at the whole idea.

Len Shackleton incurred the wrath of his Sunderland team-mates by insisting that the best way to change the wage and bonus structure was to go on strike. Signing confessions would not, he believed, help anyone: 'I am a Union member but I still have the right to form my own opinion.' His opinion was a sound one, as events would demonstrate. As it was, the signature/confession campaign made little impact on the League.

All was not lost, however, where the Union's overall strategy was concerned. Ever since the commission had suspended the Sunderland men, the Union – specifically the Management Committee and its legal advisers – had been sitting on the realization that the League and FA had blundered badly.

A member of Davies's law firm had discovered that, according to existing rules, the commission set up by the football authorities had no legal standing. Joint commissions of enquiry had never been formed before – there were no rules to accommodate them. Furthermore, any decisions they took were also open to legal challenge because there were no powers granted to such commissions – least of all to suspend men for life.

How such a basic mistake had been made was a mystery. Perhaps the fact that the FA and League had never had to worry about legal niceties – that they had always considered themselves the law where football was concerned – had dulled their legal wits. Whatever the explanation, Davies was convinced that an appeal would overturn the suspensions.

In the meantime, blissfully unaware of their mistake, the League/ FA offered the Sunderland men a second chance to 'own up'. If they did so, it was promised that their suspensions would be lifted.

This time, with the 'confessions' campaign having almost died the death, and with the appeal against the original suspensions already under way, Davies advised the men to talk.

They admitted to various illegal payments, were found 'guilty' and later punished by being stripped of part of their qualification for benefit – an odd sentence as some of the men were not even eligible for it.

The legal ramifications of the Sunderland affair would continue for some years to come, and not until 1962 would the appeal against the original commission sentence come to court.

The verdicts would then be overturned and awards to cover loss of wages and damages made to all the men concerned. Allegations of illegal payments at other clubs would continue, however: Leyton Orient, Partick Thistle and Leicester City were all to be investigated. It was a continuing nightmare for the League, discrediting the existing wages structure and calling into question the concept of the maximum wage, or at least the absurdly low maximum then in operation.

In fact, the argument where the latter was concerned was considered won: it only needed the League to concede as much. The Sunderland affair's immediate consequence, however, had been to launch the Union career of Jimmy Hill, who for the next few years would be its figurehead.

Hill has been described by one football historian as 'marginal to football culture', this presumably referring to Hill's alleged middle-class origins: son of a 'stock-broker', educated at grammar school in suburban south London, trained in insurance. In fact, Hill's father was a baker's roundsman, and his grammar-school place came as the result of his winning a scholarship. What is beyond doubt, however, is the fact that from the time he was a small boy Hill was obsessed with playing soccer, to the exclusion of all else.

Following National Service, he played briefly as an amateur under Ted Drake at Reading before turning professional with Brentford. There he was converted from wing-forward to wing-half and played alongside Ron Greenwood, developing a keen interest in the technical aspects of coaching and playing.

After three years, he moved to Fulham in 1952 and was to stay there until injury forced him out of the game at the age of thirty-three in 1961 when he moved, almost immediately, into football management at Coventry.

While at Fulham, Hill experienced both First and Second Division football and played alongside Bobby Robson, Johnny Haynes, George Cohen, Roy Bentley, Joe Bacuzzi and Tony Macedo, among others. And, though a wing-half, he had a knack of scoring occasionally important goals – during Fulham's great Cup-run in 1958 he scored in every round, including a drawn semi-final against the rebuilt Manchester United side. Swept aside in the replay by a combination of Bobby Charlton and mass hysteria, Fulham failed to reach Wembley although the following season they were promoted to Division One.

Thus, though playing for a relatively unfashionable side, Hill's playing career certainly touched the high spots and along the way he came into contact and developed ideas with some of the contemporary game's most illustrious and progressive names.

His business background certainly made him aware of the commercial possibilities then opening up for football, in particular the arrival of commercial TV with its massive advertising revenues, not to mention its insidious advertising techniques, then just beginning to have an influence on British life.

Hill embraced such developments and was not ashamed to be seen in the company of advertising executives (at one time he shared an office with one). He was prepared to participate in self-promotion and image-making (he formed the International Club to help prominent players do just that), appreciating the value of such gestures, and not feeling self-conscious about espousing the 'upward mobility' of footballers. All this caused some people within and outside the game to suspect him (indeed, accuse him) of using his position as Union chairman to further his own career.

All of which is par for the course in British society. Those who patronizingly referred to his 'romantic determination to secure for his members a place in the bourgeois world' would perhaps have preferred that footballers remained part of that 'romantic' working class so beloved of well-heeled progressive socialists/sociologists.

Jimmy Hill was more a realist than a romantic; in that sense, he was firmly centred in football culture. Yet, as he has said, in order to survive, a culture must adjust and grow.

Anyone who thought, however, that changing the name of
Players' Union to the Professional Footballers' Association in 1958
would signal a consequent softening of attitudes – a less aggressive
approach where players' demands were concerned – was speedily
disabused.

That Hill was clearly going to cause football's authorities some
trouble was demonstrated during his very first Joint Committee
meeting with the League in April 1957.

After welcoming him, Joe Richards expressed the hope that
relations between the two sides would continue to be cordial and
friendly. Hill quickly disillusioned him, announcing that earlier
declarations by the Union accepting the principles of the retain and
transfer system and the maximum wage were a dead letter.
Complete freedom was the goal.

When asked by Richards if this was 'for the good of the game',
Hill is supposed to have said, 'We're not interested in the good of
the game. We're only here to talk about our members.'

Even Jimmy Guthrie could not have put it quite so bluntly.

# 25
# *New Deal – and Eastham* 1961–63

The gradual drift towards open hostilities between the Football League and the PFA continued during 1958 and 1959. Despite the fact that personnel changes had occurred in both organizations, attitudes remained depressingly familiar, particularly where the League was concerned.

Although Alan Hardaker saw the need for changing the way professional football was run and organized in Great Britain, he remained loyal to ancient League creeds; and a significant exchange of letters with Cliff Lloyd in 1959 demonstrated this in eerie fashion.

Referring to the necessity of both the retain and transfer system and the maximum wage to the survival of the League, Hardaker cited as conclusive evidence, 'the chaotic conditions that existed before the League was formed, i.e. in 1888....'

Cliff Lloyd replied, 'This is surely a long time ago and I can hardly feel that those gentlemen who founded the League thought the maximum wage and transfer system would continue to be doggedly insisted upon without any real variation over seventy years afterwards....'

Yet the long, seemingly interminable struggle against change had been based on such ancient prejudices, and C E Sutcliffe, by

*Players' Union Management Committee, 1946. Back row, left to right: Frank Broome, Joe Wilson, Jimmy Guthrie, Joe Mercer; front row: Bob Stuart, Jimmy Fay, Sammy Crooks, Norman Low.*

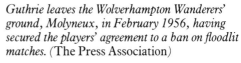

*Jimmy Guthrie addresses the TUC Conference of 1955. (The Press Association)*

*Guthrie leaves the Wolverhampton Wanderers' ground, Molyneux, in February 1956, having secured the players' agreement to a ban on floodlit matches. (The Press Association)*

*Cliff Lloyd in Fulham colours just
after the Second World War.*

*Jack Campbell, Blackburn Rovers.
Management Committee member in the
late-50s, early-60s.*

*Cliff Lloyd at his desk in the Hanging Ditch offices in the early 60s with Miss Hardman on his
right.* (The Press Association)

*Jimmy Hill talks to Arsenal players during the regional meeting to discuss the maximum wage crisis, 14 November 1960.* (The Press Association)

*Jimmy Greaves and Tommy Docherty looking sombre at the London regional meeting, November 1960.* (Associated Press)

*Hill's historic handshake with Joe Richards, League President, outside the Ministry of Labour offices, 18 January 1961.* (Associated Press)

The PFA Management Committee members celebrate after the maximum wage 'victory' in 1961. Left to right: George Davies (PFA solicitor, 1957–91), Jimmy Hill, Ian Dargie, Cliff Lloyd, Len Chalmers, Roy Wood and Harry Hough.

George Eastham (Arsenal), outside the Law Courts in The Strand before the commencement of the historic case that would see the end of the retain and transfer system, 11 June 1963. (Associated Press)

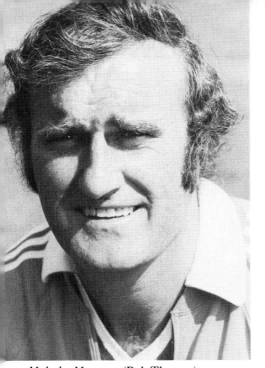

*Malcolm Musgrove* (Bob Thomas)

*Noel Cantwell* (Bob Thomas)

*PFA Chairmen 1963–78.*

*Terry Neill* (Bob Thomas)

*Derek Dougan* (Bob Thomas)

*Gordon Taylor* (Ray Harris)

*Alan Gowling* (Bob Thomas)

*PFA Chairmen 1978–88.*

*Steve Coppell* (Bob Thomas)

*Brian Talbot* (Bob Thomas)

*After twenty-eight years' service with the Union, Cliff Lloyd hands over the post of secretary to Gordon Taylor, November 1981. In 1974 Cliff was awarded the OBE, the only PFA man to receive such an honour. (Daily Mirror)*

*The former Norwich City forward, Dave Bennett, receiving a cheque for £30,000 from Gordon Taylor, 3 September 1984. Bennett was the first beneficiary of the private accident insurance arranged through the PFA. (Paul Francis)*

*Gordon Taylor hands over the keys on behalf of the Manpower Services Commission to* (left to right): *Mick Baxter, Dennis Leman and Bryan Flynn. (Steve Wright)*

writing his own highly inaccurate, self-serving League history in 1938, had made certain the myths survived intact. Even the dispute of 1960-61, which saw one of the 'two freedoms' gained at last, would not undermine those myths. Reform would be achieved in the teeth of dogged, bitter, often resentful opposition – opposition that would eventually sour any taste of victory.

Alan Hardaker, for instance, in summing up the 'strike' year a decade later, remained adamant that the players 'won' because they were able to manipulate public opinion and because Jimmy Hill had used the press in a way that he, Hardaker, had not been allowed to by his League bosses.

But Hardaker failed to grasp that public opinion was firmly on the players' side because common sense could no longer accept conditions of employment rooted in the attitudes of nineteenth-century mill-owners.

From the men on the terraces to Members of Parliament, there was a weary impatience with a League system that was, as Philip Goodhart MP described it in November 1960, 'inefficiently organized, semi-bankrupt and all too often a thoroughly bad employer'.

Thus, ultimate victory for the players would never depend on favourable press coverage. Ever since the war, it had been a matter of will. If the players wanted change badly enough, they could achieve it; and now, with a Union Management Committee capable, intelligent and well-organized enough to lead them, they appeared willing to try.

The ritual dance began in April 1960 following the PFA's AGM when four principal demands were formulated: the abolition of the maximum wage; the right of players to a proportion of any transfer fee; a new retaining system; and a new form of contract.

In June the Ministry of Labour was informed that a dispute existed and, following a joint meeting, all PFA demands were submitted to the League for its consideration.

Some five months later, on 8 November, an extraordinary meeting of League clubs offered the following: a rise in the minimum wage of £2; a wage of £10 a week to be paid to men on the transfer list; match bonuses to be paid to reserves; and the introduction of talent money.

There being no mention of substantial changes to either the maximum wage or the transfer system, the offer was rejected out of hand by the Union and, after a series of rank and file meetings held in November, December and January, the Union felt confident enough to issue a strike notice to take effect on 21 January 1961.

By 9 January, the League had moved swiftly and substantial gains seemed possible. Five more concessions were offered: longer playing contracts; the abolition of the maximum wage; the setting up of a joint committee; a minimum retaining wage per division; and testimonials for players every eight years.

With the retain and transfer system still largely untouched, the Union felt obliged to consult the members again. The players held firm and on 18 January, at 2.30 pm at the Ministry of Labour offices in London, Joe Richards, Joe Mears and Alan Hardaker sat down opposite Cliff Lloyd, Jimmy Hill and George Davies, with Ministry of Labour Conciliation Officer Tom Claro as referee, for what everyone thought would be an historic meeting.

After two-and-a-half hours of talks, the PFA men went to an adjoining room to consult with the rest of the Management Committee. At 6.45 the Minister of Labour, Mr Hare, was summoned to make an announcement to a gathering of some sixty press and TV men. Agreement had been reached concerning the retain and transfer system. The battle, it seemed, had been won!

As telegrams were being sent to all League clubs informing them that matches would be played that Saturday as usual, Jimmy Hill

# DAILY HERALD

No. 13957   H                    Thursday, January 19, 1961                    Price 2½d.

An honourable agreement | Now everyone's happy
SAYS JIMMY HILL | SAYS ALAN HARDAKER

# The PLAYERS WIN 3-1
## Soccer strike off —Pools as usual

Soccer peace—Players' chairman Jimmy Hill shakes
hands with League chairman Joe Richards.

*Premature celebrations: Jimmy Hill shakes hands with Joe Richards.*

announced: 'This is a historic moment for football in this country.'

Mr Hare commented: 'One of the things that will please the public most is the fact that this agreement was reached with great goodwill on both sides – and so the future prospects of football look really good.'

Joe Richards, League president, would only say: 'I'm not going to express an opinion. We have reached a settlement and that is enough. And it has not been easy.'

Joe Richards was wise to restrict himself to such a dour, deadpan response. Much had been achieved by the Union; but a great deal less than was at first claimed.

*" Hard luck, dear . . the strike's off."*

The agreement in respect of the retain and transfer system suggested that, once a player refused terms offered to him (and he had until 31 May to do so), he would be placed on the transfer list and other clubs notified that he was for sale. If still on the list after 30 June, he would automatically receive a minimum wage set according to his division. If not transferred by 31 July, he would be retained on a monthly contract until 31 August when the League Management Committee would sort the matter out.

Thus the 'retain' element of the system *appeared* considerably weakened, and it seemed that a player now had much more say in his future than had previously been the case. What was more, he now received a wage while waiting to move.

But whereas the PFA Management Committee had power to settle there and then – and believed that it had done so – the League Management Committee now revealed that it had no such mandate (although Jimmy Hill states in his autobiography that, when asked by Tom Claro if he had a mandate to settle, Richards replied in the affirmative).

Nevertheless, when the League Management Committee proceeded to take the package back to the League clubs to see if they would accept it, it soon became clear that the clubs were unhappy.

Indeed, at an extraordinary meeting at the Café Royal, they rejected the deal completely, Joe Richards announcing: 'Come what may, the Football League will not alter the present retain and transfer system ... it must remain an integral part of the League system....'

Predictable expressions of outrage greeted this disgraceful volte-face. Questions and statements in the Commons, banner headlines declaring that the League had 'died of shame', led back inexorably to the Ministry of Labour, and by 16 May yet another 'agreement' had been reached between the respective Management Committees. This time, however, the League representatives were careful to emphasize that they had *no* mandate.

Already, however, Hill was aware that one point in the agreement was causing the League great difficulty. This was clause four, which stated that if a player did not accept terms offered to him he should be retained but placed on the transfer list.

The League representatives, in fact, redrafted this clause to read: 'if he does not accept, the club will let it be known that he has refused terms and invites enquiries for his transfer at a stated fee.' As Hill commented 'It was a rose by any other name', and he agreed to the change. Thus, the deal was taken back to the League to be considered at its AGM on 3 June 1961.

By now, of course, the season had ended, the Union AGM had already been held and a strike was impossible until the autumn. Perhaps because the pressure was off, the League meeting turned out to be an unpleasant, acrimonious affair, the press being ejected from the room at the start to the accompaniment of derisory slow hand-clapping.

The discussion that followed saw all the old, weary arguments wheeled out: that without the 'retain' safeguard, players would 'hold the clubs to ransom'; that agents would take over; that the new agreement 'placed a premium on disloyalty'; and that no one else understood the system like they did, etc.

When it came to a vote, with almost perfect historical symmetry it was Burnley FC – Sutcliffe's old club – that proposed the whole deal be ignored. However, the clubs stopped short of such total folly, deleting instead the troublesome clause four. Without it, the 'retain' element of the transfer system remained inviolate. A player could now refuse terms and still be held (although now on a weekly wage) for as long as the club wished it.

Thus it had taken a year of meetings, arguments and brinkmanship, not to mention the expenditure of valuable nervous energy on the part of Cliff Lloyd, George Davies, Jimmy Hill and the ageing Joe Richards to return – almost – to square one.

The PFA rejected the League's 'final' offer and declared the dispute still on; in June the Minister of Labour announced in the Commons: 'No final settlement has been reached because the AGM of the Football League decided not to implement the agreement in full'; while Jimmy Hill, in a chapter of his autobiography entitled 'The Great Betrayal', wrote: 'It has now become a battle for all Trade Unionists....'

For Jimmy Hill, however, the battle was over. In December 1961, he resigned from the Management Committee to take up the post of manager of Coventry City FC.

Although Hill had been chairman of the Union for just four years, his impact had been tremendous: without exaggeration, it can be said that he introduced the Players' Union to the modern world. Before Hill, few people outside football (and many inside!) had ever heard of the Union. The 'Great Communicator' changed all that. Of his performance during the 'New Deal' negotiations, Phil Woosnam was to say: 'The way Jimmy Hill handled the affair deserves everyone's admiration. Players at last realized they could get better terms from their clubs – thanks to a brilliantly fought case by Jimmy Hill.'

He would go on to become a permanent fixture in the British game – manager, director, TV front man and entrepreneur. Opinions may vary as to his lasting contribution to the Union's history, but it certainly was the Union's good fortune to have served as Hill's 'apprenticeship' in the media.

With his departure, the 'new deal' issue unfortunately seemed suddenly to die in publicity terms, and though Tommy Cummings, the new chairman, spoke immediately after his election about the battle for the 'two freedoms' being far from over, it was decided that the Union would first wait to see if the 'spirit' of the agreement might be carried over in practice before taking further action.

In truth, the Union was now in no position to launch another full-scale assault on the system. In the first place, the mood of militancy – so crucial to the success thus far – had almost evaporated. Total unity, including the participation of top players such as Stanley Matthews and Billy Wright, had been essential in catching the public's imagination, as well as ensuring that many lower-division players 'took the plunge'.

The new 'agreement' had seen the removal of the maximum wage which meant star players could now earn high salaries – up to £100 a week in certain celebrated cases. This, it was suspected, could only weaken the commitment of the top players to sustained militant action. They now had a great deal more to lose, and without their participation strike action was pointless.

Thus the membership was now fatally divided. Not only that, but the removal of the maximum wage threatened the livelihood of many players, as it was being made clear by certain clubs that, in order to pay the higher salaries, there would have to be some trimming of playing staff – and that would mean lesser players having to go.

The majority of players would have preferred a higher maximum wage – say £25–30 a week – plus unlimited bonuses for success. Committee members such as Jack Campbell, Ian Dargie and Tony Ingham had pressed for such a deal but Jimmy Hill had insisted that the removal of the top ceiling would result in all wages going up: a 'trickle-up' effect.

In fact, in the early stages of the dispute, Alan Hardaker and Cliff Lloyd had worked out a deal that involved a higher maximum, but this initiative had been rejected by the clubs – a disastrous move, according to Hardaker.

The clubs, it seemed, had preferred the grand gesture of 'abolishing' the maximum, while attempting to impose an unofficial maximum amongst themselves – an underhand manoeuvre ultimately rendered futile by their inability to agree on a figure. In fact, individual clubs continued for many years to impose maximum figures on their own players.

The rank-and-file player was thus less excited by the achievements of the 'strike' year than might at first have been thought, for without freedom of contract, such men had little leverage when it came to negotiating a new contract.

However, by the time Jimmy Hill had left and Tommy Cummings had taken over as chairman, the Management Committee, led by Cliff Lloyd and prompted by solicitor George Davies, had become firmly committed to an alternative line of attack on the retain and transfer system – this time through the courts.

At about the same time as the Union was preparing to confront the League in April 1960, George Eastham of Newcastle United was pressing to be released from his contract.

After repeated unsuccessful requests, Eastham took the drastic step of leaving Newcastle and taking a job outside football in Surrey, working for a businessman friend.

In mid-July he wrote to the League Management Committee applying under Rule 26(b) stating that he was unable to arrange his transfer from the club and asking the League's permission to transfer. On 23 July the League Management Committee considered the appeal and decided that the matter was entirely between club and player.

As the argument dragged on and the 1960-61 football season began, the PFA saw in the Eastham affair a rare opportunity to challenge the legal nature of the retain and transfer system. Eastham was no controversial firebrand. He had conducted himself with a dignity and good sense that contrasted sharply with some of the pronouncements of the Newcastle directors (one of whom declared that he would see Eastham shovel coal before he left Newcastle).

Indeed, it was the special nature of the case, the intemperate remarks and questionable actions of certain Newcastle directors that finally convinced expert legal opinion that there was a good possibility of success.

Jimmy Hill, Cliff Lloyd and the PFA's QC had discussed the case as the dispute with the League in 1960-61 had dragged on with no prospect of victory. Despite warnings that it might cost a lot of money, they had finally decided to take the chance.

George Davies, Union solicitor, thus seized the moment and on 13 October a writ was issued on behalf of Eastham alleging that the club had deprived him and was still depriving him of the opportunity to earn his living by playing football, that in doing so the club were acting in unlawful restraint of trade, for which Eastham wished to claim damages.

There was an anxious wait to see how Newcastle would respond: the club had seven days in which to take positive action of some sort but, to the relief of Davies and the PFA, the Newcastle directorate made no move. The writ went forward.

In fact, in early November, Newcastle relented to the extent of accepting a bid from Arsenal for £47,000 for Eastham who thus re-entered the professional game amid fanfares and glory.

Understandably, Eastham was no longer interested in legal action – much pressure was put on him to withdraw, particularly as the Union 'strike' had seen the maximum wage lifted – but Cliff Lloyd impressed upon him the crucial importance of the action for all footballers and, to his credit, Eastham consented to allow the action to continue.

Thus began the Eastham saga, destined to alter the nature of professional football in England.

In a strange way, the events of 1960-63 mirror those of almost fifty years previously. Then there had been a long-drawn-out battle with football's authorities, ending in confused circumstances, to be followed three years on by a court case challenging the retain and transfer system. The catastrophic result of that court case had haunted the Players' Union ever since; and now the weight of that historic case and its consequences came to rest on the shoulders of Cliff Lloyd.

Success in the Eastham action was by no means guaranteed. Acting in restraint of trade could be declared unlawful but not illegal. The onus was on the PFA to prove that the League was acting in an unlawful way, that the restraint of trade was not justified, that it went further than was necessary to protect their legitimate interests.

The League could claim that the restraint of trade was necessary and that, without it, dire consequences would follow, for players and clubs alike, and indirectly for the public.

If the Union succeeded, the court would formally declare the system unlawful and therefore unenforceable; with such a declaration in hand, the Union could then force the League to renegotiate the standard contract to bring it in line with recognized principles of English law. In fact, the League had always contended that it would only continue with the retain and transfer system unless and until a court declared it to be contrary to public good.

It was not automatic, however, that the judge would decide in the Union's favour: and where the more specific charges concerning conspiracy and damages were concerned, expert opinion oscillated alarmingly from day to day, causing Cliff Lloyd a great deal of anguish.

By nature a worrier, he found the weeks and months of preparation an ordeal. Though the Union was solvent, it was hardly equipped to cope with massive costs and damages should the action fail. And he took the responsibility for such an outcome personally. What was more, it soon became apparent that it would be necessary for him to spend a great deal of time in court giving evidence.

Considerable amounts of detail had to be communicated to the judge and a variety of legal officials. In a sense, the case, when it was finally heard in June 1963, turned into a complete review of the workings of professional football; and all the legal preparation, the submissions, the groundwork and case-work could come to nought without a 'star' expert witness.

In fact, all the truisms, the clichés, the long-held assumptions underpinning the system were now to be given an impartial airing. How C E Sutcliffe would have relished the occasion! Unfortunately for the League, it was Alan Hardaker who stood in Sutcliffe's place; and fortunate indeed for the PFA that he was opposed by Cliff Lloyd, whose evidence and (more importantly) presentation of that evidence was to prove decisive.

Nervous, sometimes to the point of panic in the hours before the trial, Lloyd was cool and collected once he stepped into the witness box, so much so that he himself admitted: 'I think I excelled myself, I really do.'

That he was the key to the subsequent outcome of the trial was made clear by Justice Wilberforce in his summing up and judgement, given on 4 July 1963, when he made specific reference to Cliff Lloyd being 'a witness who seemed to me to be more in touch with the realities of professional football and particularly the considerations affecting the supply and interests of players than any other witness'.

In a real sense, Lloyd stood during those crucial few days for all his professional forebears – for John Devey and John Cameron,

Charlie Saer and Charlie Roberts, for Colin Veitch, Billy Meredith, Jimmy Fay and Sammy Crooks – and for Jimmy Guthrie (who could be seen throughout the trial sitting in the press gallery making assiduous notes).

It was his responsibility to put forward their arguments, express their convictions and beliefs for so long ignored, ridiculed and derided by countless League directors and FA administrators whose own arguments had prevailed for over three-quarters of a century simply because there had been no real opportunity to counter them, their ignorance bolstered by myth and crude economic power.

Perhaps if Cliff Lloyd had been conscious of his historic role he would have suffered even more nervous torment. As it was, he was able, with admirable common sense and convincing logic, to counter the manifest claims by the League that the removal of the retain and transfer system would be to the detriment of competition and the professional game as a whole.

The core of the League's defence of the retain and transfer system was that it prevented the powerful clubs taking all the best players and thus destroying 'competition'. The system protected the weak and this promoted equality, which was good for everyone and thus served the public interest.

Lloyd pointed out, however, that it was open to clubs to offer players longer contracts if they wished (instead of the one-year contracts then insisted upon) and that by staggering contracts clubs could always ensure that at the end of the season they were left with a nucleus of players, thus preventing richer clubs 'snapping up all the best players'.

He also pointed to natural checks on player movement – children at local schools for instance – and to the limit on the number of players any club could maintain. A club would employ only so many to fill a particular position and, no good forward would consider a club which already had a number of good forwards on its books. There were, Lloyd insisted, plenty of good players to go around.

Furthermore, he suggested that the removal of the maximum wage made it more rather than less likely that players would stay where they were, happy and contented rather than clamouring for a move.

Lloyd's evidence also helped Wilberforce accept the implausibility of other long-held League beliefs: that without the retention system, football would be played only in or near large centres of population (in fact, according to Lloyd, the system actually worked in *favour* of the larger towns); that clubs would be discouraged from spending large sums of money 'bringing on' players if they could not recoup that money in transfer fees (here he was able to demonstrate the relatively small amounts of money that clubs actually did spend on young players); that the system 'maintained a uniform standard of play between the various divisions' ('rather far-fetched,' commented Wilberforce); that it maintained employment for players ('conjectural,' according to the judge, whereas Lloyd accused the system of driving men *out* of the game); and that it encouraged cooperation between players and clubs and between players and players ('there is no evidence to support this,' Wilberforce concluded).

Thus the retention arguments, repeated *ad nauseam* down through the ages with little or no evidence to support them other than various crude assumptions formulated back in the 1890s, were at last reduced to rubble. Wilberforce summed up as follows:

> It is claimed as evidence that those who know best consider it [the system] to be in the best interests of the game. I do not accept that line of argument. The system is an employer's system set up in an industry where the employers have established a monolithic front and where it is clear for the purposes of negotiation the employers are more strongly organized than the employees....

Therefore, he was adamant:

> I conclude that the combined retain and transfer system as existing at the date of the writ is an unjustifiable restraint of trade....

The Union had thus obtained the sought-for declaration and Cliff Lloyd's personal nightmare was over. Gone were the days when he would be driven by taxi to the High Court confessing to George Davies, head in hands, that he was 'worried sick'. Even now, thirty years on, he cannot recall those times without a shudder.

For in a sense he had done almost single-handedly what the

profession he represented had been unwilling to do for themselves –
he had confronted Sutcliffe's ghost and laid it to rest.

In October 1963, George Eastham, the man whose case had set in
motion the dismantling of one of the strangest, most byzantine of
employer/employee relationships, stepped on to the Wembley turf
to play for England against FIFA in a celebration of one hundred
years of the Football Association.

A month later, at the PFA's 53rd AGM in Manchester, George
Davies concluded his review of the year with this tribute:

> Cliff Lloyd has always impressed us and we think also impressed
> those present when he gave evidence as being probably more
> knowledgeable and more aware of the detailed practical situation of
> the football industry than perhaps anyone else.
>
> That he manages to be so, and that in addition he manages to be
> both human and compassionate in all his dealings with everyone
> without ever losing sight of the need to be tough when necessary and
> without ever lacking the capacity to be so, is an immense tribute to
> him.
>
> That the PFA has achieved so much in recent years is an
> acknowledgement of the courage and determination of all members.
> It is also in great part a tribute to the immense skill of your
> secretary....

# 26

# *A Sort of Freedom* 1963–67

Such was the excitement caused by the Wilberforce judgement, so historic a victory did it seem, that its true significance for the immediate future of the PFA was largely ignored or misunderstood. Outright victory was claimed when, in fact, Wilberforce had awarded prizes to everyone: and the League, in particular, was quick to seize upon those parts of the summing up and judgement that appeared to offer it an opportunity to shore up the old, discredited system. Eastham would therefore prove to be a significant victory in a very long war.

Wilberforce had not, for instance, condemned the transfer system outright – only when it was combined with the draconian retention clause.

He had also dismissed Eastham's claims for damages against Newcastle United and the individuals involved in his transfer wrangle. As a consequence, the PFA had to pay substantial costs, though nothing like as catastrophic as Lloyd had feared.

The immediate aftermath thus saw the PFA in conciliatory mood, prepared to offer an olive branch to the League and renegotiate, step by step, a more equitable contract. As George Davies put it in November 1963:

It has been the policy of your Management Committee and the advice of ourselves subsequent to the Eastham decision to recognize the immediate difficulties of the Football League and Football Association. As a consequence, wherever consistent with the legitimate interests of the PFA members, no undue pressure has been exerted upon the football authorities.

The League's reaction to Eastham, however, ranged from the niggardly to the outright aggressive, Alan Hardaker at first claiming, to the incredulity of many, that the judgement only referred to the League rules as they existed in 1960. Since then, following the 'strike', changes had occurred, thus Wilberforce's judgement was now irrelevant!

At the even more obstreperous meeting of League chairmen in November 1963, Bob Lord of Burnley suggested that the clubs ignore the judgement entirely and 'take the players on' – presumably in a fight to the death. Five years or so earlier, that is probably what the clubs would have done.

Underlying all the aggressive posturing and bombast, however, was a grudging acknowledgement, not to say fear, that times had changed. The old ways were no longer acceptable; what is more, reform was desperately needed at all levels of the game, with crowds now declining in potentially disastrous numbers, the League itself in debt and, in 1962, the unthinkable really happening – a League club, Accrington Stanley, actually going out of business.

It was clear, therefore, that unless it exercised a great deal of tact, the League was in danger of doing itself even more harm. As Joe Richards warned at the '63 meeting ('The most important meeting in connection with League affairs since formation'): if they were not careful, the players would obtain *complete* freedom.

The truth was that the League, despite its problems, remained very much in the driving seat. It saw the Wilberforce judgement not as a condemnation of itself, more an inconvenience to be circumvented. As Alan Hardaker wrote in early 1964:

If clubs pay the players they are entitled to have some system – and it is accepted that this must be some system within the law – for their protection.... If a player wishes to be a professional with all the benefits financial and otherwise of the present age then he must be prepared to accept conditions of service laid down by the people who provide his wages....

To which Cliff Lloyd countered:

If the Football League Ltd want to have transfer fees and a transfer system they must agree to do it in such a way that does not demand of the player an unacceptable tie on him while he is waiting to be transferred.... It must be achieved without fettering the players. For it is the fetter that makes it unlawful.

Thus, when negotiations between the PFA and the FL to establish a new, more equitable contract began, the question of the complete freedom of the player was not on the agenda.

Critics – in particular Jimmy Guthrie – suggested that the Players' Union had made a tactical error at this crucial stage in the game's history by not pressing its advantage harder:

With the goal wide open and the opposition defence in ruins, the PFA put the ball wide.

But the facts suggest otherwise. The PFA was not a strong organization and as George Davies emphasized in 1963:

Your Association is in the unhappy position of being opposed by a powerful monopoly employer upon whose power the Eastham decision made a vital but limited impression.... The only way in which you can hope in the long term to lay sufficient weight behind the protection which you give to your members in the absence of legislation can be by establishing yourselves in a similarly strong monopoly position.

The demand for a closed shop had been raised immediately following the 1961 strike settlement. As we have seen, there had always been mixed feelings about such a policy within the Union: Cliff Lloyd, like Jimmy Fay before him, was against the idea yet adamant that 100 per cent membership was essential.

Tommy Cummings, chairman in April 1962, commented when told that one of the Spurs 'double' winning side was a non-member: 'Blackleg is a word we don't use but we are going to give this matter a great deal of thought.'

In March 1963 Jimmy Armfield proposed that a closed shop be

introduced as from 30 September that year. By November an increase in membership was announced, although this was probably due to the appointment of a delegate for every League club.

Yet even 100 per cent membership, though desirable for a number of reasons, would not have solved the PFA's problems. The Union would still have remained a relatively small organization of no more than 3–4000 members. With 'subs' at no more than £5 a year, the amount of cash it could hope to amass was modest, and a dramatic increase in the level of subs would be sure to result in a loss of members.

Without a healthy bank-balance, strike action was always going to be a gamble. With the 1961 campaign, the limits of such an approach had probably been reached – and even then the players had not been put to the test. Now, with the maximum wage gone, the earlier group 'solidarity' – all men tied to the same wage structure – had disappeared.

Money was an even more crucial fact of life where the question of further court action was concerned. Wilberforce's judgement had been a triumph, but if the League decided to dig its heels in, yet more litigation would be necessary – and where the law was concerned, nothing was automatic: the risks were immense.

Davies continually urged the PFA to investigate the possibility of raising cash from outside ventures. In 1964 the PFA Ltd was set up to coordinate such efforts. But it was clear that it would be a long time before the PFA could stand independently, particularly with regard to the provision of insurance cover to members, not to mention the Provident Fund – for both of which the Union depended heavily upon FA and League cash.

The League had never shirked from using the Provident Fund (such a positive feature in the Union's appeal to less well-off members) as a stick with which to beat the Union. In 1962, in the wake of the 'New Deal', the League Management Committee unilaterally cut the players' Provident Fund entitlement from 9 per cent to 5 per cent (of total career earnings) and many saw this as a deliberate slap in the face for the Union. Donald Saunders, of the *Daily Telegraph*, wrote:

> A number of clubs, on the whole the less successful ones, have been convinced since the 'new deal' was agreed that the players were being allowed to get far too much of their own way.

The League claimed that it could not afford to continue its contributions to the Fund because of its own debts (in 1962 a record £23,000). As mentioned, the problems of falling attendances and the threat of club bankruptcies were certainly causing great anxiety among the clubs. However, the worrying fact was that, in spite of massive injections of cash since 1959 from the pools companies, the League seemed unable to manage its affairs properly, and appeared totally incapable of reforming itself.

Although the danger signals were clear enough to Alan Hardaker, his proposals to galvanize the League by introducing more promotion and relegation, cutting down the number of League matches per season and introducing an 'appetizer' Cup competition in September, proved unacceptable to League chairmen.

The official League historian, Simon Inglis, regarded the rejection of Hardaker's 'Pattern For Football' in 1963 as a mistake second only in significance to the League's rejection of pools money in 1936. Such shortsightedness spelled danger for professional footballers. Subsequent talk of a super-league and a break-up of the existing League structure meant putting players' livelihoods at risk. The League, it was clear, was quite capable of doing great damage both to itself and its employees.

So in the immediate aftermath of the Eastham judgement, tact was needed. To press on with an all-out assault on the transfer system risked further traumatic reactions from League chairmen already sensing that the whole world was against them. The Union, in fact, offered the League a chance to save face: the old 'master–servant' relationship was going, though no one was allowed to say so openly.

Negotiations began on 19 November 1963, significantly through the new Joint Negotiating Committee – finally approved that summer, and yet another important gain for the Union.

By April the details of the new contract were settled and proved acceptable to both clubs and players. In essence, the new rules were as follows:

Every contract was now to be freely negotiated between club and player and to include, along with the basic weekly wage, everything related to bonuses, benefit payments, additional payments on transfer and talent money.

Each contract could now include one option in favour of the club for renewal on terms not less advantageous than those in the original contract and for the same period – unless mutually agreed otherwise. If the club did not want to exercise the option at the end of the original period, the player was free to go without a fee on his head.

At the end of the second period, the club had the right to make an offer to renew the contract, once again on the same terms, unless mutually agreed otherwise. If the club wanted to transfer the player, the original contract continued to run until the transfer was completed. If, however, the player was unhappy he could appeal to the League Management Committee. If this brought no satisfaction, he could take his case to an Independent Tribunal consisting of one representative from the Football League and one from the PFA under the chairmanship of the Joint Negotiating Committee chairman.

The Independent Tribunal, a key element in the new system, decided all aspects of the contract, including the eventual fee. The dates by which clubs had to notify players and by which players had to indicate their acceptance or otherwise remained the same. What was crucial, however, was that whatever the situation a player continued to receive his full wages. As Cliff Lloyd put it: 'The new agreement means that the hardships experienced by players under the old retain and transfer system have now been eliminated.'

It meant a great deal more besides. Although the 'option' clauses were quite clearly weighted in favour of the clubs, the fact that an independent tribunal eventually settled matters if the player pressed on with his demand to leave meant that clubs were increasingly inclined to meet the players' demands. As David Green, Union solicitor, put it: 'The new contract was a combination of what was written and real life.'

Because a player was guaranteed release, sooner or later, there was little to be gained by hanging on to him. It was simply too expensive. In a sense, the new system worked particularly well for men at the end of their career. Clubs had to calculate whether it was worth continuing to pay a player, often on a very good wage, or whether a free transfer would be more economical. Free transfers helped the older players as it made it cheaper for other clubs to sign them on. For the highly valuable players, the new system substantially increased their bargaining powers.

The clubs were thus able to hold on to what they increasingly saw as a vital element in their financial set-up – the inherent 'worth' of players as realized on the transfer market, while the player now had a mechanism that both ensured his financial well-being and offered freedom if keenly enough desired.

Statistics show the dramatic effect the new contract had on the movement of players. In 1963 and 1964 there were 179 and 214 men respectively held by clubs on transfer lists: in 1964 and 1965 the figures were 86 and 70, while free transfers rose from 355 in 1964 to 489 in 1965.

In an imperfect world, the professional player was now in a significantly better position *vis à vis* his employer than he had been all century. Which is not to say, as Bob Lord predictably insisted in August 1964, that 'the player today has never had it so good'.

Lord's opinions, nevertheless, were typical of many a director who would also have agreed when he declared: 'Football is in for a terrible bust-up unless the clubs stand together and refuse to be dictated to by the players any more.' Perhaps such attitudes explain the shock decision announced at the League's AGM in 1964 to axe the Provident Fund and substitute instead an insurance scheme for clubs and players.

Poverty was once again the excuse, although within days the League had negotiated an increase in the annual sum paid to it by the pools promoters from £¼m to £½m per annum.

Worse was to come. On 7 July the FA, again without warning, gave the Union six months' notice that it intended to cease paying the lump sum of £4000 towards the Insurance Scheme agreed under the 1956 TV Agreement.

It later transpired that the League had put pressure on the FA to withdraw from the scheme, thus leaving the Union with a *fait-accompli* regarding insurance.

The Union was thus battling on two fronts. Immediate protests to the League saw negotiations commence through the Joint Negotiating Committee. After an initial change of heart, the FA insisted in March 1965 that the Insurance contribution would not be continued. The Union therefore placed a ban on appearances by its members in televised Cup matches.

A truce was finally agreed on 29 April 1965 when the Union accepted a League deal offering £40,000 for the Provident Fund for players earning under £2000 per annum, plus a club-administered insurance scheme offering £750 for permanent disablement. The FA's TV money would eventually be used to set up an Education Society.

The fights over the Provident Fund and insurance proved to be the last such battles for some years. With the staging of the World Cup in 1966 and the false dawn of increased attendances in its wake, not to mention the necessity for a period of reflection on behalf of players then beginning to negotiate their own contracts for the first time, peace broke out. There was a lot to digest, much with which to come to terms.

The five years between 1960 and 1965 had seen great changes in the position of professional footballers, achieved against the back-drop of declining attendances and the ever-present fear of club bankruptcy. In fact, British football was an increasingly schizophrenic affair.

On the one hand, the glamour and riches of European club competition, plus the 1966 World Cup bringing sponsorship and TV riches; on the other, the resentment and bitterness of clubs confronted by players' new freedoms, and the resultant threat to turn the clock back to retention clauses and maximum wages.

The Union Management Committee certainly began to reflect some 'progressive' tendencies in the domestic game. Prominent and successful clubs like West Ham and Manchester United provided a significant number of Management Committee members during the sixties: Malcom Musgrove, Noel Cantwell, Phil Woosnam, Maurice Setters and later Nobby Lawton and Bobby Charlton were all invited to stand for the committee as Cliff Lloyd made a determined effort to raise the Union's profile.

Musgrove and Cantwell – and later Terry Neill – were examples of a new breed of player-coach in direct line of descent from that great innovator and teacher, Walter Winterbottom. Unfortunately, Winterbottom himself was rejected by the FA as a successor to Stanley Rous – then about to take over as FIFA chief – a rejection which perhaps indicated how the British game was failing to progress in administrative terms.

Certainly there was little room at the top for new thinking; nor could the PFA itself provide any career structure for some of the intelligent and ambitious men now rising from the playing ranks.

Someone like Phil Woosnam, who served on the PFA Management
Committee for a year before setting off for the USA where he
became commissioner of the North American Soccer League, is a
case in point.

Cliff Lloyd's tendency to invite or encourage players on to the
committee who were articulate, thoughtful men only highlighted
this wastage of talent. Men such as Freddie Goodwin, Malcolm
Musgrove, Phil Woosnam, Noel Cantwell, Terry Neill, Derek
Dougan, Terry Venables and Bobby Robson – all of whom were
elected to the committee between the years 1961 and 1967 – could
have played a significant role in changing football in the 1970s and
beyond had not both the League and the FA closed their ranks to
ex-professionals. As it was, they either became embroiled in
management and were deflected away from the centre, or they left
football entirely.

Not that club management was always a dead-end: witness the
changes Jimmy Hill attempted at Coventry City during his tenure
as manager there, introducing novel ideas that he had learned on his
trips to Canada to bring in the crowds. But such innovation
ultimately depended upon directors being prepared to take a
gamble, and such men were distressingly few and far between.

However, at least the PFA was broadening its horizons; as David
Green reported to the 1966 AGM, the Davies law firm 'have worked
with your Management Committee on the considerable and
growing number of questions that arise within the industry as a
whole and with its economic and long-term development'.

Referring to the 'specialist economic intelligence units that many
US unions now employ', Green suggested that while the PFA was
not a large union, the Davies law firm had made considerable
efforts to ensure that the Association 'had adequate briefs in
considering current issues both within the industry and with several
enquiries now being carried out at national level'.

And increasingly, as economists, government departments and
academics began to look more closely at professional football, the
emphasis where the PFA was concerned would move away from the
militancy of pitched battles into the more studious world of reports
and commissions, a context in which the PFA would gradually edge
its way more confidently into the limelight.

In 1967, to celebrate the Diamond Jubilee of the founding of the

Union in 1907, Cliff Lloyd and office secretary Miss Hardman moved into rather more spacious offices at the Corn Exchange. Lloyd, while drawing attention to the anniversary, commented:

> Never in the history of the Association has the organization been in such a strong financial position, and the Association has been successful in achieving several of the objects for which it was formed....

# 27
# *Chester and Dougan* 1968–71

In 1968 the Chester Committee – set up some two years previously by the Labour Government to enquire into the state of Association Football at all levels – published its recommendations. The committee's origins, ironically enough, lay in representations made by the League and the FA to the Government about the 'deteriorating financial position of the game and the need for cash for its improvement and administration'.

It must have made hard reading for both organizations, in particular the League, because, among its many wide-ranging recommendations and suggestions, the committee reopened the debate concerning freedom of contract. In fact, Chester went so far as to say that the existing contract system should be swept clean away.

The committee made many more suggestions, of course, but for the Players' Union this was the crucial one, affecting as it did the whole player–club relationship and thus the status of the professional player. As the report said: 'On the one hand it will provide a better moral basis for the transfer system ...' and 'the new system would add to the dignity of the professional player'.

Dignity and morals were words not often heard in the long and weary debates concerning contractual freedom, and yet they are entirely appropriate in any consideration of the next decade in the Association's life. Because the PFA would tackle – along with the central contractual issue – such diverse yet related questions as the disciplining of players by both ruling bodies, the behaviour of members on and off the field and their public image, the security of members, and their education before, during and after their playing careers.

In doing so the PFA would be addressing questions that concerned the very health of professional football as a whole – something the game's governing bodies (concerned as they were with cash and competitions) were barely alive to.

In the succeeding two decades, the inability of the Football League to maintain itself in purely physical terms – its archaic, dangerous stadiums, its outdated financial structures, its increasingly disillusioned customers – would be highlighted, criticized, agonized over. But just as shameful was the League clubs' continuing collective neglect of their own employees at almost every possible level.

Decades of indifference, not to say scorn, of modern coaching and training methods had led to a definite decline in Britain's standing as a world football power. No wonder, then, that professional players – if neglected as footballers – would be neglected as human beings.

From the casually callous treatment of the scores of young hopefuls lured into the game as 'ground-staff' or later as 'apprentices', right through to the ruthless, often heartless discarding of players of no further use, the majority of clubs' treatment of their employees had always been marked by a breathtaking ignorance.

Over the decades, the League had created, via its restrictive contract system and its disastrous 'management' techniques, a deferential, largely apathetic work-force, poorly educated, sheltered from all outside influence: a body of men who, thanks to a series of unique fines and punishments, rules and restrictions, threats, fears and insults, combined with a largely illusory prospect of riches and glory, had been conditioned to accept as inevitable and 'natural' the existing power structure within football.

Perhaps one ought not to judge too harshly the Football League Ltd. A key aspect of Britain's decline as a world manufacturing power had been its inability to invest in modern technology and training – its tendency to rake off the profits and hope that the customers would always return. Eventually, of course, they turned away.

That League football, in its monopoly situation, had perpetuated this disastrous tendency much longer than the outside world was only, alas, to be expected.

Nevertheless, its cries of woe to a government ostensibly embarking on a 'white hot technological revolution' were ironic indeed. And utterly misjudged.

After so many years of spurning the involvement and offers of help from 'outsiders', it now proffered a begging-bowl. No surprise, therefore, that when the response was so complex and challenging, the League clubs turned petulantly away, rejecting the Chester Committee's suggestions totally. They had wanted cash, not ideas. The fact that they could handle neither with much skill only made the situation the more potentially catastrophic.

For the PFA, however, the Chester Committee could not have come at a more opportune time, providing as it did a perfect blueprint for reform, a coherent, well-documented, well-researched manifesto – in a way, the natural follow-on from Wilberforce's Eastham judgement.

And though the League and the FA would exercise their irresponsible powers to ignore, reject and delay the committee's suggestions, the report stood as a beacon for reformers, and justification for the PFA's growing belief that it had an increasingly influential role to play in the future of the game.

For the PFA, the late 1960s were a time of reappraisal, of redefinition of its role. Chester had concluded that it was, in many ways, a typical trade union, giving advice to members about contracts, dealing with settlements under the Industrial Injuries Act and helping players get engagements upon the expiry of their contracts.

Yet in certain fundamental ways the PFA differed from other unions. Players' contracts were now individually negotiated in a highly competitive but limited market. Thus the role of the PFA was to try to ensure that certain general conditions were observed.

Also, Chester concluded, with the professional player's working life tending to be much shorter than in most professions (players often finishing their careers by the age of thirty-five), the Union 'has the peculiar problem of watching over the interests of boys at one end and men whose careers finish in the early thirties at the other'.

Most complicated of all, 'many aspects of the rules of the playing of football may affect the remuneration and conditions of professional footballers without the connection being direct or obvious'.

The PFA's immediate response to Chester was to draw up a list of issues and demands that touched on all these areas of concern upon which serious negotiations with both the League and the FA might be based. The latter bodies, of course, at this early stage, were theoretically committed to implementing many of the committee's recommendations, the carrot being the possible setting up of a Football Levy Board similar to the Racing Levy Board to funnel cash into the game.

At the 1969 PFA AGM, Cliff Lloyd outlined the demands as follows: changes in the option clauses in players' contracts so that they were placed on an equal footing with clubs where renewal was concerned; a proper pension scheme to replace the Provident Fund; a new standard form of contract plus a complete reform of the structure of disciplinary procedures.

Inevitably, the question of freedom of contract and the related transfer system would prove the most difficult to resolve. Chester, acknowledging that the transfer system was 'deeply rooted' in football, nevertheless suggested that it was 'not consistent with professional players' professional standing and must go'. The committee suggested that the recommended change to a system of longer contracts, with players free to move on at the end of each contract, should be gradually introduced over a five-year period in order to allow clubs to adjust their finances.

The transfer system itself would remain and men could still be bought and sold in the traditional way during the period of the contract. However, the system was subjected to quite a detailed scrutiny and the central tenet of League clubs – that the system provided poorer clubs with the opportunity to raise cash in order to continue and that it kept money circulating in the game (arguments that Wilberforce had accepted in the absence of facts and figures to prove the contention otherwise) – was confronted head-on.

To the bemusement of many League club directors, facts suggested the very opposite – that the transfer system saw a general movement of players down the divisions rather than up. According to Chester: 'Whatever may have been the position at one time, it is not now the case that lower divisions are the nursery for the First and Second Divisions and that transfer money flows accordingly from the top to the bottom....'

Once again, however, the very mechanics of negotiation would prove to be the barrier to change. The arguments might be won, the facts conclusive, but without the necessary three-quarters majority of League clubs no concrete reforms were possible.

Just as in the mid-Fifties, when the Joint Negotiating Committee had provided the League with a perfect dead end down which to shunt the Union, now the National Negotiating Committee would serve no other purpose but to absorb time and energy and nullify all effort.

Thus, by 1971, after two or three years of negotiations, an impasse was reached. Only a new Government, bringing with it new union legislation, would succeed in getting the process moving again.

Progress relating to change in disciplinary procedures would also be tortuously slow. Discipline was a complicated topic, for although seemingly concerned simply with the rules of play, it directly affected the working lives of professional players.

In 1967 David Green had told the Union AGM that the Union was watching 'with particular concern' the functioning of various tribunals, but that action would be postponed until Chester reported.

The Union's submission to Chester was based on the contention that disciplinary hearings were like being put on trial in the court of one's employer; players, therefore, should have the automatic right to legal representation. Chester did not accept that argument in total, considering a 'special elaborate system for professionals would not be acceptable'.

Nevertheless, he felt reforms *were* needed, principally at 'personal hearing' cases where there should be an independent chairman with some legal qualification, where players should have the option of legal representation, and where, if the sentence was severe, there should be a right of appeal.

Extra point was given to the demand for legal involvement by the Ernie Machin case which came to the Royal Courts of Justice in October 1972 (though based on an incident occurring in September 1970).

Quite simply, the FA got itself into a muddle because there was no one with legal expertise to point out that it was making basic mistakes.

Machin, a Coventry City player, had been sent off for apparently kicking an opponent after both men had fallen to the ground. TV film showed that the referee's report, upon which the whole FA case was based, was completely at odds with the facts.

After viewing the film, however, the FA Commission, spotting something *else* Machin had done wrong, decided to uphold the referee's decision anyway – not grasping the fact that they were sentencing Machin for another offence entirely, against which he had not been given the opportunity to defend himself.

If it demonstrated anything, the case highlighted the inadequacy of the traditional 'paternalistic' system of old men more or less making up the rules as they went along.

Derek Dougan, Management Committee member and chairman in 1970, put it rather more graphically:

> Disciplinary procedures in the game caused a great deal of heartburn. The 'courts' run by the FA were often no more than the 'kangaroo' variety. Justice was not always done nor seen to be done. Players were resentful, feeling that they would not get a fair hearing, and referees were uncomfortable appearing before the disciplinary committees to give evidence.

Player resentment and referee discomfort was brought to fever-pitch in 1971 when the FA decided, without consulting players or clubs to institute a dramatic 'clean-up' campaign which involved, as the PFA put it, 'changes in the application of the laws governing the game', resulting in a dramatic rise in the number of sendings off and bookings, etc.

Because there had been no 'warning', everyone had been taken by surprise – which had been the FA's intention. However, the resulting furore (plus the Machin case then being prepared) saw a truce arranged in early 1971 and a committee of study set up involving all interested parties. Once more, Government legislation had been important – the Conservative Government's Industrial Relations Act being a key factor. The Act granted employees the right to legal representation, as well as the right of appeal in cases of disciplinary action; so the PFA and FA were obliged to come to some kind of agreement.

The new system, eventually agreed upon in 1972, clarified the procedures and introduced a considerable 'independent' element. Under the scheme, players accumulated points for misdemeanours. Fines were eliminated and penalties were thus made uniform. Players were granted a personal hearing when charged with offences carrying heavy points penalties or when they were sent off; and they had the right of appeal to an independent chairman whenever the sentence was particularly severe.

The emphasis on disciplinary matters in the late Sixties and early Seventies, plus the PFA's desire to become involved in changing them, placed particular pressure on the PFA's Management Committee, certain of whom – Maurice Setters and Derek Dougan, for example – were no strangers to on-field controversy.

In 1968, when Noel Cantwell stepped down as chairman to become manager of Coventry (ironically Ernie Machin's team), the discipline issue seems to have affected the election of a successor.

According to Dougan, Maurice Setters ruled himself out because he felt his record would cause the Union embarrassment. Dougan had no such qualms. He felt that dedication and enthusiasm were the principal qualifications and put himself forward for chairman in competition with Terry Neill.

The committee chose Neill, though whether because (as Dougan would have it) of his 'nice, pleasant image' is arguable because, two years later, when Neill himself stood down to become manager of Hull City, Dougan was chosen – despite having been sent off twice within three weeks only a few months previously.

The only other possible candidate had been Bobby Charlton, but because he was not present when the issue had been raised, Dougan had insisted that a vote be taken there and then, and Neill backed him. Although Charlton would clearly have added greater prestige to the Union, Dougan was, in many ways, a more appropriate choice.

Throughout his long and turbulent career, Derek Dougan had always stood out as a character, an individual aware of himself and of his position *vis á vis* managers, directors and authority in general.

He once wrote that the petty forms of discipline imposed on players, and the managerial dictates they had to endure, created a wretched working environment which he compared to an open prison; and he possessed just the sort of 'quirky' character that would chafe and strain against rules and regulations that appeared to have no purpose.

'Knowing what I know now,' he wrote in 1976, 'I don't think I could ever have disciplined myself to do the mundane repetitive jobs that go along with being an apprentice'.

Jack Campbell affectionately recalls the young Dougan arriving at Blackburn Rovers from Portsmouth and the puzzled response of his colleagues: 'He was a loony! We all called him Cheyenne when he came in with his hair shaved down both sides and cut down the middle.... But he brought a lot of life and fun to the club.'

Such a character, however, was destined to cause trouble to managers, and it took him five more moves before he settled at Wolves to play his finest football.

The 'Doog', as he was known by adoring fans, was a marvellously talented and exciting player, a man whose emotions often led him into conflict with referees – yet a man who could ask seemingly illogical questions such as: 'Why is it we professional footballers are told to have more control over *our* emotions?'

In past decades such highly individual characters had turned away from the PFA and preferred to plough a lone furrow – Shackleton, Ford, James, etc. – to the PFA's detriment. Dougan, however, came to see the PFA as part of his life. He would bring down upon his head a welter of criticism, ridicule and mockery from all sides, but in a period when the professional footballer was struggling to come to terms with the new TV exposure, Dougan would serve the Union well.

In subsequent years, he would express some resentment at being likened to Jimmy Hill; yet the comparison has some truth (not least in that both men first achieved on-the-field notoriety for the way they grew their hair – Hill for his beard, Dougan for his shaven dome).

Hill had taken on – wittingly or unwittingly – not just the FA and the League but also the opinion-formers in the press, middle-class armchair critics who ridiculed Hill's 'bourgeois' pretensions, his encouragement of the idea of professional players reaching for 'the good life'.

Dougan would also find himself laughed at for his attempts to upgrade the 'image' of players, especially when he claimed that the PFA Awards dinner – a TV inspired bean-feast that he helped to initiate in 1974 – was a positive move on behalf of the whole profession. As he explained:

The image of the footballer as a thick-headed yokel who needs constant discipline and cannot be trusted to manage his own affairs is a distant throwback. The real image belongs to the PFA Awards night which I helped with Eric Woodward of Aston Villa and Cliff Lloyd to inaugurate in March 1974. The television cameras, roaming casually through groups of dinner-jacketed players, waiting to go into dinner, have presented nationwide a more articulate, self-assured image ... anyone who doubts the social progress of the modern footballer has only to switch on the Player of the Year Awards on ITV, without doubt the best night on the sporting calendar....

The Awards dinners served more practical purposes, of course. As Dougan said, they provided an opportunity for players at all levels to mix socially. 'We have on this occasion three hundred to four hundred players representing all the League clubs and they can find out what they have in common.' The awards themselves, Dougan emphasized, were democratic – all pro-players had a vote – as well as drawing attention to the 'qualities which players regard most highly in their colleagues....'

The first recipient of the Players' Player of the Year in 1974 – Norman Hunter – could hardly have been more of a challenge to

Foul *magazine's satirical cartoon on the PFA Awards.*

the perceptions of friends and foes of the PFA. At a time when pro-football was coming under increasing criticism regarding dour, defensive, not to say violent tendencies, the pro-players picked that arch exponent of the crunching tackle, Norman 'Bite Yer Legs' Hunter.

For a satirical magazine like *Foul*, which owed its existence to the disillusionment with the state of the game on and off the field, such a selection was incomprehensible.

Yet, although Hunter's selection was not consciously designed to make a point, his award certainly represented a public thumbing of the nose to critics at all levels, in particular to those in the press and the media in general.

Dougan was always keen to retain his own independence (witness his determination to always own his own house, having seen how clubs used players' accommodation as a tool of control) and to define himself (his 'way-out' hair-cuts, popularly regarded as crowd-pleasers surely having a more significant meaning).

Thus he can be seen as the perfect PFA chairman for the difficult, transitional period that saw professional football and footballers move uncertainly into the TV age.

# 28

# *CIR – and Hard Bargaining 1971–73*

It was during the 1970s that TV began to have a profound affect on professional football. In the 1950s and 1960s it had simply been a means of transmitting the action to a much wider audience – a window on the game through which people had been happy to look.

Now TV was beginning to assert itself; it was 'packaging and presenting' the game, principally via programmes of edited highlights. Panels of experts appeared, interposing themselves between the audience and the game while the camera began to poke its nose into previously 'sacrosanct' areas: down the tunnel leading to the pitch, into the dressing-rooms, on to the training pitch, even inside the team coach as it headed for Wembley.

TV was slowly, but surely, influencing what people saw and what they expected to see and, in turn, was affecting those it exposed. The football ground itself became a stage, not just for players but for the spectators as well – from singing and chanting to fighting on the terraces and even invading the pitch, everyone seemed to want to get in on the act!

Thus TV was the cause of a multitude of changes, some good, some bad, most hard to quantify. But, for the PFA, TV brought with it a commodity once in short supply – money.

TV's gradually developing economic muscle was to be both a

threat and a blessing to the Union and its members: a threat because its massive economic impact would create unbearable tensions which threatened to destroy the existing fabric of the game, and thus endanger employment prospects; a blessing because, thanks to the ever-increasing reserves of cash flowing into the Union from its share of TV contracts, pro-players were subsequently able to avail themselves of educational opportunities that transformed the profession, removing much of the fear and insecurity that had always haunted it, substituting instead horizons broader than those of which the Union's founders ever dreamed.

The advent of war in 1939 had stifled an initiative upon which Jimmy Fay had placed great store – the chance to provide for players, particularly those approaching the ends of their careers, an opportunity to acquire 'professional' skills such as accountancy or running a business.

Post-war struggles to remove the maximum wage and to reform players' contracts, etc. had seen such educational aspirations crowded out, but by the mid-Sixties the idea had been revived, prompted by the decision of the FA to pull out of the accident insurance scheme in 1964. The money provided by the FA through its TV deals ought, it was decided, to go into education instead.

By 1967 an Education Fund had been set up with a view to providing financial assistance to any member or ex-member wishing to undertake vocational training. It was pointed out at the time that the League's Jubilee Fund was available for small grants to help members cover the costs of entering courses and buying books – but the PFA had grander ambitions.

It hoped to be able to provide courses that included basic training in the practical and business side of professional football as a guide to existing players and as training for future managers and managerial staff.

Such a development was in line with changes that had occurred in British society since the war and in the nature of the 'raw material' of the professional game. Young players received a more thorough basic schooling than their pre-war counterparts and there was a greater awareness of the potentialities of education.

A significant number of youngsters signing on at seventeen had already begun training for a profession or a skill and many were forced to make a choice between football or a career in industry or the professions. While some clubs encouraged their apprentices to attend college, most did not and, for many full-time professionals, peer-group pressure plus unofficial club/manager policy tended to banish all thoughts of academic improvement.

Consequently, the determination of a player such as Gordon Taylor to push on with his higher education to study for an external degree at night school while continuing to build a successful career as a pro was the exception rather than the rule.

More typical would have been the experience of Terry Neill, chairman of the Union in 1968, who had trained as an engineer before signing for Arsenal in 1960 and who, after continuing with his studies for a time at Regent Street Polytechnic, gave them up to concentrate on football when he gained a place in the Arsenal first team.

Neill could see the advantages of having some kind of training – either academic or practical – and when he became chairman during a relatively peaceful time in the Union's history he envisaged its main task as being to help players prepare for the time when they would no longer be able to play. This, he considered, would be good both for players and for the game as a whole.

The underlying insecurity of the professional footballer had caused the game a great deal of grief down the years and had led indirectly to a number of damaging incidents, the most recent of which was the betting/fixing scandal of the early Sixties that had ended some illustrious careers.

Whilst not excusing nor even wholly explaining such behaviour, the uncertain prospects of relatively young, often unskilled men frequently led to a desperate scramble to stockpile some kind of nest-egg by fair means or foul as security against the dreaded day when 'retirement' beckoned.

Education was a more certain route to that security than the dream of a bumper 'benefit' or a hefty slice of a transfer fee. Not that many young players automatically leapt at the chance to 'improve' them-selves – and yet scores of ex-professionals would enter club manage-ment. As Chester commented, 'Few have had much, if any, experience or training in managing a commercial enterprise, or indeed, in managing people.'

The financial health of clubs would depend upon efficient and skilful management, yet according to Chester, 'We doubt whether most have yet given much attention to management.'

Once again the PFA was taking on a responsibility for the game in general that the industry's management had barely considered.

Progress on the educational front was rapid. In 1969, grants totalling £400 were disbursed (to, among others, future Union chairmen Gordon Taylor and Alan Gowling). By 1970, that total had increased to over £1000 and would continue to rise rapidly as the decade progressed.

In January 1971 the Union's first Education Officer – Bob Kerry – was appointed from among 150 applicants and the Education Fund became a separate item on the Union accounts with its own budget and charity status. George Davies commented:

> It is the start of the first systematic attempt to cope with the problems that can arise within a profession which can so easily dazzle youngsters coming into the game....

Kerry soon established links with colleges up and down the country and began developing courses specifically designed for young professionals. One interesting aspect of the increased educational activity was the sudden pressure it placed upon the League's Jubilee Fund – until then, an almost moribund institution. With Union advice and encouragement, more and more players applied to the fund for help in paying course fees – so much so that, within a couple of years, the League found it could not cope, first limiting applications to £5 a man and then, in 1974, stopping educational grants altogether. Once again, the Union was left to shoulder the burden single-handed.

In 1972, however, Kerry had been able to announce: 'Slowly but surely a situation is being created whereby anyone – especially a youngster – will be able to obtain immediate help from a suitable person at a local college.'

Not only youngsters were being helped. Courses at all levels were being gradually set up whilst individual players were being assisted, as Kerry put it, 'with problems ranging from Management Accountancy to Turf Accountancy and from Fisheries Management to Fish and Chip shops....'

The climate, Kerry continued, was definitely changing, 'and it is now easier to get both club managements and college staff to make the necessary concessions so that players can attend the college of their choice and the course of their choice....'

Firms such as Watney were sponsoring short courses; correspondence courses were being devised; while at St Helens

College of Technology the highly successful residential management course was held for the first time in 1973. Kerry noted that of the thirteen who took part, four had obtained managerial posts by the time the course started, two were subsequently appointed assistant managers, one obtained a coaching appointment, and another was promoted within his club. Men like Terry Venables, ex-Management Committee member, and Brian Talbot, future Union chairman, plus Tony Book and Alan Durban were among this pioneering group.

Initial optimism regarding club cooperation, however, would be tempered. Attempts to monitor the educational progress of apprentices in 1977 by the Education Unit were hampered by clubs' unwillingness to return simple information, leading Kerry to comment: 'Most clubs are making very little effort to help their apprentices to continue their education.'

Progress nevertheless continued, thanks to Kerry's hard work of visiting clubs up and down the country, liaising and cooperating with college principals and lecturers in an initiative unique in the history of British professional sport.

Success in this sphere must have been a source of great comfort to Cliff Lloyd and the rest of the Management Committee as the 1970s proceeded because progress towards the ultimate goals – freedom of contract and a modern pension scheme – had slowed to snail's-pace.

As mentioned, initial moves after Chester in 1968 had seemed promising, the assumption being that Chester had diagnosed the problems and the football industry simply had to work out rational ways to implement his suggestions. It took two years of patient, painstaking negotiations and discussions before it was revealed that, for the majority of League clubs, Chester might just as well have saved his energy.

A package, agreed upon by both Management Committees, was put to the League in May 1970. It included four key proposals: a pension scheme for all players; a £15 minimum wage; abolition of the option clause in players' contracts without mutual agreement; and the inclusion of apprentices in the system. However, this far from radical package was thrown out completely by the clubs, a decision that more or less ended the useful life of the National Negotiating Committee.

As Cliff Lloyd put it some time afterwards: 'It was plainly a waste of time negotiating with a body that did not have the authority to settle what had been agreed upon.'

By then, with a new Conservative Government in office and radical changes in trade union law being enacted – specifically the Industrial Relations Act of 1971 – the PFA could see alternative opportunities opening up.

The Act – which was to cause so much anguish among the mainstream Union movement – was seen by the PFA to offer 'great benefits' and on the Union solicitor's (and Roy Hattersley's) advice, the PFA remained on the Government Trade Union Register – a decision that was to lead to the PFA's expulsion from the TUC in 1973.

For the PFA, the Act offered the hope that real negotiating machinery might be set up, or that the National Negotiating Committee be given some 'teeth'. Half-hearted negotiations did continue after 1970 concerning contractual freedom but with each 'agreement' destined to come to grief at the League's AGM, the Union was increasingly convinced that an approach to the Government was its best option.

In May 1973, therefore, representations were made to the Departments of Employment and Environment which resulted in the respective Ministers of State referring the question of industrial relations between professional footballers and their employers to the Commission on Industrial Relations. This would 'seek ways to promote any improvements in their relations that appear to be necessary or desirable', and while its recommendations would not be binding, they would carry considerable weight in any subsequent case brought before the Industrial Court.

The move, coming as it did after three frustrating years, was not enough to quell some 'ripples of discontent with the lack of progress' (as the 1973 AGM put it). In fact, for the first time since the days of Jimmy Guthrie, criticism of the PFA by individuals who felt a more 'radical' approach was needed surfaced both at the AGM and in print.

In a way, such a reaction was understandable. The early 1970s were grim times for football in general. Spectators continued to desert the game in frightening numbers and bad publicity – in particular the rising tide of violence in and around football grounds, controversy relating to behaviour of players on the field, not to mention the failure of the England team to qualify for major tournaments – only added to the gloom.

The economic plight of the country – the three-day week and industrial strife – appeared to herald a collapse of the League system. Massive personnel cutbacks and club closures were forecast with a great deal of the blame for this being placed on players – particularly by Alan Hardaker the League secretary.

Critics of the PFA felt that the players were losing the initiative, that Hardaker had been able to fob off the Union with nothing substantial for years and that the CIR was just another excuse for inaction.

Eamon Dunphy, a professional with Millwall and a future journalist and writer (author of the classic pro-footballer's 'diary', *Only a Game?*) used the columns of *Foul* magazine in August 1973 to suggest that whereas much of the blame for recent Union inactivity rested with apathetic players – in particular the well-paid stars – the fact that the PFA Management Committee itself had not given a more aggressive lead was doubtless partly responsible.

'Since Jimmy Hill,' he remarked, 'no one else has emerged with the character to unite the Union behind any of its demands.'

Derek Dougan was quick to respond, but apart from reiterating the various achievements of the Union since the early Sixties (and having a dig at the fact that Dunphy himself had not, according to Dougan, paid his subs recently) there was little the Union Management Committee could say. Years had passed, with little to show for all the talking, and there was scant prospect of anything dramatic happening in the near future.

*Foul* magazine, in fact, would provide a critical, radical if unfocused voice for some years to come, dedicated as it was to opposing the 'greed, vested interests and phony glamour' that increasingly seemed to characterize the British game – typified, according to *Foul*, by pre-season competitions such as the Watney Cup – 'violent, irrelevant, glorifying only the trivial and the second-rate'.

Yet its attack on the PFA appeared at times to be based more on its dislike of the 'style' of the leadership rather than the substance, not to mention irritation with the Association for seeming to benefit from 'Tory' legislation which the rank and file union movement was fighting tooth and nail....

A year later, in October 1974, it carried a much longer article by Alan Stewart based in part on an interview with Cliff Lloyd. The

# Pretty Feeble Altogether?

Foul, *October 1974*

title, 'Pretty Feeble Altogether', sums up its approach to the Association. Once again, the PFA's relationship with its membership was attacked: the poor response of the membership being attributed to 'feeble leadership' and 'faintheartedness'. What was more, *Foul* was now able to point to sections of the newly published Government Report – the Commission of Industrial Relations – which seemed to confirm its own view by criticizing the delegate system of the Union.

The CIR had remarked that 'a substantial proportion of the players we interviewed were ignorant of the PFA's activities on their behalf ... it is often seen as being a fairly remote body having little relevance to the daily problems faced by the players....'

Cliff Lloyd commented: '... to some extent I find it hard to accept the situation as described by the CIR....' But his response to the suggestion that the PFA no longer had the 'stomach for the fight' as in the early Sixties was more specific: it was easy, he said, 'to say that our best resort is to use the courts, but it would need another player of the calibre of Eastham, not to mention a considerable amount of cash'.

Lloyd insisted, however, that the long-drawn-out negotiations in the two years following the Chester Report had proved a point and had led to the CIR Report. Time had also proved the PFA right because, 'economically and financially football can ill afford to continue with the system as it is now'.

The time, he declared, was now ripe for negotiations, and he was optimistic of success. He was also drawn to defend Derek Dougan, whom Stewart had described as 'smug', suggesting that Dougan's real aim in life was to secure a comfortable manager's job.

'Chairmen of the PFA never seem to be men with radical views; and, once there, they use the post for advertising their conformity and responsibility to club chairmen,' Stewart wrote.

Lloyd pointed out that Dougan – like all chairmen – worked extremely hard for no pay, normally during precious free time. What was more, the fact that PFA chairmen generally became managers was, according to Lloyd, all to their credit: 'This simply confirms that they possess the necessary qualifications which must surely include leadership.'

The exchange was revealing, illustrating radically different attitudes towards the Union's role and methods, not to say its ultimate aims where professional football was concerned. Lloyd clearly rejected the idea that the action of a player – whether he be a PFA chairman or not – in becoming a manager represented some sort of ideological 'selling out'.

The path chosen by Lloyd and the PFA – building a proper negotiating machinery, attempting to coax and chivvy the League into a proper negotiating situation where progress could be made via a process of mutual education – represented a rejection of the 'confrontational' tactics demanded by contributors to *Foul* and critics such as Eamon Dunphy and Jimmy Guthrie.

The CIR Report, in fact, confirmed Lloyd's optimism regarding the real possibility of progress through a proper negotiating forum. Its principal recommendation was for a new body – the Professional Football Negotiating Committee complete with an independent chairman – to be established as soon as possible.

The League's willingness to set up the body and to try to make it work was evidence of its acceptance that fundamental change was long overdue. It was also clear that both sides – players and administrators – would have to face up to certain uncomfortable truths. As Professor John Wood explained at the November PFA AGM: The Football League Management Committee were 'somewhat apprehensive about changes in the contractual position and this had been the reason given by the League for their reluctance to enter negotiations.... The Football League were now willing to negotiate but they would need convincing of the necessity for change no matter how strong the PFA's case was morally.'

The CIR Report had been helpful in this respect. When examining the transfer system, and analysing figures for the years since Chester, it had been unable to prove that the system did *not* help smaller clubs. The Report had also accepted that there was some economic basis in the fears of clubs about losing the value of players if the transfer system was abolished. Although money could not be raised on the security of players, their presence among the assets of the club meant that money on other assets could be more easily secured.

The willingness of the PFA to recognize this (while by no means approving of it) created a basis upon which the new Professional Football Negotiating Committee could begin its work.

For the League it held out the possibility that all might not be lost where the transfer system was concerned; for the Union, the concession presented it with considerable leverage with which to press for long-sought-after objectives.

# 29

# *Freedom at Last?* 1974–81

At the November 1974 AGM George Davies told delegates:

> Anything short of total freedom would be an imposition on players....
> All formulas set up were designed for one purpose, to safeguard the
> financial interests of clubs with literally no concern for the players.

Whilst echoing the beliefs firmly held by players since before the
turn of the century, such ringing declarations would eventually
prove irrelevant. As negotiations dragged on, the necessity for
compromise would become paramount and total freedom would
ultimately become a bargaining counter. Indeed, at the 1975 AGM,
Cliff Lloyd would announce that the Management Committee 'had
thought it desirable to compromise on the question of freedom of
contract despite the decision taken at the last AGM', and he would
receive enthusiastic backing from the assembled delegates.

The reason for this apparent 'retreat' was that the PFA sensed
that influence, even power, in the professional game was moving
inexorably in its direction. And though the League would delay,
prevaricate and resist during the next four years of dogged
negotiations, a peaceful revolution was under way. With the setting
up of the Joint Negotiating Committee in 1975, progress was
initially rapid. Comprising three Football League and three PFA

representatives (Derek Dougan, Gordon Taylor and Terry Venables and later on Bruce Bannister) with an independent chairman and joint secretaries, the committee's constitution provided for quarterly meetings; and it soon became clear that much of the committee's time would be spent in dealing with the apprehensions and fears of the League clubs and their chairmen.

As early as the second formal meeting, nevertheless, an outline agreement had been reached based on four principles:

> 1. During the currency of the player's contract the familiar transfer procedure would continue;
> 2. Once a contract had been completed a player would have the right freely to seek employment with another club;
> 3. A system should be devised by which the club from which a player went should receive compensation;
> 4. That compensation system should not be a serious hindrance to better employment.

It was also agreed that a pension scheme would be considered as a replacement to the Provident Fund.

The word 'compensation' was a key one, reflecting the clubs' unshakeable conviction that their very survival would continue to depend on the 'value' of a player in their 'possession'.

Thus the transfer system remained for men who changed clubs *during* their contract; the big question was, how to 'compensate' a club once the player's contract had ended and he was free to move on – a principle that was now accepted by both sides.

Quite early in the negotiations, Alan Hardaker had suggested a system then in operation in Holland called the 'multiplier'. Without knowing it, Hardaker was raising a ghost.

Back in 1899, Charlie Saer, the secretary of the Players' Union, had devised a system to replace the transfer system based upon the wages received by the player – a good guide to his worth, Charlie Saer had suggested. His scheme had been ridiculed and dismissed with contempt by C E Sutcliffe; now a League secretary was re-introducing the idea. Charlie Saer would have smiled.

The multiplier was, inevitably, more complicated than Saer's idea. Apart from wages, it involved calculations based on the age of the player, the division he was playing in and whether he was going up or down the game's social scale, i.e. from Third to First, etc.

As Hardaker put it: 'It was time to restore some sanity to the transfer market', and the multiplier was intended to do just that by removing the volatile 'free market' element and thus drastically reducing the amount of individual fees.

As early as October 1975, however, the League began quibbling over certain details of operation of the multiplier – proposing that the wage upon which calculations were to be based should be that offered by the buying club rather than the wage already being paid by the selling club.

The PFA negotiating team were adamant, however, that the original scheme should stand; and notwithstanding such 'teething' problems, the players approved the idea at the 1975 AGM, giving the Management Committee a complete mandate to press on.

In early 1976, however, it emerged that the League was pressing for the multiplier idea to be dropped altogether. Instead, it was suggested clubs should have a month in which to agree on a transfer, and if disagreements persisted then the Independent Tribunal should settle the matter.

Once again, the PFA team insisted that the multiplier must remain, although on Sir John Wood's suggestion, they conceded the earlier point regarding the basis upon which valuations should be made: it would now be the wages offered by the *buying* club rather than those of the *selling* club.

The concession brought no immediate resolution, however, and as the months dragged by, the PFA Management Committee came under increasing pressure from members to press for full implementation of the agreement.

In 1976, Jimmy Guthrie's autobiography was published containing general criticisms of the Union, calling into question the 'moderate' approach it was taking as against the 'militant' stance he considered essential.

Whether relevant or not, Guthrie's criticisms highlighted the fact that many players were unhappy, indeed afraid at the implications of the new contract under discussion. Eamon Dunphy had suggested as long ago as the 1974 AGM that Union delegates had not really understood what the new system would entail. In 1975 there were fears expressed about the influence some managers were bringing to bear on players. Managers in general appeared ambivalent towards the new freedoms promised in the agreement, and some appeared intent on waging a publicity war on the Union, predicting chaos and unemployment if 'freedom of contract' came to pass.

The Alternative Football Paper    April 1974 Number 17 10p

Cliff Lloyd was pressed by Alan Stewart in *Foul* magazine to 'tell his members exactly what was being discussed. Members, Stewart claimed, were afraid, confused and not a little frightened. And at the 1976 AGM delegates did indeed express anxiety at the way time was passing while nothing was being 'delivered'. There were also concerns at the way the multiplier might affect their rights but, as Cliff Lloyd explained, it was difficult to tell members everything that was going on. Negotiations, he insisted, were easily upset and besides, 'the players had mandated the committee to negotiate on their behalf and they must allow us to reach agreement'.

It was an awkward time for the PFA and highlighted the extent to which it was often unable to affect or counter media opinion-making. A Union publication might have helped matters. As it was, members had to rely on 'cyclostyled news-sheets' according to Dunphy – no competition for the tabloids' banner headlines.

Matters were made worse for the PFA Management Committee when in June 1977, at an extraordinary meeting of the Football League, the clubs failed to pass the new agreement. Although they supported the scheme in principle, 'with a stroke of typical genius' (according to Sir John Wood), they failed to pass the changes in regulations needed to implement it.

Negotiations recommenced through the PFNC but players' impatience was now reaching boiling point, particularly at the sight of clubs continuing to tinker and tamper with the agreement.

In September 1977, for instance, the Midland Clubs (the League had by now reorganized itself into regional groupings) mischievously suggested that the compensation formula could be manipulated in order to avoid paying a club its entitlement. Cliff Lloyd countered this by pointing out that had the clubs not insisted on altering the way the multiplier had originally been meant to work, such manipulation would not be possible.

The argument, however, was now beginning to involve individuals – particularly when it was revealed that the League had failed to pass the agreement in July because 'they had been led to believe that agreement had been reached by the PFA Chairman Derek Dougan and J W T Hill to the effect that in the event of a player deciding to leave his club at the end of his contract the clubs concerned should be free to negotiate the transfer fee for the loss of his services and this arrangement had supposedly thrown out the question of the compensation formula'.

Dougan stated that at no stage had he agreed with Hill that the compensation formula should be scrapped. All he had said was that he was 'prepared to settle the matter on the holding or buying club's offer being the basis of how the compensation was negotiated'.

He also stated quite categorically that it had never been suggested to him that the two clubs should be left to negotiate the fee. Thus the Union Management Committee passed the following resolution: 'In view of Mr Dougan's remarks it appeared that Mr Hill had completely misled the meeting of Football League clubs.'

That it should have been Jimmy Hill with whom Dougan was publicly disagreeing was ironic – indeed, given the context, not a little sad. Dougan was later to accuse Hill of going back on his earlier convictions when he had been Union chairman in the 1960s. (In Dougan's own words, Hill had become 'a poacher turned gamekeeper'.) But Hill was adamant that his philosophy had remained consistent down through the years, that even as Union chairman he had accepted the need for a transfer system and that the right of the player to move once his contract had finished had been the key principle to be established.

Hill felt that the multiplier was an unnecessary bureaucratic interference in the free market, an artificial construction that would lead, like most bureaucratic restrictions, to a 'black market'.

In fact, Hill's views on the need for a transfer market were no different from those of certain other PFA Management Committee members involved in the negotiations. Keith Peacock, for instance, always suspected that smaller clubs would need the transfer market in order to survive, while Alan Gowling agreed with Hill that without a transfer system, the spare cash would probably find its way into top players' pockets – not necessarily a good thing.

What was clear, however, was that there was a great deal of uncertainty on both sides as to what complete freedom, with no transfer system at all, would really mean. Economic models might be constructed to predict the future, but it was human beings with their fears and prejudices who would ultimately dictate events.

For Dougan, however, the transfer system remained the root of all soccer's problems. Without it, he claimed, directors would be forced to reorganize their financial arrangements, would be forced to give up relying on the illusory gains the system seemed to deliver. And though he was often pilloried by 'radical' critics as 'not having his heart in the struggle', Dougan's insistence on the multiplier demonstrates just how committed he was to fundamental change.

In fact, Dougan was one of the few people involved in football who attempted to put what he saw as the essential principles of the Chester Report into practice, lock, stock and barrel. He would often state that the Chester Report was 'his bible' and, never one for half measures, he made a determined attempt in 1974 to take over Walsall FC, a struggling club which he hoped to rescue and transform along Chestertonian lines.

That proposal fell through, but within a year he had taken a step closer to his dreams by becoming chief executive of Kettering Town FC, a non-League club in severe financial difficulties.

He was criticized in certain quarters for remaining on the PFA Management Committee while no longer a player but his reply was simple:

> It would have been impractical to get the negotiations under way and then resign as chairman to pass the complicated issues to another chairman. I was interested only in continuity which meant remaining until negotiations had been completed and the new deal implemented.

The Kettering Town experience ended in disappointment after three years mainly because of financial problems beyond his control; but in the course of his stewardship of the club he had blazed a trail, clashing with the FA over a sponsorship deal that involved putting the firm's logo on the players' shirts, but eventually seeing his dream of a 'sports complex' with the club at its centre more or less cold-shouldered by the Kettering public.

His departure from Kettering Town in 1978 and his unsuccessful

*Brendon Batson in West Bromwich Albion colours. Deputy Chief Executive of the PFA. (Terry Lake)*

*Garth Crooks, Tottenham Hotspur. PFA Chairman 1988–90. (Bob Thomas)*

*Brian Marwood, Sheffield Wednesday (then of Arsenal). PFA Chairman 1991.*

*Bob Kerry, the PFA's first Education Officer*

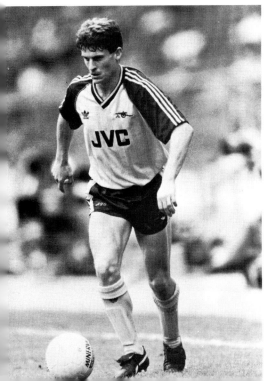

*PFA Management Committee, 1991. Back row, left to right: M Burns, G Taylor, B Batson. Front row: L Sanchez, P Nevin, B Marwood, G Twentyman, C Gibson, C Baker, G Berry. Inset: G Mabbutt. (Paul Francis)*

*PFA Administrative and Office staff. Seated: Gordon Taylor (Chief Executive). Standing, left to right: Brendon Batson (Deputy Chief Executive), Carol Brown, Karen Evans, Zöe Holmes, Tracey Clare, Mick McGuire (PFA/YT Coordinator). (Z Jacobson)*

*Footballers' Further Education and Vocational Training Society. Standing, left to right: Pat Lally (Assistant Education Officer), Mick McGuire. Seated: Nicola Wood, Micky Burns (Chief Executive), Ann Stephenson. (Z Jacobson)*

*Football and the Community Development Scheme. Left to right: Cheryl Hinds, Kevin Jardine, Kevin Glendon, Roger Reade (Chief Administrator), Natalie Coppage, Mark Holroyd, Louise Pearson. (Z Jacobson)*

*Gordon Taylor with Professor Sir John Wood CBE, for more than two decades an excellent influence for good relations within the football world.*

*Winners of the PFA's three annual awards: (left) Players' Player of the Year (for the second time), Mark Hughes; PFA Merit Award for services to the game, Tommy Hutchison; Young Player of the Year, Lee Sharpe. The PFA also selects Divisional Award Winners, eleven per division.* (Bob Thomas)

bid for the Wolves managership a few months later must only have deepened his disappointment at the Football League clubs' final rejection of the multiplier concept on 13 April that year.

The League's acceptance of the rest of the agreement and Hardaker's warning that, if the multiplier was insisted upon, the whole deal would fall, left the PFA Management Committee few options.

Following the earlier rejection of the deal and the disagreement with Jimmy Hill, the committee had consulted members at a series of area meetings up and down the country, and had received firm backing – even to the extent of strike action – for the agreement as it stood. But the PFA, if we are to believe Dougan, never really contemplated such a drastic step. In fact, Dougan was keen to point out how moderate the PFA really was:

> If Cliff Lloyd and I had been revolutionary radicals we would have exerted pressure on the industry and called footballers out on strike. This would have disrupted the game and driven away supporters on whom the game depends. At every stage of negotiations we had the good of the game at heart and showed that the PFA is not a militant movement but a progressive organization which values the interests of all that the profession represents.

Nevertheless, when it came to a vote on committee, Dougan claims he was unhappy:

> Only two of us on the Management Committee – Bruce Bannister and myself – wanted to stick it out to ensure complete freedom for footballers, but persuasive arguments were put up.... I decided it would not have been circumspect to take on the rest of the committee so a watered-down version of freedom of contract was agreed upon.

And so, at the 1978 PFA AGM, eighty years to the month after professional footballers first met to form a Union to fight the transfer system and secure freedom of contract, the most significant step along that long and weary road was ratified.

Cliff Lloyd was predictably positive about the new agreement: 'The right of the player to change clubs at the end of his contract has now been firmly established....' George Davies, however, was more circumspect:

The new regulations do attempt to provide more equality to the bargaining position. Time will tell whether the arrangements spelt out in the new regulations offer a reasonable freedom for your members.... Legally, perhaps, we are still only at the half-way house.

Dougan, however, was scathing:

I predict they'll live to regret not implementing the multiplying formula devised by the PFA in the long-term interests of the game....

The 1978 AGM, however, marked the end of Dougan's long reign as chairman. Within a few months he would become commercial director of PFA Ltd, thus maintaining a link with the organization that had become such an integral part of his life.

The 1978 AGM marked another significant milestone – twenty-five years of Cliff Lloyd serving the Union. He was now sixty-three years old and contemplating retirement. His successor – so long a problem clouding the Association's future – had already been decided upon. Gordon Taylor, the new chairman, had been asked by the Management Committee if he would serve as assistant to Lloyd for the next two years before stepping into the latter's shoes. He would thus become the first man since Jimmy Fay to have held both top positions in the Union.

Lloyd was therefore preparing for his departure in the same careful, constructive way as he had carried out the Union's affairs ever since 1953 when he had taken over from Jimmy Fay. The new standard players' agreement, then in the process of being drawn up, would provide him with the finest of monuments – indeed, with perfect timing it would come into force in November 1981, the year he was destined to step down.

Another ambition, nevertheless, remained, possibly an even more satisfying one in view of Lloyd's continuing concern for the average professional. A new pension plan, almost achieved in 1969, recommended by the CIR in 1974 and agreed in principle in 1978, had still to be negotiated with the League.

By 1980 the Players' Cash Benefit scheme, as it had come to be known, was being put to area meetings of players for their enthusiastic endorsement. The new scheme provided pro-players with something no other 'industrial' worker could boast – a lump sum payment on attaining the age of thirty-five, based on years of service multiplied by average earnings which was equivalent to between 3 and 4 per cent of a man's total earnings, plus a death-in-service benefit of up to £15,000.

A 5 per cent levy on transfer fees provided the premium for the scheme, so players contributed nothing at all. Instead, the system that had more or less called the Union into existence was now paying for each man's security.

Thus at the 1981 AGM, Cliff Lloyd could look back over thirty years of almost unrelenting toil on behalf of professional footballers and point to successes beyond the wildest dreams of men like Charlie Roberts, Herbert Broomfield, Billy Meredith and Jimmy Fay – even of Jimmy Guthrie, who had died in 1978.

The Union had now delivered a measure of financial security for each and every member, limited freedom of contract, a Benevolent Fund, accident insurance, an education scheme, legal advice relating to contracts, representation on disciplinary tribunals, representation on numerous committees concerning football's present and future, and, finally, freedom of speech. All this, and 100 per cent membership without a closed shop.

Not that Lloyd would ever claim such successes for himself alone. He would prefer to point to George Davies and David Green, of the Union's law firm; to his chairmen and Management Committee colleagues down the years, such as Hill, Dougan, Cummings, Cantwell, Charlton, Neill, Musgrove, Setters and Venables, Leighton and Leyland – all these and many others he would praise and congratulate. And Miss Hardman, the PFA office secretary for the past thirty-seven years, of whom he would say in almost awestruck tones: 'No man ever had a more loyal and devoted secretary … she was absolutely marvellous and the players don't know the debt they owe....' Because only he knew the extent to which the Union for so many years had consisted of such dedicated individuals blessed with a gargantuan capacity for hard work; only he could understand the devotion to a cause that would result in years passing without a proper holiday being taken, thousand upon thousand of miles – in trains, buses and by battered old car – travelled from club to club, player to player, dealing with hundreds of individual problems, a phone that never stopped ringing, case work that never failed to throw up some new twist, some new legal quirk.

Only he could know just how hard a road it had been and how many personal sacrifices it had been necessary to make along the way.

And yet, if satisfaction was the wrong word to describe his emotions, then pride in his profession's advances would certainly sum up his feelings as the tributes were paid to him that November afternoon in 1981 when he finally stepped down.

Inevitably, George Davies would put into words what most members were feeling:

> Cliff Lloyd's depth of purpose and endeavour, to which must be added his immense standing in the football world and his character as an individual, has provided the PFA with a consistent champion of the rights of footballers. In the period of his secretaryship the lifestyle and standard of living of footballers in the life of the community has taken a very great uplift ... and this period has seen what can fairly be described as a revolution in the conditions and financial rewards to players. He has had the loyal support of the succession of Management Committees during the whole of this period but it must be said that he has been their mainspring and much credit is due to him for the enormous changes which have taken place....

# 30

# *Gordon Taylor's Baptism of Fire 1982–84*

'I'm a product of the age,' Gordon Taylor told Patrick Barclay in 1988, commenting upon his 'high-profile' image. And yet, to be truthful, Taylor is the product of many football ages.

He was born in 1944 at Ashton-under-Lyne, just a cycle ride from Clayton and Ardwick, districts of Manchester steeped in football folklore and still haunted by the ghosts of Meredith and Roberts. Indeed, his father worked as a British Rail motor fitter at Gorton Tank amid the complex of railway line sidings and engineering works whose employees were responsible for the birth of both great Manchester sides and thus the Players' Union itself.

As a boy in the 1950s, he had cycled into Manchester to collect the autographs of men like Roy Paul and the pre-Munich Busby Babes – a football era distant enough for its heroes to remain mercifully free of today's crass commercial hype.

His own career began in the early 1960s. Signed by Bolton Wanderers, where another of his heroes – Nat Lofthouse – was second team manager, he was thrust into Wanderers' 1963-64 relegation struggle at the age of eighteen and found himself at Old Trafford confronting the resurgent Manchester United of Law,

Best and Charlton. Gordon broke his nose, Bolton lost 5–0 and were eventually relegated, after a desperate struggle that almost saw them claw their way to safety.

For a decade he would play for Bolton in the Second Division, clocking up over 250 appearances at both inside forward and on the wing before signing for Birmingham City. Playing alongside the young Trevor Francis and Bob Latchford, he helped City gain promotion to the First Division in his second season with the club. He almost reached Wembley on three occasions during his Birmingham days, but was transferred to Blackburn Rovers in 1976, only to be seriously injured in the same year. He recuperated by playing in the North American Soccer League during the summer of 1977 among the likes of Pele and Beckenbauer. He then returned to England, and later moved to Bury where his twenty-year football career ended.

Therefore, when he assumed the mantle of secretary of the PFA, his keen ambitions both for the Union and for himself were to be tempered by a mix of memory and experience, a sense of history as well as an appreciation of the game's commercial possibilities, that would serve professional football remarkably well as it plunged into the crises of the 1980s.

Upon taking office he was quoted as saying:

> All the battles the players needed to fight … against the maximum wage, for freedom of movement and now freedom of speech … have been won. What we need now is cooperation between all bodies in the game to stop the kind of disputes and mud-slinging that, I'm sure, have helped disillusion the public.

Thus, where the use of 'militant' action and of confrontation as bargaining tactics were concerned, Taylor would appear to be at one with Derek Dougan; and yet, his succession first as chairman and then more crucially as secretary, would mark a definite change of emphasis.

From Taylor's point of view, the 1978 agreement marked a new dawn for the professional game and for the pro-footballer in particular. Dougan, by contrast, had voiced (and would continue to voice) great disappointment at what had been achieved, especially when placed in the context of the Chester Report of 1968.

Taylor, however, looked to the more pragmatic industrial-relations-based CIR Report of 1974 as his guiding light. He had been brought on to the Professional Football Negotiating Committee along with Bruce Bannister in 1975 where the influence of Professor Sir John Wood had been fundamental to his Union development. Protracted negotiations, open-ended discussions inching gradually towards some kind of mutually acceptable agreement – Taylor professed to enjoy, almost revel, in the process.

Perhaps it is significant that his degree in economics was gained the hard way, by evening classes and correspondence, while earning his bread and butter as a pro-footballer rather than enjoying the luxury of three years at university on a student grant. Such an achievement both reflects and reinforces qualities of perseverence and tenacity suggesting a personality unlikely to be swayed by those around him, a stubbornness belied by his gregarious, almost benign, exterior.

In this latter respect he was straight out of the Cliff Lloyd mould. But Lloyd had grown up in a harder, more insecure world, had experienced a world war and the bleak austere years that followed. His was the more cautious, deliberate outlook of the senior civil servant feeling disinclined, indeed not entitled, to risk much.

Taylor, by contrast, had no such inhibitions. He saw himself and his role increasingly as that of chairman of the board – responsible, certainly, but entitled, if not obliged, to take risks in order that the membership should reap the bountiful harvest of the modern world.

Unfortunately, in his first year or so in office, the harvest was to prove a bitter one. Declining attendances and the onset of a severe economic recession saw an increasing number of smaller clubs facing financial difficulties. With attendance figures plummeting from 24 million in 1980 to 17.8 million in 1985, with hooliganism becoming a serious social problem (bringing with it massive policing bills) and with old grounds facing enormous costs in order to meet new safety standards, this was no longer the case of clubs 'crying wolf'.

One of Taylor's first public pronouncements in December 1981 had been to call a halt to massive transfer fees (then having passed the million pound mark on more than one occasion) which he felt were undermining the economic base of many clubs:

> The image of the game needs improving. Fans are alienated by high fees. The man in the street must wonder what's going on. He's queuing up for a weak cup of tea after standing in the rain and all he reads about are £1m fees.

According to many directors, the problem was not high transfer fees, but players' wages. It was an argument that nobody seemed likely to win: with no accurate economic analysis to prove anyone wrong, all could assert and reassert their pet theories. Peter Swales, for instance, chairman of high-spending Manchester City, suggested that fees, though high, 'kept the money in the game', whereas if it went into players' pockets it would go out of the game. Jimmy Hill, of course, had always contended that lowering fees would mean shovelling more money into stars' pockets; Gordon Taylor agreed that wages would benefit, but felt that *all* players would share in the extra cash, provided clubs were not sucked into a spiralling transfer fee market.

All such esoteric debate, however, was rudely pushed aside in January 1982 when Bristol City suddenly announced that they were sacking eight of their senior staff in a bid to avoid bankruptcy and closure. An accountant's report on the club's affairs revealed that it had debts of one and a half million pounds, and assets of only £78,000.

The eight players' contracts were worth £290,000 – thus the 'Ashton Gate Eight' were offered a redundancy package totalling £58,000 between them. The alternative, it was suggested, was the winding up of the club.

The human aspect was not lost on Gordon Taylor:

> The players have been put in a terrible position. The first words I spoke to them were assurances that, no matter what was said, they'd been given contracts they'd worked for and deserved and £58,000 just wasn't acceptable. On the other hand, we all wanted the other players at the club to have a future. It was a very delicate problem.

For the press, the resulting drama of noon-deadlines and smoke-filled rooms was perfect copy: 'The plush Dragonara Hotel in Bristol was awash yesterday with ashen-faced managers and tight-lipped players....'

But for Gordon Taylor and the PFA it was a moment of harsh truth: doom-laden prophesies (his own included) seemed to be coming true:

> We really are in grave danger. Football has been like the South Sea Bubble. The figures frighten me. Clubs have been allowed to build up overdrafts on the strength of players' values going up. In the past,

whenever the banks have started asking questions, directors have been able to say: 'Oh, Jimmy Smith can go for so much.' Now the other clubs haven't got the money to buy Jimmy Smith.... We've had warning signs for some time ... unless the game changes and there is a strong lead from the top, this is going to be just another contracting industry....

In the event, the Bristol City club survived – and the eight players agreed to go. Geoff Merrick, thirty-one-year-old captain commented:

I am heartbroken. Bitter is not a word I like the sound of. I took my boots into the ground this morning in the hope that things would not turn out the way they have but I shall still be there on Saturday to support the team....

We have gained a lot more than we would have done if we had accepted their ultimatum.

Taylor summed up:

Considering the serious financial state of the club we feel that the eight have been fairly protected. The financial terms, I believe, should be kept personal and private. There have been many changes in the final offer and we have gone through many channels of discussion. The position has been looked at by all other clubs in the country. We want to make sure that this does not happen again.

Bristol City, however, would not be the last club that would find itself being approached by Taylor during a hectic couple of months that saw him rushing from town to town, 'trouble-shooter' style, working out 'rescue packages', lending cash, looking for ways to keep his members in employment. It was, as George Davies put it, 'a baptism of fire' for Taylor, but one from which he emerged triumphant. At the beginning of March 1982 he was profiled in the *Daily Mirror*:

Gordon Taylor stepped into soccer's most unenviable pressure-cooker with his eyes open. Just as well. His big difficulty now is finding the time to close them.

'Yes, the bags underneath are becoming a bit of a fixture,' says the beleaguered PFA secretary – Bristol City, Darlington, Hull, Halifax – the files on his crisis-packed desk are inches thick. And this personable, highly articulate leader of 2900 playing members knows that every phone-call could be the next SOS.

Taylor has driven 77,000 miles in eighteen months from his Lancashire home – plus numerous train-trips to London.

'Playing the game was certainly a lot easier,' says the thirty-seven-year-old who has leaned on his economics degree – and the union's accountants and lawyers – to unravel club balance sheets of doom and gloom in this season of threatened shut-downs....

Apart from giving the PFA a tremendous publicity bonanza, the 'crisis' and Taylor's pivotal role in it had the effect of putting the League and its apologists on the defensive. Clearly, any club going out of business meant a loss of jobs for players. But Taylor, during these hectic months, managed to present both himself and the Union as 'guardians' of the old League philosophy – determined to see the structure survive, despite the shortcomings of those ostensibly in charge.

For one thing, he simply did not believe that certain clubs threatened with bankruptcy had thought hard enough about how to solve their financial problems, had not looked around for alternatives involving the council, the supporters and the local community.

He warned of the damage done by simply cutting out 'uneconomic' units in the way that Beeching had closed down railway stations in the 1960s – stations that in the 1980s could have solved critical transport problems. Not enough was being done, he felt, by the larger clubs to persuade smaller clubs not to commit hara-kiri. In fact, he declared:

> There are a few people in football who want to see a Super-League, want to see the end of the small-town team but the whole magic of the game is that small clubs like Ipswich, Swansea, Norwich and Northampton can come up. Little teams living in hope. To disqualify them from that hope is to begin the end of football.

It was a theme he would virtually make his own, as suddenly he was being presented as the man holding everything together, the man to whom everyone was looking for answers:

Throughout all the recent traumas Taylor remains optimistic about the future of most of his members, despite clubs showing a lot of financial irresponsibility and overstretching themselves.

'I can see some light at the end of the tunnel. Even managers now ring up to seek our advice. And the League cooperates because they know our intentions are genuine.'

The League, in fact, had done more than cooperate. In early March it had agreed to give the PFA the power of veto over clubs that tried to avoid bankruptcy by forming a new company, and it also underwrote PFA loans to clubs by agreeing to channel the club's share of pooled monies directly to the PFA.

In effect, the Football League had to deal with Taylor. With its public image so poor at that point, it could not afford to be seen as obstructive to an organization whose philosophy and practice looked to the public to be so positive and constructive.

Even so, underwriting loans was not the same as lending hard cash: the League Management Committee argued that if it helped one club it would be obliged to help them all. Yet there was a definite indifference to the fate of smaller clubs in trouble, an attitude that flew in the face of the League's own traditions. League president Jack Dunnett was quoted as saying:

It's true I believed in natural wastage. If a community couldn't sustain a football club I didn't see why it should be propped up. We were quite prepared to see the League slimmed down to ninety or even seventy clubs. We certainly weren't going to provide special arrangements under which clubs who were teetering on the edge would have been allowed to avoid paying tax or their creditors.

No doubt this seemed sound in crude economic free-market terms, but the economic struggle in the early Eighties was a many-sided one. Football was under siege. So much was wrong with the professional game and so many fans were deserting it. It had a crisis of 'identity' on its hands. And yet football's 'crisis' was the country's crisis, too. Clubs in economic trouble were at one with individual industrial towns in similar straits. The economic recession, bringing large scale unemployment, caused widespread despair. Football clubs were often the focal points of such communities and to keep them going was a small but sometimes significant contribution to keeping up people's morale. As Taylor put it:

> The League believes in natural wastage, whereas we think that clubs
> have a debt to supporters to stay in existence.

This, according to Taylor, was the true 'identity' of football,
confirmed by the fact that on occasions he was welcomed more by
local supporters and councillors than by the club's directors.

In fact, Taylor and the PFA often received little but abuse from
certain beleaguered chairmen who persisted in attempting to lay
their financial troubles at the feet of players. Sam Rourke, Halifax
Town chairman, faced with the collapse of his club, attacked the
PFA 'for the way they have got more and more money for players,
many of whom would be on the dole at the end of the season'.

There remained a substantial residue of anti-player feeling,
blaming 'freedom of contract' and the 'removal of the maximum
wage' for soccer's financial ills. But increasingly it was being
realized that clubs themselves – directors in particular – were the
architects of their own destruction. The fact that players could not
now be sacked, or held on the retain and transfer list, or paid on a
sliding scale that had no bottom rung, merely closed off the
traditional avenues of escape for many poorly run, inefficient club
administrations. The anger and resentment expressed towards the
'massive pay packets' was often the gut reaction of men who were
now finding themselves with no alternative but to talk to Gordon
Taylor and his specialist insolvency accountant as part of the price
of survival.

Furthermore, the idea that wages were the cause of the economic
crisis in football could now be disproved by real figures. Industrial
historian Braham Dabscheck has revealed that, as a share of total
football income, players' wages for the years 1981, 1982 and 1983
represented only 48 per cent, 46 per cent and 43 per cent
respectively, while earlier research concerning the seasons 1955–6,
1965–6, and 1980–1 put the share at 43 per cent, 43 per cent and 49
per cent respectively.

The figures indicate that after the introduction of the new
transfer/compensation system in 1978, there was an initial shift in
the distribution of income to players, but that gradually the players'
share of income returned to more traditional levels. Further
research has revealed that the vast majority of players only earned
modest incomes. In 1981 only eight players received more than
£50,000 a year: this had only increased to forty-one by 1985, while

total salaries during the same period had only increased by 10 per cent with salaries rising more slowly in the Third and Fourth divisions. Indeed, the median salary between 1981 and 1985 increased from £8108 to £11,101.

Thus Gordon Taylor could confidently rebut accusations of greedy players, indeed could point instead to the 'greed' of bigger League clubs which insisted upon home clubs keeping all gate receipts, on the majority of prize money being awarded to 'winners' (usually big clubs), on TV money going principally to big clubs, and on pools money being channelled to such clubs for the loss of their star players on international calls.

Taylor's rejection of the impending 'Super-League' idea – increasingly suggested as 'inevitable' – caught the mood of the average supporter. Super-Leagues might represent a kind of economic reality but there was nothing very romantic about them, and nothing to stir the imagination. Moreover, as he commented at the beginning of the 1982–3 season, 'such sentiments betray the traditions of our game, the underlying strength of the Football League acknowledged as the most competitive throughout the world'.

His nostalgia and rhetoric were laced, however, with pragmatism. At the PFA's 1982 AGM it was decided that if the Super-League idea was put forward seriously by the top clubs, then the PFA would press ahead for complete contractual freedom for players and thus 'smash' the transfer system: 'Complete freedom would effectively abolish the transfer system – and provide a complete deterrent to a break-away.' Taylor added:

> We could have gone for this in 1978 but voted not to because we committed ourselves to upholding the present ninety-two club structure of the Football League. But there has been a lot of talk recently about big clubs being approached by individuals with a view to the future of the Watfords, the Swanseas and all the town clubs....

The 1978 agreement had been considered by some to have 'legalized' the transfer system, that is, protected it from legal challenge. However, the Kerry Packer case and subsequent successful moves by cricketers against the TCCB, would seem to have reopened the debate, particularly where a player's 'right to work' might appear to be in danger of being infringed by a 'monopoly' employer in the Football League.

Whether instrumental or not in halting the move towards a Super-League in 1982, the PFA's unequivocal declaration of intent was proof, if proof were needed, that it was now a major player in football politics.

Nevertheless, its new-found strength and influence could still be fundamentally undermined by football's parent bodies. Much of the PFA's confidence stemmed from its healthy bank-balance, the lion's share of which came from TV revenues passed on to it by the League and the FA. While the latter bodies tended to divide up their shares into relatively insignificant portions, the PFA's share (totalling between £300,000 and £400,000 per annum) arrived in one lump. While much of the money was put to good use by the rapidly expanding Education Society and in providing services to PFA members, a significant proportion was invested; so there was a fair amount left that could be loaned to clubs in need.

In November 1983, however, the FA decided, for reasons known only to itself, that it was going to cut the amount it paid to the PFA by 60 per cent – from £100,000 to £40,000 (this after the FA had successfully negotiated a massive increase in TV fees).

The FA was offering, in fact, less in total than it received for televising one match. Reaction to the move was swift and angry. A ban on PFA members' appearances in televised Cup ties was threatened, with top players such as Kevin Keegan of Newcastle and Phil Thomson of Liverpool pledging their teams' support. This resolute action took the FA by surprise and within a fortnight it agreed to talk. The £100,000 was restored – but the PFA had to agree to shoulder all Benevolent Fund obligations (with which the FA had previously helped) to players past and present.

It was an unnecessary squabble, made more unpleasant by FA chief Bert Millichip's remarks concerning the effects of players' freedom of contract which he declared had been 'a disaster. It has changed the whole balance of power. The word "loyalty" is no longer in football's dictionary.'

Nevertheless, such confrontations involving players as 'rank and file' threatening to withdraw their labour were now to become a rarity in PFA/FA/League relations, particularly as the PFA, in the person of Taylor, continued to insist that the traditional Union stance of 'them and us' was irrelevant, if not futile.

Taylor eschewed 'political' stances. The PFA, for instance, remained outside the TUC, was more 'independent' than its opposite number in Scotland which was affiliated to the GMU and thus, according to Taylor, 'a more political group'.

Taylor's own father had been a diligent and dedicated AEU official and so he was no stranger to orthodox trade unionism – but his insistence that all conflict could be resolved by discussion, that somewhere a position could be found that satisfied everyone, and that it was incumbent on all concerned to stick to it until an agreement was reached, emphasized common ground rather than separate camps.

Of course, from the PFA's viewpoint, this was not a new idea. Jimmy Guthrie and Derek Dougan apart, its leadership had always been moderate and constructive, anxious to talk and desirous of amicable relationships with both the FA and the League.

Taylor's determinedly corporatist approach to labour relations was made easier, however, by key personnel changes at the League headquarters. His predecessor, Cliff Lloyd, had been unfortunate in having to deal with two League secretaries – Fred Howarth and Alan Hardaker – neither of whom had made life easy for him, nor seemed particularly concerned for players and their problems. Meaningful communication with Howarth had hardly existed. Lloyd had been able to build more of a relationship with Hardaker, but the latter always regarded the players with a mixture of suspicion and disdain (mixed with some envy) while his ego had to be constantly fed with banner headlines proclaiming his name – often created at the expense of dialogue with the PFA.

When Taylor became secretary, Hardaker had already gone, replaced by the somewhat more approachable Graham Kelly. Taylor's predilection for picking up the phone or driving over to Lytham rather than writing a letter was thus made much easier.

There was also the fact that Taylor's Management Committee – the chairmen in particular – very much shared his own political outlook. Nor were they inclined to seek publicity for themselves.

Alan Gowling, Taylor's immediate successor, regarded himself as politically 'right of centre', while Steve Coppell, who succeeded Gowling, made his own position clear:

> I was not going into the job as a reformer like two of my predecessors, Jimmy Hill and Derek Dougan. My responsibility was administration and to ensure that the members knew what was happening to their £12 a year.

Industrial action, Coppell declared, was never discussed: the settlement with the FA in 1983 was a 'gentlemen's agreement' reached after 'sensible discussion'.

The fact that there was a rapid turnover in chairmen in the early 1980s also tended to emphasize Taylor's pre-eminence in the organization, a fact endorsed by his personal style and increased exposure in the press.

Alan Gowling might well have made more of an impact than he did; unfortunately his football career was prematurely cut short at the end of the 1981–2 season when Bolton Wanderers released him. Gowling had served on the Management Committee since 1975 and was, like Taylor and Coppell, a graduate – indeed, he obtained an MA on the basis of a thesis studying the relationship of professional players to the Union. However, he chose to leave football entirely, and built a career in industry.

Steve Coppell also saw his tenure as chairman cut short, in his case because of injury. Coppell was due to be succeeded by Bob Latchford who within a few months was signed by a Dutch club and thus was ineligible to accept in the post.

It would not be until 1984, therefore, when Brian Talbot was elected chairman, that the occupant of this key post could begin to make any sort of an impact on the public's consciousness.

Talbot would always emphasize the fact that he was not chairman to push the players' case alone. Rather, he was looking to the interests of 'the whole game':

> I would like to think that the PFA was an organization for the benefit of football, not just being a Union to make players greedy....

Thus Gordon Taylor's philosophy would be faithfully endorsed by the chairmen to whom he nominally reported, not to mention a Management Committee that was gradually changed to reflect his own attitudes and approach:

> Cliff Lloyd had tended to encourage 'big names' on to the committee to give the Union more of an image, to get more of an impact. My approach was that it was more important *what* you were than *who* you were.

By a judicious mix of informal encouragement and co-option, therefore, the committee came to consist of men like Malcolm Lord, Ray Treacy, Paul Hart, Ken Allen, Dave Cusack and John

Deehan – hard-working pros neither super-stars nor nonentities – very similar in career terms to Taylor himself.

Consequently, the early 1980s were destined to be a time of great change for the PFA. Some changes were planned for and eagerly anticipated; others, tragically, were not. Coppell's unfortunate departure coincided with a grievous blow to the Union – the death of Bob Kerry, the education officer.

Kerry – bearded, pipe-smoking, enthusiastic advocate of Union principles in general and the education of young footballers in particular – died on a charity fun-run in October 1983. Steve Coppell, still trying to come to terms with the premature end of his career, wrote:

> It acted like a cold shower and suddenly everything was in perspective. Here I was, twenty-eight years old and in comparatively good health. Bob was forty-two and married with four children.

A year later, Eileen Hardman, after forty years as office secretary to the Union, also died. She had been the last remaining link with Fay's wartime Union – indeed, she had started working for the Union when it was situated in a one-room office over Fay's Southport shop.

Travelling in to work each day to the Corn Exchange from her home in Appley Bridge, a devout Catholic with a lively sense of humour, she had ruled the Union office for decade after decade, had seen Jimmy Fay, Sammy Crooks, Billy Meredith, Jimmy Guthrie, Jimmy Hill and Cliff Lloyd come and go.

Her own passing, therefore, was a sure sign of the changing times: no more lunchtime card-games with Cliff Lloyd, no more sandwiches eaten in the local churchyard: within two years of her death the Union offices would leave the Corn Exchange to which Fay had brought them back in 1930 and move across the city to Mosley Street, into a high-tech neo-Georgian office block complete with word-processors, computers and fax machines.

For Gordon Taylor, one senses, the move clearly represented a necessary break with a past that had rarely seen the PFA in a position of influence, let alone of equality, with the other two football organizations. As the 1980s progressed, however, that would all change.

# 31

# *Building for the Future* 1985–88

As the Football League approached its hundredth anniversary in 1988, it was in greater danger of breaking up than ever before. Paradoxically, as the Players' Union approached its ninetieth birthday in the same year, it had never been healthier.

Repeated newspaper predictions that Gordon Taylor would be lured to Lytham St Annes in the late 1980s can thus be seen as inevitable. Like a precious talisman, possession of which would solve all problems, Taylor was fêted and courted, was the subject of countless newspaper feature articles and the focus of endless speculation. Yet by the end of the decade he would still be with the PFA – much to its members' collective relief.

In many senses, his celebrity status was a reflection of the PFA's growing confidence, a good deal of which was attributable to Taylor's own efforts but which, it can be argued, was inevitable anyway, given the turbulent football times. For as catastrophe and calamity rocked the professional game in the mid-Eighties, with the Football League seeming at times to have lost the desire to continue in existence, and with the FA unable to provide a coherent, authoritative lead, only the PFA remained unsullied and somehow aloof from the squabbles over money and power.

Only the PFA leadership could act in the knowledge that behind it was a united membership committed to a simple aim – to keep the League system intact. Taylor's success was thus both a personal triumph and a triumph for his organization.

As 1985 opened, the League was arguing with itself and the TV companies over new deals: how much would be paid, whether the number of live matches would be increased, whether sponsors' names should be prominently displayed on shirts. Personalities clouded the issue; as Robert Maxwell clashed with Philip Carter, accusations of vested interests abounded.

At this point the PFA was very much on the sidelines, though continuing to lend substantial amounts of money to smaller clubs who were quite clearly not going to gain much from the increased TV revenue.

The collapse of the TV negotiations, however, sent ominous reverberations through the game. The PFA's substantial income temporarily ceased, and at the 1985 AGM Mike Birch, accountant and auditor, suggested that a substantial increase in membership subscriptions was advisable (from £15 to £20 a year). After all, subs contributed a mere £27,000 while Union expenditure on education, accident insurance, hardship grants and general administration amounted to almost £350,000.

By then, however, tragedy had struck. Fire at Bradford City, collapsing walls at Birmingham and at the Heysel Stadium in Brussels, caused over a hundred deaths. The lethal combination of decaying superstructures and declining standards of public behaviour was reducing professional football in Great Britain to its knees.

The response was predictable. Excluded from Europe indefinitely, banned from selling alcohol in grounds, saddled with ever-increasing costs to modernize and make safe outdated stadiums, and deprived of TV revenue, the larger League clubs decided that, once again, their future lay in a Super-League. And, once more, the PFA – Gordon Taylor in particular – was propelled into the argument.

This time it was not simply a matter of announcing opposition to the Super-League concept in general terms and hoping the idea would eventually blow over. As the secret meetings and negotiations between the chairmen of the bigger clubs continued into late 1985, it became clear that something drastic was about to happen.

Clubs such as Manchester United, Everton, Liverpool, Tottenham and Arsenal – the 'Big Five' – appeared to be in deadly earnest. The League system had, according to men like Philip Carter of Everton and Martin Edwards of Manchester United, to be radically altered. The Fourth and Third Divisions had to be cut adrift. Top clubs could no longer afford to be part of an unwieldy obstructive out-of-date organization like the Football League. Everyone was being dragged down into bankruptcy and ruin.

Gradually, however, a pattern emerged from the welter of rumour and panic-inducing headlines. The initial Super-League idea was shelved but the First Division clubs issued an ultimatum to those in the Second Division to join them in a breakaway, or the First Division clubs would go it alone.

Discussions began between the two leagues, the nub of which concerned money. The top clubs wanted the entire TV revenue, all sponsorship monies plus an abolition of gate levies; in short, a complete financial break with the lower clubs. The Third and Fourth Division clubs were understandably alarmed and frightened. However, realizing that little could be done without the players' consent, and that the plans were a clear threat to players' jobs, they turned to Gordon Taylor who, in November 1985, began to act as unofficial arbitrator, go-between and catalyst.

He was doing what he did best – searching for a solution, gradually edging suspicious and essentially antagonistic parties closer together – but he was not just a peace-maker. He carried with him a substantial mandate from his membership that committed him to hold out for certain minimum criteria, the most fundamental of which was retention of all ninety-two Football League clubs within the existing League structure:

> If the players in the First and Second Division clubs are prepared to support their Third and Fourth Division colleagues then we can influence the changes for the benefit of all members and the game. Remember that many of today's top players either started or will finish in the Third and Fourth Divisions....

Gradually, by exerting pressure on the associate members (the Third and Fourth Division teams) and extracting concessions from them, Taylor was able to bring the bigger clubs back into the fold. He convinced the lower clubs that they must agree to promotion and relegation in and out of the Football League itself, something they had consistently opposed. In fact, the two clubs involved in proposing and seconding the change – Rochdale and Halifax – could well have been in danger of relegation themselves.

As regards TV money, it was conceded that larger clubs ought to have a bigger slice of the cake but a system of potentially lucrative play-offs was suggested to settle certain promotion places to help compensate for the sacrifice. A reduction in Division One also meant more clubs and more matches in Division Two.

Taylor also calculated that TV money ought to be divided according to the percentage of spectator support each division attracted. Thus, the First Division roughly accounted for 50 per cent of total support and should therefore receive 50 per cent of the TV revenues. The remainder was divided 25 per cent to the Second Division and 25 per cent jointly for the Third and Fourth Division clubs.

By 26 November, Everton chairman Carter was emphasizing: 'There has never been any intention on our part to cut the Third and Fourth Divisions away....'

Once again, Gordon Taylor and the PFA were being presented in the best possible light, headlines such as 'Gordon Battles For The Minnows' and 'The Voice of Reason' eloquent testimony to the influence he was able to bring to bear on events.

On 18 December, at an hotel near Heathrow, agreement was finally reached on a restructuring package to embody much of what Taylor had set out to achieve – all clubs to survive within a traditional league system which had been altered to give a slightly reduced First Division more money and increased power to influence future events on a restructured Management Committee.

The Super-League idea had not been completely banished, of course – it would return with a vengeance in 1988 – but the negotiations of 1985–6 did confirm Taylor's pre-eminence in the game; indeed, it was openly suggested that he should somehow 'run' pro-football.

The Super-League advocates had certainly thought as much: during the negotiations Taylor had been offered the secretaryship of the proposed new streamlined League. Had he accepted, it is arguable that the idea would have been approved and the Football League destroyed. As Taylor commented afterwards: 'I suddenly felt that the future of the game was settling on my shoulders.' He dispelled suggestions of altruism in his decision to turn the idea down by expressing suspicion: 'You could read it two ways – they thought I had the administrative qualities for the job or they were trying to buy off the opposition.'

But leading a Super-League would have run counter to every one of his professed beliefs in the true significance of football – its meaning for ordinary people, its 'grass-roots' origins and its ultimate strength. He had experienced the heady days of the American pro-soccer boom: 'I played in America. I saw all the razzmatazz of the Cosmos and others. I was at Las Vegas when they had Trevor Hockey driven on in a tank wearing a Fidel Castro uniform. They had bands, cheer-leaders, half-time dog-racing and parachutists. "Gordon", they said, "you guys don't know how to sell the game." '

But selling an artificial glamorized product had led ultimately to disillusion and collapse. The NASL seemed unable to reach down and connect with localities, schools and kids in the streets. It was a brilliant commercial success for a short while, in certain highly profitable locations – but it had died. To rush British football towards such a fate seemed to Taylor to fly in the face of logic. As he put it, 'There has got to be sensible change, but it must be gradual. You can't write off ninety-seven years of history overnight.'

Thus the offer of a Super-League commissionership was simply unreal. Taylor, it could be argued, had bigger ambitions, now centred within the PFA which, by 1986, was a burgeoning organization.

The removal of the Union offices from their traditional home in Hanging Ditch to the high-tech Georgian-style office block close by the G-Mex centre on Lower Mosley Street and the new luxury Midland Hotel helped to underline the dramatic changes that had occurred in both the Union's 'image' and the scope of its activities since the early 1980s.

Taylor had always professed a keenness to develop the educational role of the Union – it had been one of the reasons why he had originally joined the Management Committee – but he was not alone in this.

As we have seen, as far back as the late 1930s secretary Jimmy Fay had been trying to organize professional training courses for members and many PFA/Union chairmen such as Terry Neill, Derek Dougan, Alan Gowling and Steve Coppell – not to mention Cliff

Lloyd, of course – had all expressed a desire to see professional footballers given help and encouragement to develop more than just their footballing skills.

The good work of Bob Kerry had seen the Educational Society (since 1980, in partnership with the League) expand considerably – in the year of his untimely death some 343 grants had been made, totalling £22,479 to past and current PFA members. This would always remain the major sphere of the society's work but in 1983 the PFA began an involvement in the education and training of younger players that was to revolutionize, indeed replace, the old apprenticeship system.

It was an example of the PFA acting against the trend, an example, to use Taylor's terms, of 'accepting reality (in this case the Government's YTS scheme) and using it to our advantage'.

In 1983 Pat Lally, assistant education officer, reported that over 500 boys had been taken on by eighty-two clubs under the YTS scheme. The Education Society had been appointed the managing agency for football schemes and the PFA had been given the general responsibility for the welfare and training of all trainees who were expected to join the PFA at the same rate as apprentice professionals.

Trainees were covered by the League Accident Insurance Scheme and Union delegates were encouraged to take an interest in both the football and the educational side of trainees' lives, and 'to make sure it [the scheme] is carried out properly'.

YTS, in conventional TUC terms, was regularly derided and denounced as a means of 'exploiting' young people without jobs and it is true that a weekly wage of £29.50 (in the first year) and £33.50 (in the second year) was rather low. For pro-footballers with experience of *real* exploitation as old-style apprentices, confined to sweeping the terraces, cleaning seats and the occasional kickabout at the end of the day, such criticisms meant little. At a time when clubs were finding it hard to make ends meet and were cutting back on the development of young players, sacking coaches and disbanding youth teams, here was an offer of cash to take youngsters on.

By 1984 the Education Society could claim that the scheme had helped to double the average number of schoolboys entering football. Some 10 per cent of them had played first team football and half of them been taken on for a second year. Over £1½m had been put into the scheme, and over the next few years that would rise to £3m: money which paid wages, travelling expenses, lodging allowances and reimbursement to clubs for their outlay, as well as the fees for educational courses at local colleges.

By 1985, YTS in football would be organized in six regions with coordinators employed to develop the scheme, and Gordon Taylor could claim that the scheme had 'rejuvenated youth development at many clubs'. 1986 saw predictions of over 1000 boys being received onto the scheme and in 1987 the Education Society's success was reflected in the award of Approved Training Organization status from the MSC. In 1991, only one club in the league system – Watford – remained outside the scheme.

Now any schoolboy approached by a scout had a standard procedure to follow. Leaving school at sixteen, if offered a chance by a club, he would be registered as a football trainee and would join the YTS scheme. This involved day-release at a college plus other aspects of the football industry, e.g. groundsmanship and office administration. A boy could still sign on as a full pro at seventeen, though the PFA encouraged them to see the YTS scheme through, while all YTS trainees enjoyed the same freedom of contract as a full professional.

Much of the good work in developing the scheme was the responsibility of Micky Burns who had taken over as education officer after Bob Kerry. A qualified schoolteacher, Burns had an impressive amateur career with Skelmersdale United (winning amateur international caps) before turning professional with Blackpool in 1969.

In 1974 he joined Newcastle, leaving in 1977 after taking part in what was dubbed at the time a 'player-power' attempt to influence events and policy at the club following the sacking of manager Gordon Lee. Along with Alan Gowling and Geoff Nulty, he was considered a key 'rebel', although the players achieved little.

After Newcastle he was player/coach at Cardiff, then went to Middlesborough where he was youth team coach for a year. Two years back in education followed, as a lecturer in Middlesborough, before he was appointed Education Officer in 1984.

His work and that of his assistant Pat Lally was not the stuff of headlines and yet the ultimate impact of YTS can be regarded as one of the most significant developments in the pro-game. By 1989, just six years after the PFA took responsibility for the scheme, a manager like Dave Mackay (then of Doncaster) could claim: 'The scheme has probably been the saviour of the Third and Fourth Divisions.... Without it we couldn't entertain signing apprentices.'

In that year, six out of eight YTS boys had been signed on by Doncaster as full pros while the whole of the club's Youth Cup Final Team were YTS trainees – many of them worth potentially substantial transfer fees.

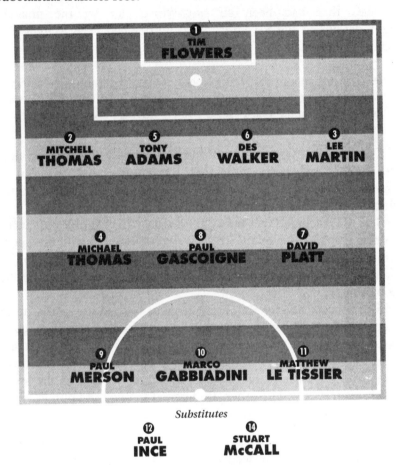

*The YT Squad. 90 Minutes magazine, 1990*

The scheme saw hundreds of boys given a chance. In 1983, the year the scheme started, there had only been thirty-three apprentices in the whole of the Fourth Division. In 1989 Crewe alone had twenty-one YTS students on their books. The success-rate of trainees now securing contracts through YT (successor to the YTS) is claimed to be astonishingly high. Mick Burns, YT national coordinator, believes it ranges between 50 and 60 per cent. At Sunderland the rates have been four out of seven in 1990, seven out of nine in 1989 and six out of eight in 1988. Sunderland's youth development officer reflected that in the old apprenticeship days only one in ten would make it. Thus the youth policies that had been all but wiped out by the financial depradations of the Seventies and Eighties had been dramatically revived. But as Gordon Taylor commented:

> It's not just about producing players. It gives them the opportunity to learn other skills – coaching, refereeing, administration and commercial enterprises, hotel and catering, communications, computers, first-aid and life-saving....

That the PFA through its Education Society should have been developing and controlling this revolution must be seen as vindication of an historic struggle, a triumph of the common sense that has been one of its chief characteristics down the century.

The YTS scheme was not to be Burns's only significant success working 'against the grain'. In 1985, in conjunction with the Sports Council, he began to investigate the possibility of arranging a national programme to involve professional footballers and the community.

The concept had its philosophical roots back in the 1968 Chester Report – the opening up of clubs to involve local people, young and old – and had been given extra impetus in the Seventies and Eighties by the despair of not knowing what to do about hooliganism. The tragedies of Heysel and Bradford, as well as the losing battle against crowd disorder, threatened to sever the public's links with the national game. Mickey Burns wrote:

> I work within the football industry and I am particularly interested in the development of football as our national sport. We want to promote our national game and I feel that a community programme is a way of promoting it in the community and rejuvenating the interest of years gone by. We want to develop an interest among young people and introduce them to good practices in the game and, hopefully, to develop a better spectator response to the game.

Burns had other aims in mind for the scheme, in particular, to open up employment prospects for ex-professionals who would be the principal workers on the scheme; it would also be an opportunity to involve ethnic minority groups in football and build up a relationship between them and the game; and it would maximize the use of club facilities, re-establishing traditional links between clubs and the local community.

It was an experiment, a 'new concept', and one that seemed likely to fail. Football and community schemes had been tried before. In 1978 Denis Howell, Minister for Sport, had allocated extra money to be dispersed through the Sports Council to League clubs to be used in attempts to 'involve young people in sports'. Some £1m had been spent, but bureaucracy and confusion as to aims and objectives had led to accusations that clubs had simply taken the money to improve or add facilities while failing to involve the types of youngster intended. Ex-professionals had occasionally been employed as 'motivators' but there was considerable scepticism as to end results.

The PFA Education Society was to have a much greater impact. A pilot scheme was established in 1985, on a budget of £300,000 supplied by the MSC, involving six north-western clubs ranging in size from Manchester United to Oldham Athletic. It created sixty jobs, many taken by ex-professional footballers.

Roger Reade was appointed chief administrator with a management team including Brian Kidd (ex-Manchester Utd), Pat Howard (ex-Newcastle Utd), Dennis Leman (ex-Manchester City) aned Mick Baxter (Preston North End). Statistics abound: in two years 2500 visits were made by pro-players to local schools and youth clubs: over fifty ex-players worked as supervisors in charge of club projects; by 1987 the scheme had been extended to involve thirty clubs with over £1m being funnelled through the MSC, and over 300 jobs had been created. In June 1989 Taylor commented:

> At all clubs where the scheme has been introduced attendances have increased and the behaviour of the crowd has improved dramatically.... The concept of bringing club and community together is one that will benefit the game in the long term in generating supporters. The stronger this becomes, the more healthy the game will become....

Scepticism regarding such efforts and claims are inevitable. The philosophy behind such a massive enterprise is admirable; the end results difficult to quantify. Family enclosures, mini-vans for school visits, youngsters learning 'good habits' and shunning

hooliganism, the 'smile being put back on to the face of football....' –
it could mean as much or as little as you wanted it to. Can a football
club become a community centre? What exactly is a 'community'
anyway?

The USA football experiment had attempted to build its audience
in similar fashion: encouraging family groups, involving more
women, closer links between pro-players, establishing football
'clinics' in schools and clubs, and providing entertainment before
and during the match. Yet it had all ended in financial disaster.

A principal reason for failure, however, had been the lack of TV
exposure. Without TV coverage, the pro-game had made little
impact on the national psyche, although the game had thrived at
school and college level.

In Britain, the problem was inverted: TV falling over itself to pour
millions into the game while the live audience appeared to be turning
away, the raw material in danger of drying up.

Arguments as to the real and lasting achievement of the Football in
the Community Programme will no doubt continue, but a significant
side-effect of the PFA's pioneering work – the involvement of both
the FA and the League – may well have repercussions that go far
beyond what was initially envisaged for the scheme.

In 1989 the FA, without involving the PFA, began to develop its
own national community programme. Such duplication of effort was
soon recognized as wasteful, particularly as the PFA's scheme
already involved over fifty League clubs. Thus began a painfully
slow process of amalgamation between the PFA, the Football
League and now the FA, under the umbrella of the Footballers'
Further Education and Vocational Training Society. This is a unique
body in football's long history, involving as it does the three principal
football bodies in equal partnership in a scheme that embraces all
aspects of education (YTS as well as FA coaching schemes) and the
community programme.

The Society's board of directors consists of three directors from
each organization plus joint secretaries (Gordon Taylor from the
PFA and David Dent from the League) under an independent
chairman, Professor Sir John Wood, CBE. A national programme is
at present under discussion funded to the tune of £4m from the
Football Trust and administered from the PFA offices in
Manchester.

The PFA's hope is that this body will act as a catalyst for

fundamental change in the set-up of British football – an amalgamation of all three bodies into one coherent body, something the
PFA has been urging for some considerable time. It would certainly
seem to have more possibilities than the recent troubled League
plan to share power with the FA.

# 32

# *Taylor of the League?* 1989–90

1987–8 – the centenary season of the Football League – saw attendances at League matches rise for the second year running. Some 18 million people watched Football League matches while more than 20 million attended all competitive professional games, with gate receipts put at a record £60m.

Yet anxiety about the future remained the keynote. League clubs were still banned from Europe, every major international tournament carried with it the threat that England might also be banned if its 'fans' misbehaved, while the government's identity card scheme looked set to decimate attendances and break the link between the traditional fan and the national game. Not surprisingly, perhaps, the summer of 1988 saw the League go into yet another of its (by now) regular, disturbing convulsions.

The 1985 'crisis' had been caused by the larger clubs panicking at the prospect of losing money, having been banned from Europe and unable to secure a TV deal. In 1988 it was the opposite – the prospect of too much money.

The arrival of satellite TV – in this case BSB – saw the bidding for football television rights raised to dramatic heights. The BBC/ITV 'cartel' had kept fees artificially low for decades: now the lid was lifted. In fact, a lucrative deal with BSB and BBC seemed to have satisfied most parties, but when the smaller clubs voted to end the payment of 'compensation' money to clubs featured on live matches (in case their actual attendance fell significantly) the old Super-League idea was raised once again. ITV, excluded from the original deal, approached several of the larger clubs and offered £1m to each for exclusive live coverage. With cash like that on offer, the break-up of the Football League seemed inevitable.

Accusations of secret deals and the involvement of key League Management Committee figures only increased the intrigue and hastened the deadlock. Once again, Gordon Taylor was summoned – along with Brendon Batson, assistant secretary – to act as mediator.

It was 1986 all over again, even to the extent that the ultimate settlement, whereby the First Division clubs took 75 per cent of all TV revenues, leaving 25 per cent for the remaining three divisions, was only facilitated by the PFA agreeing to accept yet another cut in *its* percentage share. Although there was more money in cash terms (the deal with BBC/BSB was eventually worth £44m over four years, with the PFA receiving £550,000 per year) the percentage had been reduced from 10 to almost 5 per cent.

Gordon Taylor justified the cut to delegates at the 1988 AGM as necessary because, 'I considered that it was essential for the clubs to come to an agreement before the start of the season and put an end to the bickering and bad publicity which the game had received.'

Nevertheless, the 1988 crisis and its resolution marked a period of relative uncertainty for the PFA. The departure of Graham Kelly, secretary of the League, to become chief executive of the FA led to calls for Gordon Taylor to be offered the League post. A spate of newspaper articles and features thrust him into the public eye again: no one else seemed remotely as well qualified for the job, and both he and the League appeared willing to entertain the idea.

Yet there were serious doubts as to the advisability of such a move. The League AGM of 1988 rejected out of hand a PFA resolution to penalize clubs with poor disciplinary records, and failed to take the opportunity to elect Bobby Charlton on to the Management Committee when such a move would have attracted much positive publicity. The League clearly remained as blinkered and inward-looking as ever.

The prospect of taking over the secretaryship to become a 'servant' of the clubs thus had little appeal. As Brian Glanville wrote: 'What

Taylor clearly doesn't want to do is to find himself sucked into the maw of the League expending so much time and energy sorting out the various factions.'

Moreover, the suspicion and resentment of players on the part of directors and administrators remained as strong as ever – witness Charlton's rejection. So Taylor turned the idea down.

As a response to the threat of his departure, the PFA, prompted by chairman Brian Talbot, created a new title – chief executive – and Taylor signed a five-year deal. He then declared his intention of pressing for a closer working relationship between the PFA, League and FA:

> I strongly believe and hope that what will be taken on board is the idea of a steering committee made up of the president and chief executive of the League, the chairman and chief executive of the FA and the same people from our own Association so that we could have a consistent body that works together and speaks for football with one voice.

Taylor's refusal to become League secretary had nonetheless been influenced in no small way by the apparent state of flux and disunity on the League Management Committee itself. The future of both chairman Carter and Management Committee member David Dein were in doubt following their questionable involvement in the TV dispute. Indeed, Carter was ultimately voted out of office – the first League chairman to suffer such a fate.

His successor, Jack Dunnett, was also soon on his way; in June 1989, after leaving Notts County and failing to get re-elected as a Division Two representative with Portsmouth, he resigned and another election was arranged, one that would eventually drag Gordon Taylor back into the arena.

For over a year, the League had continued without a full-time secretary. As far back as January 1988, a head-hunting agency had drawn up a short-list and in August had announced the candidates who included Glen Kirton, press officer of the FA, David Griffiths, former chief executive of Wembley Stadium, Trevor Phillips, the League's commercial director and Ronald Allison, TV executive and former Buckingham Palace press secretary.

Unable to agree, Dunnett and the Management Committee had called upon another firm to look for more candidates not necessarily from football, but his own resignation had halted the process yet again.

However on 11 August, at a Football League EGM, Bill Fox of Blackburn Rovers was elected as the League's new president, and announced to a startled world that part of his electoral 'platform' had been the appointment of Gordon Taylor to the post of League chief executive.

Taylor, interviewed the following day, explained that he had agreed to take the job, subject to certain conditions including PFA approval, because:

> I just could not stand by and allow someone with very little knowledge of and no real feel for the game to take over such a vital position. The task which awaits me at the Football League may prove to be impossible but at least I'll know I had a go.

Fox declared that 'the chief executive will have far-reaching powers and that is why it is so important that the person occupying the position knows exactly what it is all about'.

Fox had apparently made his approach to Taylor little more than two weeks before the election and Taylor had been swayed by Fox's promises:

> He persuaded me that the time was right to take what in all honesty has been a very difficult decision.

Oddly enough, given the crucial importance of such a move, neither man appeared to have persuaded, nor even informed, their respective Management Committees. Not surprisingly, there was an immediate outcry.

Three League Management Committee members – John Smith of Liverpool, Doug Ellis of Aston Villa and Robert Chase of Norwich – were determined to oppose Taylor's appointment, even though Fox insisted that he had the backing of the clubs ('I have been elected by the 92 League clubs and my platform included Gordon Taylor').

His opponents, however, insisted that he had acted unconstitutionally by negotiating secretly with Taylor before he had the authority to do so. They were also annoyed that the expensive and delicate 'short-list' process had been scuppered. Taylor, they pointed out, had refused to apply before and thus had disqualified himself. What was more, the suggestions by Fox that Taylor would have extra 'far-reaching' powers – which had not been included in the earlier job description – made various members of the Management Committee nervous and suspicious, particularly when Taylor himself outlined those powers:

> I see my role as running the League from day-to-day, making financial and commercial decisions and influencing policy with reference to the Management Committee but answerable only to the president and having complete security of tenure.

The opposition to Taylor's appointment presented the PFA Management Committee with the opportunity it had apparently been waiting for. In a sense, Fox had attempted a publicity 'coup': by suddenly announcing Taylor's appointment, he had gambled that any opposition would be swept aside on a tide of enthusiasm, and had the decision been greeted with unanimity and loud hosannahs the PFA would have found it hard to resist. However, once Fox's opponents had demonstrated their determination not to be 'steam-rollered' (and Fox himself failed to deliver or confirm his promises), Garth Crooks, PFA chairman, was quick to act.

A Management Committee meeting was called in London on Monday 14 August, and what was to have been a press conference endorsing the move became a meeting to stop it. The Management Committee asked Taylor to honour the agreement he had signed less than a year previously.

Crooks confessed to having been shocked when Taylor had first informed him of his decision to leave and join the League should Fox win the election. Whilst recognizing that Taylor was struggling with a difficult decision, feeling a responsibility and sensing an opportunity to have a greater control over the game's destiny, Crooks was nevertheless angry that Fox had not considered it necessary to consult with the PFA and himself, or even to ask permission to approach their chief executive. Furthermore, the response to Fox's victory from defeated opponents had convinced him that the prospect of unity at the League was now remote.

Thus, the hastily convened Management Committee attended by Nigel Spackman, Colin Gibson, Trevor Morgan, Crooks and David Mercer – PFA lawyer – was adamant. Taylor must stay. Crooks explained:

Events since last Friday have satisfied the committee that Gordon could not be guaranteed the support and backing he enjoys at the PFA if he joined the League.

Their decision dealt a body-blow to Fox's strategy and placed Taylor in an awkward situation:

I accept the reasons and the decision because I don't want to go and leave bad blood behind me.... I am not going to say I am disappointed, but I would have relished the challenge, given the opportunity by both sides....

With Fox left battling on alone to secure his own position (and even trying to persuade Taylor to join a list of interviewees for the League post he had originally said was Taylor's for the asking!) questions were now asked as to Gordon Taylor's own judgement in allowing both himself and the PFA to become embroiled in such a fiasco. It was suggested in the press that he had been 'naive' in expecting support from the entire League Management Committee and that, having declined to apply for the FA and League positions in previous years, he must now 'contemplate his sparkling career stagnating for the foreseeable future'. Taylor himself was to make no further public statements about the whole affair. If he felt that he had been let down, or even betrayed by Fox, he appeared content to let others judge. As for his career 'stagnating', he considered the PFA offered more than enough challenges for the time being.

Perhaps the whole episode can be attributed to the pressure of events. 1989 had been, by anyone's standards, a traumatic year. The Hillsborough Disaster had occurred in March and had placed a great deal of strain and emotional pressure on many people in football, even those not directly involved with Liverpool FC.

Taylor had been present at most of the commemorative services as representative of the PFA and had been deeply affected by the sense of collective grief. The PFA Awards dinner, held the Sunday following Hillsborough, had been restructured and became a sombre occasion, with a minute's silence, prayers and a collection that raised £12,500 for victims' dependants. In July Taylor wrote:

Life can never be the same again after Hillsborough: it must change to make sure that football is never again thus scarred, but there are too many people offering catch-penny solutions to million pound problems.

The Government's identity card scheme would solve nothing, he continued:

> However, if football spends the summer arguing over the TV package and the size of the First Division, going to tribunals over transfer fees and arguing over playing surfaces rather than trying to sort out some way forward, then we will deserve to be dragged screaming through the government's hoop ...'

As a powerful chief executive of the League, he might have had the opportunity to try to prevent another Hillsborough. Fox's offer represented a chance for him to get to grips with the organization that – whilst not entirely to blame for soccer's manifold problems – still had a maddening propensity to stick its head in the sand and ignore reality.

His decision to remain with the PFA, therefore, must have caused some soul-searching despite Garth Crooks's diplomatic comments:

> Gordon fully understands and accepts our reasoning. He has set a marvellous example to everyone in football that contracts are there to be honoured by all....

The determination by the PFA Management Committee not to budge and to insist that Taylor serve out his contract must be seen, however, as positive, despite criticisms that it had been 'selfish' and 'not in the interests of the game as a whole'.

Gordon Taylor's rapid rise to prominence in British football had tended to eclipse the rest of the Management Committee and overshadow the role of the chairman – even though Brian Talbot had proved an effective partner for some four years. Taylor's successful style entailed taking personal initiatives while counting on the support of a membership that trusted him implicitly. He considered regular, detailed consultation with the members to be unnecessary and even a hindrance to effective decision-making. Thus, it had appeared – understandably perhaps – that at times Gordon Taylor *was* the PFA. Now the Management Committee had asserted itself.

It reminded Taylor of priorities he had set; and Crooks even went so far as to reiterate something Taylor had called for the previous year when once again declining to put forward his name for the

League secretaryship: 'We would like to think Gordon could become the leader of a steering committee with the PFA, League and FA.'

Crooks would say, on more than one subsequent occasion, that Taylor was 'our man … we're keeping him because we believe that the players need him and we believe that we are the most important body in football – representing the players that play the game. And if he's going to do it – steer that committee – he'll do it bringing the players with him.'

The PFA could therefore be said to have demonstrated its independence and safeguarded its integrity. The League could not expect to be allowed simply to 'lift' their chief executive. Moreover, the incident established the role of the chairman – in this case Garth Crooks – as a force to be reckoned with in the PFA.

Crooks had joined the committee as long ago as 1982 when still at Tottenham Hotspur with whom he won a FA Cup winner's medal and a League Cup runner's-up medal. A decade earlier, as a thirteen-year-old boy, he had watched George Eastham score the winning goal in the 1972 League Cup Final for Stoke City – the club he joined as an apprentice and where he played alongside Peter Shilton, Gordon Banks and Mike Pejic.

At Spurs Crooks had teamed up with Steve Archibald to form an exciting strike force and might have been selected for England had it not been for a certain 'lack of desire' on his part, a commitment to the game that he freely admits was not 100 per cent.

By 1983 he was on loan to Manchester United, before being transferred in 1985 to West Brom for £100,000. The move was not a success and in 1987 he joined Charlton Athletic.

The first black player to score in an FA Cup Final, the first black chairman of the PFA, Crooks was in 1989 a representative of the changing face of British football. When he turned pro in the 1970s, black players were rare. His initiation into the hard, cruel world of professional sports was made more of a trial by the virulent, unceasing abuse that came echoing down from terraces famous and infamous.

He recalls playing as an eighteen-year-old in front of the Kop at Anfield when the cruel and tasteless 'witticisms' rendered him isolated and alone, almost an embarrassment to his playing colleagues. At St James Park his manager actually took him off rather than let him face the endless barracking. And yet, like all black players, he knew he had no choice but to persist. As he put it:

If you couldn't cope, you fell foul of the industry.... No black player has been spared it – one has to deal with it and get on with it because sport offers an opportunity, one of the few areas where you can get on, doing what you do best, where talent is allowed to come through.

In a sense, whether he accepts it or not, Crooks is a test case. Not where the Union is concerned – at the playing level if we are to believe what most successful black players say, colour is no longer an issue. But where the crucial next step of management is concerned, questions loom.

Since the war, of all Union chairmen, only Jimmy Guthrie and Alan Gowling have not either become managers or taken jobs of similar quality in football. Crooks – intelligent, and self-assured – would seem ideally suited for similar elevation. Yet he expresses (defensively perhaps?) a certain ambivalence, a 'lack of ambition' – a definite acknowledgement that whoever takes that first step into the unknown will be  ubjected to almost unbearable scrutiny. His subsequent move into journalism and punditry suggests he will not be the one to expose himself to such an ordeal.

The challenge is one that Brendon Batson, however, deputy chief executive of the PFA, would appear eager to embrace. The controversy over Gordon Taylor's on-off appointment as League chief executive had, as well as projecting Garth Crooks into the limelight, also highlighted the role Batson played in the PFA. Whether he considered himself ready and willing or not, he was openly discussed as a possible successor to Taylor. Having been Taylor's deputy since 1984, he was ideally placed.

Six years older than Crooks, Grenadan-born Batson can also claim for himself 'pioneering' status. He came to England in 1962 at the age of nine, having never seen or played football before. By 1965, however, playing for Waltham Forest Boys, he caught the eye of George Male, scouting for Arsenal, and after a brief apprenticeship he signed for the Highbury club in 1970.

Four years of what he termed simply 'frustration' followed before he secured a transfer to Cambridge United where at last he earned a regular first-team place. When manager Ron Atkinson moved to West Bromwich, he took Brendon with him and for four years he was part of a flamboyant West Brom side that included Cyrille Regis and Laurie Cunningham. Always an astute publicist, Atkinson dreamed up the 'Three Degrees' stunt to highlight the fact that for the first time black players were making up a quarter of a full League side. Batson enjoyed the exposure, whilst confessing that it might have gone on 'one publicity shot too many'.

Although West Brom never quite managed to win a major trophy, the team played exhilarating football and it was a good time for Batson – unfortunately all too brief. By 1982 his career was almost over. Severe cartilage damage necessitated a series of operations that eventually resulted in retirement in 1984.

By then he was on the Union Management Committee, impelled by an innate curiosity, a desire to learn more about contracts, a natural tendency to speak his mind.

He applied for the managership of Cambridge but felt that, at thirty-one, he was probably a little young. Then suddenly, Gordon Taylor offered him the newly created position of Union assistant secretary.

Brendon confessed that he found it hard: for the first year he was 'clinging on for dear life', the experience made all the more difficult and painful by having to watch contemporaries continue their playing careers. The PFA job was something he 'had to grow into'. It was also somewhat chastening: 'People were always phoning the office and automatically asking for Gordon – Gordon and the PFA being synonymous of course.'

But he persisted and has clearly not only grown into but with the job. He still cherishes management ambitions, however, and is aware of the need to make that breakthrough. It is clear, Batson feels, that only in such a way – black players becoming coaches and managers – will the unpleasant odour of racism that pervades the majority of League grounds be dispelled. Referring to the small numbers of black fans on the terraces, he asks, 'Why should black people go into privately owned stadia to watch fellow blacks being subjected to abuse, or to be subjected to abuse themselves?' He also confesses himself disappointed that few clubs make overt references to the problem in their programmes, or that TV commentators and pundits studiously ignore the clearly audible abuse echoing around grounds during live transmissions; and he welcomes the Taylor Report's recommendations that action of some sort should be taken.

The playing profession itself, he considers, sets an example of integration and toleration 'second to none', but the absence of black managers 'leaves a lot of questions unanswered'. Batson appears anxious to provide a few answers.

In the meantime, he looks set to become a central figure in the PFA of the 1990s, particularly in relation to new ventures such as the financial company – PFA Financial Management Ltd – acquired in 1989.

The new company was established to provide members with an all-embracing financial advice service and will help explain to younger members the comprehensive range of benefits that now flow from membership of the PFA. These include personal and legal help with everything from contracts to private pensions and personal insurance; details and advice on organizing testimonials; the taking out of private medical insurance for free and immediate treatment (including the specialist injury clinic at Lilleshall); a non-contributory Cash Benefit Scheme that ensures every player a substantial lump sum on retirement; an automatic accident insurance scheme linked to the player's club; severance pay when a player is not offered a new contract, and help finding a new club; the longstanding Benevolent Fund; death benefit up to £400,000 to help provide for dependants; and the Education Society and Football and Community Scheme for help when a player retires and is seeking a new career.

Gordon Taylor was concerned that many young professionals did not realize all the PFA had to offer, particularly when the problem of players' agents became acute in late 1989. He commented:

> The situation is extremely frustrating for the PFA bearing in mind the top class advice available to all our members on finance, tax, savings, wage and contracts for example for a professional fee based on an hourly rate or subscription cost alone.

Brendon Batson demonstrated the advantages of the new company in this respect when, along with the Union's financial experts, he was instrumental in arranging the first £1m goalkeeping transfer – Nigel Martyn from Bristol Rovers to Crystal Palace – a service that cost the player no more than £200, in stark contrast to the massive percentage 'cuts' taken by some agents for similar work.

It was inevitable, of course, that the PFA would become involved in the controversy over agents and their apparently increasing influence in the modern game. In 1989 FIFA was anxious to establish a code of conduct for players' agents, while prominent managers complained in the popular press that top players were being unsettled and manipulated by unscrupulous men interested only in earning massive cuts from transfer fees and other 'external' payments.

In a sense, it was history come full circle. The malign influence of 'agents' was just another manifestation of the age-old fear of the financially liberated player. Nothing is new in football, including the double-standard applied by those in control of the game. Clubs had used agents from the very beginning of professionalism in order to secure players in the teeth of fierce opposition. But that was considered 'business'. For the player to behave in such a way was a 'threat to true sport'.

The question of agents does, however, highlight one of the continuing contradictions of the PFA – an association-cum-union dealing with a majority of young men earning no more than respectable salaries, yet characterized by 'stars', many of whom are independent companies in their own right. Brendon Batson has described the PFA as being 'a large boys' club – its members mostly young men who need advice and help in handling their careers until they are old enough to look after themselves'.

Thus where standards and codes of conduct are concerned – particularly in the perilous world of professional football – the PFA can only go so far in controlling what its members do. The same limited role applies to the vexed question of foul play; it can lay down guide-lines, agree schedules with the FA and exhort players to set good examples, but at the same time it must be seen to be protecting its members, even when they are committing misdemeanours. It is a difficult tightrope to walk.

But the 'greedy' player, the 'irresponsible' player, are caricatures as old as professional football itself. The PFA was formed to fight such myths, to protect and ultimately liberate players from the 'solutions', i.e. the maximum wage, the retain and transfer system, and disciplinary procedures that smacked of the armed forces.

That the Association will never be entirely successful in banishing the unsavoury images peddled in the 'popular' press will be due more to the endless capacity of football fans for believing the fantasies woven by journalists than to any lack of application on the Association's behalf. For the football industry is like almost no other in having a work-force composed of young men who are simultaneously creators of wealth and valued assets in themselves – both producers and products. As such, they are the objects both of veneration and scorn, as much a part of our dreams as they are of the real world.

It is, nevertheless, a touch ironic that the organization formed to represent the 'greedy' players, the 'mercenaries' who had no real regard for 'true sport', should be fighting with such skill, resourcefulness and commitment for a League system based on locality and community, on justice and even on dreams rather than on crude commercial muscle.

Ironic, too, that the organization staffed by men for so long mocked and derided for their supposed ignorance and simple-mindedness should, in the few short years it has been at the heart of affairs, have demonstrated such admirable good sense that it has eclipsed its venerable 'masters' both in terms of public esteem and confidence.

# *Epilogue*

The 1990 World Cup, with the success of both the England and Ireland teams, breathed new life into the British game. The subsequent re-entry of English clubs into European competitions, the departure of certain Government personnel and their replacement by individuals prepared to look at football and its problems more sympathetically and constructively only confirmed a general impression that better times were on the way.

It has, inevitably, not been all plain sailing. Increased cash for ground improvements from a reduction in the Government levy on betting, and the abandonment of the unpopular membership scheme have been tempered by an increasing tendency for police forces (not to mention satellite TV companies) to manipulate – even distort – major competitions, while problems on the field caused by FIFA's directive *vis-à-vis* the 'professional foul' have placed great pressure on referees, linesmen and players.

This latter issue, and the continuing controversy concerning the use by the FA of TV evidence in the disciplining of players found the PFA once again calling for more even-handed justice. Players such as Paul Davies and Tony Adams, plus both Arsenal and Manchester United clubs were 'convicted' and punished largely on the basis of TV recordings viewed after the event. Gordon Taylor commented:

In an age of technology there is a need to further fine tune our disciplinary system with a right of review of a sending-off offence where there is substantial visual evidence of an error of judgement. At the moment the only redress is to ask the referee to reconsider his decision in the light of the evidence presented to him in the aftermath of the game. The decision should be taken out of his hands so as to be consistent with those cases at Highbury and Old Trafford where the 'TV Referee' was used to over-rule decisions made by the man in the middle.

The first sign that the FA were listening to the PFA followed the sending-off of Watford's Keith Dublin by FIFA referee Keith Hackett. The decision was subsequently quashed after the FA had viewed video evidence. However, it is clear that the lessons of the Ernie Machin affair of some twenty years earlier have still not been completely digested.

Where the vexed question of the 'professional foul' was concerned, the professional player found his behaviour on the field once again the subject of intense scrutiny. The PFA's approach was largely one of trying to clear up the confusion surrounding the interpretation of FIFA's directive by referees up and down the country. If players are uncertain as to the consequences of their actions or when they see one player booked and another sent off for committing the same offence, the inevitable consequence will be anger and frustration, emotions easily transmitted to the terraces.

As the controversy reached its peak in December 1990 and January 1991, the PFA took the initiative and, with the League, arranged a series of six regional meetings, inviting referees, managers, players and administrators along to talk about the problem. A common consensus eventually arrived at was that, within the penalty area, unless there was violent conduct, a caution and a penalty-kick should be sufficient punishment for the cynical foul. To go further, the PFA felt, was 'unwarranted, unnecessary and counter-productive to entertainment, leaving an uneven contest.'

The problem remains, however, that referees continue to interpret the rule in different ways, and the problem was further exacerbated for professionals by the fact that the culprit was given the same initial three-match ban as a violent-conduct offender. After PFA pressure the professional foul now carries a one-match ban.

Inevitably, the question of TV's pervasive influence was raised at the regional meetings – in particular the practice of showing close-ups of players swearing and spitting. Significantly, it was a referee, Vic Callow, who commented:

> It's a pity that such moments are highlighted and relayed into people's homes.... I feel it is unfortunate that these things could undermine much of the good work being done as I feel there is a big improvement in standards of behaviour both on and off the field....

In this, at least, referees and players would appear to be at one. However, that refereeing standards have also come under scrutiny has opened up another area of debate in which the PFA has definite, if controversial, views that run counter to those of many referees.

With FIFA's decision to sanction the introduction of professional referees in Italy in 1993/4, the question of paying the men in black in this country appears to be a matter of when, not if. The PFA's attitude has been clear for some time: it backs the idea and is also adamant that ex-professional players would make good referees. Clearly, as an alternative career for ex-pros the idea would appear attractive, although with FIFA's insistence that World Cup officials should be no older than forty, long-term employment prospects seem limited.

However, the suggestion implicit in all this – that professionalism would improve standards and efficiency – reveals a growing gulf of understanding and diminishing common ground between professional players and amateur referees. In this, professional footballers are no different from other professional sportsmen such as tennis-players and cricketers, all of whom appear happiest when judged by fellow professionals – as Gordon Taylor has put it: 'Professional control of a professional game'.

Ironically, controlling the professional game in the wider sense became the most contentious issue of 1991, one that threatened to plunge the game once more into confusion and chaos.

Relations between the two governing bodies, the Football League and the Football Association, had been under strain for some time. The FA's decision to reduce the 'sentence' imposed by the League on Swindon Town following the latter's 'conviction' regarding illegal payments clearly angered League officials, while the League's own comprehensive plan for fundamental change – 'One game, one team, one voice' – unveiled in October 1990, certainly unsettled the FA.

The League were calling, in effect, for an historic amalgamation of the two bodies (with no mention, incidentally, of a role for the PFA).

From the outset, the scheme looked doomed, not least because the FA's initial lukewarm response brought forth threats from certain League Management Committee members that they would withdraw their clubs from the FA Cup and their players from the England squad if the FA were not co-operative.

Gordon Taylor was convinced such an amalgamation would fail. In August 1990 he commented:

> Because of their different characteristics ... amalgamation would be like asking two dinosaurs to come together creating a dodo that would not survive in the face of modern-day problems.

Taylor's own proposal was unambiguous:

> I really feel there needs to be a flexible structure including the PFA because without our involvement the chances of success would be non-existent. I would support moves by the FA to implement a football 'cabinet', comprising the heads of different spheres of influence within the game and providing an effective response without being bogged down by red tape and sectional interests. Each would represent his own autonomous body but each would have to accept the authority of the 'cabinet'.

Garth Crooks took the idea a little further, voicing fears the PFA had:

> The tragedy is that football's legislative hierarchy only calls upon the PFA as a last resort and purposely sidesteps it when the game's policies are being formed. It has never been the style of the PFA to broadcast its successes but they are many. I know only too well the frustration of the management committee and, unless the PFA have equal involvement in the proposed steering committee at some convenient stage, there will be confrontation.

The confrontation, when it came, did not at first involve the PFA, however. Taking almost everyone by surprise, the FA launched its own reorganization plan in April 1991 entitled 'Blue-print For Football'. The work of Graham Kelly and Charles Hughes, it took the radical step of proposing the creation of a

Premier League of eighteen top teams to be run by an independent management committee but ultimately under the control of the FA. The League, far from being an equal partner, would be left to run the Second, Third and Fourth Divisions.

The FA's motives for such drastic surgery were simple. The Football League's earlier decision to return to a twenty-two team First Division angered those who felt that England's top players played too much football to the detriment of the national side. Such a return to the past was also evidence that the League was still unable to govern itself consistently or coherently, being unable to deliver what it promised. The FA had thus decided to reassert itself as the supreme ruler of football in England.

The immediate accusations by the League that its First Division had been 'hi-jacked', was the beginning of a bitter war of words between the two bodies. The PFA, ignored now by both the League and the FA in their reorganization plans, took its time before pronouncing, but Gordon Taylor's response was clearly a pointed reminder to all concerned that the PFA could make or break any such scheme:

> People can have blueprints until they are blue in the face but, unless the players believe the proposals are in the best interests of the game, they are going down a road that leads to a dead end.

With previous abortive Premier League proposals in mind, Taylor continued:

> In 1986 I had to say that the players have always been united and are aware of their roots. No matter what people may think the players do care about the game as a whole, possibly more than most of the other people involved in it. The players are no longer a back-burner issue. I am proud of having 92 clubs and 2,000 full-time professionals and 1,200 on Youth Training programmes.
>
> Our contracts and commitments are with the League. We hear a lot of criticism about the way our football is run but the control of the players and clubs is better in this country than virtually every other country in the world.

But where actual decisions were concerned, Taylor concluded there could be none with so little detail available: 'Everybody's firing shots and nobody can see where we are going because of the smoke. I'm waiting for the smoke to clear.'

During May 1991, the Government had become concerned at the continuing bad publicity the FA/League split was generating. With its commitment to implementing the Taylor Report and its reducing of the betting levy to provide considerable extra funds for the Football Trust, it was disturbed at the sight of the two major governing bodies in the game so fundamentally at odds – and threatening to tear the professional game apart.

Thus Minister for Sport Robert Atkins approached Garth Crooks in the latter's capacity as chairman of the Pro-Sport Liaison committee and a meeting was arranged with Gordon Taylor and new PFA chairman Brian Marwood. Once again the PFA was being asked to act as mediator – only this time it was also being asked to put forward its own blueprint for change and the manner in which the game should be governed.

The PFA now has a great deal of responsibility resting upon its shoulders. Having achieved the goals set for it by men like Meredith, Cameron, Roberts, Fay, Guthrie and Lloyd – goals that necessarily concerned the welfare of its own members – the hope and expectation is that the Association can go on and play an equally constructive role in maintaining some kind of sane balance not just between the principal governing bodies but also between the almost unlimited financial promise (and threat) of the satellite TV age, and the much narrower but more justified demands of the spectating public whose hopes remain affectionately local and enduringly loyal and yet whose interests have been so scandalously neglected.

As Gordon Taylor told guests at the 1991 PFA Awards dinner:

> Let us remember that the spectators are the game's biggest sponsors (£100 million in gate receipts) and we depend on their loyalty for our livelihood – the move to quality and comfort cannot exclude them and concern itself only with corporate men in glass booths, expense account football symbolized by 'Never mind the result, just pass the champagne'.

Billy Meredith, never one to ignore the financial side of being a professional footballer, nevertheless commented on his enduring love-affair with playing the game, 'My heart was full of it.' It is in that spirit that the PFA – an organization staffed almost exclusively by ex-players whose roots go deep into the communities upon whom football depends – must surely go forward: seeking always to promote and protect only those things that will ultimately prove to be 'for the good of the game'.

# Appendix One: PFA Chairmen

John Devey (1897–1898)

Exelsior; Aston Unity; Mitchell St George; Aston Villa

Captained Aston Villa to five championships and two FA Cup wins, including the Double in 1897. Won three England caps and represented the Football League twice. A skilful, individual player, in both inside forward positions. Fast and clever on the ball but also a hard worker. Formed a famous partnership with Athersmith of England. A good cricketer, he played for Warwickshire; also a keen baseball player. Eventually became a director of Aston Villa.

Robert 'Bob' Holmes (1897–1899)

Preston Olympic; Preston North End

Played his first game for Preston First XI during the 1885/6 season, playing twenty games including one against Earlstown Wanderers which Preston won 19–0. Bob learnt much of the trade of full-back from his skipper, the famous N J Ross who was probably the best full back of the era, and when Ross went to Everton, Bob claimed the full-back position for himself. Making his League début in the first ever League game versus Burnley, having already played in the 1888 Cup Final and having gained a full England cap, Bob went on to captain Preston, the Football League and England for whom he appeared seven times. At the end of the 1899/1900 season he retired as a professional but was retained as an amateur. He later took up refereeing and coaching. Made 300 League appearances for Preston (one goal) and thirty-five FA Cup appearances (one goal).


Jack Bell (1897–1898)

Dumbarton Union; Dumbarton FC; Everton; Celtic; New Brighton Tower; Everton; Preston (later manager/coach)

'Bell has plenty of weight, runs fast and is a rattling good shot,' it was written of Jack Bell, who stood nearly six feet. A winger, he won ten Scottish caps and scored five goals in the process, as well as winning the Scottish League Championship with Dumbarton. On the losing Everton side in the Cup Final of 1897 (against John Devey's Aston Villa) he went to Preston and helped that great club regain First Division status in 1904. An exciting but tough player.


Harry Mainman (1907–1910)

Burton Swifts; Reading; Notts County

A skilful tackler and hard worker ('Wraps his legs round forwards like an octopus'), he captained Reading for five years and eventually retired there as a publican in 1911.


Evelyn Lintott (1910–1911)

Woking; Devonshire; Plymouth Argyle; Queen's Park Rangers; Bradford City; Leeds City

'Never flags from start to finish. Adept with either foot, clever in obtaining the ball but the use he makes of it to his forwards is his strong point.' A left back, he went to Guildford Grammar school and later qualified as a teacher at Exeter Training College. With Woking he captained the side to a Surrey Senior Charity Shield in 1904 and represented Surrey in County matches. Was a teacher in Willesden while playing for Queen's Park Rangers. In 1908 won an England amateur cap versus Ireland and went on to win seven full England caps. Joined the 15th Battn. West Yorks (The 'Leeds Pals') and was the first professional footballer to hold a commission (Lieut.). Killed in action on the first morning of the Somme offensive.

Colin Veitch (1911–1918)

Rutherford College; Newcastle schools; Newcastle

A strong, thoughtful half-back, cool and steady and very much a tactician (he pioneered team talks at half-time while at Newcastle), he captained Newcastle on many occasions, turning out for the club 321 times during his 15 years with them, during which time they were League Champions three times (1905, 1907 and 1909) and Cup Winners five times (1905, 1906, 1908, 1910 and 1911). He also won six England caps. After the war he coached Newcastle reserves until 1926. He then managed Bradford City for two years before turning to journalism full-time. A multi-talented man, he was a playwright, producer, composer and actor of some merit. Became a lieutenant during the war and qualified as a teacher. A socialist.

Charlie Roberts (1919–1921)

Darlington St Augustine's; Bishop Auckland; Grimsby Town; Manchester United; Oldham Athletic

One of Manchester United's great players, joining the club in April 1904 for £600. He played 299 League and Cup games for them, most of them as captain. The club won the League twice (1908 and 1910) and the Cup once (1909) while Roberts won three full England caps and made 9 Football League appearances. He joined Oldham in August 1913 for £1,750 and under his captaincy the club achieved their best-ever League position as runners-up to Everton in 1915.

Retiring because of injury he managed Oldham for a short spell before leaving football to concentrate on his confectionery business (which still flourishes today in Manchester). A great captain and leader, constructive at centre half and almost unbeatable in the air.

Jimmy Fay (1921–1929)

Southport Blue Star; Southport Working Lads; Chorley; Oswaldtwistle Rovers; Oldham Athletic; Bolton Wanderers; Southport

Remarkably consistent player, missing only one first-team game in six seasons from 1905 to 1911, Jimmy Fay was part of a famous Oldham team that lifted the club from obscurity into Division One of the FL. As an emergency inside right (he was normally a half-back) in season 1909–10 his 26 goals from 21 matches helped Athletic clinch promotion from Division Two as runners-up to Manchester City. Made 128 appearances for Bolton between 1911 and 1921 and gained a Football League representative cap, his third, against the Scottish League in 1919 when 35 years old. Had a sports outfitters in Southport for most of his life.

Howard Matthews (1929–1930)

Oldbury St John's; Langley St Michael's; Burslem Port Vale amateur; Burton United; Oldham Athletic; Port Vale; Halifax Town; Chester

Son of a well-known amateur goal-keeper, Howard Matthews was of comparatively slight build for the position. Nevertheless he was a fine player and a model footballer on and off the field. A civil servant by profession and a life-long teetotaller and non-smoker he was probably the oldest player in League football when he was playing for Halifax in his 45th year. One Football League XI appearance v Irish League 1909. Made 344 appearances for Oldham Athletic.

Arthur Wood (1930–1931)

Southampton; Clapton Orient

Son of Harry Wood, Wolves inside right and trainer of Portsmouth.


Dave Robbie (1931–1936)

Renton; Bathgate; Bury; Plymouth Argyle; Rochdale

Made 420 appearances for Bury during the years 1921 to 1934/5 during which time he scored 101 goals. He was a right winger and tall for the position (5ft 10ins). A solid club-man he joined Plymouth Argyle as player coach in 1936/7 and stayed two years. Later went into business as a private physiotherapist.


Albert 'Sid' Barrett (1936)

Fairbairn House Boys; West Ham Boys; Leytonstone; West Ham; Southampton; Fulham

Cool stylish wing-half with a flair for attack. Won four England amateur caps while with Leytonstone. Toured South Africa with an FA XI in 1929, and won one full England cap v Ireland 1930. In ten seasons with Fulham made over 400 appearances. Emigrated to South Africa in 1954.


Sammy Crooks (1937–1946)

Durham City; Derby County

Between 1927 and 1947 Crooks played 445 League and Cup games for Derby County scoring 111 goals. Despite his frail appearance, he was fast and tricky and had a sharp footballing brain. He was England's outside-right 26 times before the war and was picked for the Football League four times. After the war he became Derby County's chief Scout and later in 1950 Shrewsbury Town's Secretary/Manager. Originally a miner.

Jimmy Guthrie (1945–1957)

Luncarty Boys; Perth Thistle Juniors; Scone Thistle; Dundee; Portsmouth; Crystal Palace

A tough, uncompromising half-back, he was a good leader, captaining the Portsmouth side to a surprise FA Cup win in 1939 and a Southern Cup Final in 1941. Coached Crystal Palace after the war.


Jimmy Hill (1957–1961)

Brentford; Fulham

An enthusiastic, wholehearted rather than skilful player, he holds the club record of scoring five goals in an away match. Not a prolific scorer at inside right, he nevertheless scored crucial goals during Fulham's 1958 Cup run, and helped the club to promotion to Division One in 1957. Almost 300 appearances for Fulham, he went straight into management at Coventry, guiding the club from the Third Division to the First. Subsequently Managing Director of Coventry, he then became a director of Charlton, only to return to Fulham to chair a group attempting to save the club from extinction. TV executive and pundit, he once ran the line during a First Division game at Highbury.


Tommy Cummings (1961–1963)

Hylton Colliery Welfare; Burnley; Mansfield

Joined Burnley in 1947. A commanding centre-half, relying on positional skill and judgement. He played for England 'B' and also represented the Football League and probably would have gained further honours but for the brilliance of Billy Wright. Won League Championship medal and Cup runner's-up medal with Burnley before going to Mansfield in 1963 as player-manager. Now a publican.

Malcolm Musgrove (1963–1966)

Lynemouth Colliery; West Ham United; Leyton Orient; assistant manager Leicester City; Manchester United; manager Torquay United

Direct goal-scoring winger – second only to Jimmy Ruffell as the highest-scoring West Ham winger of all time with 83 goals. A member of the Second Division championship team of 1958, he moved to Leyton Orient for £11,000 in 1962. Became coach at Orient under Dave Sexton, then assisted Frank O'Farrell at Leicester City and Manchester United. Made 298 appearances for West Ham (Cup and League) and another 83 appearances for Orient.

Noel Cantwell (1966–1967)

Cork United; West Ham United; Manchester United; Coventry City, Peterborough United; Boston Tea Men

Swashbuckling, attack-minded full-back, thick-set and skilful, he gained 36 Irish caps and won championship medals with Manchester United as well as captaining the side to an FA Cup win in 1963. With West Ham, formed a famous partnership with John Bond which was a major factor in West Ham's promotion in 1958. As a manager, he took Coventry to sixth place in Division One and took Peterborough United from the Fourth to the Third. Over 250 League and Cup appearances for West Ham and another 150 for Manchester United, he was voted Irish Footballer of the Year in 1958/9.

Terry Neill (1967–1970)

Bangor (Northern Ireland); Arsenal; Hull City

A well-built centre-cum-wing-half, Neill joined Arsenal in 1959 and spent most of his career at Highbury as a utility player although by 1965/66 he had gained a regular place alongside Ian Ure in the heart of the Arsenal defence. In July 1970 he joined Hull City, playing over 100 League games for the 'Tigers' before stepping up into the manager's chair. Made 59 appearances for Northern Ireland and had a spell managing the national side. Today he runs his own business.

Derek Dougan (1970–1978)

Portsmouth; Blackburn Rovers; Aston Villa; Peterborough; Leicester; Wolverhampton Wanderers

A marvellous extrovert centre-forward. Dougan had great skill on the ground and was quite capable of winning any aerial battle. Played for a number of clubs but only settled down with Wolves whom he joined in March 1967 and for whom he turned out some 244 times scoring 93 goals. In all his career totalled 532 appearances and over 200 goals. A great favourite with most fans, he won 43 Northern Ireland caps. For a short time was chief executive of Kettering Town FC and has since gone into public relations on his own account.

Gordon Taylor (1978–1980) (see Secretaries)

Alan Gowling (1980–1982)

Manchester University; Manchester United; Huddersfield; Newcastle United; Bolton Wanderers; Preston North End

Combined powerful shooting with pace and craft. After completing a degree at Manchester University, signed professional for United in 1967, making 77 appearances, scoring 21 goals. With Huddersfield and Newcastle he made another 220 appearances and scored another 88 goals. Retired from League football in 1984 and now works in industry.

Steve Coppell (1982–1984)

Tranmere Rovers; Manchester United

Completed degree at Liverpool University before signing

professional forms for Tranmere in 1974. Made 40 appearances and scored ten goals before being signed by Manchester United in 1975. With the Old Trafford club he made 392 League and Cup appearances, scoring 70 goals, at the same time appearing for England 42 times. Reached the Cup Finals of 1976, 77 and 79 and the Milk Cup Final in 1983. Retired because of injury in 1983 and took over as manager of Crystal Palace in 1984. Noted for his all-action, fast, direct style and a good crosser of the ball.

Brian Talbot (1984–1988)

Ipswich; Arsenal; Watford; Stoke City; West Bromwich Albion

Ipswich-born, he joined his local League team on leaving school in 1969, making 177 League appearances for the Suffolk side. An industrious, goal-scoring mid-fielder who never gave less than 100 per cent, he won a Cup Final medal under Bobby Robson in 1978 after which he moved to Arsenal. In six years with the Gunners he clocked up over 300 League, Cup and League Cup appearances, made two more Cup Final appearances and a European Cup Winners Cup Final. In 1985 he moved to Watford, then to Stoke and finally to West Bromwich where he appeared 74 times in the League as player/manager. This brought his total League appearances to over 600. He is now manager of Aldershot. A great servant of the PFA, he was Chairman for five years until 1989.

Garth Crooks (1988–1990)

Stoke City; Tottenham Hotspur; Manchester United; West Bromwich Albion; Charlton Athletic

Snappy little striker. Born and educated in Stoke, joining City as a 16-year-old in 1974. He scored 53 goals for Stoke in 162 League and Cup games before moving to Tottenham Hotspur in 1980. He made another 160-plus appearances for Spurs, scoring 68 goals. He retired in 1990 having won two FA Cup Final medals, been capped four times at Under-21 level and equalling Spurs club record of scoring eight goals in eight consecutive games. A prolific TV performer, he is now making a new career in TV production and presentation, as well as chairing the Pro-Sport liaison committee which operates under the auspices of the CCPR.


Brian Marwood (1990–    )

Hull City; Sheffield Wednesday; Arsenal; Sheffield United

Talented, speedy forward at home on either flank, he began his first-class career with Hull City as an apprentice in 1976. After 158 League appearances (and 51 goals) during which he helped the Tigers to promotion from the Fourth to the Third Division, he joined Sheffield Wednesday, for whom he made 128 League appearances, scoring 27 goals. During his three seasons at Arsenal he won an England cap and a League championship medal. In 1990, he joined Sheffield United and was elected to the Chairmanship of the PFA following Garth Crooks's resignation.

# Appendix Two: PFA Secretaries

Charles Saer (1898–1899)

Fleetwood Rangers; Feb 1897 Blackburn Rovers; Sep 1897 Leicester Fosse; cs 1898 Stock County

'Cheerfully charismatic', skilful goalkeeper who might have had an international career with Wales but for the pre-eminence of J Trainer. Helped Leicester Fosse to their best defensive record during his single season with the club. Studied to become a teacher. First job was in Ffestiniog at a higher grade school, he then moved to a job on the school board at Fleetwood Lancs. Injured a knee in 1899 and gave up the game.

John Cameron (1897–1901)

Elmbank, Parkhouse; Queen's Park (amateur); Everton 1897; Spurs 1898

Skilful, ball-playing centre-forward; won a full Scottish cap in 1896 when still an amateur in a 3–3 draw with Ireland. A clerk with Cunard, he joined Everton as an amateur, eventually turning professional in 1897/8. Moved to Spurs as player/manager and guided them to Southern League championship in 1899/1900 and the FA cup the following year. Left Spurs in 1907, a year before they were promoted to Division Two. Returned to Scotland; was a journalist, contributed to books on football and coached. Was coaching in Germany at the outbreak of the First World War and was interned for the duration. Returned to Ayr in 1919 and managed the home side for a season.

Herbert Broomfield (1908–1910)

Northwich Wednesday; Northwich Victoria; Bolton Wanderers; Manchester United

Considered a brave, skilful goal-keeper, if unlucky. Dislocated his shoulder and collar-bone shortly after moving to Bolton Wanderers. Then broke his nose in a reserve-match come-back. Played just 28 times for Bolton's first team between 1902–07; controversially dropped during Bolton's FA cup campaign of 1906 for missing training due to concern over his painting and decorating business in Northwich. Transferred to Manchester United in 1907; played only a handful of games before retiring from football. A businessman, trained civil servant, amateur artist, he left football to concentrate on developing a new rubberized football, a patent bought from Billy Meredith.

Alfred Sydney Owen (1910–1913)

North Stafford Nomads; Northern Nomads; Jan 1907 Stoke; July 1907 Stockport County; April 1908 Stoke; Sept 1908 Leicester Fosse; 1911 English Wanderers; July 1911 Blackpool; Nov 1912 Stoke

A forceful inside or outside left, whenever business commitments or amateur internationals would permit; originally a full-back at Stoke, but converted to the forward line so successfully he was selected for a senior England trial in Jan 1919, scoring once for the Whites v Stripes at Anfield but not subsequently winning a full cap. Won Amateur international caps v Sweden, Ireland, Holland, Belgium and Ireland again during which he scored 6 goals. A trained chartered accountant, he resigned from the PFA in

February 1913 to take up a coaching appointment in Budapest.

Harry Newbould (1913–1929)

Derby St Lukes

A qualified accountant, Newbould was appointed assistant secretary of Derby County FC in 1896. He was promoted to secretary some years later and became manager of the club in 1900. In July 1906 he moved to Manchester City as Secretary/Manager and helped rebuild the club following the bribery scandal of 1905. Became secretary of PFA (Players' Union) in 1913 and remained in the post until his death in 1929. In his youth a fine sprinter, an attribute that equipped him well as a right-winger in his youth.

Jimmy Fay (see Chairmen) (1929–1953)

Cliff Lloyd (1953–1982)

Helsby; BICC Cables; Liverpool; Wrexham; Brentford; Fulham; Bristol Rovers

Son of a footballing father, fourth of six brothers, Cliff joined Liverpool in 1936 as a full-back; the 1939–45 war ended his hopes of playing in the First Division for the Reds but during his army career he played for Wrexham, Fulham and Brentford and appeared for London Division, The Army and the Combined Services. After the war he remained with Fulham for another five years, coached Lisleby in Norway and finally moved to Bristol Rovers for a season in the early Fifties. Became Players' Union Secretary in 1953. Retired in 1982.

Gordon Taylor (1981–     )

Bolton Wanderers; Birmingham City; Blackburn Rovers; Vancouver Whitecaps; Bury

Originally an inside forward before establishing himself as a winger with Bolton in the Sixties, playing over 250 games for them, mainly in Division 2. Signed for Birmingham in December 1970 and linked up with Trevor Francis and Bob Latchford to win promotion to Division 1 in 1972 (the season he joined the PFA Management Committee). After losing to a Bobby Moore-led Fulham at Maine Road in a 1975 Cup Semi-Final replay, he returned to help Blackburn Rovers avoid relegation to Division 3. Played in the North American Soccer League in the summer of 1977 with Vancouver Whitecaps (beating the New York Cosmos of Pele and Beckenbaur 5-3). Returned to Blackburn before joining Bury in 1978. FA Coach, London University External BSc (Econ) (1989), Honorary MA from Loughborough University in 1986 for services to football. Over 500 Football League games and over 50 goals.

# Appendix Three: Team Line-ups for the Three Scottish Union vs. English Union Fund-raising Matches

28 April 1898 at Ibrox Park, Glasgow

Scottish XI (0) 1 (Smith)

M Dickie (Rangers)
J W Welford (Celtic)
D R Gardner (Third Lanark)
B Breslin (Hibernians)
D Russell (Celtic)
N Gibson (Rangers)
P Murray (Hibernians)
J McPherson (Rangers)
J Campbell (Celtic)
A McMahon (Celtic)
A Smith (Rangers)

English XI (1) 2 (Wheldon, Milward)

J W Robinson (New Brighton Tower)
R Holmes (Preston NE)
D Storrier (Everton)
H Wilson (Sunderland)
R Chatt (Aston Villa)
J T Robertson (Everton)
W C Athersmith (Aston Villa)
F Becton (Liverpool)
J Bell (Everton)
G F Wheldon (Aston Villa)
A Milward (New Brighton Tower)

15 March 1899 at The Crystal Palace, London

Scottish XI (1) 2
(Divers, Millar)

English XI (1) 1 (T Smith)

J W Sutcliffe (Bolton Wanderers)

D McArthur (Celtic)
N Smith (Rangers)
D Storrier (Celtic)
N Gibson (Rangers)
H Marshall (Celtic)
B Battles (Celtic)
J Campbell (Rangers)
R Walker (Hearts)
J Divers (Celtic)
J Millar (Rangers)
J Bell (Celtic)

R Holmes (Preston NE)
W Williams (West Bromwich A)
J R McNaught (Tottenham H)
A Chadwick (Southampton)
J W Crabtree (Aston Villa)
W C Athersmith (Aston Villa)
T Smith (Tottenham H)
W Wigmore (Gainsborough
Trinity)
H Wood (Southampton)
H Bradshaw (Tottenham H)

26 March 1900 at Ibrox Park, Glasgow

Scottish XI (1) 2
(Gibbons, Hamilton)

English XI (0) 0

J Hillman (Burnley)

H G Rennie (Hearts)
R Davidson (Celtic)
B Battles (Celtic)
N Gibson (Rangers)
R G Neil (Rangers)
W Orr (Celtic)
J Hodge (Celtic)
T Gibbons (Third Lanark)
R C Hamilton (Rangers)
G T Livingstone (Hearts)
A Smith (Rangers)

R Holmes (Preston NE)
J Blackett (Wolverhampton
Wanderers)
W Bull (Notts County)
H Stringfellow (Portsmouth)
H Griffiths (Wolverhampton
Wanderers)
J Cameron (Tottenham H)
J Settle (Bury)
W Toman (Everton)
G F Wheldon (Aston Villa)
J Millar (Wolves)

(Note: The J Campbell of Celtic in 1898 is a different player from
the J Campbell of Rangers in 1899)

With acknowledgements to Keith Warsop

# Bibliography

Books

*The Book of Football*, Amalgamated Press, 1906

Cameron, John, *Association Football and How To Play It*, Health and Strength, 1908

Catton, J H *The Rise of the Leaguers*, Sporting Chronicle, 1897

Chester, Sir Norman, *Report of the Committee on Football*, HMSO, 1968

Coppell, Steve, *Touch and Go*, Collins/Willow, 1985

Crampsey, Bob, *The Scottish Footballer*, Edinburgh, 1978

Dabscheck, Braham, 'Defensive, Manchester', in R Cashman and M. McKenna *(eds) Sport in History*, St Lucia, 1979

'*A Man or A Puppet*' *The FA's Attempt to Destroy the AFPU*, School of Industrial Relations, University of New South Wales, Australia, 1990

Dougan, Derek, *How Not To Run Football*, All Seasons Publishing Ltd, 1981

Douglas, Peter, *The Football Industry*, George Allen and Unwin, 1973

Eastham, George, *Determined to Win*, Sports Book Club, 1964

Fabian, A H and Green, G, *Association Football* (IV Vols), Caxton, 1960

Fishwick, N, *English Football and Society*, Manchester University Press, 1989

Ford, Trevor, *I Lead the Attack*, Stanley Paul, 1957
*Foul Book of Football No. 1 Best of Foul 1972–75*, Foul Pubs, 1976
Franklyn, Neil, *Soccer at Home and Abroad*, 1955
Gibson, A and Pickford, W, *Association Football and the Men Who Made It*, Caxton Publishing, 1906
Guthrie, J, *Soccer Rebel*, Davis/Foster, 1976
Hardaker, A, *Hardaker of the League*, Pelham Books, 1977
Harding, J, *Football Wizard*, Breedon Books, 1985
Hill, J, *Striking for Soccer*, Sportsman's Book Club, 1961
Inglis, S, *League Football and the Men Who Made It*, Collins/Willow, 1988
Keeton, G W, *The Football Revolution*, David & Charles, 1972
Levine, P, *A.G. Spalding and the Rise of Baseball*, Oxford University Press, 1985
Mason, Dr Tony, *Association Football and English Society*, Harvester Press, 1980
PEP, *English Professional Football Planning*, XXII, 1966
Redhead, S, *Sing When You're Winning*, Harvester Press, 1984
Tischler, S, *Footballers and Businessmen*, New York, 1981
VamPlew, W, *Pay Up and Play The Game*, Cambridge, 1988
Wagg, S, *The Football World*, Harvester Press, 1984
Wright, Billy, *The World's My Football Pitch*, St Paul, 1953

Newspapers/Magazines (pre 1945):

*Thomson's Weekly News*
*Lancashire Daily Post*
*Sporting Chronicle*
*Daily Dispatch*
*Athletic News*
*Bolton Cricket and Football Field*
*Saturday Post*
*Topical Times*
*Daily Sketch*
*Sports Pictures*
*Red Letter*
*Football Field*

# Index

**\* Denotes magazines, newspapers or books**

\* *Abaris*, 9, 11, 22, 30
Aberdare FC, 134
Aberdeen FC, 164
Accrington Stanley FC, 290
Adams, T., 367
AEU, 339
Allen, K., 340
Allison, G., 129
Allison, R., 356
American Professional Soccer League, 249
American Soccer League, 163
\* *Answers*, 135, 136
Appleton, W.A., 72, 73, 74
Archibald, S., 361
Armfield, J., 291
Armstrong, K., 263
Arsenal FC, 123, 129, 143, 145, 164, 165, 172, 173, 174, 175, 241, 284, 311, 362, 367
Ashcroft, J., 59
\* *Association Football and the Men Who Made It*, 33
Aston Villa FC, 33, 34, 35 36, 74, 98, 99, 100, 110, 114, 117, 119, 129, 185, 198, 269
\* *Athletic News*, 6, 13, 30, 41, 53, 54, 57, 61, 89, 92, 94, 107, 111, 113, 118, 132, 135, 136, 149, 150, 167
Atkins, R., (MP), 372
Atkinson, R., 362
Atlantic Charter, 209
Atterby, (Plymouth Argyle), 86
Ayr Utd FC, 33

Bacuzzi, J., 253, 274
Bangor City FC, 171, 184
Banks, G., 361
Banner, A., 247, 248, 261, 264
Bannister, B., 320, 325, 331
Barclay, P., 329
Barnes, 86
Barnsley FC, 144, 217
Barr, J., 224
Barrett, A., 197
Bastin, C., 173, 197, 253
Batson, B., 355, 362, 363, 364, 365

393

Batson, J., 234–6, 241
Baxter, M., 351
BBC, 186, 354, 355
Beadles, H., 181
Beasley, P., 253
Beattie, A., 198
Beckenbauer, F., 330
Beeching, E., 334
Bell, J., 8, 10, 15, 16, 20, 22, 33, 42
Benevolent Fund (Players Union), 29, 47, 101, 102, 103, 107, 139, 218, 327, 338, 364
Bentley, J.J., 6, 10, 27, 45, 46, 57, 72
Bentley, R., 274
Best, G., 330
Birch, M., 343
Birmingham, C., 330, 343
Blackburn Rovers FC 19, 86, 110, 185, 268, 306, 330
Blackpool FC, 348
Block Accident Insurance Policy, 231, 242
Bloomer, S., 13, 33
Bohemians, FC, 198
Bolton Wanderers FC, 10, 38, 39, 143, 253, 329, 330, 340
Bond, 'Dickie', 95, 96
Book, T., 313
Boston FC (USA), 164
Bourne, (Crystal Palace), 135
Bowman, J., 182
Boxhall, D., 224
Boyle, (Rochdale), 261
Bradford City FC, 43, 85, 96, 114, 131, 343, 350
Bradford Park Avenue FC, 269
Bradley, S., (ASE), 123
Bradshaw, F., 15, 16, 110, 123
Bradshaw, 'Tiny', 253
Brelsford, W.H., 144
Brentford FC, 253, 273
Bridgett, A., 89, 94
Bristol City FC, 34, 62, 146, 332, 333

Bristol Rovers, FC, 248, 253, 364
Britton, C., 172
Brook, E., 171, 197
Brooklyn FC (USA), 164
Broome, F., 211, 213, 227, 247
Broomfield, H., 42, 43, 48, 50, 55, 56, 57, 59, 60–72, 76, 78, 80, 81, 82, 85, 86, 101, 103, 110, 129, 178, 185, 203, 327
Brown, A., 213, 247
BSB, 354, 355
Buchan, C., 129, 142, 143, 148, 166, 173
Buchan, J., 96, 97
Buckley, (Major) F., 220
Bulganin, N., 236
Bull, W., 42
Burgess, H., 42
Burnley, FC, 22, 53, 131, 154, 229, 281, 290
Burns, M., 348, 355
Bury, FC, 166, 171, 330
Busby, M., 172, 253

Calderhead, D., 8
Callow, V., 369
Cambridge United FC, 362, 363
Cameron, J., 11, 13, 16, 18, 25, 28, 29, 31, 32, 33, 43, 203, 285, 372
Cameron, J., (Newcastle), 43
Campbell, J., 257, 267, 268, 269, 282, 306
Cann, S., 209
Cantwell, N., 296, 297, 305, 327
Cardiff, FC, 171, 181, 348
Carter, P., 343, 345, 356
Carver, J., 172
Cassidy, J., (Celtic), 164
Cassidy, J., (Man. City), 38
Catton, J., 43, 162
Celtic, FC, 9, 10, 15, 33, 39
Chapman, H., 129, 143, 158, 167, 172, 173, 174, 175
Charing Cross Hotel, 246
Charlton Athletic FC, 224, 361

Charlton, R., 274, 296, 305, 327, 330, 355, 356

Charnley, T., 92, 146, 177

Charterhouse Hotel, 43, 73

Chase, R., 357

Chedgzoy, S., 164

Chelsea FC, 34, 44, 110, 131, 173, 174, 224, 263

Chester Committee/Report, 299, 301, 302, 303, 311, 313, 316, 317, 324, 330, 350

Chesterfield FC, 63, 149, 150, 151, 153, 248

Chorley FC, 142

Clapton Orient FC, 98, 119, 135, 171

* *Clarion*, 70, 80

Claro, T., 278, 280

Clayton, R., 268

Clegg, J.C., 26, 39, 63, 64, 74, 76, 78, 79

Cohen, G., 274

Coleman, T., 120

Collins, A., 86

Commission on Industrial Relations (CIR), 314, 315, 316, 317, 326, 330

Community Programme (FFEVTS), 350, 351, 352, 364

Cook, W., 144

Cooper, T., 253

Coppell, S., 339, 340, 341, 346

Copping, W., 173

Corn Exchange Building, 245

Cordell, H.P., 181

Coventry City FC, 274, 281, 297, 304, 305

Cowen, S., 171, 197

Craig, C.J., 42, 43

Crewe Alexandra FC, 349

* *Cricket and Football Field* (Bolton), 8, 9, 10, 12, 24, 30, 62

Crompton, R., 62, 81

Crooks, G., 358, 360, 361, 362, 370, 372

Crooks, S., 185, 196, 197, 198, 201, 204, 206, 209, 210, 211, 212, 213, 215, 216, 218, 219, 220, 221, 247, 286, 341

Croydon Common, FC, 98

Crump, C., 77, 78, 102

Crystal Palace, FC, 63, 95, 134, 135, 364

Cuff, W., 172, 202, 213, 214, 215, 216, 218, 219, 225, 227

Cullis, S., 209

Cummings, T., 267, 282, 283, 291, 327

Cunningham, L., 362

Curran, P., (MP), 72

Cusick, D., 340

* *Cupid and Football Answers*, 136

Dabscheck, B., 336

* *Daily Express*, 182

* *Daily Dispatch*, 79

* *Daily Herald*, 214, 265

* *Daily Mail*, 135, 182

* *Daily Mirror*, 333

* *Daily News and Westminster Gazette*, 182

* *Daily Sketch*, 60, 61

* *Daily Telegraph*, 292

Dargie, I., 267, 282

Darlington FC, 333

Davies, G., 267, 269, 270, 271, 272, 273, 278, 281, 283, 284, 287, 288, 289, 291, 292, 297, 312, 319, 325, 327, 328, 333

Davies, J.H., 43, 45, 46, 74

Davies, L., 166, 171, 181, 184

Davies, P., 367

Dean, (Dixie), 164, 165, 175, 185, 198, 202

Deehan, J., 341

Dein, D., 356

Dent, D., 352

Derby County FC, 6, 7, 103, 197, 218, 219

Devey, J., 8, 9, 20, 22, 32, 33, 285

Dickson, J., 176
Dodds, J., 160
Doncaster Rovers FC, 182, 349
Donovan, T., 222
Dougan, D., 297, 304–8, 315–17, 320, 323–7, 330, 339, 346
Downie, A., 42
Doyle, D., 9, 10, 33
Drake, T., 273
Drewry, A., 259
Dublin, K., 368
Duncan, (Dally), 209, 211
Dundee FC, 220
Dundee United FC, 152
Dunlop, W., 81
Dunnett, J., 335, 356
Dunphy, E., 315, 317, 321, 322
Durban, A., 313
Durham City, 146, 197

Eastham, G., 283, 284, 288, 289, 290, 291, 293, 301, 316, 361
Edelston, J., 171
Education Society, 296, 310, 311, 313, 338, 347, 348, 350, 351, 364
Ellis, D., 357
Elliot, T., 123
Elliot, W., 241, 247
Empire Pools, 218
Evans, A.J., 42
Everton FC, 9, 10, 11, 15, 16, 34, 36, 72, 119, 148, 149, 152, 161, 164, 172, 173, 198, 229, 345

Fagan, W., 253
Farquarson, T., 198
Fay, J., 103, 129, 142, 144, 156, 162, 168, 169, 170, 172, 173, 174, 177, 178, 180, 182, 184, 185, 187–194, 199, 201–12, 216–21, 223, 227–2, 234, 240–43, 245–7, 252, 255, 257, 266, 267, 269, 286, 291, 310, 326, 327, 341, 346, 372
Fazakerly, S., 144, 145

FIFA, 162, 234, 288, 296, 364, 367, 368, 369
Finney, T., 249
Firmani, E., 255
Flavell, B., 250
Fleetwood Rangers FC, 19
Fletcher, E., 129, 171
Flint Town FC, 253
Football Association, 1, 3, 4, 9, 12, 13, 17, 18, 20, 22–4, 26–8, 31, 32, 35–7, 43–50, 53, 55–60, 62–5, 68–70, 72–82, 84, 86, 88, 95–7, 102, 103, 107–9, 120, 121, 124, 135, 139, 150, 162, 164, 167, 178, 191, 192, 194, 199, 218, 222, 229–35, 239, 240, 254, 259, 261, 264, 270–73, 288, 290, 292, 295, 297, 299, 301–6, 324, 338–342, 352, 359, 361, 368–72
FA Benevolent Fund, 46, 108, 109, 112
★ *Football Chat*, 28, 29, 31
Football League, 1–9, 11–13, 15, 20, 22–8, 30–35, 37, 40, 45, 49, 53, 58, 81, 84, 86, 89, 92, 94, 97, 98, 100–103, 107–109, 111, 116, 121, 124–7, 131, 132, 135, 138, 149–54, 167, 186, 189, 191–6, 199, 204, 208, 210–16, 218, 222, 224, 225, 229, 230–32, 237, 239–41, 254–9, 261, 264, 266, 270–73, 275–7, 280, 281, 284, 286, 289–95, 297, 299–303, 306, 314, 317, 319, 321, 322, 325, 334, 335, 337–9, 342–5, 352, 354–9, 361, 369–72
Football League Management Committee, 31, 43, 47, 88, 91, 94, 103, 111, 112, 113, 121, 123, 131, 132, 134, 136, 138, 146, 151, 153, 172, 178, 190, 192, 193, 201, 213–16, 219, 224, 225, 227, 234, 258, 260, 279, 280, 283, 292, 294, 313, 317, 335,

355–9, 370
Football League Mutual Insurance Federation, 55, 109, 154, 187, 198, 211
Footballer's Regiment, 120
* *Football and Sports Survey*, 234
Football Trust, 352, 372
Ford, T., 250, 306
Forster, J. (Report), 239, 240, 259, 260, 271
* *Foul*, 308, 315, 316, 317, 322
Fox, W., 357, 358, 359, 360
Francis, T., 330
Franklyn, N., 250
Friendly Societies Act/Register, 11, 258
Fresh Air Fund, 68
Fulham FC, 34, 63, 98, 248, 253, 270, 274

Gallagher, H., 177
Gee, A., 72, 73
GFTU, 61, 62, 64, 68, 69, 72, 73, 74, 76, 78, 81, 82, 254
GMU, 339
Gibbons, S., 198
Gibson, C., 358
Gilbert and Sullivan, 91
Gillespie, T.B., 164
Gillespie, W., 144
Glanville, B., 355
Goodhart, P., (MP), 276
Goodwin, F., 297
Goslin, (Bristol City), 171
Gough, H., 144, 145
Gowling, A., 312, 323, 339, 340, 346, 348, 363
Griffiths, D., 356
Griffiths, T., 198
Grimsby Town FC, 10, 146
Green, D., 294, 297, 303, 327
Greenwood, R., 273
Greyhound Racing Association, 176
Grundy, H., 144, 184, 185

Guthrie, J., 204, 205, 208–13, 215–18, 220–23, 225, 227, 228, 230–32, 234–7, 240–52, 254–58, 260–69, 271, 275, 286, 291, 314, 317, 321, 327, 329, 341, 362, 372

Hackett, K., 368
Hacking, J., 171
Hackney Borough Council, 119
Hagan, J., 209
Halifax Town FC, 333, 336, 345
Halse, H., 123
Halton, R., 247, 248
Hamill, M., 164
Hamilton, T., 161
Hammonds, 243, 245
Hampton, H., 33
Hannah, G., 10
Hansen, (Liverpool), 172
Hapgood, E., 197
Hardaker, A., 266, 270, 276, 277, 278, 282, 290, 293, 315, 320, 325, 339
Hardinge, H.W.T., 123, 125, 173
Hardman, E., 298, 327, 341
Hardy, S., 80, 129
Hare, (Minister of Labour), 278, 279
Harper, W., 164
Harper, T., 184, 185
Hart, P., 340
Hartley, (Liverpool), 16
Hartley, W., 191, 192, 193
Hattersley, R., 314
Haynes, J., 274
Henderson, A., 74
Henshall, H., 128, 129
Heysel, 343, 350
Hibernian FC, 10, 97, 198
Hill, J., 257, 258, 261, 264, 267–85, 297, 306, 315, 323, 325, 327, 339, 341
Hill, J., (Burnley), 164
Hill, T., 259
Hillman, J., 39

Hillsborough, 359, 360
Hilton, F., 166
Hinchcliffe, T., 63, 99, 109, 135, 151, 194, 267
Hobson, (Sheff. Utd), 160
Hoby, A., 223
Hockey, T., 346
Hogg, W., 250
Hold, O., 242, 243, 248, 264
Holdsworth, E., 128, 129
Holmes, R., 8, 9, 10, 16, 17, 18, 20, 25, 26, 32
Holmes (Sheff. Utd), 160
Holt, J., 16
Hough, H., 267, 268, 269
Howarth, F., 193, 199, 209, 210, 230, 231, 234, 259, 260, 266, 339
Howell, D., 351
Hughes, R., 166
Hull City FC, 305, 333
Hulton, E., 36
Hunter, N., 307, 308
Hyde Road, 36, 38

Ibrox Park, 13
Imperial Hotel, 42
Independent Tribunal, 294
Industrial Relations Act, (1971), 304, 314
Ingham, T., 267, 268, 282
Inglis, S., 293
Insurance Act (1911), 102
International Board, 9
Ipswich Town FC, 334
Isaacs, G., (MP), 230
ITP Pools, 218
ITV, 354, 355

Jack, D., 173
Jackson, A., 177
James, A., 161, 173, 174, 175, 176, 177, 249, 306
Jenkin, E., 171
Jobey, G., 197

Joint FA/Players Union Insurance Policy, 261, 263, 295
Joint Negotiating Committee (National), 293, 294, 295, 303, 313, 314, 322, 331
Joint Standing Committee, 234, 235, 237, 246, 248, 255, 258, 259, 275, 303
Jones, Di, 38, 39
Jones, T., 249
Jordan, J., 249
Joy, B., 234
Jubilee Fund, 193, 202, 310, 311

Karno, F., 44
Keegan, K., 338
Kelly, G., 339, 355, 370
Kerr, Dick, (FC), 161
Kerry, W., 312, 313, 341, 347, 348
Kettering Town FC, 324
Kidd, B., 351
Kingaby, H., 95, 98, 99, 100, 101, 102, 110, 152, 153, 240
Kirton, G., 356
Kirwan, (Spurs), 32
Kitchen, F., 44
Kitchen, J.E., 144

Lally, P., 347, 348
Lancashire Association, 23
Lancashire and Cheshire Federation of Trades Unions, 70
Lancashire Combination, 23
* *Lancashire Daily Post*, 8, 9, 16, 18, 20, 23, 26, 29, 30
Lancashire League, 26
Lancashire Referees Association, 23
Latchford, R., 330, 340
Law, D., 329
Lawrence, J., 49, 72, 112, 128, 134, 135, 136, 142, 146, 156, 172
Lawton, N., 296
Lawton, T., 229
Leadgate FC, 134
Leddy, H., 142, 149, 150, 151, 152,

153, 154, 157, 171
Lee, G., 348
Leeds United FC, 173
Leicester City FC (Fosse), 19, 24, 85, 273
Leighton, T., 327
Leman, D., 351
Levitch, F., 46
Lewis, J., 41, 47, 59, 60
Leyland, H., 327
Leyton Orient, 98, 273
Liddell, W., 253
Lintott, E., 85, 86, 91, 94, 119
Lintott, S., 107
Lipsham, B., 42, 43, 86
Liverpool FC, 11, 16, 34, 72, 119, 120, 146, 148, 172, 196, 247, 253, 268, 359
Lloyd, C., 245–8, 252–4, 257, 258, 260, 261, 263–5, 267–9, 276, 278, 281–91, 294, 296–8, 302, 307, 313, 315–17, 319, 322, 325–8, 339–41, 346, 372
Lofthouse, N., 329
Lord, W., 290, 295
Lord, M., 340
Lovell's Athletic FC, 198
Low, J., 172
Low, N., 213, 234
Luncarty, 220
Lush, (Mr Justice), 154
Lyons, (Ginger), 77, 95, 96

Macedo, T., 274
Mackay, D., 348
Mackay, N., 198
McCombie, A., 42, 43
McCracken, W., 129
McDowland, 86
McElwain, B., 234
McGregor, W., 1, 3, 4, 5
McGuire, (Wolves), 221
McIntyre, (Morton), 164
McKenna, J., 43, 114, 115, 124, 125, 146, 147, 148, 186, 196

McMahon, J., 42
McNaught, J., 15
McNeill, H., 8, 20, 22
McPherson, (Liverpool), 172
Machin, E., 303, 304, 305, 368
Mainman, H., 42, 43, 63, 64, 65, 68, 69, 85, 99
Male, G., 362
Maley, T., 36, 39
Maley, W., 39
Mallalieu, J.P., 218
Malvern College, 129
★ *Man and Superman*, G.B. Shaw, 91
Manchester Athletic, 71
Manchester City FC, (Ardwick), 15, 34, 35, 36, 37, 38, 48, 65, 77, 96, 97, 103, 117, 120, 128, 134, 171, 197, 229, 256, 332
★ *Manchester Evening News*, 41, 72
Manchester Royal Infirmary, 44
Manchester United FC, (Newton Heath), 34, 35, 37, 38, 43, 45, 47, 48, 65, 69, 70, 71, 72, 74, 77, 81, 94, 107, 114, 128, 171, 274, 296, 329, 344, 351, 361, 367
Mangnall, D., 223, 234
Mannion, W., 249
Marchi, T., 263
Martyn, N., 364
Marwood, B., 372
Matthews, H., 142, 144, 168
Matthews, S., 214, 282
Maxwell, R., 343
Maypole Public House, 17, 18
Mears, J., 278
Meecham, P., 16
Mercer, D., 358
Mercer, J., (Snr), 120
Mercer, J., 172, 213, 215, 216, 217, 234, 252, 253
Meredith, W., 15, 34, 36, 37, 39, 40–44, 49, 50, 57, 58, 62, 63, 66, 67, 73, 74, 76, 78, 80, 82, 94, 99, 101, 108, 120, 128, 129, 135,

143, 171, 185, 193, 203, 266, 267, 271, 286, 327, 329, 341, 372
Merrick, G., 333
Merthyr Tydfil FC, 143
Middlesborough FC, 32, 36, 38, 86, 110, 173, 348
* *Midland Daily Telegraph*, 182
Midland Hotel, 47, 213, 214, 225, 346
Millichip, B., 338
Millwall FC, 315
Ministry of Labour, 180, 224, 225, 227, 230, 234, 237, 239, 240, 277, 278, 280, 281
Minister of Sport, 235, 351, 372
Minshull, R., 247
Mitchell, (Notts County), 164
Mitten C., 250
Moncton, W., 222, 240
Morgan, T., 358
* *Morning Herald*, 30
Morris, G., 59
Mountford, G., 250
MSC, 348, 351
Muirhead, T., 164
Munroe, (Wolves), 12, 20
Mulhearn (Boilermakers Union), 123
Musgrove, M., 296, 297, 327

National Arbitration Tribunal, 227
National Union of Railwaymen, 70
Needham, E., 13, 32, 81
Neill, T., 296, 297, 305, 311, 327, 346
Newbould, H., 86, 97, 103, 104, 107, 114, 115, 129, 139, 149, 150, 154, 165, 168, 169
Newcastle Amateur Operatic Society, 91
Newcastle People's Theatre, 91
Newcastle United FC, 34, 35, 36, 44, 46, 53, 70, 72, 81, 94, 114, 128, 171, 172, 229, 283, 284, 289, 348

Newport Association FC, 134
New Tredegar FC, 143
New York Cosmos, 346
New York Giants, 164
Norris, H., 43, 124
North American Soccer League, 297, 330, 346
Northampton Town FC, 334
Northern Nomads, 85
Norwich City FC, 134, 334
Notts County FC, 25, 129, 229, 356
Nulty, G., 348

Oakley, A., 230, 257, 266
* *Old Fogey* (Athletic News), 6
Oldham Athletic FC, 72, 86, 124, 128, 139, 143, 144, 185, 351
Old Swan Hotel, 115
Old Trafford, 37
Owen, S., 85, 86, 87, 90, 92, 94, 101, 102, 103, 105, 110

Packer, K., 337
Pantling, H. H., 144, 145, 184
Parker, R., 248
Parker, T., 174
Parlby, J., 37
Parsonage, G., 63, 77
Partick Thistle FC, 164, 273
Paul, R., 250, 329
Peacock, K., 323
Pejic, M., 361
Pele, 330
Pennington, J., 98, 103, 124, 128, 142, 148
* *People*, The, 182, 223, 271
* *Perseus*, 26
Peterborough City, 99
Phillips, T., 356
Pickford, W., 50, 180, 181
Piercy, 86
Players Cash Benefit Scheme, 326, 327
Player's Charter, 222, 232, 239, 246, 257

Player's Union Athletic Festival, 105, 106, 107
Player's Union Magazine, 107, 108, 110
Plymouth Argyle FC, 85, 143, 184
Pontypridd FC, 134
Portsmouth FC, 31, 204, 210, 220, 221, 306, 356
Powell, I., 223
Premier League, 371
Preston North End FC, 33, 38, 86, 128, 129, 161
Priest, F., 32
PFA Annual Awards, 306, 307, 359, 372
PFA Financial Management Ltd, 364
Professional Football Joint Negotiating Committee, 317, 318, 319
Professional Football Players and Trainers Union (1918), 123
Provident Fund, 228, 230, 231, 232, 234, 255, 256, 259, 260, 292, 293, 295, 296, 302, 320
Prudential Insurance Company, 230

Queens Park FC, 16
Queens Park Rangers FC, 85, 223, 248
Quested, L., 253

Racing Levy Board, 302
* *Railway Review*, 70
Rance, C., 123
Rangers FC, 9, 164
Rawlings, A., 171
Rawlinson (KC), 100
Reade, R., 351
Reading FC, 55, 57, 68, 217, 273
Reagan, (Norwich City), 257
Regis, C., 362
Reinstatement of Civil Employment Act (1946), 213
Richards J., 266, 269, 275, 278, 279, 280, 281, 290
Richards, S., 265

Rinder, F.W., 47
Roach, (Justice), 187
Robbie, D., 166, 171, 177, 184, 185, 196, 221
Roberts, C., 42, 43, 62, 71, 76, 81, 82, 83, 87, 88, 89, 103, 110, 120, 123, 124, 125, 126, 127, 128, 129, 135, 139, 141, 142, 144, 169, 173, 177, 178, 184, 203, 206, 232, 286, 327, 329, 372
Robertson, (Everton), 16
Robey, G., 44
Robinson, T., 114
Robson, R., 274, 297
Rochdale FC, 345
Roost, W., 267, 268
Rose, W., 6
Ross, J., 8, 17, 38
Rourke, S., 336
Rous, (Sir Stanley), 228, 230, 234, 235, 261, 296
Rushton, 20
Russell, M., 142, 143, 166, 184
Ruth, (Babe), 165

Saer, C., 10, 15, 17, 18–25, 30, 32, 286, 320
Sagar, C., (Everton), 172
Sagar, C., (Man Utd), 42
Salter, (Mr Justice), 154
Sanderson, S., 206
* *Saturday Post*, 120
Saunders, D., 292
Saul, 86
Scott, E.J., 180
Scott, L., 8, 88
Scottish Players Union, 10, 218, 234
Seed, J., 224
Selfridges, 175
Setters, M., 296, 305, 327
Sewell, J., 255
Shakespeare, W., 91
Shackleton, L., 229, 250, 272, 306
Sharpe, I., 105, 197
Sharp, J., 86

Sharp, S., 171
Shaw, B., 91
Shaw, J., 128, 129, 142, 173
Shea, D., 123
Shearman, M., (KC), 100
\* *Sheffield Guardian*, 70
Sheffield, I.L.P., 70
Sheffield United, 46, 114, 144, 145, 160, 173
Sheffield Wednesday FC, 34, 110, 114, 134, 145, 172, 173
Shilton, P., 361
Simmons, J., 144
Skelmersdale United, 348
Skene, L., 98
Sloan, P., 249
Smith, E., 222
Smith, J., 357
Smith, (Sheff. Utd), 160
\* *Soccer*, 234, 235, 241
\* *Soccer Rebel*, 242
Somerville, J., 8, 10, 38
Southampton FC, 15, 31, 166
Southend United FC, 267
Southern League, 2, 5, 9, 12, 15, 20, 26, 34, 47, 86, 88, 98, 111, 112, 127, 143
Southport General FC, 143
South Shields FC, 128, 129, 142, 173
\* *South Wales Evening Express*, 181
Spackman, N., 358
Spalding, A.G., 165
Spikesly, F., 10
\* *Sporting Chronicle*, 102, 121, 153
Sports Council, 350, 351
\* *Sports Pictures*, 136, 151
Spottiswoode, 135
Spread Eagle Hotel, 11, 25
Stephens, L., 247
Stephenson, C., 129, 172
Stewart, A., 315, 316, 322
Stewart, W., 16
Stillman, 227
Stockport County FC, 24

Stoke City FC, 85, 182, 250, 361
Storrier, D., 16
Strangs Pools, 218
Stuart, R., 213, 227
Sturgess, A., 144
\* *Sunday People*, 265
Sunderland Albion FC, 10
Sunderland FC, 34, 35, 72, 74, 86, 94, 114, 143, 171, 172, 173, 270, 271, 273, 350
Sutcliffe, C.E., 18, 20, 22, 23, 27, 31, 47, 53–5, 57, 58, 84, 87, 88, 90, 92, 94, 99, 100, 102, 107, 111, 113, 114–16, 121–8, 131, 132, 134, 136, 148, 151–4, 157, 158, 164, 165, 167, 178, 180, 181, 185–93, 196, 199, 201–3, 276, 281, 285, 288, 320
Sutcliffe, J.W., 38
Swales, P., 332
Swansea City FC, 334
Swift, (Chesterfield), 63
Swinden, G., 173, 231, 232, 234, 235, 241, 242, 247
Swindon Town FC, 369

Talbot, B., 313, 340, 356, 360
Tate, J., 184, 185
Taylor, G., 311, 312, 320, 326, 329–48, 350–52, 355–64, 367, 369–72
Taylor Report, 363, 372
Terrington, Lord, 227
TCCB, (Test and County Cricket Board), 337
\* *Thames Valley Times*, 182
Thompson, E., 209
Thompson, P., 338
\* *Thomson's Weekly News*, 48, 49, 54, 62, 66, 80, 82, 94, 96, 99, 107, 108, 112, 120, 135
Thornley, I., 42
\* *Times, The*, 74
\* *Topical Times*, 136, 151–153, 157, 167, 188, 189

Tottenham Hotspur FC, 15, 16, 28, 29, 31, 32, 33, 34, 43, 110, 114, 119, 123, 146, 229, 263, 291, 361
Trades Dispute Act, (1906), 35
Trades Union Act, 11
Trades Union Congress, (TUC), 61, 70, 81, 225, 254–60, 314, 338, 347
Trainer, J., 19
Tranmere Rovers FC, 149
Treacy, R., 340
Troup, A., 152
Turnbull, A., ('Sandy'), 42, 71, 120
Turnbull, J., 45, 46
* *Truth*, 68

Utley, G., 142, 143, 144, 166

Variety Artists Federation, 44
Veitch, C., 47, 49, 53, 67, 70, 72, 76–81, 85, 86, 89, 91, 99, 102, 107, 110, 114, 119, 123, 126, 128, 135, 172, 203, 286
Venables, T., 297, 313, 320, 327
Vizard, T., 129

Walden, F., 129
Walker, T., 224
Wall, F.J., 120, 180
Walsall FC, 269, 324
Walton, F., 243, 246, 249, 257, 264, 265, 267
War Emergency Act, 225, 227
Wardle, G., 254
Wass, H., 198
Watford FC, 348
Watney's Cup, 315
Webb, C., 214
Wedlock, W., 62
Wells, W., (ETU), 123

Welsh, D., 234
West Bromwich Albion, 98, 241, 361, 362, 363
West Ham United, 296
* *Western Mail Ltd*, 181
Wheldon, H., 44
Whitley Council, 228
Whittaker, T., 173
Wigan Athletic FC, 175
Wilberforce, (Justice), 285, 286, 287, 289, 290, 292, 301, 302
Wilkinson, (Manchester City), 43, 63, 96
Wilson, J., 213, 215, 216, 217, 218, 222
Winter, D., 247, 254
Winterbottom, W., 296
Woking Town, FC, 85
Wolverhampton Wanderers, 166, 220, 221, 306, 325
Wood, A., 166, 171, 184
Wood, H., 8, 10, 15, 166
Wood, J., (Prof. Sir), 317, 321, 322, 331, 352
Wood, R., 267
Woodward, E., 307
Woosnam, P., 281, 295, 297
Workman's Compensation Act, (1906), 35, 47, 55, 97, 109, 188, 190, 199, 207
Workington Town FC, 181
Wright, W., 251, 282
Wright, H., 107

Ye Old Royal Restaurant, 50
Yorkshire and District Trades and Labour Council, 70
YTS (YT), 347, 348, 349, 350, 352, 371

Zetters Pools, 218